DYNAMIC
ARGUMENT
BRIEF EDITION

DYNAMIC ARGUMENT

BRIEF EDITION

Robert Lamm
Arkansas State University

Justin Everett
University of the Sciences

 **WADSWORTH**
CENGAGE Learning

Australia • Brazil • Japan • Korea • Mexico • Singapore • Spain • United Kingdom • United States

WADSWORTH
CENGAGE Learning

Dynamic Argument, Second Edition
Robert Lamm and Justin Everett

Senior Publisher: Lyn Uhl

Publisher: Monica Eckman

Acquisitions Editor: Margaret Leslie

Development Editor: Laurie Dobson

Assistant Editor: Amy Haines

Editorial Assistant: Danielle Warchol

Associate Media Editor: Janine Tangney

Executive Marketing Manager:
   Stacey Purviance

Marketing Coordinator: Brittany Blais

Senior Marketing Communications
   Manager: Linda Yip

Senior Content Project Manager: Carol
   Newman

Senior Art Director: Jill Ort

Senior Manufacturing Planner: Betsy
   Donaghey

Senior Rights Acquisition Specialist:
   Jennifer Meyer Dare

Production Service/Compositor: Integra

Text/Cover Designer: Bill Smith Group

Cover Image: Bill Smith Group

For product information and technology assistance, contact us at
Cengage Learning Customer & Sales Support, 1-800-354-9706
For permission to use material from this text or product,
submit all requests online at **www.cengage.com/permissions.**
Further permissions questions can be emailed to
permissionrequest@cengage.com.

Library of Congress Control Number: 2011939242

ISBN-13: 978-1-111-84135-5

ISBN-10: 1-111-84135-7

Wadsworth
20 Channel Center Street
Boston, MA 02210
USA

Cengage Learning is a leading provider of customized learning solutions with office locations around the globe, including Singapore, the United Kingdom, Australia, Mexico, Brazil and Japan. Locate your local office at **international.cengage.com/region**

Cengage Learning products are represented in Canada by Nelson Education, Ltd.

For your course and learning solutions, visit **www.cengage.com.**

Purchase any of our products at your local college store or at our preferred online store **www.cengagebrain.com.**

Instructors: Please visit **login.cengage.com** and log in to access instructor-specific resources.

Printed in the United States of America
1 2 3 4 5 6 7 15 14 13 12 11

BRIEF CONTENTS

CONTENTS

CHAPTER 4
Researching Arguments 90

CHAPTER 5
Writing Process:
Planning Arguments 132

CHAPTER 6
Writing Process: Drafting Arguments 156

CHAPTER 7
Writing Process: Revising and Editing Arguments 187

CHAPTER 8
Using Sources, Avoiding Plagiarism 211

CHAPTER 9
Arguing Visually 240

CHAPTER 10
Using Logic 272

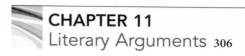

CHAPTER 11
Literary Arguments 306

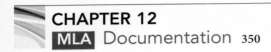

CHAPTER 12
MLA Documentation 350

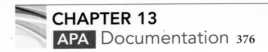

CHAPTER 13
APA Documentation 376

You may have heard the saying, "Life is a banquet, and most people are starving." In the same sense, life is an argument, and most people are speechless. Effective persuasion is one of the most essential skills students will need to succeed in their education, career, and life in general. *Dynamic Argument* helps student writers acquire the practical skills they need to join life's debate. We wrote this book as a down-to-earth guide to understand the arguments of others and to create arguments in response.

The writing process is the foundation of this book. Three chapters follow a student's process as she creates an essay on the issue of plagiarism: Planning Arguments, Drafting Arguments, and Revising and Editing Arguments. Other chapters are process oriented, focusing on how to read critically, conduct research, and use sources without plagiarizing.

Dynamic Argument also features readings and visuals that engage the lives that students live today as citizens, consumers, and members of families. It avoids prepackaged and antiseptic pro or con, conservative or liberal viewpoints—what we like to call "canned arguments"—that do not encourage critical or creative thinking. By allowing students to avoid binary thinking and instead explore ambivalence and ambiguity, *Dynamic Argument* challenges students with fresh material that has no preconceived viewpoint. Students in a *Dynamic Argument* classroom engage topics that speak to them. They develop their own points of view, work out logic independently, and determine their own approaches to persuasion.

New to This Edition

▶ **A new chapter, "Literary Arguments."** Chapter 11 shows how interpretations essentially are arguments that use textual and research evidence to support claims. It includes definitions and examples of many literary terms, examples of literary arguments written by scholars and students, and guidelines for writing an essay, a literary review, and a "modest proposal." Unlike chapters in other books that focus only on the jargon of literary analysis, this chapter focuses on applying the principles of argument in the context of reading and responding to literature.

▶ **New student essays.** All were written by our students during class-testing of new material.

▶ **Sequenced *writing process* chapters with *unified examples*.** Planning Arguments, Drafting Arguments, and Revising and Editing Arguments follow a student's steps as she writes on the topic of plagiarism. This allows the book to focus not only on the logic of writing arguments, but the in-depth, step-by-step process of drafting arguments from start to finish.

▶ **Updated MLA and APA guidelines.**

Features

▶ ***Really* process oriented.** *Dynamic Argument's* Rhetoric section (Part 1) takes the *process* of writing seriously in sequenced chapters that help students plan, draft, revise and edit, and research their writings. Techniques, models, and guided practice make the process clear and as easy as possible. Reflecting the recursive nature of the writing process, these chapters can be revisited productively whenever the student is working on a writing assignment.

▶ **Visually appealing.** The visual appearance of the text is inviting and dynamic, with creative formatting, abundant illustrations, entertaining-yet-instructive cartoons, and four-color layouts varying the presentation. Its many photographs provide additional interest and context for the discussion of contemporary issues and challenges. Page layout was designed with the look and feel of a web page so that it could be read the way most students read today—hypertextually, moving in nonlinear order between elements. Chapter 9, "Arguing Visually," presents full-color visual arguments on a variety of contemporary and significant issues, encouraging students to read visual arguments critically and to use visuals within their own arguments. This chapter introduces students to elements of visual rhetoric and the fundamental elements of design while providing them with practical advice on how to integrate tables, graphs, charts, and other visual elements into their documents.

▶ **Nontechnical.** The terminology and examples used to present argument, rhetoric, and process are nontechnical and user-friendly, with the goal of helping the student become a better writer. The pedagogical approach is not an end in itself. Our approach to logic is not overly prescriptive. *Dynamic Argument* helps students discover persuasion through both the process of logic and the process of writing.

▶ **More useful material.** The Rhetoric (Part 1) contains the kinds of examples, advice, and materials that teachers often have to provide as supplements to a text. There are chapters on "Using Sources, Avoid Plagiarism: Quoting, Paraphrasing, Summarizing and Synthesizing" and on "Arguing Visually," revision and editing guides, many models of writing (including student-written essays), and many tips contained in sidebars and textboxes.

▶ **Dynamic approaches for today's diverse classroom.** Today's students are asked to interact with each other, lead discussions, participate in group activities, and use a wide variety of learning styles from hands-on practice to the creation and interpretation of visual texts. *Dynamic Argument* takes advantage of current research in multiple intelligences, cooperative learning, and other learning styles. By offering strong visuals and group-oriented exercises, it addresses the needs of both traditional and nontraditional learners.

▶ **Spoken like a mentor:** The style of the book's exposition is cordial. It addresses one reader—the student. Its tone is that of a one-on-one conference between a student and a rather pleasant instructor who is at once challenging and encouraging. We have extensively class-tested this material with our own students, who have been candid and generous in helping us to shape both pedagogy and voice.

Organization

The brief version of Dynamic Argument includes Part 1, "Rhetoric" section. The full version of *Dynamic Argument* consists of two sections—the Rhetoric and a Reader—with a glossary.

Part 1, "Rhetoric" Part 1, the Rhetoric section of *Dynamic Argument*, comprises eleven chapters sequenced to lead students through the complete process of writing and two chapters that provide the basics of MLA and APA documentation styles. Conceptually, Part 1 is based on three pedagogical concepts integrated into every chapter:

▶ **Elements of argument.** Chapter 10, "Logic," introduces Classical, Toulmin, and Rogerian approaches to argument. Earlier chapters provide an essential introduction to claims and support that students need to begin developing their arguments while later chapters provide more in-depth information on the logical structure of arguments.

▶ **Rhetoric.** The rhetorical context is made memorable with **PASS**: Purpose, Audience, Structure, and Style. This acronym, used throughout the text, keeps students focused on key features of strong arguments.

▶ **The process of writing.** Planning, drafting, revising (with editing), and research are given their own respective chapters. Separate chapters on MLA and APA citation styles provide clear, easy-to-follow examples of key print and electronic sources, as well as student models of MLA and APA research papers.

Resources for Students

Book Companion Website Visit cengagebrain.com to access valuable course resources. Students will find an extensive library of interactive exercises and animations that cover grammar, diction, mechanics, punctuation, research, and writing concepts, as well as a complete library of student papers and a section on avoiding plagiarism. The site also offers a downloadable Instructor's Manual.

Online Instructor's Manual Available for download on the book Companion Website, the Instructor's Manual is designed to enhance the experience of teaching with *Dynamic Argument*. Each chapter of the Instructor's Manual (IM) has a corresponding chapter in the textbook. Recurring IM contents for the Rhetoric (Chapters 1–13) include a *Chapter Summary* (main ideas), *Approaches to Teaching* (general suggestions for assignments), *Learning Goals* (chapter objectives), *Key Terms* (definitions), and a *Guide to Practices* (answers to questions and specific suggestions on teaching).

CourseReader: Argument (ISBN: 1111769656) This fully customizable online reader provides access to hundreds of readings, audio, and video selections from multiple disciplines. This easy to use solution allows you to select exactly the content you need for your courses, and is loaded with convenient pedagogical features like highlighting, printing, note taking, and audio downloads. YOU have the freedom to assign individualized content at an affordable price. The CourseReader: Argument is the perfect complement to any class.

Acknowledgments

We are grateful to our universities and colleagues for their assistance. At Arkansas State University, we thank Jerry Ball, Chuck Carr, Dixie Keyes, Sam Gennuso, and Bryan Moore. At the University of the Sciences, we thank Andrew Peterson, Shannon Marquez, and Cristina Hanganu-Bresch. At West Chester University, we thank Deirdre Pettipiece.

We thank our students for their contributions to this text. At ASU, we thank Janet Barnett, Kerri Bennett, Faith Bruns Reeves, Anna Carling, Brittany Einhorn, Erin Flagg, Charles Mueller, Stephen W. Pogue, and James Southard for contributing their writings and models. At USciences, we thank Hetal Shah, Joellen Freeman, and Priya Panchal.

We are indebted to our former instructors and colleagues at the University of Oklahoma for the education and experiences they provided us: Peter Smagorinsky (now at the University of Georgia), Michael Angelotti, Robert Con Davis-Undiano, the late Michael Flanigan, David Mair, Ronald Schleifer, Alan Velie, and Kathleen Welch. We also acknowledge the broad membership of the Council of Writing Program Administrators, the Philadelphia Council of Writing Program Administrators, and particularly the sage advice provided by the WPA List, without which much of this book would not have been possible. Finally, we acknowledge the National Writing Project, whose instructional methods have influenced this book's process-based approach to writing.

For their helpful guidance and suggestions through the development of *Dynamic Argument*, we would like to thank the following reviewers:

Cathryn Amdahl, Harrisburg Area Community College
Shannon Beasley, Arkansas State University
Jamie Berthel, Danville Area Community College
Cristina Hanganu-Bresch, University of the Sciences in Philadelphia
Ron Brooks, Oklahoma State University
Becky Childs, Coastal Carolina University
Leila Marie Crawford, Atlantic Cape Community College
Linsey Cuti, Kankakee Community College
Anthony Di Renzo, Ithaca College
Patricia Dunmire, Kent State University
Mia Eaker, The University of North Carolina at Charlotte
Steve Hecox, Averett University
Ellen Johnson, Arizona State University
Tiffany Morin, University of North Carolina at Charlotte

Shelley Palmer, Rowan-Cabarrus Community College
Deirdre Pettipiece, West Chester University of Pennsylvania
Suba Subbarao, Oakland Community College
Ralph Velazquez, Rio Hondo College

Of course, we owe a lifetime of gratitude to our "textbook widows and orphans": Rob's wife, Martha, and children, John, Alexi, and Mark; and Justin's wife, Diana, and daughter, Hannah.

Finally, we owe gratitude to the wonderful staff of Cengage Learning, in particular Margaret Leslie, Acquisitions Editor, English Composition; Laurie Dobson, Development Editor; Carol Newman, Senior Content Production Manager; Katrina Wilbur, Project Manager; Sue Brekka, Text Permissions, Tux & Tales Publishing Services; Scott Rosen, Image Permissions, Bill Smith Group; Stacey Purviance, Executive Marketing Manager; and Melissa Holt, Marketing Manager.

Robert Lamm
Arkansas State University

Justin Everett
University of the Sciences

DYNAMIC

ARGUMENT

BRIEF EDITION

Argument, Rhetoric, and Process

A blank page or computer screen is the traditional starting place for writers. It symbolizes limitless potential. Like all writers, you will learn to fill the blank page as you go—cautiously at first and eventually with growing confidence and skill. Each of the thirteen chapters in *Dynamic Argument* has tips and examples that will guide you in your exploration of writing and help you master the methods needed to complete your writing assignments. You might even learn to fill the blank page with great thoughts that amaze readers and change the world.

Introduction

1

COLUMBIA / THE KOBAL COLLECTION

An argument is a connected series of statements intended to establish a proposition.

—Monty Python's Flying Circus, "Argument Clinic" sketch

In a comic sketch performed by the British comedy ensemble Monty Python's Flying Circus, a man walks into an "argument clinic" hoping to debate with one of the staff. After paying a fee, he first wanders into a room where he is subjected to verbal abuse before finding the right room where he hopes to enjoy an argument (see photo). He becomes dismayed when the arguer stubbornly disagrees with everything said. Finally, frustrated, the would-be arguer blurts out, "An argument is a connected series of statements intended to establish a proposition." We agree with this definition, and we add that *an argument is a dynamic process*—an exchange of ideas intended to change a person's thoughts and actions.

THE DYNAMICS OF ARGUMENT

Argument changes the world. It shapes the way people think and allows them to change their minds about deeply felt, but unexamined, beliefs. It motivates people to behave differently, providing them with reasons to take action or to halt. As a result, countries wage war or seek peace. People gain or lose civil rights. Those accused of crimes are convicted and jailed or acquitted and freed. Business deals are made or broken. Personal relationships form, break up, or mend. Politicians are elected or defeated. All these activities are set into motion and resolved through a dynamic process of change known as argument.

What Is an Argument?

Argument is both product and process. The word can refer to *a thing*, such as the completed text of a conversation, speech, or piece of writing. Another meaning is less static and more dynamic: *Argument is the process of giving reasons to change the way one thinks or acts.* By seeking change in people, argument may affect everything touched by humans.

Chances are that when you first saw the word *argument* in this book, other possible definitions came to mind that are not applicable. Let's consider those other meanings before putting them aside.

Argument Is Not . . . One way to define a term is to clarify what it is *not*. As practiced in this book, argument is not a verbal duel, not quibbling, not a shouting match, not a quarrel, not a rant. Unfortunately, yet understandably, the word *argument,* as commonly used, carries some negative connotations. That kind of outcome is loud, emotional, and counterproductive.

Argument Is Not Quite . . . Another way to define a term is to qualify it, which means to tell under what conditions it is or is not true. It is true that argument can be adversarial, meaning that one side can be pitted against another as in court trial: The prosecutor offers one interpretation of a crime; the defense offers a different one. In a court of law both sides claim their interpretation is true and provide reasons in the form of evidence and explanations to influence the judge or jury to think and act a certain way— that is, to reach a verdict in favor of only one side.

In writing, effective arguments are seldom one-sided: A reader depends on a writer to present a fair account of all important aspects of the issue being discussed. Because the written product may be the reader's only source of

Successful arguments convince an audience to accept a claim.

information, the writer acts as both the prosecution and the defense to present a kind of verdict, a *claim*. A reader who feels misled will usually reject not only the writer's argument but also the writer's credibility in all other matters.

Argument Is... Our definition of argument—*"establishing valid claims by giving reasons to change the way one thinks or acts"*—is used throughout this book. The desired "change" is expressed as a claim, which is any statement

ARGUMENTS CONSIST OF CLAIMS AND SUPPORT

Claim: A claim, also known as an argumentative thesis, is an assertion that needs support—specific reasons—to be accepted as true. Claims fill our public and private lives. Politicians make claims about one another and about public policy: "This law is immoral"; "That candidate is uninformed"; "We should (or should not) carry out certain policies." Advertisements claim that you should buy certain products. In your daily life, you deal with claims in many forms, such as friends wanting your help or you wanting theirs, people making excuses, perhaps you explaining why a teacher should accept late homework or change a grade. All of these examples are claims, and all are supportable by reasons.

Support: Support consists of any reasons you provide to convince an audience to accept your claim. A skeptical audience always wonders, "Why should I accept your claim?" Support lets you answer with "Because...." The "because" of support consists of (1) evidence and (2) explanations of how the evidence applies to the claim.

Evidence: Evidence is information that proves or strongly suggests the claim is true or valid. For example, if you were to make a claim about the legality of downloading music from the Internet, the evidence supporting that claim would be specifically related to downloading—statistics about how just or unjust the punishment is, how much revenue is lost by music companies, stories about legal prosecutions, or appeals by musicians to stop stealing from them. Evidence includes expert opinions, facts and statistics, history, personal experience, scenarios, and specific examples—almost anything that backs the claim. (See Chapter 2, Claims and Support, for more information.)

Explanation: Evidence often needs to be explained, either because the evidence itself is unclear or because its relevance to the claim needs to be spelled out explicitly. For example, if you cited the Geneva Convention as evidence that suspected terrorists should be tried in a military tribunal rather than in civil court, you might explain how laws that apply to conventional military personnel apply also to paramilitary fighters and "nonnative combatants." Explanations take the form of clarification, interpretation, application, analysis, synthesis, and evaluation.

that needs proof before acceptance. "Reasons" are the support for the claim in the form of evidence and explanations.

Argue Within the "Zone of Reasonable Skepticism"

Fair arguments take place in what we call the "zone of reasonable skepticism." This means that the audience is not yet persuaded by the claim the arguer is presenting, but is willing to fairly weigh the evidence against the claims without unreasonable bias. All audiences bring their own perspectives—biases—when they consider an argument. If they are so attached to their own position that they are unwilling to consider the claim, then the argument is a waste of time for both the arguer and the audience.

Disbeliever ⟵——————————————⟶ **Supporter**

Someone who *refuses* to consider your claims and evidence, no matter how convincing.

Zone of Reasonable Skepticism
An appropriate audience for your argument should not already believe your claim is true, nor should they dismiss it out-of-hand. They should be *willing* to fairly weigh your evidence and consider the *possibility* that your argument is valid.

Someone who *already believes* your position is true and does not need to be convinced.

As you plan your argument, you can create a zone of reasonable skepticism by (1) selecting an audience that is willing to consider your claims or (2) adjusting your claims and support to fit an audience that is not so open. Creating a zone of reasonable skepticism is like the jury selection process for a trial. The trial attorneys will try to eliminate those who already believe the defendant is innocent or guilty as well as those who will not "play by the rules" by considering proof that is "within reasonable doubt." Once the jury is selected, the attorneys will tailor their evidences to the values and biases of the jury.

Although some audiences will be homogeneous, many others will be heterogeneous, holding varied and sometimes conflicting beliefs. Environmentalists, for example, would have similar concerns about issues such as clear-cutting of rainforests, while the larger population would have a wider assortment of concerns—the need for more logging jobs, corporate profits, cheap building materials, increased farmland, or fewer government restrictions. As you craft an argument, you must consider the audience, tailoring your claim and support to fit its particular beliefs. (See Chapter 5, Planning Arguments, for more information about understanding audiences.)

Cornered   by Mike Baldwin

"What's important is that we found some common ground. Let's try not to get bogged down over who found it first."

Successful arguments find common ground.

PRACTICE 1.1	Reasonable Skepticism: Arguing for Different Audiences

Working individually or in groups, consider the following purposes for writing arguments and their associated audiences. Explain whether the audiences are appropriate for the arguments and why. If the audiences are appropriate, how would you approach each situation and why would you take that approach?

1. You are writing a letter home to your parents to ask them to send you money for living expenses. Would you tell them about any or all of the following: (a) your part-time job, (b) your classes and grades, and (c) your social activities? Explain.

2. Your education depends on student loans, but budget cuts to financial aid have become an issue in an upcoming election. You will make two appeals: (1) you'll visit a retirement home to encourage elderly voters to support government assistance to students, and (2) you'll write an editorial for the student newspaper in which you encourage fellow students to become activists in support of financial aid. In what ways will your appeals to these two audiences be different and similar?

Establishing Common Ground through Conflict Resolution

In some cases, people are so opposed to each other's positions that they do not easily hear what the other person is saying. Because these positions are so far apart and often refuse to hold certain beliefs or values in common, they are necessarily outside the "zone of reasonable skepticism." One way to address this problem is to find ways to acknowledge and incorporate opposing views into your argument.

Carl Rogers (1902–1987) was a humanistic psychologist who believed the best way to resolve this problem was for the individual making the argument to be required to state the opponent's position to the opponent's satisfaction before putting forth the individual's own position. Such Rogerian rhetoric—stating an opposing viewpoint before stating your own—can have the effect of pacifying a potentially hostile audience. Summarizing and respecting the

---

→ USE CONFLICT RESOLUTION IN CLASS DISCUSSIONS

In-class discussions of issues may create conflict. However, these arguments need not be adversarial. Below are some guidelines for conducting a productive discussion.

▶ **Begin positively.** Begin by establishing your points of agreement on elements relevant to the issue. Then narrow the argument to points of disagreement. A background of agreement provides a comfortable setting when disagreement comes to the foreground.

▶ **Take turns setting the agenda.** Each participant helps decide which part of the issue should be discussed. For example, if the issue is national health insurance, one person may be concerned about the impact on the federal deficit while the other may be more concerned about the suffering of the uninsured. An exception to this rule is when the arbitrator sets the agenda.

▶ **Don't interrupt.** This includes not only verbal silence but also avoiding body language and facial expressions that convey negative reactions.

▶ **Respond positively.** As the other person speaks, nod or offer a brief word of agreement such as "Yes." Avoid reacting emotionally, especially if your reaction is not in sympathy with the speaker. Positive body language—showing interest and openness—is encouraged. Work at creating a supportive atmosphere.

▶ **Postpone disputing facts or opinions.** Factual disputes may not be resolvable during the session. You may even discover later that some of these were not worth discussing anyway. Immediately arguing about facts and opinions may sidetrack you from learning the main source of disagreement and discovering possible solutions to the conflict.

▶ **Restate the other person's position briefly and in your own words.** This approach allows you to check whether you understood not only the idea being expressed but also the feeling behind it. You can begin these statements with phrases such as "You think . . . ," "You seem to feel . . . ," or "What I hear you saying is . . . ."

▶ **Ask for clarifications.** A nonadversarial way of doing this is to re-use the speaker's own words: "What do you mean when you say that national health insurance will lead to death panels?"

▶ **Listen for omissions or evasions.** You can sometimes learn much from what the person has not mentioned. Omissions may indicate what the other person hasn't considered; evasions may reveal what the other person is reluctant to confront.

PRACTICE 1.2   Understanding Conflict

In a brief writing or a group discussion, recall a disagreement (from your personal experiences or a television talk-show debate) that degenerated into a quarrel or even a fight. What was it about? What went wrong? Could you have resolved the conflict in a better way? How? Did the experience have an effect on the way you now deal with disagreements?

PRACTICE 1.3   Conflict Resolution

Working in groups or in a class discussion, practice conflict-resolution techniques to better understand a point of view with which you currently disagree. In your discussion, try to find a middle ground that everyone can agree on. Select an issue that already is on your mind or choose an issue from the options given below. Apply Carl Rogers's method (state your opponent's position to his or her satisfaction before stating your own). How might this approach help make your audience more receptive to your point of view?

1. Should students who are caught cheating on exams at your college or university be expelled?
2. Should illegal immigrants have access to public services such as education and health care?
3. Should people be profiled by law-enforcement agents?
4. Should artists who portray or advocate violence be held responsible when their fans or viewers behave violently?
5. Should public laws regulate the practices of certain religions?

opposing views can go a long way toward making a potentially hostile audience more willing to listen to your argument with an open mind.

Conflict resolution seeks common ground and consensus building, often with an acceptable compromise as the end result: "win-win" rather than "win-lose." Conflict resolution during a class discussion can help you to rehearse and refine your arguments and to accommodate opposition as you draft and revise your essay.

Why Study Argument?

There are personal reasons for learning how to argue effectively: Good arguing skills bring many benefits. For example, they can help you make wise decisions in all phases of your life, from life-altering personal issues, such as whether and whom you should marry, to social and civic matters, such as which policy or candidate you should support. Even better, your arguing skills can help resolve both personal and professional disagreements diplomatically, with less chance of a situation degenerating into a quarrel.

In this sense "the ability to argue well" is part of most job descriptions, whether it is stated directly or implied. Consider these examples from several different professions:

▶ Executives make decisions that are essentially claims—developing and marketing a new service or product—guided specifically by whatever evidence is presented about the market for that service and guided generally by the belief that the company must be profitable.

▶ Doctors make decisions that are essentially claims—treating illnesses based on evidence of symptoms and knowledge of the effectiveness of various treatments—guided primarily by the ethical codes of the Hippocratic Oath.

▶ Lawyers argue cases, whether for or against a client's particular position. They must sway a judge and sometimes a jury to reach the desired verdict.

▶ Scientists argue for or against theories. They also must argue for grants and for legal permission. Sometimes they must argue for political action, as in cases such as global warming or stem-cell research.

▶ Salespeople argue the merits of their products and services, often needing to overcome the skepticism of a customer or client.

▶ Teachers argue for or against philosophical, aesthetic, and scientific ideas to give their students the tools to develop good critical-thinking skills.

Lack of good arguing skills can result in errors of judgment, both small and disastrous, and can cause conflict with others that otherwise could have been avoided. People who cannot evaluate claims, evidence, and explanations are easily misled or cheated. They sometimes must depend more on chance or blind faith because they cannot make well-reasoned decisions.

PRACTICE 1.4   Arguments at Work

Many careers involve some kind of decisions or controversy. In addition, you may be debating internally on which career to choose.

1. Name a possible career and list arguments for and against pursuing it.

2. Name some issues that are argued within the career. (For example, physicians argue the pros and cons of "mercy killing.")

Argument Supports Democracy In addition to the personal benefits afforded by good argumentative skills, the ability to argue effectively has a public benefit: Logical argument is fundamental to the survival of democracy. In a democracy, where all citizens have a right to influence social and political policies, poor decisions can be catastrophic on a national or even global scale. Good citizens understand and practice argument as the best available process for reaching decisions.

PRACTICE 1.5 Argument and Democracy

Respond to the following quotation (through a short writing or a group discussion). How does it relate to argumentation?

> "Democracy is the recurrent suspicion that more than half the people are right more than half the time."
> —E. B. White (*1899–1985*)

Three Persuasive Appeals: Authority, Emotion, and Logic

Claims and support are linked to logic, but using logic is but one of three ways to persuade an audience. These three persuasive appeals are sometimes referred to by their original Greek names: *ethos* (authority), *pathos* (emotion), and *logos* (logic).

How might audiences respond differently to this ad before and after Tiger Woods' admitted adultery? How does this affect the ad's persuasive power?

The next time you see a television commercial or view a print advertisement, pause a moment to think about how it persuades you. Very often, advertisements use an authoritative appeal, using a celebrity spokesperson that you respect. Ads sometime appeal to your emotion, perhaps promising that the product will make you look successful or sexy. Ads sometimes are logical, offering evidence such as test results or statistics to convince you of the product's superiority.

Authority (*Ethos*) Getting readers to read what you have written and respect what you are saying requires you to appear to your audience that you understand what you are discussing. This does not mean that you must necessarily be a leading expert in the field or create an overbearing tone when you write, although some degree of knowledge and self-confidence is part of this perception. The Greek word *ethos* is the same root found in the word *ethical*; it is sometimes translated as *character* or interpreted as *trust*. If your readers trust your character, they will be receptive to the claims and support you present.

There are two ways to enhance your authority as a writer: (1) become an "instant authority" through research and (2) use an authoritative yet reasonable tone.

▶ **Become an "instant authority."** If you know very little about your subject, you can become informed by researching your topic. In this way, you can, in effect, "borrow" the authority of experts in the field. You should also present alternative viewpoints fairly when you write your arguments.

▶ **Sound authoritative.** Once you have researched your topic and borrowed the authority of your sources, you will be more likely to create an authoritative voice in your writing. Your tone of voice should carry confidence and a sense of authority without seeming arrogant or closed-minded.

Emotion (*Pathos*) The emotional appeal helps establish common ground with your readers by demonstrating your sympathy for their values, beliefs, and worldview. It can be a powerful tool. Think of how President Obama's "Hope" poster helped voters identify with him on a personal level by appealing to their emotional need to see their lives improve. The emotional appeal has the added benefit of increasing your ethos with your audience: Once you have established a sympathetic connection, audience members are more likely to view you as a reliable and authoritative source of information.

AP Photo/Manny Garcia/Shepard Fairey

Which of the persuasive appeals were at play in the Obama "Hope" poster of the 2008 election?

Pathos can be overplayed to the point that its emotional element causes the claim to be forgotten. Consider Superbowl commercials that are so humorous you fail to notice which product is being advertised. Pathos also can be too disturbing, such as an anti-abortion ad displaying a bloody fetus pinched between a pair of forceps. The audience may be so repulsed that it refuses to consider the issue.

Logic (*Logos*) The logical appeal is equated strongly with argument. Based on claims, evidence, and specialized kinds of explanations, logic is considered a reliable means for reaching decisions. Logic refers to the reasoning and critical thinking that undergirds the structure of an argument. Logic usually takes two forms: *inductive* and *deductive* reasoning.

Inductive reasoning draws general conclusions from several examples: specific to general. For instance, if you interview ten of your classmates and find out that eight out of ten prefer Professor Smith over Professor Williams, you would infer that Professor Smith is more popular.

Deductive reasoning, on the other hand, begins with an established principle that leads to a particular conclusion: general to specific. This reasoning is illustrated by a logical equation called a *syllogism.* A syllogism begins with a *major premise* (a general principle), followed by a *minor premise* (a specific example); together, these statements lead to a conclusion. For example:

> Riding a bike every day makes you healthy. (*Major premise*)
> Joe rides a bike every day. (*Minor premise*)
> Therefore, Joe is healthy. (*Conclusion*)

The problem with deductive reasoning—sometimes called Aristotelian or formal logic—is that a conclusion can be logically valid without being true. (What if Joe has terminal cancer?)

In *Dynamic Argument*, our method is less formal than Aristotelian logic. We explain argument in terms of "claim, evidence, and explanation" rather than in terms of a syllogism. (See Chapter 2, Claims and Support, and Chapter 10, Using Logic, for more information.)

PRACTICE 1.6	Using Authority, Emotion, and Logic

Make a claim about each of the following issues, and support your claim by using each of the three appeals—emotion, authority, and logic. Because you haven't researched these topics, your support probably will have to be speculative or invented.

1. Are the enhanced screening techniques now used at many airports a violation of privacy?

2. Should chain restaurants be required by law to list nutritional information on their menus?

3. Should higher education be free to all students?

4. Is cyberbullying free speech, protected under the First Amendment?

5. To prevent potential threats against the American public, should the government have access to everyone's personal records, including what individuals choose to read in the library or view on the Internet?

Truth and Belief

What is the relationship between argument and truth? The ancient Greeks, who are credited with bringing the arts of argumentation and rhetoric to Western civilization, believed that truth is absolute, pure, and eternal and was out there waiting to be discovered by philosophers. Today we live in an era that is more relativistic and in which truth is often considered tenuous and subjective. It often seems that the only truth today is the idea that there is no absolute truth.

Of course, truth is not relative in the sense that we can violate the laws of nature, but the values we hold true are largely constructed by our cultural beliefs. How an audience responds to a particular issue—Islam, cyberbullying, mental health, health insurance, or genetic engineering—is guided by what it believes to be fundamentally true about what is important in life. One argues by aligning elements of your position with the values of the audience.

Take marriage, for example: Do you believe it is a holy sacrament created by a divine being? If so, your underlying belief probably is based on religious teachings that a supreme being established rules to guide human behavior. Yet others define marriage primarily as a social contract established by government. Still others see it is primarily a romantic bond between two people. Is it a union of any two (or more) people, or should it be limited to pairs specified by race, religion, gender, age, and so on? Is the union temporary or for life? On top of all these possibilities, do you insist that others should conform to your beliefs—that "there ought to be a law"? However you define marriage, it is your underlying cultural beliefs that guide you.

PRACTICE 1.7   Truth and Claims

For the following issues (or others selected by your instructor), list a claim that particular people make. For each claim, speculate on the belief that underlies it. What do those people believe to be true?

1. Who is responsible for the national debt?
2. To what extent should funding of entitlements such as Medicare, Social Security, or the military be affected by the national debt?
3. What, if anything, should be done about people who hire undocumented workers (illegal immigrants) and pay them at rates below the minimum wage?
4. What restrictions should there be on genetic engineering?
5. Are some poor people being oppressed by society, or are they ultimately responsible for their own station in life because of the choices they make?

WRITING ARGUMENTS

The Writing Process: Planning, Drafting, Revising, Editing, Presenting, Reflecting

Writing includes more than just the physical act of assembling words into visible messages that convey meaning. It also encompasses the mental activities of the writer, including all preparations before and follow-up activities after the physical activity. This comprehensive view of writing is known as the *writing process*. The writing process can be described as consisting of sequential phases—planning, drafting, and revising—although in practice these phases tend to overlap and repeat as the writer discovers what else needs to be done. In other words, the earlier parts of the process are *recursive* (recurring as needed). After the rhetorical and argumentative features are finalized, the writing process terminates with stages that usually occur only once (*nonrecursive*): editing, presenting, and reflecting.

▶ **Planning:** The planning stage of the writing process helps you create arguments by discovering and organizing your claims, evidence, and explanations. Also known as prewriting, it can make writing remarkably easier. Planning includes understanding the assignment, generating material, and organizing.

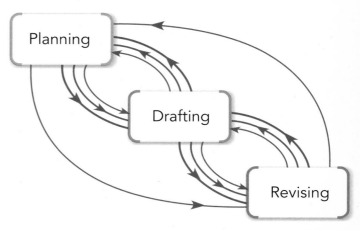

Parts of the writing process are recursive, repeating as needed.

(These techniques are demonstrated in Chapter 5, Planning Arguments.)

▶ **Drafting:** Also known as *composing,* the drafting phase involves putting the arguments into particular words, sentences, paragraphs, and overall structure. Drafting is characterized by the many decisions you must make at the verbal level—diction (word choice), syntax (sentence formation), and organization. It seldom is an orderly process because the text will evolve partly according to early planning and partly through trial and error as the drafting occurs. Often you will resume planning when new ideas are needed or engage in revision briefly while drafting. (These techniques are demonstrated in Chapter 6, Drafting Arguments.)

▶ **Revising:** The word *revision* literally means to "view again." Also known as rewriting, the revising phase is characterized by changing any part of the writing that affects the meaning of a text. When revision reveals that more ideas are needed, the writer may return to planning. You might use a rubric (criteria describing qualities of writing) and feedback from peers, teachers, or editors to help "view again" with fresh eyes. If time allows, you might set the text aside for a while so as to gain a new perspective on it. (These techniques are demonstrated in Chapter 7, Revising and Editing Arguments.)

▶ **Editing:** Editing is the "correctness" phase of the writing process. Known also as copy editing, proofing, or proofreading, this phase involves making sure the usage, spelling, punctuation, and other conventions are acceptable. Editing can be aided by various software packages attached to word processors. Experienced writers postpone most editing until after they finish the revision process. Otherwise, time may be wasted editing text that will be changed or deleted later. Even worse, the flow of drafting may halt while the writer deals with technical details. (These techniques are demonstrated in Chapter 7, Revising and Editing Arguments.)

▶ **Presenting:** Also known as sharing, publishing, or submitting, this phase is when the writer makes the text public in any way. In most college classes, presenting is accomplished by sharing with classmates and by submitting the work to an instructor. It also may involve reading the text in public or circulating it electronically (via e-mail or Web) or in print. In the workplace, virtually all written works are presented to other employees, administrators, or clients as memos, letters, reports, and proposals.

▶ **Reflecting:** You learn from your experiences in life, and writing is one of those experiences. You may learn more if your writing process and products become the subject of reflection, perhaps even the impetus of further writing. Writers sometimes keep a "writer's journal" that is focused on any writing they contemplate, work on, complete, or admire—anything writing-related.

Rhetoric: Purpose, Audience, Structure, and Style

As you write an argument, you must make choices about the best ways to communicate. These choices can be divided into four major considerations:

▶ **Purpose:** What effect on the audience are you seeking?

▶ **Audience:** Who will read (or hear or view) your argument?

▶ **Structure:** What form, genre, or organization will the writing take?

▶ **Style:** What attitude or "voice" will your writing display?

These four considerations—purpose, audience, structure, and style (known by the acronym PASS)—provide the basis for a broad set of rules or guidelines for writing effectively that are known as *rhetoric*. Perhaps without realizing it, you have been learning and practicing rhetoric all your life, communicating in different ways with different kinds of people—friends, teachers, police officers, romantic interests.

The *purpose* is the goal of your communication. In a general sense, your purpose is to argue and to change the audience's thoughts or actions.

→ PURPOSE AND THESIS

We write to attain a purpose—to express our feelings, to entertain, to inform, or to argue. The implied or stated purpose for a particular piece of writing is its central idea—that is, its thesis.

Sample Thesis Statements for Purposes of Writing

▶ **To express:** "When I turned 21, it was the best year of my life!"

▶ **To entertain:** "When I was one-and-twenty / I heard a wise man say / Give crowns and pounds and guineas / But not your heart away."—A. E. Housman

▶ **To inform:** "In most states, 21 years is the minimum age for purchase of liquor."

▶ **To argue (claim):** "The legal age to vote should be 21, not 18."

An argumentative thesis is called a claim. It differs from other statements of purpose primarily because it is controversial, requiring reasons for an audience to accept it. Keep your primary goal in mind when you write. Arguers sometimes get sidetracked into primarily informing or entertaining an audience or venting their personal feelings.

PRACTICE 1.9   Analyzing Rhetoric

For the following paragraph, analyze the major rhetorical features and explain your analysis by referring to specific parts of the passage. Answer these questions about rhetoric:

1. Purpose: What effect on the audience does the author seek?
2. Audience: To whom is the argument addressed? Who would reject it?
3. Structure: What form, genre, or shape does the writing take?
4. Style: What attitude or voice does the writing display?
5. In what ways could the author use rhetoric differently, perhaps more effectively?

"The war on terror is in truth nothing more than an excuse for using aggressive means to open Middle Eastern oil resources to Western corporations—the very corporations that fund the political campaigns of those who engage in the war-making. All talk of terror here is deception, and the shameful and hypocritical war in Iraq is, in fact, a counterproductive effort that will do nothing except worsen the very predicament whose improvement was its stated objective."

—*Excerpt from a student's essay*

However, you will always have a specific purpose for arguing—specific opinions or specific actions desired. In writing, that specific purpose forms your thesis, your argumentative claim.

The *audience* consists of the readers, listeners, or viewers of your argument. In everyday communications you may understand your audience well enough to write or converse freely, such as with a friend. More generally, audiences can vary in so many ways (and may even be imaginary scenarios) that it may be overwhelming to comprehend all of the possibilities:

▶ **Physical characteristics:** Age, race, and gender. For example, an older audience may have different values than a younger audience regarding tastes in music and fashion or ideas about morality.

▶ **Background:** Ethnic group, level of education, geographic or national origin, heritage, religion, politics.

▶ **Size, variety, and distance:** Large or small groups, mixed or uniform, near (in your presence) or far (whom you'll never meet).

Structure is the recognizable form that your argument takes. Written arguments are found in the form of essays, certainly, but also as personal letters, ads, print versions of speeches, memoranda, editorials, and blogs (Weblogs). Structure also includes the way you organize your ideas within a form, such as comparison/contrast or narration. Your audience, purpose, and style will influence your choice of structure. For example, a letter might influence a friend, whereas a letter to the editor of the local newspaper might influence a community.

Style is how you say something. It is influenced strongly by your purpose, audience, and structure. An informal letter to a friend might begin, "What's up, man?" whereas a letter to a senator might begin, "The Honorable Paul Ryan." Style includes voice, which essentially is your personality being expressed through the writing. Your voice is conveyed by your distinctive word choices, sentence formations, and organization as well as by the attitude and tone you convey toward your audience and subject. You vary your writing style to suit the occasion, much the same way that you wear informal clothes to relax with friends but dress up in formal attire to attend a wedding or dinner party.

STUDENT ESSAY

Read the student essay, "Childhood Obesity: Introducing the Fat Card," and complete the associated practice exercises.

PRACTICE 1.10	Before You Read

Working individually or in groups, consider your opinion of the problem of childhood obesity in America.

1. Are more of today's young people getting fat than members of previous generations? What makes you think so?

2. If you think childhood obesity is increasing and creating health problems, what might be the cause?

3. Do you think the responsibility for making people healthy rests with society or with the individual? In other words, can you blame McDonald's for making you fat?

4. Examine the essay's title. What does it suggest about the author's thesis?

Janet Barnett

Dr. Robert Lamm

Composition II

14 April 2011

Childhood Obesity: Introducing the Fat Card

Nationwide, childhood obesity has increased threefold over the last thirty years, rising to affect a total of nine million obese children ("New Grants Program"). Obesity is creeping up on a majority of children as they eat junk food and rest on their derrieres while watching television and playing video games. It is easy to blame fast-food restaurants and advertisers for enticing children to want supersized portions of junk food. Moreover, it is parents and guardians who provide children with fattening food choices and hours of unlimited television time exposing children to advertisements. Many children will not make wise nutritional choices for themselves; therefore, parents should set examples and encourage children to develop healthy eating habits and active lifestyles.

In an effort to inform parents and guardians about how their children rate according to acceptable standards of height and weight, many state governments have ordered schools to provide body mass index information in the form of a health report card—sometimes referred to as a "fat card" ("Massachusetts..."). Although this information alone cannot change the weight of a child, ideally it will make parents and guardians take the initiative to help their children eat healthier and become more physically fit. Some parents fear that too much emphasis is already put on children to be thin, even without the humiliation of a fat report card. Most students and parents resent schools reporting student body mass information and forcing changes in nutrition and exercise.

Barnett 2

   Child nutrition and physical activity are the responsibility of adults in the home. Unfortunately, in the United States, approximately 60 percent of adults are overweight. Based on the assumption that children have environmental influences from obese adults, it is not surprising that one-fourth of our high school students are obese or are at risk of becoming obese. Obese children have shorter life expectancies and will cost the government a phenomenal amount of money in health care. According to Claudia Wallis, overweight adolescents have a high risk of becoming overweight adults (68). Many obese students may not be able to work when they are older if they do not change their lifestyles. Only long-term behavior and health improvement will guard against adult obesity, which is the second leading cause of preventable death in the United States ("New Grants Program").

   Because so many students are failing the nutrition and exercise practicum, the government has had to take necessary steps to change junk-food habits in American children (Avery). Schools are taking on the tasks of monitoring students' health and adapting fitness goals and junk-food intake while at school.

   Some states, such as California, are seeking nutritional standards under which healthier food choices would replace junk food in school vending machines (Sprague). Many schools are afraid if they have to stop selling junk food in vending machines and cafeterias, school programs will suffer because junk food yields high profits. Schools do not want to lose money, and children do not want to give up junk food; but the risks of being overweight are greater.

   Obese students are at risk of developing diseases such as heart conditions, hypertension, and diabetes. Type II diabetes is up

800 percent in the last ten years. Prevention is the best combatant against these diseases caused by obesity.

Promotion of fitness, wellness, active lifestyles, clinical intervention, preventive screenings, and health education are keys to defeating obesity in children and adults nationally ("New Grants Program"). Parents are the most suited to make these changes for children, but it seems the task will be easier if schools help in providing healthier foods and improved physical education plans.

In addition, the health report card will hold parents and guardians accountable for information regarding their children's fitness and provide assistance if necessary. The health report card is a good reminder for parents and students as long as too much emphasis is not placed on the report, causing students who are not overweight to go on starvation diets that could lead to serious food disorders.

Works Cited

Avery, Sarah. "Childhood Obesity Raises Worry, Debate at National Summit." *Knight Ridder Tribune Business News*, 4 Jun. 2004. Web. 8 Apr. 2011.

"Massachusetts Public Schools to Issue 'Fat' Report Cards on Students." Associated Press, 8 Apr. 2009. Web. 9 Apr. 2011.

"New Grants Program Aims to Prevent Obesity through Promoting Physical Activity." *The Daily Record*, 16, Apr. 2004. Web. 8 Apr. 2011.

Sprague, Mike. "California State Senator Seeks Junk-Food Ban for Schools."

Knight Ridder Tribune Business News, 26 Mar. 2004. Web. 8 Apr. 2011.

Wallis, Claudia. "Guess What F Is for? Fat." *Time*: 15 Sep. 2003: 68. Print.

PRACTICE 1.11   Understanding the Essay

1. Identify the writer's central claim (thesis statement). What secondary points does the author make to support the main idea?

2. What sort of evidence does the author provide? Examine the paragraphs one at a time. Are any supporting ideas not really supported?

3. Does the author acknowledge an alternative point of view? Explain.

4. In your own words, summarize the author's (a) argumentative purpose, (b) target audience, (c) method of organization (How does she "break up" the topic into arguable parts?), and (d) style (How does she use language appropriate to the target audience?).

5. How does the author appeal to the audience's logic? How does she attempt to establish an authoritative voice? How does she work to make an emotional connection with the audience?

PRACTICE 1.12   Responding to the Essay

1. Do you agree or disagree with the author's claim and supporting ideas? Did the author change your prior opinion in any way? How?

2. Where is the author's support stronger? Where is it weaker? Explain.

3. Does the author's omission of another point of view affect your willingness to believe what she has to say? In what way?

4. What, if anything, would you change about the essay's organization and content? Is there anything missing that you would add?

5. Which of the appeals (logic, authority, emotion) do you think is strongest in this essay? Which is weakest? Why do you think so?

6. Name the essay's greatest strength and most significant weakness. Explain your answer.

Looking Back at Chapter 1

▶ Argument pervades our lives—in some ways reflecting the way we are but in other ways trying to change thoughts and actions and shape the way we will be.

▶ The pervasiveness of argument in our culture makes its study significant and weighty in ways you may find surprising: You can argue back.

▶ This book aims to provide the experiences, guidance, and tools that will make you a skilled arguer in your studies and in life.
  1. How to recognize the issues in their various forms
  2. How to analyze, evaluate, and respond to arguments
  3. How to effectively present claims, evidence, and explanations
  4. How to utilize authority, logic, and emotion when you argue
  5. How and why you should argue honestly
  6. How to analyze and evaluate the written forms of arguments and write your own arguments using rhetorical principles: audience, purpose, structure, and style

Suggestions for Writing

▶ Search though magazines and locate advertisements. What claims do they make, and how do they support those claims?

▶ Write a journal entry describing and reflecting on your best and worst experiences with writing.

▶ Brainstorm a list of issues that intrigue you and affect your life. Write an essay responding to one of those issues.

▶ Think of one change that would benefit your hometown. Write a detailed letter to the city council explaining what that change is and why it should be made.

Claims and
Support

2

AP Images

A *claim with support*—this is the simplest definition of an argument. A claim is any assertion that your audience won't accept without the support of more information. Support provides evidence as well as helpful explanations of how the evidence is relevant.

This chapter's opening epigraph is a Chinese proverb: "How can one beam alone support a house?" Imagine for a moment that an argument is like a house. A claim resembles a roof, in the sense that it thematically covers

{
How can one beam
alone support a
house?
—Chinese Proverb
}

all the text and needs support—not by beams, but by reasons in the form of evidence and explanations. Without the right kind of support arranged in rhetorically sensible ways, an argument collapses like a shoddily constructed building. To make your argument sturdy, you need to be as familiar with claims and support as a carpenter is with blueprints and building materials.

This chapter will help you to discover arguable claims and to support them with appropriate evidence and clear explanations.

CLAIMS

A claim asserts that something is true, but some element of uncertainty or disagreement prevents others from accepting that statement. Arguments always are based on one or more claims, with the goal of convincing *reasonable skeptics*—people who don't already accept your claim as true, but are willing to weigh the evidence with an open mind.

You encounter claims every day. Some are about public issues, advocated by politicians and interest groups: "Undocumented immigrants should (or should not) be given a path toward citizenship." Other claims are more personal, such as "You should exercise more."

Not All Statements Are Claims

Non-argumentative writings have other primary goals, such as expressing emotions for personal benefits (e.g., a diary, a journal), entertaining readers creatively (e.g., novels, poems), or informing others with noncontroversial facts (e.g., expository writing). Your understanding of claims will help you avoid drifting into writing for non-argumentative purposes. Also, you will be able to better analyze and critique the way others argue about an issue. Finally, understanding claims will help you reach the decision every writer must make: "What do I want to say?"

Claims Are Relative

A claim is relative, meaning that its degree of controversy depends on the audience to whom it is addressed: One audience may fully agree with your position on an issue, whereas another may disagree completely. Consider, for example, two different claims (theories) about the origins of life on earth: evolution and intelligent design. A claim based on intelligent design would be controversial at a conference of scientists, whereas some church congregations would accept intelligent design as a reality, not as a claim. Similarly, evolution is doubted by some religious people but accepted by many scientists as a fact.

A Claim Is the Thesis of Your Argument

An argument usually presents one *major claim* that functions as a thesis statement, the main idea of a piece of writing. A major claim always needs support
in the form of evidence and/or explanations. For example, you might argue
about one of the many issues of the Deepwater Horizon oil spill of 2010. You
might assert that is was (or was not) preventable, that clean-up methods were
effective (or ineffective), that spilled oil did minimal (or catastrophic) damage
to the ecosystem of the Gulf of Mexico, or that a particular party is to blame.
However, other aspects are not claims, such as that fact that the spill did occur.

A Claim Can Act as Supporting Evidence

A *supporting claim* is offered as evidence to back the major claim. Whenever evidence contains some element of uncertainty or disagreement, it
must be treated as a claim and must be given its own support. For example,

---

→ TYPES OF CLAIMS

Fact: Is/was it real?
  Existence: Does/did it actually exist?
  Occurrence: Does/did it actually happen?

Cause/Effect: How or why does it work?
  Cause: What made, makes, or will make
  it happen?
  Effect: What happened, happens, or will
  happen?

Value: How is it judged?
  Quality: How "good" or "bad" is it?
  Ethics/Morality: How "right" or "wrong"
  is it?

Proposal: Should something be done?
  Policy: What should be done?
  Procedure: How should it be done?

Identity: What is it?
  Definition: What are its characteristics?
  Classification: To which group does it
  belong?
  Resemblance: What does it resemble?
  Comparison/Contrast: How is it alike or different?

Maxppp/Landov

**During the Libyan rebellion of 2011, dictator Moammar Gadhafi claimed
that all his people love him, in spite of evidence to the contrary. Unsupported
claims are rarely successful.**

if your major claim was that the Deepwater Horizon oil spill was preventable, then your evidence might be that more government inspections could have saved the day. However, that supporting statement is itself a claim needing proof.

Five Types of Claims

To make claims more understandable, we have sorted them into five types: *fact*, *cause/effect*, *value*, *proposal*, and *identity*. You may find that some of your claims fit more than one category, but don't let that be a problem: your main goal is to argue a position, not to label a claim. In other words, let your *argumentative purpose* govern the type of claim you use—don't let a predetermined claim type dictate the structure of your argument. The thesis statement of an argument usually fits into one of these categories. By contrast, the support you supply for the thesis statement often consists of a combination of many types of claims.

- ► *Fact* claims make assertions about what is real or not real.
- ► *Cause-and-effect* claims make assertions about how or why things happen.
- ► *Value* claims make judgments.
- ► *Proposal* claims make assertions about what should be done.
- ► *Identity* claims make assertions about what something is.

Fact Claims: Is or Was It Real? Fact claims make assertions about whether something is or ever was an actuality, answering the question, "Is or was it real?" These claims sometimes deal with whether an event occurs or ever occurred. In courtrooms, lawyers may debate whether a crime was committed. Likewise, historians debate whether Viking or Chinese explorers discovered America before Columbus. Fact claims may also focus on whether a person, place, thing, or phenomenon exists or ever existed. For example, global warming—a theory that human pollution is contributing to a greenhouse effect—has been the subject of much argument.

> **EXAMPLES OF FACT CLAIMS**
> Could it be that man-made global warming is the greatest hoax ever perpetuated on the American people?
>
> —Senator James Inhofe, Senate Standing Committee on
> Environment and Public Works

The warnings about global warming have been extremely clear for a long time. We are facing a global climate crisis. It is deepening. We are entering a period of consequences.

—Al Gore, former vice president

Facts Change Over time, the unearthing of new evidence has shown many earlier claims of fact to be erroneous. For example, from ancient times until the fifteenth century, European astronomers believed the Earth was the center of the universe; later astronomers such as Copernicus and Galileo discovered new evidence showing the Earth revolved around the Sun.

Facts Overlap into Other Claims If you say it is a fact that Barack Obama was not born in the United States, you may also be arguing an identity claim based on defining "certification of live birth" as being different from "birth certificate." If you say it is a fact that a particular movie is outstanding, you may also be arguing a value claim based on criteria not shared by everyone.

PRACTICE 2.1	Fact Claims

1. What is arguable about the following claims of fact?
   a. Immigrants take jobs from U.S. citizens.
   b. Global warming is only a theory.
   c. The government should provide financial aid for students.
   d. Islam is a violent religion.
   e. Political metaphors such as "crosshairs" or "reload" lead to political assassinations.

2. State a claim of fact that you have heard or read—a statement that some people accept as valid but others reject. What makes this claim arguable? What evidence and explanations support it? Are there alternative claims of fact?

3. State your own claim of fact about a controversial issue. Who would agree or disagree with your claim? How would you defend your position?

Cause-and-Effect Claims: How or Why Does It Happen? Claims of cause and effect argue how or why something takes place. When you argue that an action (or the lack thereof) leads to a particular result, you are making a cause-and-effect claim. Your auto mechanic might warn you that if you don't change the oil in your car regularly, its engine will burn out. Your professor might argue that if you do not do your homework regularly and with care, it will be impossible to get an A in the class.

Non Sequitur © 2005 Wiley Ink, Inc. Dist. by UNIVERSAL UCLICK. Reprinted with permission. All rights reserved.

Understanding cause-effect relationships can help people avoid undesirable consequences.

Cause-and-effect relationships might seem obvious, but in many arguments this kind of link is not immediately clear. An effect might have more than one cause, a cause might have several effects, or the evidence connecting two events might be inconclusive. Because causal relationships are rarely simple, they can be some of the most challenging arguments to make.

When you make a claim about cause and effect, you may want to focus on either a cause or an effect: You'll name a known effect and then claim a cause or causes, or you'll name a known cause and then claim an effect or effects.

Cause Claims: What Made, Makes, or Will Make It Happen?
Cause claims are argued when an effect is known but the cause is uncertain.

EXAMPLE OF A CAUSE CLAIM
Research conducted . . . at Harvard reveals that even among people who claim to have no bias, the more strongly one supports the ethnic profiling of Arabs at airport-security checkpoints, the more hidden prejudice one has against Muslims.

—Margo Monteith, "Why We Hate"

In this example, the cause—a subconscious prejudice against Arabs and Muslims—leads to the effect of supporting racial profiling at airport security stations.

Cause claims may focus on past, present, or future effects, depending on when the effects are presumed to take place.

Effect Claims: What Happened, Happens, or Will Happen?
Effect claims are argued when a cause is known but its outcome is uncertain.

EXAMPLE OF AN EFFECT CLAIM

More than in the past, children are viewed as a project by perfectionist parents. Today's parents are imposing on their kids a violence of raised expectations. They are using their children for their own needs. We've decreased the threat of physical violence but increased the psychological violence.

—Steven Mintz, *Huck's Raft: A History of American Childhood*

In this example, the focus is on the effect. The cause—parents who drive their children to excel as a sort of status symbol—results in the effect—psychological damage to the children.

Like cause claims, effect claims may focus on past, present, or future effects.

Causal Chains Some cause-and-effect claims deal with a sequence of events called a causal chain. In a causal chain, each effect becomes the cause of another effect. On March 12, 2011, the world witnessed how one catastrophe can lead to another: The magnitude 8.9 earthquake in northeast Japan caused a tsunami that caused meltdowns at the Fukushima nuclear plant that caused an economic crisis not only in Japan but also in countries dependent upon Japan's production of materials.

Courtesy of Hasbro, Inc.

The game Mouse Trap is based on a causal chain: each effect causes another effect.

Vicious Circles Some causal chains are actually causal loops known as vicious circles, such as the historic feud between the Hatfield and McCoy clans: A member of one family shoots a member of the other family, setting off a series of revenge killings. Sociologists and economists speak of the "cycle of poverty," a self-perpetuating situation in which the deprivations associated with having a low income produce new generations of poor people. It is possible to write an entire essay that focuses on a cycle of causes and effects. For example, in the diagram on page 33, domestic-abuse counselors argue that a "cycle of violence" within an abusive relationship (1) begins with an incident of violence, (2) which is followed by making up, (3) which results in a period of calm, (4) which is followed by a period of renewed tension, (5) which eventually explodes into a new incident of violence, and so on.

PRACTICE 2.2   Cause and Effect Claims

1. In a journal entry or group discussion, make claims about the following issues as (1) effects and then as (2) causes. What evidence is available? Who would agree or disagree with your claims of cause and effect? Why?

   a. Millions of undocumented immigrants.
   b. College students unable to pay for tuition.
   c. Radicalization of American Muslims.
   d. Unaffordable health care.
   e. Increasing national debt.

2. Name a cause or effect that you have heard or read about. What claims do some people make regarding this cause? Who would disagree? Why?

3. Name a cause or effect that interests you. What claim would you make? Who would agree or disagree with your position? Why? How would you defend your claim?

Value: How Is It Judged? Value claims make judgments about things, answering the question, "How is it judged?" These claims examine specific features or criteria and assess them using standards or a scale. The assessment can be quantitative, which usually means that numbers are involved, or qualitative, which usually means that the assessment is stated in words. Assessments often rank the thing being assessed (e.g., "top of the class") or simply accept or reject the thing (e.g., a "pass/fail exam").

Value claims can be classified as either quality or moral/ethical, based on the kinds of standards applied.

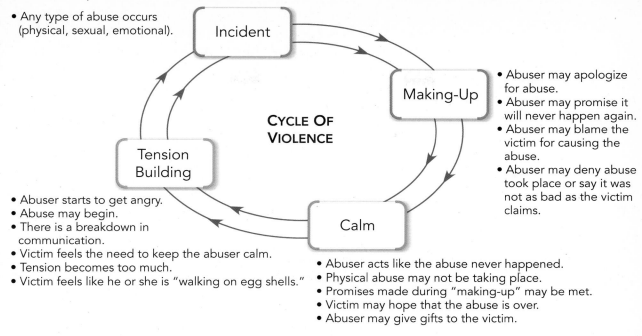

- Any type of abuse occurs (physical, sexual, emotional).

Incident

Making-Up

- Abuser may apologize for abuse.
- Abuser may promise it will never happen again.
- Abuser may blame the victim for causing the abuse.
- Abuser may deny abuse took place or say it was not as bad as the victim claims.

CYCLE OF VIOLENCE

Tension Building

- Abuser starts to get angry.
- Abuse may begin.
- There is a breakdown in communication.
- Victim feels the need to keep the abuser calm.
- Tension becomes too much.
- Victim feels like he or she is "walking on egg shells."

Calm

- Abuser acts like the abuse never happened.
- Physical abuse may not be taking place.
- Promises made during "making-up" may be met.
- Victim may hope that the abuse is over.
- Abuser may give gifts to the victim.

Cause and effect sometimes result in a self-perpetuating cycle, such as the "cycle of violence."

Quality Claims: How Good or Bad Is It?   Quality claims assert that a person, place, thing, or event fulfills a function at a particular level of competence. Typically the writer acts as a critic, reviewer, grader, or other kind of evaluator of the quality of performance.

EXAMPLES OF QUALITY CLAIMS

The scenery, effects, and balletic, iconic combats are perfectly wonderful, but there's an emotional black hole where the hero should be.

> —Joe Morgenstern, "Lucas Goes to the Dull Side" (review of *Star Wars Episode III*)

All Libyans love me.

> —Moammar Gadhafi, Libyan dictator, during the rebellion of 2011

The criteria used to evaluate performances may range along a high-to-low scale, as in the following examples:

▶ Hotels and restaurants are rated on the quality of service: "four out of five stars."

▶ Dramas are rated on aesthetic qualities such as the script, costumes, and actors' performances: "two thumbs up."

▶ Employee performances are rated according to a supervisor's expectations: "excellent," "good," or "bad."

When making quality claims, it is important to use criteria that other people can share. For example, film critics assess the acting, screenplay, musical score, special effects, and other features that an audience values. Critics, judges, and reviewers try to maintain as much objectivity as possible, avoiding claims based on idiosyncratic, personal tastes. For example, saying "I hate spicy foods" is such a highly personal critique of Cajun cuisine that a mixed audience will find the information in a restaurant review containing this phrase of little use when looking for a place to dine.

"Dude, I got the answers for the test in Ethics class from my frat brother ... you want 'em?"

Moral/ethical arguments make judgments about conduct.

By permission of Russ Wallace and Creators Syndicate, Inc.

Moral and Ethical Claims: How "Right" or "Wrong" Is It?

Moral and ethical claims judge human behavior by applying a code of conduct based on a religious or philosophical belief system. These types of claims emerge when someone (1) matches a standard to a situation or behavior, (2) establishes a moral/ethical standard where none previously existed, and (3) resolves conflicts between competing moral/ethical standards (for example, between mercy killing and allowing someone to suffer). The moral/ethical scale of values typically ranges from right to wrong, from good to evil, or from moral to immoral. Depending on one's belief system, this scale may or may not include a middle ground or "gray area."

EXAMPLES OF MORAL OR ETHICAL CLAIMS

Advocates of the gay and lesbian movement have the responsibility to set forth publicly their alternative proposals.

—*Wall Street Journal* editorial

Contrary to a lot of scary rhetoric, a healthy cloned infant would not be a moral nightmare, merely the not-quite-identical twin of an older person.

—Virginia Postrel, "Should Human Cloning Be Allowed? Yes, Don't Impede Medical Progress"

Most people make moral/ethical decisions, following their consciences or moral compasses—in fact, a lack of conscience is considered a defining trait of a sociopath. Conscience goes beyond an individual's conduct, spilling over into public affairs and taking many forms. Although "separation of church and state" limits religion-based influence on some public issues, it doesn't prevent people from "voting their conscience." Codes of conduct, such as an honor code against cheating, try to make a boundary between ethical and unethical behavior. For example, your professor may discuss plagiarism in your class. When she tells you that representing someone else's writing as your own is like stealing, the professor is making an ethical argument.

The argument that women and children should be rescued first in a disaster is a moral choice based on conscience and a sense of right and wrong.

PRACTICE 2.3   Value Claims: Quality

1. For each of the following (1) give an example of a quality claim and (2) evaluate the example based on qualities you select. Briefly explain your evaluation.

   a. Creative artist or work (film, television, stage, music, art, writing)
   b. Politician or political party
   c. Law or public policy

2. Describe a quality claim that you have heard or read. Who would agree or disagree with it? Why?

3. Select something that interests you and briefly evaluate it. Name and explain the qualities you believe to be important. Who would agree or disagree with your position? Why?

PRACTICE 2.4   Value Claims: Moral and Ethical

1. For each of the following, take a moral or ethical stand. Which criteria are you using? Who might agree or disagree with your values?

   a. Some ethnic groups are more dangerous than others, so they should be profiled for searches and other means of investigation.
   b. Activists have a right to demonstrate at funerals of the kinds of people they oppose.
   c. Because of limited funding, some sick people should be denied health care.

2. Describe a moral/ethical claim that you have heard or read. Who might agree or disagree with it? Why?

3. Make a claim about something moral or ethical that interests you. Which values influence your claim? Who might agree or disagree your position, and why?

Proposal Claims: Should Something Be Done? When you make a proposal, you try to convince an audience that it should take a specific course of action. Familiar examples of proposals are those issued regularly by the American Medical Association and the U.S. Department of Health, which suggest dietary habits that could improve health and longevity. Dietary proposals often are supported by other kinds of claims such as classification (food groups) or value (degree of healthiness of particular foods).

Proposal claims have two possible aims: prescribing *what* should be done (policy) and indicating *how* it should be done (procedure). Policy and procedure are closely related, and sometimes you may find yourself synthesizing the two

By permission of Chip Bok and Creators Syndicate, Inc.

Proposal claims argue what should be done, such as "eat healthy foods." Identity claims classify the foods we should eat.

AP Images

What policies should governments enact to be better prepared to respond to disasters?

into one argument. On other occasions you may be more concerned with one aim than the other. For example, you may want to propose or revise a policy without getting into the details of its implementation, or you may want to propose or revise an implementation plan for an existing policy.

Policy: What Should Be Done? Policies can be rules, guidelines, or laws. They help guide decision makers, enabling them to treat people or situations in a consistent and fair manner. When policies lack consistency or fairness, they are likely to be challenged and eventually revised or repealed.

EXAMPLE OF A POLICY CLAIM

If cities are to survive in Europe or elsewhere, they will need to face this latest threat to urban survival with something more than liberal platitudes, displays of pluck, and willful determination. They will have to face up to the need for sometimes harsh measures, such as tighter immigration laws, preventive detention, and widespread surveillance of suspected terrorists, to protect the urban future.

—Joel Kotkin, "City of the Future"

Procedure: How Should It Be Done? A claim of procedure is intended to persuade an audience that a policy should be carried out in a specific way. For example, if your community had a policy of restricting possession of handguns, you might propose a buy-back program through which people could turn in handguns for cash; this procedure would be an alternative to procedures such as having the police execute search warrants in homes and other methods that might be either objectionable or ineffective.

© Robin Nelson/Photo Edit

Students with cognitive disabilities receive help while enrolled in a special degree program. Should institutions create special bachelor's programs for people who are mentally challenged?

PRACTICE 2.5 — Proposal Claims: Policy and Procedure

1. For each of the following issues, write a policy and then propose procedures for implementing that policy:

   a. Cyberbullying: What should be done?
   b. National debt: What should be done?
   c. Financial aid for college students: What should be done?

2. Describe a proposal that you have heard or read. Who would agree or disagree with it? Why?

3. Choose a problem that concerns you. Write a proposal that will remedy this problem. In what way do you think your proposal will be beneficial? Is your proposal practical?

EXAMPLE OF A PROCEDURE CLAIM

Given the gravity of the terrorist threat, vigorous questioning [of prisoners] short of torture—prolonged interrogations, mild sleep deprivation, perhaps the use of truth serum—might be justified in some cases.

—*The Economist* editorial

Identity Claims: What Is It? Identification is the ability to assign a name to something by observing its characteristics. The ability to identify is so basic to our lives that we probably take it for granted.

Identity claims are based on descriptive details known as criteria (also called descriptors, qualities, characteristics, or features). Criteria provide a kind of checklist that helps answer the question, "How do I know what this is?" For example, if you define an activist as "a person who believes that direct, visible action is necessary to attain a political or social goal," then the criteria are expressed in the key words: *person, direct action, visible action,* and *social* or *political goal.*

The methods we use for identification include defining, observing resemblances, classifying, and comparing/contrasting.

By permission of John L. Hart FLP and Creators Syndicate, Inc.

Identification claims are based on criteria that are descriptive.

Definition Claims: What Are Its Characteristics? Definition claims identify something by detailing its characteristics or features. For example, "An activist is a person who believes that direct, visible action is necessary to attain a political or social goal." Most definitions are not controversial, but they become claims when they are not accepted by all or part of an audience.

Features: Definition often places the specific thing being defined within a larger category and then distinguishes it from other classes within the larger category. Other means of definition include telling what it is not, giving examples, and explaining derivations, root words.

EXAMPLE OF A DEFINITION CLAIM

Cyberbullying is "any use of information and communication technology to support deliberate and hostile attempts to hurt, upset, or embarrass another person."

—Anne Collier, "Cyberbullying in the Workplace"

Resemblance Claims: What Does It Resemble? Sometimes you may identify things by indicating what they resemble. Resemblance claims can help an audience understand something complex or unknown by showing how it mimics something simpler or more familiar.

Features: Resemblance uses simile, metaphor, or analogy. Explanation of the similarity or difference often accompanies the statement of resemblance.

EXAMPLE OF A RESEMBLANCE CLAIM

At first glance, the correlation between piracy and terrorism seems a stretch. Yet much of the basis of this skepticism can be traced to romantic and inaccurate notions about piracy. An examination of the actual history of the crime reveals startling, even astonishing, parallels to contemporary international terrorism.

—Douglas R. Burgess, Jr., "The Dread Pirate bin Laden"

Classification Claims: To Which Group Does It Belong? Classification claims offer a system for splitting a large group of people, places, objects, or events into smaller groups. People are classified by race, gender, age, education, career, nationality, religion, height, weight, blood group, hair color, and many other ways. For example, "Political demonstrators may be classified four ways: activists, rabbles, subversives, and crazies."

Features: The categories can be presented in different ways: order of importance, alphabetical order, order of appearance (e.g., geological or historical eras). The components of a large group often can be arranged continuously between two extremes, as with human IQ values. A range (spectrum or continuum) usually is divided into subgroups, even when none are obvious, such as the way the U.S. Department of Agriculture divides healthy eating into five categories represented as a plate of food.

EXAMPLE OF CLASSIFICATION CLAIM

The spectrum of body decoration incorporates body painting, body adornment, and body modification.

—Janice Selekman, "A New Era of Body Decoration"

Comparison and Contrast Claims: How Is It Alike or Different?

Comparison and contrast claims identify something in relation to something else: Features of one thing are shown to be similar to or different from the features of the other thing. Claims based on comparisons and contrasts tend to point out the unexpected: how two "different" things are unexpectedly alike, or how two "identical" things are surprisingly different.

Features: If the comparison/contrast runs more than a few sentences, it often is organized by either a "Point by Point" or a "Block" method.

EXAMPLE OF A COMPARISON AND CONTRAST CLAIM

The negative effects of cyberbullying are often more serious and long-lasting than those of traditional forms of bullying for several reasons. First, the internet provides a veil of anonymity. . . .

—Alison Virginia King, "Constitutionality of Cyberbullying Laws"

PRACTICE 2.6	Identity Claims: Definition, Comparison/Contrast, and Classification

1. Define a term (a concept, thing, or role) connected to an issue that interests you. Consider terms such as civil disobedience, terrorism, American Dream. Here is an example: "Cyberbullying is psychological assault through electronic means."
2. State a resemblance between a term and something similar. For example, "A cyberbully is like a sniper, concealed but determined to psychologically wound a victim."
3. Compare/contrast a term to something similar. List the points of comparison and/or contrast. For example, "Cyberbullying is like bullying but is different in means of contact (anonymous vs. face-to-face) and method of attack (psychological vs. physical)."
4. Classify a term as part of a larger group containing three or more categories. For example, "Hate crimes include cyberbullying, bullying, gay-bashing, and ethnic slurs."

→ TWO WAYS TO ORGANIZE A COMPARISON AND CONTRAST

When your comparison/contrast extends to several sentences or paragraphs, choose a way to organize: *point-by-point* or *block method*.

▶ *Point-by-point* uses the major points of comparison as text units. Discuss everything about one characteristic or point before moving on to additional points. The advantage is that it keeps the differences and similarities very clear.

▶ *Block method* uses the separate subjects as text units. Discuss everything about the first subject before discussing the second subject. The advantage is that it keeps each subject clear, but the distinctive differences and similarities are less clear than with point-by-point.

Point-by-Point Comparison/Contrast Guidelines

▶ Address the similarities and/or differences of both subjects one point at a time.

▶ Follow the same order of the two subjects under each point (usually).

Point-by-Point Outline: Comparing Conventional Bullying and Cyberbullying

  I. Introduction (usually naming the two subjects being compared and why)

  II. First point (e.g., topic names "method of contact")

    a. First subject (conventional bullying: usually face to face)

    b. Second subject (cyberbullying: usually anonymous)

  III. Second point (e.g., method of abuse)

    a. First subject (conventional bullying: usually physical)

    b. Second subject (cyberbullying: usually psychological)

  IV. Third point (e.g., audience)

    a. First subject (conventional bullying: usually limited to a small group or community)

    b. Second subject (cyberbullying: can be global, through the Internet)

  V. Conclusion

Block Method Comparison/Contrast Guidelines

▶ Discuss all points for the first subject before transitioning to the second subject.

▶ Follow the same order of points for each of the two subjects (usually).

Block Method Outline: Comparing Conventional Bullying and Cyberbullying

  I. Introduction (usually naming the two subjects being compared and why)

  II. First subject (conventional bullying)

    a. First point (method of contact usually is face to face)

    b. Second point (method of abuse primarily is physical)

    c. Additional points as needed

  III. Second subject (physical bullying)

    a. First point (method of contact usually is anonymous)

    b. Second point (method of abuse primarily is psychological)

    c. Additional points as needed

  IV. Conclusion

SUPPORT

A claim seldom stands alone: You must convince the doubters. Support your claim with evidence and with explanations of how the evidence fits the claim.

akva/Shutterstock.com

Support is not automatic. It requires research.

Evidence

Evidence gives support to a claim by connecting it to the real world. Evidence helps answer the question, "What proof is there that the claim is valid?" Your answer could consist of many categories, or kinds, of evidence: anecdotes, expert opinions, facts and statistics, history, scenarios, and specific examples.

Anecdotes Anecdotes are real-life accounts of situations or events that have happened to you or to others. They usually are specific and limited, lacking the significant number of cases typical of statistics. However, story-telling techniques (narration and description) can make anecdotes very vivid and appealing to an audience.

EXAMPLE OF AN ANECDOTE
Megan was a thirteen-year old middle-school student who engaged in an online relationship with a purported fellow teen, Josh Evans, through the popular social networking site MySpace. What began as a friendly and flirta-tious exchange of messages escalated into a barrage of cruel and insulting attacks that drove Megan, who suffered from clinical depression, to take her own life. Megan's mother found her hanging in the closet by her neck from a belt the day of Josh's final posting: "The world would be a better place without you."

—Alison Virginia King, "Constitutionality of Cyberbullying Laws"

Expert Opinions   You could quote, paraphrase, or summarize the opinion of an expert or experts on an issue. The opinion can carry much weight if it is based on research, analysis, and interpretation. Of course, experts disagree on many things, so the opinion of only one may not be enough to convince an audience.

EXAMPLE OF AN EXPERT OPINION

Chief Justice Roberts, writing for the majority, acknowledged "uncertainty at the outer boundaries as to when courts should apply school speech precedents. . . ."

—Alison Virginia King, "Constitutionality
of Cyberbullying Laws"

Facts and Statistics   Any evidence that an audience will accept at face value can be considered a *fact*; you may support a claim using facts from science or other sources. A statistic is a fact based on numerous cases. Although statistical evidence may not be as vivid as an anecdote or a scenario, it often can more accurately reveal the "big picture."

EXAMPLE OF STATISTICS

Even though suicide rates have decreased 28.5% between 1990 and 2004 among young people, upward trends were identified in the 10- to 19-year-old age group in 2003–2004 (Center for Disease Control and Prevention, 2007).

—Sameer Hinduja and Justin W. Patchin, "Bullying,
Cyberbullying, and Suicide"

History   What happened in the past could resemble the present and thus be used as a precedent or analogy.

EXAMPLE OF HISTORY

The Tuskegee study is the most notorious episode in the history of American medical research. Begun in 1932, . . . more than 400 of the men were known to have syphilis and were never treated; some of them unknowingly transmitted it to wives and children; many died of the disease.

—Anonymous, "Don't Let It Happen Again"

Scenarios   You can produce hypothetical or fictionalized accounts. Like anecdotes and personal experience, scenarios can be vivid and dramatic. They can also illustrate what *might* happen.

EXAMPLE OF A SCENARIO

Imagine, for a moment, that a disease like this exists—it affects babies in the womb, is often fatal, but may be treatable using some very fancy new technology. The treatment (which is experimental and not guaranteed to work) involves injecting the unborn fetus with a special extract of human cells. The only drawback is that the cells are derived from living adults. The cells in question must be "harvested" from adults suffering from Alzheimer's disease or Parkinson's disease [who are to be] humanely and quietly killed and their cells used to save the lives of babies. A disturbing scenario—one which would hopefully never be allowed to happen. But the exact reverse of this is, apparently, fine.

—Ed Walker, "We Must Not Kill to Cure"*

Specific Examples You sometimes will offer a sampling of evidence to represent a larger body of evidence. Some examples are brief, consisting only of naming the evidence; these brief examples may be illustrative without claiming statistical significance. Other examples may be detailed, perhaps involving description, narration, or other techniques.

EXAMPLE OF A SPECIFIC EXAMPLE

The cartoon carnage that ends each episode of *South Park*, when the character meets different grotesque deaths, has echoes of the comic dismemberment suffered by a stupidly obstinate knight in *Month Python and the Holy Grail* (1975)—not to mention the cretinous head-bashing of the Three Stooges.

—Anonymous, "Moreover: It's Stupidity, Stupid"

PRACTICE 2.7   Finding Evidence

Make a claim about an issue that concerns you. Using the following list as a guide, speculate about the kind of evidence you might find:

▶ Expert opinions

▶ Facts and statistics

▶ History

▶ Personal experience

▶ Scenarios

▶ Specific examples

*Ed Walker, "We Must Not Kill to Cure" Hospital Doctor. *Sutton:* Apr 29, 2004. p. 13 (1 page). Reprinted by permission of the author.

Explanations

Evidence hardly ever "speaks for itself," yet inexperienced writers too often move from one piece of evidence to the next prematurely, leaving their audience to figure things out for themselves. Poorly explained evidence can not only frustrate a reader but also leave the writer struggling to find enough words to fulfill a minimum-length requirement. Explanations can appear before a piece of evidence (as an introduction), after a piece of evidence (as a follow-up), or both. Also, explanations may be combined in various ways—that is, you may explain evidence using more than one approach.

The explanations listed below are based on a system known as Bloom's taxonomy, which identifies six ways we can understand things: knowledge (clarification), comprehension (interpretation), application, analysis, synthesis, and evaluation.

Knowledge (Clarification): Clarify to Make Sure the Evidence Is Understood

You can explain to ensure that evidence is understood on a basic, literal level. This kind of explanation is known as clarification, or "making clear." Clarification typically entails some kind of repetition. Although repetition and redundancy often are a waste of words, at other times they are necessary to ensure the reader understands your meaning. Paraphrase, summary, and emphasis are types of restatements that help clarify evidence.

Paraphrase: Restate to Translate Some evidence may need to be repeated in more familiar terms. Paraphrasing can make slang, technical jargon, or dialect more intelligible; it can also use synonyms to make important points more clearly relevant to a claim.

> **EXAMPLE OF PARAPHRASING**
> Ann L. Flynn, a psychologist who is associate director of the Counseling Center at College of the Holy Cross, cited the trauma and searingly personal sense of violation that accompanies a sexual assault as another reason such crimes are underreported. "In terms of whether it gets reported, there's a good reason for why not," Flynn said. "It's a medical, psychological, criminal event. When a person is raped, they're responding to the immediacy of their emotional, medical state."
>
> —Ian Donnis, "Campus Rape: A Hidden Problem"

Summarize: Restate to Abbreviate Putting the evidence "in a nutshell" makes it easier to grasp.

EXAMPLE OF SUMMARIZING

In "The Challenge of Legalizing Drugs" . . . Joseph P. Kane, S.J., presents a compelling description of the devastation wreaked on our society by drug abuse, but draws some troubling conclusions supporting the legalization of drugs. . . . The solution, he concludes, is to legalize drugs while at the same time (1) changing attitudes within our society about drugs, (2) changing laws and public policy, and (3) providing drug education and treatment to all those who want it.

—Gerald Lynch and Roberta Blotner, "Legalizing Drugs Is Not the Solution"

Emphasize: Restate to Highlight Sometimes one part of the evidence is more relevant, revealing, or startling than other parts. Emphasis helps your reader see the key points.

EXAMPLE OF EMPHASIZING

The point is not that consensual sex always involves an explicit "yes, I want to have sex with you," but that nonconsensual sex always involves, at best, a failure to be sure that sex is wanted.

—Richard Orton, "Date Rape: Critiquing the Critics"

Interpretation: Speculate on Its Deeper Meaning and Significance Sometimes evidence requires an interpreter who can "read between the lines," putting a kind of "spin" on it. If a statistic shows the unemployment rate as 5.4 percent, is that to be regarded with alarm or relief? Your interpretation will put the data into perspective.

EXAMPLE OF INTERPRETATION

It took 71 eggs to produce a single [cloning] success, and in the best case, the embryo grew to only six cells before dying. That's not a revolution. It's an incremental step in understanding how early-stage cells develop.

—Virginia Postrel, "Should Human Cloning Be Allowed?: Yes, Don't Impede Medical Progress"

Application: Explain How the Evidence Applies Application can be important when the connection between the evidence and the claim isn't immediately clear. An analogy, for example, involves "applying" the principles underlying one thing to another, seemingly different thing.

EXAMPLE OF APPLICATION

For more than 3 billion years, biological evolution has guided the colonization of our planet by living organisms. Evolution's rules are simple: Creatures that adapt to threats and master the evolutionary game thrive; those that don't, become extinct. And so it is with the threat posed to the United States by terrorist networks such as al Qaeda. If the genus Americanus wants to overcome this latest challenge to its existence, it must adapt its defense mechanism accordingly.

—Raphael Sagarin, "Adapt or Die"

Analysis: Explain the Parts Analysis is like a dissection, dividing a whole into its parts and explaining how they work separately and in unison. When an argument is complex, breaking it down into smaller pieces helps the audience understand it more readily.

EXAMPLE OF ANALYSIS
Three horrors come to mind: First, the designing of our descendents, whether through cloning or germ-line engineering, is a form of generational despotism.

—Eric Cohen and William Kristol, "Should Human Cloning Be Allowed? No, It's a Moral Monstrosity"

Synthesis: Relate It to Other Claims or Evidence One claim or piece of evidence may interact with others, supporting each other piece or disagreeing with it. Synthesis brings two or more arguments together, allowing for comparison/contrast, rebuttal, or accumulation of mutually supporting points. Synthesis is discussed in Chapter 8, Using Sources, Avoiding Plagiarism.

EXAMPLE OF SYNTHESIS
The ideas of integration and assimilation were key to earlier versions of America's historical narrative, be it the assimilation of European immigrants at the turn of the century, like those in *The Godfather*, or the motive for integration that defined Martin Luther King Jr.'s ideology and that of the civil rights movement.

—Todd Boyd, *The New H.N.I.C.*

Evaluation: Explain Its Value Sometimes evidence needs qualification: an explanation of how reliable and complete it is. Rebuttals often use evaluation to dismiss the other claims or evidence as being weak or erroneous.

EXAMPLE OF EVALUATION
The best discussion I have seen of the role and influence of music in the lives of today's young people occurs in the "Music" chapter of the late Allan Bloom's 1997 book, *The Closing of the American Mind*.

—Lloyd Eby, "The World & I"

PRACTICE 2.8   Explaining Your Own Evidence

For an essay you are currently writing, select a piece of evidence and explain it using Bloom's taxonomy. How many ways of explaining can you apply to it? Which way(s) seem most effective?

PRACTICE 2.9   Before You Read

1. What do you think of when you hear the word *bullying*? What do you already know about *cyberbullying*? Why is it considered controversial? If you don't know much about this topic, how could you find out more?
2. What do you think of when you hear the phrase *freedom of speech*? Should this freedom have limits? What problems might be caused by free speech? What problems might be caused by limiting free speech?
3. What does the essay's title, "Cyberbullied to Death," suggest to you about the topic? What do you think the essay will claim? What kind of evidence and explanations do you think the author will use?
4. Glance over the essay quickly. Look at the "Works Cited" page. What does it tell you about what the writer will argue?

David J. Green/Alamy

Cyberbullying can happen anywhere at any time.

STUDENT ESSAY

In the following essay, a student discusses the issue of cyberbullying. We suggest you complete the "Before You Read" Practice prior to reading this essay, and then answer the questions that follow the reading.

Flagg   1

Erin Flagg

Dr. Robert Lamm

Composition

14 February 2011

Cyberbullied to Death

"Sticks and stones may break my bones, but words will never hurt me." I vividly remember my parents comforting me with this proverb when I would come home from elementary school upset about another student calling me an ugly name. However, bullying has taken a new turn in recent years. Not only is bullying verbal, but it has also gone viral. Sent online or as text messages, harsh comments travel much further than they once did and can resonate much longer. This new form of bullying is referred to as *cyberbullying*. Sadly, it is leading some students to take their own lives: they are cyberbullied to death.

The issue of cyberbullying raises four questions: First, how does cyberbullying become lethal? Second, at what point does cyberbullying become a crime? Third, how adequate are the existing laws? Finally, what must yet be done to protect victims of cyberbullying?

First, we should consider the question of how cyberbullying can push its victims toward suicide. Cyberbullying consists of "willful and repeated harm inflicted through the use of computers, cell phones,

and other electronic devices" (Hinduja and Patchin, "Bullying . . ."
208). The harm ranges from brutal e-mails to harsh postings on
Facebook or other electronic media. Similar to traditional bullying,
cyberbullying causes its victims to undergo negative effects: low self-
esteem, depression, and suicidal thoughts (Hinduja and Patchin,
"Cyberbullying . . ." 1).

However, cyberbullying can be more extreme than traditional
bullying. Rather than just name-calling on the playground in front of a few
people, cyberbullying can be posted widely, instantly, and permanently,
twenty-four hours a day. Escape is impossible and the effects are
psychologically devastating. Research shows that damages were
"heightened when the student had no idea who was doing the bullying,
which increased the feelings of powerlessness and fear among targets"
(Hoff and Mitchell 659). The resulting depression and suicidal tendencies
have prompted the Centers for Disease Control and Prevention to
characterize cyberbullying as an "emerging public health problem"
(qtd. in King 849).

Our second major question concerns the point at which
cyberbullying crosses the line from childish misbehavior to crime. To
answer this question, consider Megan Meir, a thirteen-year-old girl from
Missouri. She committed suicide in 2006 after being cyberbullied by
"Josh Evans," who actually was Lori Drew, the mother of one of
Megan's friends:

> Megan . . . engaged in an online relationship with a purported
> fellow teen, Josh Evans, through the popular social networking
> website MySpace. What began as a friendly and flirtatious
> exchange of messages escalated into a barrage of cruel and

insulting attacks that drove Megan, who suffered from clinical depression, to take her own life. Megan's mother found her hanging in her closet by her neck from a belt the day of Josh's final posting: "The world would be a better place without you." (King 846–847)

By definition, Lori Drew was a cyberbully who willfully caused harm through an electronic medium. But to what extent is she a criminal, accountable for a victim's suicide? Although reasonable people might find Lori Drew culpable, there are two major legal complications that stand in the way of justice: freedom of speech and a lack of adequate legal protection for victims.

First, cyberbullies may be protected under First Amendment "freedom of speech" precedents (King 864). Although communities and states often set standards for speech in schools, acts of expression outside of schools are a different matter. For that reason, Lori Drew's "free speech" was protected as she used her home computer to cyberbully Megan Meir. This protection of speech was affirmed by the United States Supreme Court: speaking for the majority of justices, Chief Justice John Roberts observed "uncertainty at the outer boundaries as to when courts should apply school speech precedents."

Another legal loophole for cyberbullies is that the cause-and-effect of harassment and suicide is difficult to prove under existing laws (Bennett). Some prosecutors instead have prosecuted under related yet clearer charges, such as stalking or harassment. However, this indirect approach is impractical:

> [T]his approach heavily burdens prosecutors, who must find an arguably applicable law and build a case that satisfies the

requirements of a law intended to fight *offline* problems. Cybercrimes have unique features and raise special evidentiary issues that might not be adequately addressed by simply stretching old laws to fit new crimes. (King 855)

Our third major question concerns the adequacy of existing laws. This question can be answered by the Megan Meir/Lori Drew case: Lori Drew, the cyberbully associated with the suicide of Megan Meir, ultimately was convicted of nothing. Because her offense did not fit existing statutes under the federal Computer Fraud and Abuse Act, Lori Drew was able to beat the charges against her: "Judge Wu aptly recognized the ill fit of the CFAA to Drew's case, noting that 'there is nothing in the legislative history of the CFAA which suggests that Congress ever envisioned . . . application of the statute [to cyberbullying]'" (King 857). Although forty-five states now have anti-bullying laws, still they often are inadequate. For example, in Arkansas the law prohibits cyberbullying narrowly, only if it "presents a clear and present danger" of injury or "substantial disruption," and only within the schools, not outside the schools (King 860).

Finally, we should consider the question of what now must be done to protect victims from cyberbullying. The threat of cyberbullying in our society is on the rise, and ultimately it will continue to increase if preventative measures and strict actions are not taken. Legislators must decide who needs protection more, the bullies or the victims. It is our responsibility to stand up to cyberbullies before they bully another victim to death.

Works Cited

Bennett, Jessica. "From Lockers to Lockup." *Newsweek.com*, 4 Oct. 2010. Web. 6 Feb. 2011.

Hinduja, Sameer, Justin Patchin. "Bullying, Cyberbullying, and Suicide." *Archives of Suicide Research* 14:3 (2010): 206–221. Print.

Hinduja, Sameer, Justin Patchin. "Cyberbullying: Identification, Prevention, and Response." *Cyberbullying Research Center* (2010): 1–5. Web/PDF. 31 Jan 2011.

Hoff, Diane L. and Sidney N. Mitchell. "Cyberbullying: Causes, Effects, and Remedies." *Journal of Education Administration* 47.5 (2009): 652–655. Print.

King, Alison Virginia. "Constitutionality of Cyberbullying Laws: Keeping the Online Playground Safe for Both Teens and Free Speech." *Vanderbilt Law Review* 63:3 (2010): 845–884. Print.

PRACTICE 2.10   Responding to the Essay

1. Study the introductory paragraph. What does the author intend to accomplish with this paragraph?
2. What is the thesis of the essay? Where is it located? Is the thesis strongly stated or implied? Is there a forecast of main points?
3. How well is the essay organized? Are the topics and transitions clear? Explain any organizational strengths and weaknesses.
4. What evidence does the author cite? Is the evidence adequate to support the claim(s)? Are the explanations adequate?
5. Examine the conclusion. How does it relate to the thesis and/or to the forecast of main points?
6. If you were peer-reviewing this essay, what would you say were its best features? What suggestions for improvement would you offer to the author?

Looking Back at Chapter 2

▶ Arguments always are based on claims, always with the goal of convincing reasonable skeptics of the claims' validity.

▶ Claims state that something is true, but some element of uncertainty or disagreement prevents others from immediately accepting that statement.

▶ The thesis statement of an argument usually will be one of five kinds of claims: fact, cause/effect, value, proposal, and identity.

▶ Claims always need support in the form of evidence and explanations.

▶ Evidence gives support to a claim by connecting it to the real world. Evidence helps answer the question, "What proof is there that the claim is valid?"

▶ Evidence includes anecdotes, expert opinions, facts and statistics, history, scenarios, and specific examples.

▶ Common methods of explaining are clarifying, interpreting, analyzing, applying, synthesizing, and evaluating.

Suggestions for Writing

▶ Choose an argumentative article and read it carefully, examining its claims and support. Write a short evaluation of the effectiveness of the argument.

▶ Use the Practice activities in this chapter to guide your planning for writing your own essay on an issue.

▶ Choose an argumentative article and read it carefully. Using some of the same evidence employed by the article, write a refutation of the article by providing an alternative explanation.

3 Reading and Responding

This chapter opens with a quotation from Aaliyah. Before her death in a plane crash, she was a rising star. As a hip-hop singer and song writer, Aaliyah was aware of how deep language can be. Her lyrics, which encourage listeners to open their minds and read between the lines, remind us that the meaning of a text—whether it be a rap song or even an essay in a college textbook—depends not only on the words but also on the efforts of the audience. In a way, Aaliyah sings of critical reading.

Critical reading is a dynamic process of not just reading the lines but also "reading *between* the lines." *Critical* does not mean that you read solely with the intention of finding fault, but rather that you play the role of a *critic*, examining the material's strengths and weaknesses as you explore its meanings and rhetorical methods.

When you read a novel, an article in a magazine, or a Web site you process and interpret what you read against a complex background of personal experience. As a researcher, you bring with you a body of knowledge, and opinions, and perhaps skepticism about the topic at hand. You bring prejudices—a tendency to be enthusiastic or skeptical about the issue—as well as personal experience and knowledge.

As a researcher you learn to read the information you collect with an open mind. This means that you conduct an inventory of your prior knowledge and beliefs about the issue; you read and re-read your sources for their messages and methods of organization, to annotate, and finally to evaluate and respond to what you have read.

> ### Topic, Issue, and Claim
>
> A *topic* is a subject that is under consideration. For example, rap music is a topic. An *issue* is something related to the topic but more specific and controversial. Rap music issues include violence, disrespect for women, cultural identity, obscenity, freedom of speech, and social/political activism. When you take a side on an issue, you propose a claim, such as the following:
>
> - Even if their lyrics are offensive, rap artists have a constitutional right to freedom of speech.
> - Because rap artists are public figures, they should be held to the standards of morality in the communities in which they live.

READER RESPONSE: HOW YOU READ

Your opinion of what you read changes as you work your way through an article, book chapter, government document, or Web site. Although you progress linearly, from left to right and from top to bottom, you also work backward and forward simultaneously—scribbling notes in the margins; reevaluating your knowledge of the topic, the author, and the argument; reconsidering earlier thoughts; and anticipating what might come in the next sentence or paragraph. You might even jump around in the document, reading captions of photos, information in text boxes, studying illustrations, or checking out the references at the end of the chapter. When you evaluate information on a Web site, you read hypertextually rather than linearly by following links, watching videos, and reading different parts of the site—or even other sites—out of the order in which they may have been intended. Your opinion changes dynamically as you move from word to word, sentence to sentence, paragraph to paragraph, Web site to Web site.

Consider this sentence from the opening paragraph of John McWhorter's "Mean Street Theater," a commentary on rap music:

> Last fall pioneer rapper Jam Master Jay was murdered in his Queens, N.Y., studio at 37, leaving behind a wife and children.

As you read sequentially from the first word to the final period, you apply cognitive thinking skills that build meaning as you go. Let's reconstruct a possible phrase-by-phrase sequence of critical reader-responses prompted by McWhorter's sentence about Jam Master Jay:

> Last fall pioneer rapper Jam Master Jay . . .

The mere mention of this person's name and profession, depending on your cultural mindset and opinion of rap music, may be positive or negative. Now we add a bit more:

> . . . was murdered . . .

Your reaction at this point, unless you are completely hostile to rap and its associated musicians, is probably one of sympathy. A little more:

> . . . in his Queens, N.Y., studio at 37 . . .

While the first part of the phrase might be viewed as mere information, what does the mention of his age imply? With most people, their reaction would be, "That's too young to die!" However, a rap-hater might respond, "Serves him right! How'd it take so long?" Now let's finish the sentence:

> . . . leaving behind a wife and children.

The tragedy is complete. Regardless of your opinion of rap music and rappers, you probably feel sympathy for Jam Master Jay at this point. McWhorter has piqued your interest and earned your ear, if only for a moment.

By reading carefully and tuning in to your responses, you'll gain understanding not only of a text's argumentative and rhetorical strengths and weaknesses, but also its possible uses in your own argument.

PRACTICE 3.1   How You Read

In a brief writing or group discussion, reflect on the following questions.

1. Do you like to read? Why or why not? Before you answer, take into account the many kinds of reading you do every day—e-mails, text messages, Web sites, social networking profiles, and other things you might not normally associate with "reading."

2. Do you like some kinds of reading better than others? Which do you like best? Which do you like least? Why?

3. How much and what kind of reading do you think your future career might require? Does your ability as a reader affect your career plans? Why?

4. When you read critically, what are some of the things you do to improve your understanding of the text?

QUESTIONING CRITICALLY

There is no single "tried and true" method of critical reading. Instead, most textbooks offer tips, guidelines, or lists of things to do while reading. We suggest that you pursue one major strategy: **Ask questions constantly about what you read.**

Asking Questions

Critical readers know how to ask the right kinds of questions about a reading—questions that go beyond the stated facts. The psychologist Benjamin Bloom classified and described six cognitive skills that often are used as a guide for questioning. Known as Bloom's taxonomy, this system begins with knowledge (understanding the stated meaning of the text) as the most basic type of questioning and then builds by levels: comprehension (interpreting the deeper meaning and significance), application (considering uses for the text), analysis (considering how specific parts of the text function separately and in unison), synthesis (relating the material to other texts and to prior knowledge), and evaluation (judging the qualities of the text). Bloom's taxonomy can lead you to ask questions that you might not otherwise have considered. (For more about Bloom's taxonomy, see Chapter 2, Claims and Support; Chapter 5, Planning Arguments; and Chapter 6, Drafting Arguments.)

→ BLOOM'S TAXONOMY QUESTIONS FOR CRITICAL READING

Knowledge/Clarification: Understanding the Stated Meaning or the Knowledge Conveyed Who is the author? What is the title? Where and when was the text published? What issue(s) does the text address? What is the claim? What evidence and explanations are provided? What beliefs are stated? How would I paraphrase or summarize the text?

Comprehension/Interpretation: Inferring Deeper Meaning What is implied but not stated directly? What unstated beliefs lie behind the claims? How does my point of view differ? How does the author use rhetoric (e.g., style) to help make the argument?

Application: Using the Text How does the text apply to real-life situations? How can I use these arguments for my own purposes, such as for support or for rebuttal? How might others use or misuse these arguments? Which argumentative techniques should I adopt or avoid in my own writing? Which rhetorical techniques should I adopt or avoid in my own writing?

Analysis: Understanding Parts in Relation to the Whole Where are the claims, evidence, and explanations expressed in the argument? What are specific instances of rhetorical techniques? How do the parts function separately and in relation to other parts and to the whole?

Synthesis: Relating the Text to Other Texts and Personal Experience Do I have personal experiences that relate to the arguments in the text? To what collective point of view, belief, or "school of thought" does this text belong? How does that school of thought compare to others? What other arguments exist? How do other arguments compare? How do the rhetorical strategies used by this author compare to those employed by other authors?

Evaluation: Judging the Text How well does the text present its major and supporting claims? How valid and convincing are the evidence and explanations? Is the support relevant and sufficient? Do the arguments appeal to the beliefs of the audience? How effective are the rhetorical techniques?

Focusing Questions

As a critical reader, you constantly ask the kinds of questions in Bloom's taxonomy, but not aimlessly. Those questions will be guided by your goals of arguing and writing about a particular issue. You will want to focus your questions in three ways: (1) culturally, about your beliefs and those of others; (2) argumentatively, about the claims, evidence, and explanations; and (3) rhetorically, about the purpose, audience, structure, and style of an article.

1. **Questions about cultural context**
   a. What is your opinion of the topic or issue?
   b. What prior knowledge, experience, or beliefs do you hold that influence your opinion?
   c. What is your emotional reaction to the subject matter?
   d. Where did you see the argument—in a magazine or on a Web site, for example—and how does this context influence how you approach the text? (*Example:* Reading an article about rap music in the *New York Times* as opposed to a popular music Web site may lead you to have different expectations about what the text will say.)

e. Has your opinion of the subject matter changed any as a result of the reading? Are you firmer in your prior opinion, or have you changed your mind?

2. **Questions about argument**
   a. Where are the claims and support located in the passage?
   b. Which kinds of claims are made and which kinds of support are provided?
   c. Are the claims (thesis statement and supporting claims) arguable?
   d. Is the support—evidence and explanations—adequate? Why or why not?
   e. How could the claims or support be modified to appeal more strongly to you or to a larger audience?

3. **Questions about rhetoric**
   a. **Purpose:** Where does the author state a purpose? What is the purpose? Is it stated or implied?
   b. **Audience:** Is the audience appropriate, considering the topic and purpose? Why or why not? Could you describe the intended audience of the text in any detail? Is the audience too narrow or too broad to be useful in accomplishing the purpose?
   c. **Structure:** Is the form (e.g., essay, letter, speech) appropriate to the purpose and audience? What are its strengths and limitations? What other forms would have been possible? How well is it organized?
   d. **Style:** Does the style (e.g., word choices, sentence structures) accomplish the purpose and reach the audience in question? Why or why not? What is the author's tone? Is the tone appropriate? Do you get a sense of the author as a person? How?

→ KEEPING A READING JOURNAL

When you are investigating any subject for the purpose of writing about it, keeping a journal can be an excellent tool. The journal can help you solidify your reaction to what you have read and make it easier for you to later react to the reading in a formal argument. A double-entry journal can help you separate your understanding of a text (in the form of a summary, for example) from your response to a text (in the form of an analysis or evaluation).

Summary McWhorter argues that the negative image of blacks can be blamed largely on rap music.

Response This may be partly true, but the "thug" image is not just a brand. It is also reinforced by news reports, especially in urban areas. Does this mean that news reports should be censored because they present a negative image of some African Americans? McWhorter also ignores the positive images associated with some rappers, as well as the philanthropy and the charitable work they do in their home communities.

Reading Culturally

To read culturally means to consider your personal place or "niche" in the dominant culture—your beliefs, values, background, prejudices, and the like—in relation to the "niche" represented by the text you are evaluating. It may be helpful to realize that what we broadly call "culture" is actually a conglomeration of subcultures based on religion, race, gender, education, upbringing, national or regional origin, personal interests, and many other criteria. Clearly, members of these subcultures are highly diverse. Most of the time your cultural mindset is different—sometimes **very** different— from that represented by what you read. If you are a conservative Protestant from the Midwest, for example, you may approach an article advocating gay marriage with a degree of reservation. Because your beliefs and opinions often affect your attitude toward a subject even before you have read the first word of the argument, it is important for you to examine your own cultural point of view prior to reading. In other words, be aware of your opinion as you approach a text. Try to notice the ways that a particular argument affects your opinion as you read—or even after you have read and have thought about or discussed what was proposed.

PRACTICE 3.2	Reading Rap Culturally, Argumentatively, and Rhetorically

Use the culture, argument, and rhetoric "focusing questions" to guide your critical reading of the following passage. Written by Chuck D, founder of the rap group Public Enemy, and excerpted from an article titled "The Sound of Our Young World," it first appeared in *Time* magazine. Record your responses (e.g., as a journal entry) or share them in a group discussion.

Astrid Stawiarz/WireImage/Gettyimages

In addition to making music, Chuck D writes and speaks about rap and its culture.

"[R]ap . . . is in the earth-wide sound stream . . . ready to pulse out to the millions on the wild, wild Web. It's difficult to stop a cultural revolution that bridges people together. . . . Watch, feel, and listen. It's only just begun."

—Excerpted from Chuck D

PRACTICE 3.3	Reading Other Topics Culturally, Argumentatively, and Rhetorically

Use the "focusing questions" to guide your critical reading of an article or passage that is relevant to a topic of interest to you. Record your responses as a journal entry, or share them in a group discussion.

PROCESS OF READING: PREVIEWING, READING, AND RESPONDING

Like writing, reading is a dynamic process. Reading occurs in three stages, commonly known as previewing, reading, and responding. It is possible to proceed through these steps one at a time, though in reality most readers move back and fourth between the steps in the process.

Previewing

Previewing is the first step of the reading process. It can help make the reading process easier and more productive by giving you a context—that is, by situating the reading inside a broader picture. Previewing usually considers reflecting on the (1) topic and issues, (2) title, (3) author, and (4) features of the text. You can use questions to guide your previewing activities.

- ▶ **Topic and issue:** What do you already know, factually? What do you probably need to know? What is your current opinion? Are you flexible, or are you set in your opinion?

- ▶ **Title:** What can you learn from the title?

- ▶ **Author:** What do you know or need to know about the author?

- ▶ **Text:** What do you learn from the form (e.g., article, letter), formatting, and organization (e.g., headings of sections, tables, and charts)?

Previewing Topics and Issues To be a responsive and thoughtful reader, it is important to "tune in" to your own knowledge, opinions, and preconceptions about a particular topic. Your prior experiences with an issue will not only affect your level of interest in the issue, but also influence whether you approach a topic enthusiastically or cautiously. Take inventory of your prior knowledge, beliefs, and information gaps.

PRACTICE 3.4   Previewing the Topic and Issues
of Rap Music

Use the questions below to guide your preview of the topic and issues of rap music. These questions can be used in brainstorming, journal writing, or group discussion.

- ▶ What do you already know (facts, key words, important issues)?
- ▶ What else do you probably need to know?
- ▶ What is your current opinion?
- ▶ Are you flexible, or are you set in your opinion?

PRACTICE 3.5   Previewing Your Own Topics and Issues

Use the questions below to guide your preview of a topic and issues that interest you. These questions can be used in brainstorming, journal writing, or group discussion.

▶ What do you already know (facts, key words, important issues)?

▶ What else do you probably need to know?

▶ What is your current opinion?

▶ Are you flexible, or are you set in your opinion?

Previewing a Title   Titles have a dual function: to inform the reader about the content and to attract the reader's interest. Readings intended primarily to inform (such as science articles) tend to have very information-packed titles—for example, "The Effects of Eight-Week Foci of Instruction on the Quality of Argumentative Essays Written by First-Year College Composition Students." Novels, short stories, poems, and similar works have titles meant to attract interest—for example, *The Da Vinci Code.* The titles of argumentative writings usually need to be informative yet still attract interest. To do so, they sometimes combine a title and subtitle, as in "Mean Street Theater: An Awful Image for Black America." Titles can convey information on several levels, ranging from general to specific: topic, issue, claim, and even an author's attitude. For example, "Stop the Madness!" conveys information about the claim, indicating the kind of action being proposed.

Because you will add titles to each of your own essays, you can benefit from learning more about how titles are crafted by other writers.

PRACTICE 3.6   Previewing a Title

Consider the following list of titles. Rate your interest in each one on a scale from one to ten. Which is the most engaging? Which is the least engaging? Which is the most informative? Which is the least informative? Explain.

1. "Mean Street Theater: An Awful Image for Black America" (article by John McWhorter)
2. "The Sound of Our Young World" (article by Chuck D)
3. "Taking the 'Rap' for Violence in Music" (student essay)
4. "Rap Music" (student essay)
5. *The Language Police* (title of book about censorship)

(continued)

(continued)

6. "The Importance of Hip Hop and Rap: A Question of Resistive Vernaculars" (academic source)

7. *Get Rich or Die Tryin'* (movie title)

8. *Doggumentary* (CD by Snoop Dogg)

PRACTICE 3.7	Informative Titles

Working from the table of contents of this book or from your own knowledge, make a list of five titles. Then explain in what ways they are interesting and to what degree they are informative.

Previewing the Author Sometimes you may already know something about the author; at other times you may have to conduct some research to learn about him or her. Frequently you can obtain author-related information from the Internet. Books sometimes provide information about the author, and essays occasionally are prefaced with a headnote, a biographical paragraph found at the beginning of an essay. You will find headnotes in many collections of essays as well as in the reading selections found in the latter portion of this book. As you preview the author, consider questions such as these:

► What do you already know about the author (other writings, public statements, reputation, background, personal information)?

► What have you learned from your research directed at learning about the author (such as checking Web sites or reading *Who's Who?* or a headnote)?

► Do you trust the author's expertise?

► Do you trust the author's integrity?

PRACTICE 3.8	Previewing the Author

Read the headnote below, and then answer the following questions. These questions can be answered in brainstorming, journal writing, or group discussion.

1. What do you already know about the author (other writings, public statements, reputation, background, personal information)?

2. What have you learned from the headnote?

(continued)

(*continued*)

3. Do you trust the author's expertise?

4. Do you trust the author's integrity?

John McWhorter

© James Leynse/ Corbis

After receiving his Ph.D. in linguistics from Stanford University in 1993, John McWhorter served as a post-doctoral fellow at the University of California at Berkeley, where he served as associate professor of linguistics. He now is a senior fellow at the Manhattan Institute's Center for Race and Ethnicity. A specialist in Creole languages and typology, he has written extensively about Creole languages, Black English, dialect, and language change. His books include *Losing the Race* (2000), *The Power of Babel* (2002), *Winning the Race: Beyond the Crisis in Black America* (2006) and *All About the Beat: Why Hip-Hop Can't Save Black America* (2008). McWhorter was also a contributing editor to *The New Republic* and *City Journal*. His writings on race argue that African Americans have held themselves back culturally by emphasizing victimization instead of individual responsibilities. A politically conservative African American, McWhorter argues in his article "Mean Street Theater" about rap's effects on racial identity.

Good schools!

What do these words mean?

What else has he written? Check out these for more info.

What other articles on rap music has he published?

Previewing the Text A preliminary scan of a text often will reveal features that can help you as you read. Headings of sections, for example, work much like titles, giving you a notion of what the major parts of the reading will discuss. The lengths of paragraphs may suggest something about how thoroughly the topics are discussed. Sentence length hints at how easy or challenging the reading will be. Highlighting (boldface letters, color fonts, italics, underlining) are signs that the author is adding aids; conversely, a lack of highlighting probably means that you will have to work more diligently to uncover key points for yourself. Illustrations (pictures, charts, graphs) may indicate a kind of rest break in the reading; they also offer graphic alternatives to otherwise linguistic information. The presence or absence of bibliographic references (works cited) indicates how scholarly the text will be.

PRACTICE 3.9   Previewing the Text

As you scan the paragraphs of McWhorter's "Mean Street Theater" that follow, analyze the following features: headings, paragraph length, sentence length, highlighting, illustrations, and bibliographic references. What do these features reveal about the reading?

Reading

The second stage of the reading process involves the actual reading of the text. As you read, you'll continue to ask questions. In addition, you'll annotate the text by marking it with your questions, observations, and concerns.

On the following pages, you will read McWhorter's essay a few paragraphs at a time. The first three paragraphs have been annotated with commentary to help you understand how cultural, argumentative, and rhetorical factors affect the reading process. Study the paragraphs below, and reflect on the questions below each passage as you read.

The paragraph on the next page involves readers on several levels:

▶ **Cultural:** Most arguments will affect you on a personal level in one of two ways: They will give you confidence in the author (by showing that he or she is an expert on the subject at hand, for example), or they will tug at your heartstrings. Although some of the information in the paragraph below—like the second through fourth

---

→ ANNOTATING ARGUMENTS

To annotate something means to respond to a text in writing, frequently in the form of marginalia (i.e., annotations in the margins of the paper). You may choose to bracket words, sentences, or paragraphs that seem important to you. Alternatively, you may underline, circle, use asterisks, or even use a highlighter to draw attention to particular parts of the text. You may also write notes, sometimes between the lines of text itself, but usually in the margins. You may pose questions ("What does *sybaritic* mean?"), paraphrase what you think the author is saying ("He is arguing that rappers are getting rich at the expense of their race"), or evaluate the argument ("Weak evidence here").

Annotating what you have read, whether one article or many, will give you the opportunity to think about your own position on the topic at hand, consider the mistakes others have made, and ultimately sharpen your own approach to your subject.

Guidelines for Annotating a Text

Here are some general guidelines that will be useful whenever you read and mark a text:

1. Mark difficult passages, words, and phrases you did not understand. You can develop your own "shorthand," perhaps using symbols for some remarks. Here are some suggestions:

   ?   A question mark next to a passage can show you don't understand.

   !   An exclamation mark can show your surprise about a statement.

   *   A star or asterisk can show you think a statement could be valuable.

   Q   A Q can mark a statement you think is quotable.

   __ Underlining can mark an important passage such as a major claim.

2. Highlight points that "stand out" or seem otherwise important to you. Don't over-highlight, however, because it will make the important points indistinguishable from minor points.

3. Indicate (circle) words that are important or need to be defined.

4. Use lines to connect passages, showing relationships between related ideas.

5. Jot down a restatement of the central ideas in the margin.

Note: John McWhorter's entire article "Mean Street Theater" is presented sequentially on pages 68-75, but it is interrupted frequently with commentaries that model the techniques of critical reading. Each of the fifteen paragraphs is numbered to assist a reading of the whole piece.

Mean Street Theater: An Awful Image for Black America

JOHN McWHORTER

Paragraph 1

Engaging hook!

Rappers put their kids in the line of fire?

Look up info on these guys.

Negative tone. Emphasis on rapper's family—not him.

<u>There goes another one.</u> Last week 21-year-old Savannah-based rapper Camoflauge was shot to death in front of his <u>toddler</u> son. Only two months before, New York rapper <u>Freaky Tah</u> was killed, at age 27, shot while leaving a party. Last fall pioneer rapper <u>Jam Master Jay</u> was murdered in his Queens, N.Y., studio at 37, leaving behind a <u>wife and children</u>.*

Funeral of Jam Master Jay.

© Reuters/CORBIS

*Mean Street Theater: An Awful Image for Black America, by John McWhorter. *The Wall Street Journal,* May 30, 2003. Copyright © 2003, John McWhorter. Reprinted by permission of the author.

sentences—shows that the author holds some sympathy for rappers and knows something about rap (which may give you some faith in what he has to say), most of the information is designed to evoke sympathy for the dead men. Note especially the "lead sentence" that both involves your emotions and implies the problem illustrated by the rest of the paragraph—that rappers are dropping like flies.

► **Argumentative:** It is notable that this paragraph lacks argumentative structures—there is no major claim or thesis statement. Is this a problem? If so, can you explain why?

► **Rhetorical:** The paragraph uses carefully selected words to pique your interest. It uses emotional appeals to keep you interested in the topic and encourage you to move on to the next paragraph. Does this paragraph do enough to successfully indicate the problem (rap = violence) that will be treated in the remainder of the essay? What does the word *pioneer* imply? Does it help gain your sympathy or otherwise keep you engaged? Who would you guess the intended audience to be? Does the paragraph "speak" to you? Why or why not?

Paragraph 2

Such carnage puts in a certain perspective the mantra that black America is so often taught: "Why can't whites see blacks as equals?" Many claim that a big problem is the depiction of blacks in the media, and there is a point here—but no longer the "whitey did it" point that many suppose. Today the biggest image problem for blacks comes from neither the movies nor television but from the rap industry. The most popular music in black

* America presents a grim, violent, misogynist, sybaritic black male archetype as an urgent symbol of authenticity.

Negative tone again. Effective, though. Good use of question.

Trivializes serious social problems.

Strong claim but one-sided. Look up words.

The preceding paragraph is more complex than the first one, which engaged your emotions so as to encourage your interest in the topic.

► **Cultural:** While McWhorter does less in this paragraph to engage your emotions, the two quotations are provocative. Each one operates on both emotional and rhetorical levels. What is your emotional response to these quotations?

▶ **Argumentative:** Does this paragraph include a thesis statement (major claim)? What is it? How do you know it is the thesis of the essay? The first two sentences make a counterargument—they present a point of view that runs counter to the point McWhorter will make. How do they function argumentatively? (How will they function to help McWhorter prove his point?) How do they function rhetorically? (What is the persuasive advantage of presenting an alternative view first?)

▶ **Rhetorical:** How do the two quotations affect you rhetorically? Who is the target audience? How might a black person respond to the quotations? How might a white person respond? How does the context of these quotations (the feelings of blacks regarding stereotyping by whites) affect your response to them? What sort of stereotypes of blacks do these quotations imply? Do you know what the words *misogynist, sybaritic,* and *archetype* mean? Look them up. What does their use imply about the intended audience?

Now briefly consider the first two paragraphs together. How do they function together to create an "introduction" for the argument? Is it a good idea to split introductory material into two paragraphs? Why or why not?

Acknowledges positive side but does not give enough credit.

Look up bio.

Is this the fault of the rapper or the teachers?

"Gutter" may be the common feeling of many American blacks. Many below poverty line. How did McWhorter grow up? Privileged?

Paragraph 3

Fans object that there is plenty of hip-hop with <u>constructive</u> messages. True, but it's the "thug" brand that sells best. How many hip-hop magazines would there be if the music delivered only positive messages? <u>Camoflauge,</u> despite his searingly profane, violent lyrics, was regularly invited to speak at Savannah <u>high schools</u>. In the hip-hop world, "keeping it real" is everything, and the <u>gutter</u> is considered the "realest."

▶ **Cultural:** Here the words that appeal to the emotions also have rhetorical impact. The use of "hip-hop" words such as *thug, gutter,* and *realest* have negative emotional connotations while invoking notions of "Black English."

▶ **Argumentative:** English teachers often instruct students to write paragraphs that begin with topic sentences followed by specific examples. Is that what McWhorter does? Which minor claim forms the topic sentence for this paragraph? Now look at the fourth sentence. How does McWhorter use evidence to back up his claims? Is it effective? Why or why not?

▶ **Rhetorical:** How does the counterargument presented in the first sentence function on a rhetorical level? (How is it used as a persuasive device in conjunction with what follows?) What role does the word *True* play in convincing the audience that rap music creates an image problem for black people in America?

Paraphrasing and Summarizing Arguments

Paraphrasing is putting someone's text into your style—that is, "into your own words." *Summarizing* is putting someone's text in far fewer words. Both techniques can be used to help you read critically. (See Chapter 8, Using Sources, Avoiding Plagiarism, for more on paraphrasing and summarizing.)

Paraphrasing has two major uses: to add the ideas of others to your own writing and to help you understand what others mean. Researchers use paraphrasing as an alternative to quoting sources: The imported material blends together smoothly with the researcher's own prose. Later in this textbook you will learn paraphrasing techniques that can enhance your writing while allowing you to give proper credit to your sources and thereby avoid plagiarism or "literary theft." In this chapter you will use paraphrasing to help you understand what you read.

A reader often must "translate" or "decode" the written material. This kind of paraphrasing may be as simple as restating a word or phrase, or it may involve more complex, longer portions of text. When you read critically, you essentially paraphrase the material, putting the entire text into your own words, albeit usually without actually rewriting the original text. Occasionally, however, you may find that rewriting the original in your own words helps you not only understand a text but also evaluate both its strengths and its flaws.

Consider this sentence from McWhorter's article about rap music:

> The most popular music in black America represents a grim, violent, misogynistic, sybaritic black male archetype as an urgent symbol of authority.

The sentence contains "elevated" diction—words you might encounter only in an intellectual discussion. You may understand some, most, or all of the words, depending on your previous experiences as a reader. You may need to look up words in a dictionary, including words that you thought you understood but that may have special meanings in the context of the sentence. After conducting such a translation, however, you may discover that the sentence is still difficult to understand.

How would you express McWhorter's sentence in your own writing style? Here is one student's paraphrase of it:

> Rap makes the "ideal" black man look like a dangerous women-hater who cares only about his own pleasure.

Is McWhorter's meaning clearer? Was the paraphrase accurate? Was it complete? For example, did the student clarify what McWhorter meant by "urgent symbol of authority"? What do you think that phrase means?

Paragraphs, too, can be paraphrased. Consider the fourth paragraph in McWhorter's article:

Focus on aggression and anger.

Implies it contributes to violence.

Good use of supporting detail from videos. But what good do these guys do?

Language here implies a danger of a real revolution? Over the top!

Paragraph 4

And most hip-hop, whatever its "message," is delivered in a <u>cocky</u>, <u>confrontational</u> cadence. The "<u>in your face</u>" element is as essential to the genre as vibrato to opera, reinforced as rappers press their faces close to the camera lens in videos, throwing their arms about in poses suggesting <u>imminent battle</u>. The smug tone expresses a sense that hip-hop is sounding a wake-up call, from below, to a white America too benighted to listen. I can count on hearing about a "hip-hip <u>revolution</u>" from at least one questioner at every talk I give these days.

Here is one student's paraphrase of the preceding paragraph:

> According to John McWhorter, the majority of rap, regardless of its meaning, is performed in a self-confident, combative style. The aggressive performance is as basic to the art form as brush strokes are to painting, emphasized as hip-hoppers thrust their visages toward the lens of the camera of a televised video, waving their arms while striking poses like battling warriors. The self-satisfied sound conveys the idea that rap is an alarm bell rung by the underprivileged to awaken American Caucasians too dense to understand. McWhorter wagers that he'll hear a comment about a "rap revolution" from at least one person attending each speech he gives nowadays.

Again, is McWhorter's meaning clearer? Was the paraphrase accurate? Was it complete? Is word-substitution enough to make the paraphrase "in your own style"?

Read the fifth paragraph of McWhorter's essay, and paraphrase it on your own.

Paragraph 5

But unfocused cynicism is not a promising platform for a revolution. The Hip-Hop Summit Action Network, for instance—founded by rap impresario Russell Simmons—has attempted to 'bridge hip-hop and politics' and does deserve credit for its proposed voter registration drive. But then what does the organization want 'the hip-hop generation' to vote for? Mostly the bromides that have disempowered blacks for decades.

Consider the sixth and seventh paragraphs of McWhorter's essay, which have been annotated for you:

Paragraphs 6 and 7

Stuck in the idea that urban schools fail because of inadequate funding, the group corralled marchers to support the teachers' union opposed to New York Mayor Michael Bloomberg's education budget. It also stuck it to President Bush for invading Iraq and has protested advisory labels on rap CDs.

One has to wonder whether the Action Network will ever sponsor "summits" [supporting the welfare reform now improving countless black women's lives or urging the Bush administration to give more money to faith-based initiatives.] By focusing on the issues that lend themselves to street theater, the organization proposes a "revolution" committed more to the thrills of acting up than to the mundane work of helping people in need.

> Diction: "corralled" sounds like they're being forced. Implies animals. Makes them sound stupid. Logic: Just because McWhorter doesn't agree with these initiatives, it doesn't make them wrong.
>
> Implies that the Action Network doesn't care. What makes him think these will work? How many rappers go to church?
>
> Without "street theater" there would have been no civil rights movement!
>
> Check on his claims about AN. Some rap groups must be doing good. Is "acting up" bad? What about Martin Luther King, Jr.? Rosa Parks?

Clearly, this passage could have been annotated in many other ways. The important thing to consider, however, is that the reader has engaged the writer in a conversation by asking questions, commenting, and paraphrasing what has been said. There are probably as many ways to carry on this conversation as there are ways to write. Ultimately, you must develop your own approach to critical reading.

Read the last few paragraphs of McWhorter's essay. Annotate them, and then answer the questions that follow the reading.

Notes

Paragraphs 8-15

Of course, "hip-hop intellectuals" would disagree, celebrating hip-hop as an expression of inner-city frustration. But frustration does not require music so willfully alienated and nihilistic: None existed during the centuries when all blacks endured injustice much more concrete. In any case, hip-hop elicits identification across classes, having become a kind of "musica franca" for black identity. One often sees well-heeled young black executives get into their new cars and turn on the same spiky rap that the inner-city black man listens to.

Hip-hop, in short, is not a message from the streets but a histrionic pose. Producers coach aspiring artists to glower for photos. "I"m valid when I"m disrespected," an aspiring black rapper told a reporter for the *New York Times* in 2000, in an article from its "How Race Is Lived in America" series. The piece ended with his recording a CD whose strident vulgarity and sexism chilled the article"s writer. The rapper knew the truth—he was indulging in an act that sells, pure and simple.

In the grand view, hip-hop may be seen as a typical American phenomenon—one part the cowboys-and-Indians tradition of heroic conflict and one part the recent "Bobos in Paradise" syndrome of celebrating countercultural gestures as "real." *The Sopranos,* in its violence and vulgarity, shares this mixed cultural parentage. But that TV show is not intended as a guide to living for all Italians. Hip-hop, by contrast, is linked to a particular racial identity. Yes, numerically it has more white listeners. But hip-hop"s fans would be up in arms against anyone who claimed that the music was rooted in white culture rather than an African American consciousness.

And what a dismaying symbol of identity for a race just past misery. Rappers slip acrid slams at their rivals into recordings, nurturing "battles" to sell CDs. It was such provocations that likely led to the deaths of Tupac Shakur and "Biggie" Smalls. And that brings us back to "rap and rap sheet," in the artful phrase of the music critic Kelefa Sanneh. Rapper 50 Cent was recently arrested for harboring assault weapons in his car. DJ Funkmaster Flex physically assaulted a female rival DJ in New York last fall. In 2000, a brawl at the Source Hiphop Awards shut the ceremony down—right after a video tribute to slain rappers!

"But white people act up too." Yes, but Garth Brooks does not bring a "piece" to the Grammys, and Martin Scorsese does not get into ugly scuffles on the street. There is a fine line between playing the bad boy and becoming one, and in the "hip-hop community" too often violence jumps out of the quotation marks and becomes a tragic reality.

But calls to combat hip-hop are useless for the moment. As Judith Rich Harris showed us in *The Nurture Assumption,* children identify with their peers more than with their parents. Blacks under a certain age feel this music is their poetry, rattling off extended selections as readily as Russians recite Puskin. It's not going away.

But this is a lowdown, dirty shame. I am just old enough to remember when whites were making the sourest, nastiest pop music while blacks were making the sweetest and truest. White kids listened to hideous screaming, while funk and soul were black America's soundtrack. As a kid in the 1970s I was conscious of that contrast and proud of it. The civil rights protesters a decade before, who made the lives of the "hip-hop generation" possible, would have been appalled to hear the likes of Jay-Z, and we would be hard-pressed to claim that they would have been somehow missing something in that judgment. They accomplished a lot more, too, than any rapper's sideline donations to community efforts ever will.

The staged alienation of the hip-hop scene shows black Americans celebrating attitude over action at best and violence over civility at worst. For 350 years white America told blacks they were beasts. Now a black-generated pop music presents us to whites and ourselves as beasts, while a cadre of black intellectuals celebrate this as "deep" and black impresarios glide by in their limos calling it a "revolution." Revulsion is more like it.

PRACTICE 3.10   Understanding "Mean Street Theater"

1. Identify the primary claim (thesis statement) and the minor claims (supporting statements) in the essay. (It would be valuable to compare your answers to those of your peers to see whether you have identified the same sentences.) Write the sentences word for word, then paraphrase them (put them in your own words without distorting the original meaning).

2. Does McWhorter recognize a point of view other than his own? Are you able to adequately understand the other viewpoint? Explain.

3. Does McWhorter support all of his claims with adequate evidence?

4. Do you consider McWhorter to be a trustworthy, authoritative source? Explain.

5. Who seems to be the target audience? How can you tell? Would McWhorter's view be received with sympathy by that audience? What do you think his target audience is like in terms of race, class, education, politics, and interest in the arts?

6. What is McWhorter's tone? Is it formal or informal? Is it well suited for his audience? Do you think his audience was receptive to his claim? Explain.

Responding

Determining where reading ends and responding begins is difficult, because the acts of reading and responding inevitably occur together. Paraphrasing, annotating, and writing in your reading journal are all aspects of reading as well as elements of responding. At some point, however, you may decide to respond to the text in a more formal way. Perhaps you may write a refutation, a sort of argument in which you explain why you disagree with another argument. Alternatively, you may write a synthesis, in which you discuss how one argument relates to others that consider similar issues. Ultimately, your response will probably involve reacting to the writings of others as you construct your own argument.

PRACTICE 3.11   Responding to "Mean Street Theater"

1. Read the first two paragraphs and last two paragraphs of McWhorter's article. How effectively do they introduce and conclude the content of the essay? Are they misleading in any way? How?

2. Do you agree or disagree with McWhorter's analysis of rap and its culture? Explain.

3. Evaluate McWhorter's use of evidence. Where is it strongest? Where is it weakest? Why?

4. If you had written this article, would you have spent more time discussing the rappers' point of view? What advantage would this approach offer?

5. Identify the greatest strength and the greatest weakness of the argument. Explain your answer.

WORKING WITH MULTIPLE ARGUMENTS

When you investigate written arguments on your own, you will encounter a variety of viewpoints on any given argument. In the news media, political and social issues are often debated in terms of liberal versus conservative, for and against, pro and con. While some issues readily lend themselves to this sort of division (considering whether a law should be passed, for example), most issues have many dimensions. You will encounter people who are strongly in favor of an idea, people who are firmly against the idea, and people who fit somewhere in between the two extremes. To complicate matters further, arguments you read will not always neatly "line up." That is, they will rarely talk about the same aspects of the issue being debated. As a reader, you must consider the overall issue and determine what the various arguments have in common. Some will agree (more or less); others will disagree (more or less). You must decide which features are worth comparing to gain an overall picture of what is at stake.

Refutations

When one argument directly responds to another argument, it is often called a refutation (see Chapter 6, Drafting Arguments, for more on refutations). When someone refutes another argument, the refutation depends on the original source for its central claims, and often for its organization and support. The argument that follows, "Hip-Hop Activism Buds Beautifully," is a direct response to McWhorter's essay.

Hip-Hop Activism Buds Beautifully

OPIO LUMUMBA SOKONI

Opio Lumumba Sokoni is an activist, attorney, and writer who was educated at Howard University. He has worked for the Drug Policy Alliance and Amnesty International, where he worked on issues related to the use of excessive force by police. In addition to his frequent writings on the Internet, his articles have appeared in *Black Commentator*, the *Washington Times*, and the *Boston Globe*. He has written on the drug war, the disproportionate treatment of African Americans in the criminal justice system, and, of course, hip-hop.

Before You Read

1. What is your reaction to the name Opio Lumumba Sokoni? How does it compare to the name John McWhorter?
2. What does the title, "Hip-Hop Activism Buds Beautifully," imply?
3. What do you think this author is likely to say in his argument? What does a quick scan of the document tell you?

"Hip-Hop Activism Buds Beautifully"

1   Harry Belafonte stated to me in an interview that entertainers have the responsibility to speak out on issues concerning the community. He also said that entertainers are so often used to take people's minds off real issues and that entertainers who do not act are part of the problem. In a recent *Wall Street Journal* article entitled "Mean Street Theater," written by John McWhorter, he called social and political contributions to the community made by rappers' "sideline donations." About the recently slain rap artist Camoflauge, McWhorter writes, "Despite his searingly profane, violent lyrics, [he] was regularly invited to speak at Savannah high schools." This article could have been more appropriately titled, "Mean Muggin' Hip Hop."

2   There's more. The article went on to run off other artists (i.e., Tupac, Biggie, and Jam Master Jay) as products of the genre. Never mind the failings of law enforcement, who have yet to find the killers of any of these men. But, they could find any small-time hustlers in the hood and lock them up for years and years for a nonviolent offense (i.e., drug possession).

3   This brings me to the most appealing part of the piece. While the author gave credit to Russell Simmons's Hip-Hop Action Network for setting a goal to register millions of hip-hop voters for the 2004 elections, he asked a poignant question: "What does the organization want the hip-hop generation to vote for?" If for nothing else, his article should have been printed for this query.

4   It is true that hip-hop has to have a political issue or issues to mobilize around. And we got issues; no doubt about that. Well, Russell Simmons, P Diddy, Jay Z, and many other hip-hoppers are right on point in their effort to address what should be the number one issue to focus hip-hop activism—fighting against the failed war on drugs. These celebrities are doing exactly what Mr. Belafonte says is expected of them.

5   This is a perfect issue for hip-hop activism because the lives affected the greatest are in the same communities that hip-hop most represents. In addition, the unchecked drug war is now devastating lives in white communities. But what makes this an even greater issue for the hip-hop generation is the fact that it is The Issue of our time.

Source: "Hip-Hop Activism Buds Beautifully" by Opio Lumumba Sokoni. Alternet, June 10, 2003. Reprinted by permission of the author.

READING SELECTION

6   No other cause has as many moving parts as the issues associated with the failed drug war. First, the war on drugs has created a prison population that should be an embarrassment to any rational person. I do not know any African American who does not have a personal connection to someone in jail for a drug crime. Most of the over 2 million people in jail are nonviolent, low-level drug offenders who would be better in treatment, therapy, job training, and/or on a job than in jail. But instead, the war on drugs has delivered young bodies to jails that are used to support the heartbreaking reality of the prison industrial complex.

7   Second, our babies are in foster care in high numbers because their parents have been given long sentences, usually for minor use or possession charges. In Washington, D.C., an estimated 70 percent of the children who are in foster care are there directly or indirectly due to drug addiction. There are no studies that show prison as being better than treatment for a parent.

8   Finally, aside from the other civil and human rights problems related to the war on drugs (i.e., a person losing the right to vote or a person being denied financial aid for college), there is the matter of racism. The fallout from the drug war has been more devastating than the KKK lynchings of the 1920s. Young people are racially targeted, set up, captured, convicted, sentenced, and jailed at a staggering rate.

9   A 2000 Human Rights Watch report confirms that in Wisconsin a black man is fifty-three times more likely to go to prison on a drug charge than a white man. This rate is reported to be the second highest in the country and more than four times the national average. Only Illinois ranked higher—there, a black man is fifty-seven times more likely to go to prison on a drug charge.

10   In New York, 94 percent of the people sentenced under the Rockefeller drug laws are from black and Latino communities. That's right, 94 percent. Debra Small, who works for Drug Policy Alliance, says that the Rockefeller drug laws are the granddaddy of the federal mandatory sentencing laws. A low-level drug offender can be sentenced to fifteen years to life if convicted.

    I recently met a victim of the Rockefeller drug laws named Anthony Papa who is the painter of *15 Years to Life: Self-Portrait*. Anthony spent twelve years in a maximum-security prison for passing an envelope containing 4 ounces of cocaine. When asked about this law, he says, "The millions of dollars being spent to house nonviolent persons can be used to feed the hungry, put shoes on children's feet, and spent on education."

11   Russell Simmons's Hip-Hop Action Network has decided to work with Mothers of the New York Disappeared and other activists, celebrities, and organizations to change these laws. A victory in New York could have a domino effect among other states that have adopted similar drug policies. Further, this may be the catalyst to make drug policy reform front and center in the 2004 elections.

12   Hip-hop is coming into political maturity and can work to change some of the realities that are reported so vividly in rap lyrics. It is so fascinating how music has always been a part of social action in the black community. During slavery, coded songs were used to take persons to freedom. In the civil rights movement, marchers sang songs like "Ain't Gonna Let Nobody Turn Me Round." Now, there is an entire genre that is budding into full political awareness. How beautiful. And, it does not look like a mere "sideline donation" to me.

Responding to the Reading

1.   Do you think Sokoni is an authority on the subject of hip-hop activism? Who is more authoritative for you—Sokoni or McWhorter? Explain.

2.   In what ways is Sokoni's audience different from McWhorter's audience?

3. What is Sokoni's thesis (argumentative claim)? Do you sympathize with Sokoni's view? In what way does it address or respond to McWhorter's primary claim? Explain.

4. Does Sokoni provide adequate evidence and explanations to support his claims? Explain.

5. How well has Sokoni refuted McWhorter's argument? Be specific.

6. What points does Sokoni make that are unique to his argument and do not depend on McWhorter's argument?

7. Name one significant strength and one significant weakness of Sokoni's essay. Why do you make this judgment?

Synthesizing Arguments

One of the tasks you may face as you prepare to write about an issue is determining how a particular text relates to other texts, in what has been termed the "universe of discourse." Everything we know relates to something else in this universe of discourse; understanding how an argument relates to other arguments is called synthesis. Synthesis helps a reader tease out details of how different texts relate to one another—how they agree and disagree, where their ideas come together, and where they diverge.

When you write a synthesis, you compare and contrast what different writers have to say about the same subject. In this case, your thesis will generally report on the significant similarities and differences between two or more arguments (or other sources) you have read. A synthesis can be comparative, meaning that it doesn't make critical judgments about one text or the other. A synthesis can also be analytical, meaning that it judges the quality of particular arguments. Finally, a synthesis can be evaluative, meaning that it argues one writer is correct and another writer is wrong.

Understanding the "Universe of Discourse"

Perhaps the easiest way to think about the universe of discourse is to consider all mass-distributed discourse (ads on billboards, television shows, articles in newspapers, postings on a Web site) to be part of the same giant conversation. Think about the last time you went to a party: The room was probably filled with people, not talking in a single large mass, but conversing in various smaller, more intimate groups. Texts function in the same way. They respond to each other. Even if one author does not directly respond to another author (such as when a reader writes to a newspaper complaining about a particular view expressed in an editorial), writers often address common issues so that, in effect, they seem to be talking to one another.

PRACTICE 3.12 Writing a Synthesis

Choose one paragraph from McWhorter's argument and one paragraph from Sokoni's response. Make sure that they are linked, such that McWhorter makes a claim and Sokoni then responds to it in his argument. Write a synthesis of the paragraphs.

READING AND PREWRITING

Critical reading techniques and prewriting techniques overlap. Already in this chapter you've seen methods of questioning, journaling, previewing, annotating, paraphrasing, summarizing, and synthesizing. Other methods include listing, mapping, and freewriting—all of which are described below. (For more on prewriting techniques, see Chapter 5, Planning Arguments.)

Listing

Listing is just what it sounds like—making a list of as many items as you can come up with on a given topic. Let's say your first idea is to write about issues related to rap music. Just write "rap music" at the top of the page and jot down all of the single words or short phrases that come to mind. Try not to let yourself write less than ten entries at the first try. Then look back through the list and circle one or two items that interest you most. Put this at the top of the next list and keep going until you have a fairly focused topic. You can then use this topic as the basis for exploring issues.

LISTING FOR RAP MUSIC

Drugs	Biggie Smalls
Money	Kanye West
violence against women	Lil' Kim
kill cops	Jay-Z
murder	50 Cent
obscenity	free speech
glamour	clothes
shiny jewelry	influences kids
Aaliyah	

Mapping

Another technique is mapping (also called clustering). It can be used to generate ideas or to organize the ideas already generated by listing/brainstorming. Begin by writing your key concept in the middle of a blank page and begin branching out from it. Unlike listing, mapping helps you map out complex relationships between ideas and helps you create complex hierarchies of relationships. The first time you do it you will probably generate only a few ideas, but as you practice you will learn to break your ideas down into complex and interesting diagrams. When you see one "branch" of the diagram developing in a particularly interesting way, you know you are on to something. You can then use these ideas to further develop your thoughts with a focused freewrite.

Focused Freewriting

Exploring ideas with free-form prose has long been a popular method of generating ideas and exploring opportunities to focus a writing project. The best approach is to begin with a focused freewrite by writing the general topic—such as "rap music" at the top of the page. Then allow your ideas to flow freely without being concerned about writing coherent paragraphs, complete sentences, or polished prose. There are just a few basic rules to follow:

▶ *Get it down.* Don't worry about errors in punctuation, spelling, or grammar. The most important thing is to let the ideas flow as quickly and freely as possible. If you get stuck, repeat an idea until another one occurs to you.

▶ *Time yourself.* Don't allow yourself to stop, even if you run out of ideas. The best thing to do is set your cell phone timer to a specific time limit—say 10 minutes—and write down everything that pops into your head within the time period. Don't even worry if it is off topic. Just keep writing!

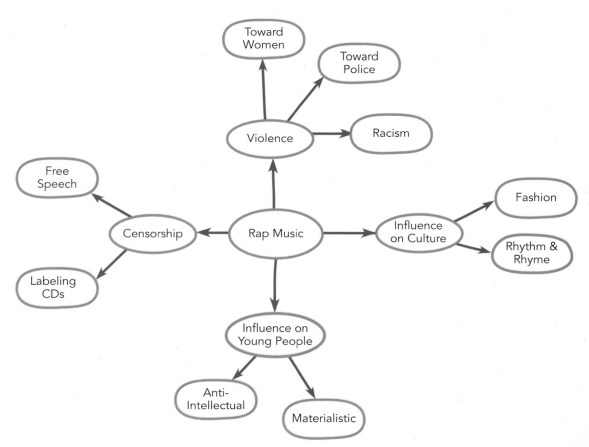

▶ *Use looping.* After you've finished the freewrite, go back over it and look for key ideas. Underline or circle things that "jump out at you" as potential topics. Choose one idea and then do a focused freewrite on it. This is called "looping."

Love the driving rhythms. Social themes, like 2PAC: "When it rains, it pours. They got money for wars but can't feed the poor." Not sure about the difference between rap and hip-hop. I like the way some performers mix rap and rock. Rap-rock. Eminem is OK, kind of comic. Wasn't he sued by his own mother for defamation of character? Like Coolio's "Gangsta's Paradise": "As I walk through the valley of the shadow of death .I take a look at my life and realize there's not much left."Great rhymes and they fit the song. Like Kanye a lot, but his lyrics are not for kids. Sometimes I think rap is losing its shock value. I mean, where do you go after f-word and n-word? Not thrilled about the n-words and f-words and like it less when they're cut from a good song. Messes up the song and you still know what words they cut.

PRACTICE 3.13   Critical Reading and Prewriting

Go through a sequence of prewriting activities for topic that interests you.

1. List
2. Cluster
3. Freewrite

STUDENT ESSAY

Working individually or in groups, consider this student's response to rap music.

PRACTICE 3.14   Before You Read

1. What is your opinion of rap music and hip-hop culture now, after reading and responding to McWhorter's and Sokoni's arguments? Has your opinion changed in any way? Explain.
2. What does the title of the essay suggest to you? What do you think the writer might argue?
3. Scan the essay. What do you think the major divisions of the argument are? Who is the target audience?

Kerri Bennett

Dr. Lamm

Composition

22 May 2011

    Taking the "Rap" for Violence in Music

Whether or not one appreciates rap music, its prevalence cannot be ignored. In traffic, its aficionados treat other drivers to rap by pumping up the volume of oversized car speakers, booming teeth-rattling rhythms into any automobile within range. Channel surfing the television reveals music videos of rappers snarling their lyrics while striking menacing poses. A trek through a mall or other public places becomes a fashion show featuring youths dressed in droopy pants and draped heavily with gaudy, bling-blingish jewelry in imitation of their favorite rap entertainers. Since its emergence from the break-dancing competitions in the 1970s and 1980s, rap has evolved into one of the most popular and influential genres of music among America's youth.

    Of course, the danger of rap music lies in neither its fashion statements nor its driving rhythms. The threat is in its message, a litany of catchy phrases encouraging its audience of young children and teens to commit violence against women and other groups. These young fans of rap are impressionable. Noted child psychologist Judith Rich tells us that instead of looking up to their parents, the young use other youths as role models (McWhorter 3). Shock-rocker Marilyn Manson confirms that musicians lead their young fans: "Music is such a powerful medium now. The kids don't even know who the president is, but they know what's on

MTV. I think that if anyone like Hitler or Mussolini were alive now, they would have to be rock stars" (qtd. in Brownback 3). As Manson suggests, artists have far-reaching influence. Recent evidence to support Manson's statement can be found in a Pew Research Center poll conducted in 2007, which "found that 71 percent of African American adults felt that rap had a bad influence on society, while other polls show that a majority of black teenagers feel that rap music is too violent and degrades women" (qtd. in Beaver 108). That extreme violence is not confined merely to the lyrics of songs. In the world of rap, brutality seems to change quickly from an act for the cameras and the words of songs to real guns, knives, or rape (McWhorter 3).

Snoop Dogg (born Calvin C. Broadus, Jr.), a rap music mogul whose lyrics have a violent message, is a popular figure among teens and collegiates, and as such was selected by student vote to perform last month at the University of North Carolina. In an article written prior to the performance, Snoop Dogg's music is described as "lyrical and behavioral misogyny" (Moran). The author, Matthew Moran, cites some of Snoop Dogg's album art and public appearances which degrade women by portraying them as sex objects and blatantly comparing them to dogs kept in houses and on leashes. Moran also mentions several demeaning lyrics from Snoop Dogg's songs. For example, in 2004 "Can You Control Yo Hoe?" was released—a song in which the speaker says, "You've got to put that bitch in her place/Even if it's slapping her in her face . . . This is what you force me to do/I really didn't want to put hands on you" (Broadus). Though supporters of rap music as a form of self expression claim that these images, songs and performances are mere fantasies, Moran believes, "The truth is that we, and children especially, are very impressionable when it comes to violence and misogyny in music." He also cites an experiment conducted in 2008 which indicates "that listening to Eminem's sexist lyrics also increases negative attitudes toward women" (Moran). These findings are difficult to dismiss considering the content of Eminem's songs.

Eminem (born Marshall Mathers) is another rap music icon, and whether voluntarily or involuntarily, he also serves as a role model. Regrettably, his lyrics are rife with violence and with hatred toward women, describing acts of rape and murder in gruesome detail and even aiming some of his most brutal lyrics toward his own mother and the mother of his daughter (Mathers, "Kill"). He is also aware that young children look up to him, as the lyrics to his rap "Stan" indicate: in it, he describes a six-year-old who considers the rapper to be an idol and wants to be like him. Like many other rap singers, Eminem is criminally cavalier as a role model.

What should we do to stop the violence? Contrary to the suggestions of some extremists, the answer is not to ban rap music: the First Amendment does give rappers the right to "spew their poison" (Hoyt 3). Although freedom of speech may seem to allow the problem, it can also be the solution because the media have the right—indeed, the responsibility—to denounce and expose any person or artistic work that could be harmful. Unfortunately, even though newspapers and magazines are aware that rap songs are violent and misogynistic, they still endorse them as entertaining. For example, Eminem's *Slim Shady* met with approval from *Arizona Republic* music critic Victor Barajas: "It's mean-spirited, profane, shocking—and actually quite entertaining if not taken too seriously" (qtd. in Hoyt 2). Ideally, the media can do better.

The news media should act as a spotlight, a kind and informative "Note Nanny" for parents, issuing warnings about particularly obscene or violent music. Magazines, newspapers, and television have the means, opportunity, and mandate to expose the nature of objectionable lyrics in reviews, editorials, and columns so that an informed and concerned public can guide and protect their young. The ironic solution to the problems presented by a constitutionally protected freedom to produce rap music lies not in repression of the arts but in the freedom of the media to expose rap's dark side to the light of reason.

Works Cited

Beaver, William. "Rap and the Recording Industry." *Business & Society Review*. 115.1 (2010): 107–120. *Business Source Complete*. EBSCO. Web. 25 Apr. 2011.

Broadus, Calvin C., Jr. "Can You Control Yo Hoe?" *Rhythm & Gangsta*. Snoop Dogg, The Neptunes, 2004. CD.

Brownback, Sam. "Free Speech: Lyrics, Liberty, and License." *Vital Speeches of the Day*. 15 May 1998: 454–56. Print.

Hoyt, Michael. "An Eminem Exposé: Where Are the Critics?" *Columbia Journalism Review* 1 Sept. 2000: 67. Print.

Mathers, Marshall. "Kill You." *Marshall Mathers LP.* Interscope Records, 2000. CD.

—. "Stan." *Marshall Mathers LP.* Interscope Records, 2000. CD.

McWhorter, John. "Taste: Mean Street Theater." *Wall Street Journal* 30 May 2003: W15. *ABI/INFORM Complete.* ProQuest. Arkansas State U Lib., Jonesboro, AR. Web. 25 April 2011.

Moran, Matthew. "Be Wary of Sexism in Snoop's Lyrics." *The Daily Tar Heel.* DTH Publishing Corp., 22 Mar. 2011. Web. 25 Apr. 2011.

PRACTICE 3.15 Understanding the Reading

1. What is the author's argumentative purpose? Who is her target audience? How can you tell? Do you agree with the author's primary claim (thesis statement)?
2. What claims does the author use to support her thesis? Does the author fail to provide any supporting ideas that have occurred to you? What are they?
3. Does she recognize any views other than her own? Explain.
4. How does the author attempt to establish authority and appeal to the emotions of her audience?
5. Name one significant strength and one significant weakness of the argument. Explain your answer.

Looking Back at Chapter 3

▶ Critical reading is a process involving previewing (thinking about the topic), reading (understanding, annotating, and analyzing the argument), and responding (evaluating and writing about what you have read).

▶ Reading is a dynamic process. Rather than moving neatly from previewing to reading to responding in a linear fashion, you are more likely to switch back and forth between these functions, often performing all of them at once.

▶ Writing about critical reading involves asking questions about what you have read:

  ▶ How the argument is situated culturally—how it relates to you, to its audience, and to the culture in general;

  ▶ How it functions logically—how well it presents claims, evidence, and alternative points of view;

  ▶ How it functions rhetorically—how it utilizes purpose, audience, structure, and style to establish authority and maintain an emotional link with its audience.

▶ Critical reading and prewriting overlap. Those techniques include questioning, annotating, paraphrasing, summarizing, synthesizing, listing, mapping, and freewriting.

Suggestions for Writing

▶ Select an argument or arguments from the readings in this chapter or other readings in this textbook. Critically read the argument(s). Then write one or more of the following:

  1. An analysis and evaluation of the argument
  2. A response to the argument
  3. A synthesis of one argument with another argument
  4. An analysis and evaluation of the rhetoric within the text(s)

▶ Choose an article on a subject of interest to you. Apply critical reading strategies, annotating the text thoroughly. Work on developing your own system of annotation.

▶ Summarize McWhorter's article or another article of your choosing.

▶ Paraphrase a paragraph from one of the readings in this chapter or from an article of your choosing.

▶ Synthesize information from two or more readings about a topic or issue that interests you.

4 Researching Arguments

A claim requires support in the form of evidence. But where does the evidence come from? Sometimes you may be able to draw upon your firsthand observations or you may have gone through enough training to be an expert on some subjects. At other times your personal experience regarding the subject under investigation may be limited. That is when research becomes vitally important. As its root word indicates, *research* is a search for facts, studies, testimony, and other forms of evidence that can help you reinforce your knowledge of an issue so that you can write about it authoritatively. Because research helps you to become more confident and knowledgeable about the issue you are writing about, along with careful writing, it helps you establish your *ethos*—your sense of reliability and expertise—on the matter at hand. In short, it helps your reader have more confidence that you know what you are writing about, and this helps you persuade your audience.

THE PROCESS OF RESEARCH

The research process involves three stages: *planning*, *exploring*, and *evaluating* sources.

▶ In the **planning stage**, you identify an issue, formulate a research question, and develop a plan for finding the answer to that question.

▶ In the **exploring stage**, you divide your strategy into phases, usually based on the types of sources you plan to use (serial publications, books, the Internet, government documents, and so on) and follow the "trail of evidence" as you move from one source to another. For example, if you notice that certain ideas, people, or other sources are discussed repeatedly as you conduct your research, then you also need to explore these trails of evidence.

▶ In the **evaluating stage**, you determine whether the evidence is sufficient to answer your question and support the claims you wish to make. If the answer is no (and it usually is no the first time through), then you must return to one of the earlier stages of the research process.

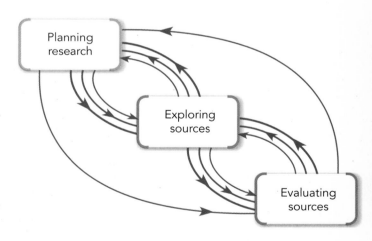

Like the process of writing, the process of researching is recursive: You may need to return to any part of the process at any time. Typically, you will return to the exploration stage to locate more information. Sometimes, though, you will go all the way back to the planning stage, perhaps even to rewrite your research question if you discover that it is too narrow (for example, you can't locate enough evidence) or too broad (to adequately argue the case, you might have to write much more than required by the assignment).

PLANNING RESEARCH: FROM RESEARCH TOPIC TO RESEARCH QUESTION

Research usually begins with a topic—something you want to investigate. Sometimes your instructor will assign the topic. At other times you will choose your own topic, perhaps selecting from a list or coming up with it on your own. A topic by itself is not very useful, because it usually is broad and doesn't give your research much direction or focus. The topic needs to be narrowed to an issue—something that is arguable that falls within the *zone of reasonable skepticism*. Even better, you should try to phrase the topic as a *research question*. Then you can seek to discover the answer to the question. Doing this not only will help you think of your issue in terms of an argument, but also will provide direction for your research. Once you have completed your research and believe you have found the answer to your question (or at least have obtained an opinion or some perspective on it), you can rewrite the question in the form of an initial claim or working thesis for your paper. A *working thesis* is an experimental version of your major claim; it is open to changes as new information comes to light. If you already have enough knowledge about your issue (or at least an opinion about it), then you may be able to write a claim instead of a research question, but you should be prepared to further refine this statement as your research progresses. In some cases, it may not even be advisable to write a working thesis at such an early stage in the process. The research question, and the research itself, can help you explore your issue and discover your thesis as a part of the overall planning process. (For more on developing a thesis and discovery techniques, see Chapter 5, Planning Arguments, and Chapter 6, Drafting Arguments.)

Donna Day/Getty Images

Some people argue that excessive television or computer time and diseases related to childhood obesity are connected.

Let's illustrate this idea with an example. Sarah, a college student, has decided to investigate the declining health of America's youth. As a Phys Ed major, she is much interested in this, particularly because she has a little brother who is overweight and suffers from childhood diabetes. Following the guidelines in Chapter 5, Planning Arguments, she does some initial brainstorming in the form of mapping and a freewrite. She realizes the topic is very complex and encompasses many distinct issues, including childhood diabetes, lack of exercise due to spending a lot of time at the computer, and diets consisting of too much fast food. Like many of us, she turns to the Internet to help her locate some ideas that can help her focus her topic. About an hour of searching leaves her more confused than ever, with most of the sites providing superficial information. She realizes that she should have followed her teacher's advice to plan carefully before beginning her research, and returns to her brainstorming exercises. She ultimately decides to focus on fast food, and specifically on supersizing, to help her define a research question for her project. Here is her initial research question:

> What contribution has "supersizing" made to childhood obesity, and what should be done about it?

At this point, Sarah can begin planning her research, because she has a specific purpose in mind. This two-part question provides her with two directions for her research: (1) does supersizing contribute to childhood obesity and (2) what policies are being considered to counteract this effect? Already she knows the first part of the question will lead to a causal argument and the second part to a policy argument. Now she needs to consider what kinds of sources are likely to supply her with information about these two related issues. She might begin by looking into news stories about these issues. While these sources will likely be superficial, they will provide her with clues that will allow her to follow the "bibliographic trail" that will lead to the reporter's original sources and beyond. With some luck, she may locate some scientific studies that link supersizing to obesity, which will set her up nicely to make a policy argument for regulating fast-food meals targeting children. After some research, she is able to turn the question into a working thesis:

> Since fast food may be a significant contributing factor to childhood obesity, laws should be enacted requiring restaurants to post nutritional information on menus.

Now Sarah can begin organizing her research notes and planning the content of her argument.

Following a Bibliographic Trail

Often, you will come across useful information in a source but will not find the "answer" to your research question. However, your efforts may not have been wasted: One of the best ways to find sources is to look at the bibliography at the end of an article or book on the same subject you are investigating. Even if the article, book, Web site, or news story itself isn't very useful, its list of references may lead to something better. It is rather like being a detective following a trail of clues. In fact, the absence of references is usually a good sign that the source is superficial and should not be trusted.

Types of Sources: Primary and Secondary Research

Research can involve either obtaining information in person—that is, through *primary research*—or reading what others have written about a particular topic—that is, through *secondary research*. If you learned about the college you are attending by visiting the college, taking a tour, and speaking to students and instructors, you were conducting primary research. If you learned about the college through the Internet, you were engaging in secondary research.

Primary Research Some types of research projects call for primary research, especially in the sciences, social sciences, and education. These projects may involve visiting a place (a school or nursing home), interviewing people or conducting focus groups (teachers, students, patients, nurses), or executing a study (determining the number of part-time students who attend your school). When you decide to conduct interviews, a university is a goldmine—it employs experts on wide variety of subjects. If you conduct this type of research, you will probably have to carry out secondary research in the library as well to give you the appropriate background with which to pursue the primary research project.

Secondary Research In many academic classes, you will be asked to write research papers that are based on secondary research. To use the library's resources successfully, you should understand how your library organizes this information.

How Your Library Classifies Sources Most libraries divide resources into five general areas: books, periodicals, reference works, government documents, and media. The nature of your topic will help you decide where to focus your search, and your instructor can help you plan the focus of your research. Periodicals generally contain the most up-to-date information, while books hold the most extensive information. You will usually begin with reference materials such as electronic databases and other specialized bibliographies. In addition, you may use encyclopedias or other reference materials that your university holds or can access over the Internet. (Databases and services such as ProQuest, InfoTrac, and Ebscohost have vastly "expanded" the holdings of even the smallest libraries.) Government documents are usually housed in a special area, and may range from land records to extensive research reports. Media resources should not be overlooked. In addition to films and recordings, your library may own CD-ROMs that contain useful information. The best way to begin planning your research—even before you write your research question—is to visit your library and discover what sorts of resources it offers that are related to your topic.

→ CONDUCTING AN INTERVIEW

An interview is a form of primary research that can yield information that might otherwise be difficult to find or perhaps not even available from any other source. Your interview will be more productive if you plan ahead.

Make an appointment. An interviewee will have to allot time for you; indeed, you may have to wait days or longer to get adequate time for an interview. When you make the appointment, you should inform the interviewee briefly of the nature of your project (subject and possibly your working thesis). This step will ensure that you don't waste your time on someone who can't provide the information you need. Also, give an estimate of how long you think the interview will last.

Prepare a list of questions in advance. As much as possible, target the questions to relevant issues and to specific gaps in your research. In addition, prepare a few broad-spectrum questions that might lead to results you couldn't anticipate. Your interviewee might want to see the list before you arrive, allowing for some reflection or research.

Use a digital recorder, if permissible. A recording not only provides exact quotations for later use, but also lets you reflect on the interviewee's tone of voice and other nuances. Ask in advance for permission to record.

Take copious notes. Write down some statements in brief form—you don't want the pace of the interview to depend completely on your speed as a transcriber. Important points, especially if quotable, should be written verbatim. Ask the interviewee to repeat some key statements, especially if you plan to quote him or her directly. Even if you use a recorder, don't expect it to completely replace your notes: Recordings sometimes are unintelligible or suffer from technical failures.

Check back with the interviewee before publishing. This courtesy usually is appreciated greatly. No one wants to be misquoted, especially in writing: The misquote could be an embarrassment that is requited endlessly by others. Your source may want to refine the phrasing a bit, because the impromptu nature of oral interviews sometimes results in awkward sentences or inaccurate wording.

Send a "thank you" note. This courteous gesture need not be elaborate. In many cases, an e-mail message will suffice.

Make a record of the date, time, and location of the interview. You'll need this information as you document your sources. For more information on documenting an interview, see Chapter 12 (for MLA documentation style) and Chapter 13 (for APA documentation style).

Obtain Institutional Review Board (IRB) permission for the research, if applicable. Though review and approval for primary research is almost always required of graduate students, some institutions require undergraduates to obtain permission to collect data, including conducting interviews, by applying for permission through the Institutional Review Board. IRB approval is usually needed only if you go off campus to conduct your study, and only then if you plan to present the data in a public forum. Ask your professor if this is required at your institution. Ask early to allow time for the board to review your request.

Obtaining Electronic Books These days, obtaining books your library does not own is not limited to interlibrary loan. Thanks to the efforts of volunteers, many out-of-copyright books are available for free on the Internet. If your research involves books that are at least 70 years old, then this may be a viable option for you. Online, one of the largest repositories of out-of-copyright books is Project Gutenberg. Another valuable resource is Google Books, where you can download and print PDF files of the actual physical books. If you have an e-reader, out-of-print books can usually be downloaded for free or for a nominal fee. If your library does not have a book you are looking for, it may own an e-reader and will download the book for you to consult. Of course, you

→ FOCUS GROUPS

Although interviews are good methods of conducting primary research, focus groups are a good method to employ when you would like to gain information from multiple individuals on a range of opinions. Because you ask questions of a whole group rather than an individual, you may get richer insight into the question you are investigating because participants can follow up on each other's answers. If one person has little to say about one question, another person may provide insight. Focus groups can be very dynamic, with individuals disagreeing and taking the conversation in new directions. As a researcher, you should pursue those lines of discussion and see where they lead. Some guidelines for focus groups include:

Limit the size of the group. Too many participants can make the conversation chaotic and difficult to interpret. Five or six participants is an ideal size. Too few and the conversation falters; too many, and no one can get a word in edgewise.

Limit the number of questions. Because you will give everyone a chance to talk, limit your questions to ten. Even then it is easy for the group to go on for more than an hour.

Write focused, open questions. Avoid questions that can be answered with a simple yes or no. Instead, write questions that allow the participants to tell their own stories and provide insight.

Follow up on answers. If someone says something intriguing you did not anticipate, then ask them to elaborate. This may lead your research in new directions.

Video the session. Even when you record the session, you may find it difficult to know who is speaking when. A video camera set up in the corner as a backup to your audio recorder can help you determine who was speaking when you're not sure.

Provide snacks. Nothing will open up your participants like a bowl of chips or candy. Providing a little food, or even bottled water, can help put your participants at ease and in a mood to talk.

Using Interlibrary Loan

Although the Internet and electronic databases are valuable for obtaining articles and government documents, at present copyright laws usually limit online access to books your library does not already own.

Not long ago, if you wanted to obtain a book through interlibrary loan, you had to process your request very early in the semester if you wanted to receive the book in time for it to be useful in your research. Electronic streamlining has since made it very easy to get books though interlibrary loan. Today, they often will arrive within a matter of days. You may be able to request a loan directly from the database where you found the reference just by entering your name or student identification number.

→ INTEGRATING ELECTRONIC AND CONVENTIONAL RESEARCH

You will probably integrate information gleaned from library research with information obtained from electronic sources. However, if your library has a good collection, begin there. Even if you intend to use primarily electronic resources, your librarians can assist you in locating appropriate resources. Also, your library may have access to specialized databases such as Ebscohost, ProQuest, Lexis Nexis, Project Muse, and ERIC that you may not be able to use from home. For more on electronic research, see the "Electronic Research" section later in this chapter.

can download a more recent book to an e-reader or tablet PC if you are willing to pay the downloading fee.

How to Evaluate a Topic Evaluating a topic to plan your research is a part of the prewriting stage of the writing process. Your goal should be to narrow the topic to an arguable issue, and eventually develop a working thesis to help you focus your project. Many activities that are useful for brainstorming a topic for an essay that does not require research are useful

PRACTICE 4.1   Narrowing a Research Topic

Working individually or in groups, evaluate the general topics in the following list. Select one, and use freewriting, listing, or clustering to narrow the topic so that it could become the basis of a research question.

1. Islam and the West
2. Student loans
3. Immigration control
4. Cyberbullying
5. Plagiarism

Richard Ellis/Getty Images

Here a group of first-generation American citizens say the Pledge of Allegiance. What issues surrounding immigration to America—legal or otherwise—can you think of that are relevant today?

PRACTICE 4.2   Writing a Research Question

Choose the topic you explored in Practice 4.1 or another topic that interests you, and write a research question for it. Critique your research question in small groups or in class. Is it too narrow? Too broad? Is it researchable? Where might you locate information on this topic?

for those projects that do require it. Writing lists, clustering diagrams, and freewriting can all be used to narrow down a topic and discover an issue (see Chapter 5, Planning Arguments, to learn more about these methods). Initially, you can brainstorm based on your prior knowledge about a particular topic or something you learned in class. As your topic becomes

> **LEVELS OF SOURCES**

Librarians, instructors, and researchers often classify sources by their degree of originality, labeling them as different levels—primary, secondary, or tertiary—depending on the relative distance from firsthand information.

Primary Sources Sources are considered primary when they result from direct experience, such as an article written by scientists to describe the results of their experiments, the diary of soldier during a war, or statistics from surveys. Primary sources are valuable because they are close to the original experience and are not influenced by the analysis, editing, and interpretation added by other people.

Secondary Sources Secondary sources use or build on primary sources. Examples include a textbook that reports on the history of scientific research, a biography that interprets someone's diary, or a proposal based on statistics from surveys.

These secondhand sources may be more comprehensive than primary sources and have the benefit of expert interpretation, analysis, and commentary.

Tertiary Sources Tertiary sources are overviews of fields of information. Dictionaries, encyclopedias, directories, indices, and bibliographies are frequently used as tertiary sources. An index or bibliography is a source of sources, listing many different primary or secondary sources and telling when and in which media they were published. Annotated bibliographies include a brief summary of the content of the source, and many indices include abstracts or longer summaries. Libraries make tertiary sources available as reference books or electronic databases. Writers often begin their research with tertiary sources to gain an overview and to find appropriate primary and secondary sources.

more focused, however, you may need to conduct some preliminary research before you narrow it into an arguable issue.

CONDUCTING RESEARCH

After you have developed a plan of attack, you will have to physically locate the sources that will provide some insight into your working thesis or research question. Inevitably, you will run into difficulties. Books may be checked out. Pages may have been torn out of journals. The sources you find may supply only superficial information. Much-needed Web sites may deny you access or cannot be found. When this happens, it is a good idea to sit down and review what you have found. Remind yourself that your goal is not just to "fill up" your paper but to provide adequate support for your working thesis or provide insight into your research question.

Your research is complete only when you have enough information to adequately back up the claims you will make in your argument. Sometimes you may have to reevaluate, or even rewrite, your research question or working thesis. Don't hesitate to return to the planning stage and rethink the focus of your project if necessary. If you must refocus, do so early in the process. The worst time to discover that you can't find enough information about your project is the night before it is due.

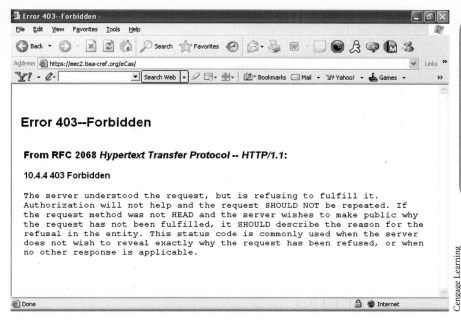

Cengage Learning

Limited access, especially from home, can make Internet research frustrating.

EVALUATING SOURCES

The main way you will evaluate your sources is by reading your sources *critically*. This involves several processes:

► Previewing what you will read

► Annotating the text

► Responding to the text

► Organizing with other texts

→ WIKIPEDIA WARNING!

It is sometimes very easy to go to Wikipedia and other online resources as a first stop when conducting research. While it is fine to consult Wikipedia (or similar community-based resources) as an initial step, it is very important that you trace down the original sources used in the Wikipedia article to make sure that they are legitimate. In many cases, Wikipedia articles are not cited at all, or may cite Web sites or other sources that contain erroneous information. Because Wikipedia and similar sources can be edited by anyone, the information they contain is often incorrect. Instead, use legitimate online sources for which you can verify the accuracy of the information.

Previewing What You Will Read

Previewing means you try to understand the context of something you will read. You can ask questions about the topic, author, title, or publisher. You can also briefly examine the length of a piece, getting an idea about its tone and its level of complexity.

Who Is the Author? Occasionally you will happen across a piece of writing by a famous person, or at least by a person whom you recognize. Ask yourself whether this person will be recognized and respected by the audience. Additionally, as you conduct research, you will start seeing the same names over and over. When a person has written repeatedly about a particular subject, he or she is often (but not always) knowledgeable about the subject area. Sometimes you can obtain information about an author by looking for a headnote, reading a foreword to a book, or looking up the author in the library or on the Internet. These days, many active writers have home pages or maintain blogs that tell more about them and their writings.

What Does the Title Imply? Sometimes a title will tell you almost nothing about the content of the article or book in question. At other times the title may imply a great deal. For example, *War and Peace* tells you more about the content of Tolstoy's novel than *Hamlet* tells you about Shakespeare's play. Often, the title will tell you something about the point of view presented in the writing. You would naturally expect a different viewpoint from an article entitled "We Need Stem-Cell Research Now" than you would from an article called "The Immorality of Stem-Cell Research." Titles can sometimes help significantly in deciding how you will eventually classify the information you have found.

Who Published the Piece? Publishers can be more important than you may realize. Certain publishers will carry more clout (*Wall Street Journal* and *Time*), while others may be particularly liked or disliked by a given audience. A politically conservative audience, for example, is likely to look positively upon articles from *National Review* and negatively upon articles from *New Republic*. Also, you can expect academic journals to provide more rigorously examined information than popular magazines do. As you become familiar with different publishers, you will also become familiar with the unique viewpoint that each offers.

What Does Skimming Tell You? If you skim a piece before you read it carefully, you will get an idea about its length and complexity. Look for section headings, sidebars, illustrations, and other features that can tell you something about the text. This information will help you decide how much time it will take you to carefully read and annotate the article. You may also

→ RELIABILITY OF INTERNET SOURCES

When using sources found on the Internet, you will find that some texts are co-published on the Internet and in print. If you use these sources, you should credit both the print source and the Internet source. When you use Internet-only sources, scrutinize them with care. While many Internet-only sources are very good, always remember that *anyone* can publish on the Web. The Web site where the information is published can help you gauge the reliability of the source in question. If a Web site has a long history and is well respected, then you can approach the source with the same level of confidence as you can a reputable print source. Conversely, be wary of information found on personal Web pages.

Warning: Some very legitimate looking Web sites are sources of inaccurate (or even blatantly false) information. Just because a Web site looks professional does not mean the information it publishes is reliable. If the Web site is unknown to you, research the name of the site, or the authors of some of the articles found on the site. Using this approach, you may find a watchdog group that has revealed the Web site as misleading. Often such watchdog sites will provide you with sources of legitimate information.

PRNewsFoto/AutoMD/AP Images

Reliable databases such as AutoMD are good sources of Internet-based information.

be able to identify the major and minor claims, as well as gain a sense of the article's level of difficulty. A complex academic piece will usually take more time to read and annotate than an article from a popular magazine. The lengths of paragraphs (short ones typically contain less information), illustrations, and the presence of a bibliography can all help you prepare to read.

Responding to the Text

Responding to the material you have gathered in your research is not something that begins after you have read the article, made note cards, taken notes, and written down summaries, paraphrases, and quotations. Responding actually begins when you preview your reading, and it continues as you annotate your text and take notes. However, after you have absorbed your source, it is a good idea to evaluate its information in depth and make some decisions regarding where it fits into your research project, if at all. (You should never be afraid to toss out a source that "just doesn't fit.") One way you can evaluate a source is to consider once again the particular strengths of the author, the reputation of the publication, the applicability to your research question or claim, and the rhetorical strength of the text.

Author   When authors are well known, their "reputations precede them," meaning that the public is aware of their biases and degree of credibility. Other times, you may have to investigate authors to discover whether they are specialists in a field and trustworthy in their judgment and in the presentation of their claims.

Is the Author an Expert?   Whenever the perception of an issue depends on having knowledge beyond common experience, a *reasonable* audience will pay attention to opinions from experts. For an issue such as censorship, for example, an audience will want to hear from experts on morality to understand certain values, from lawyers to understand legal aspects, from sociologists and psychologists to learn how images and language affect people, and from artists to appreciate free expression. When using an expert as a source, you may want to inform your readers: "Dr. John McWhorter, a Senior Fellow at the Manhattan Institute, states. . . ." An audience will also weigh the opinions of capable nonspecialists who have taken the time to conduct research into an issue. When using a nonspecialist as a source, you will need to determine that his or her research has been adequate—for example, a list of references at the end of a publication helps indicate the extensiveness of the research. Conversely, you should be wary of an opinion that comes from a nonspecialist who has not conducted adequate research or who might have misunderstood or misrepresented the facts.

How Trustworthy Is the Author? All people have biases—points of view that may influence their opinions. The credibility of authors depends partly on their biases and partly on how reasonably and fairly they deal with those biases. For instance, journalist George Will has a reputation for being moderately conservative and fair-minded, whereas radio personality Rush Limbaugh is known for his unflinching right-wing convictions and extreme positions. A center-of-the-road audience would probably be skeptical about most opinions offered by Limbaugh but would give strong credence to opinions offered by Will. A strong bias may lead authors to overlook or downplay evidence that contradicts their points of view while overestimating the value of other evidence that supports their claims. Even honest people can be blinded by their convictions. Of course, some people are dishonest and will purposely present false claims and evidence to further their goals.

When the reputation of a writer is unknown, you should exercise extra caution before accepting any of his or her conclusions. You can check authors' credentials through reviews of their works, by searching the Internet for entries about them, or by consulting other experts. Some databases are devoted to the backgrounds of authors: Internet authors can be checked through <http://www.writers.net>, for example. A number of *Who's Who* editions, both general and specific to various disciplines, may be useful as well.

Publication Information about a publisher can help you evaluate your source. Publishing houses, periodicals, and sponsors of Web sites have histories and biases that can be researched. As you check the credentials of publishers, you will want to note how specialized and how trustworthy they are.

How Specialized Is the Publication? Some periodicals, such as *Newsweek* and *Time,* have broad interests and appeal to a very diversified readership. Their articles tend to be short, moderately detailed, and aimed at the nonexpert, although some of the feature articles may go into more length and depth. Publications with broad readerships tend to provide information on a "secondary" level that has been summarized, interpreted, and perhaps simplified. Other periodicals, such as the *Journal of the American Medical Association* (*JAMA*), have a readership of specialists; few readers outside the field of medicine would understand the terminology and data presented by *JAMA,* for example. Professional journals often present data that are "primary" in nature, appearing there for the first time.

Articles from specialized journals have high credibility because they are written and reviewed by experts. By contrast, articles from popular magazines may require more evaluation because the authors might not be specialists and the articles might not be reviewed by experts before publication. If a book is published by a university press, it has probably been reviewed by experts.

How Trustworthy Is the Source? Like authors, many publications are well known and are preceded by their reputations. Editors of respected publications accept responsibility for what they publish, often demanding that authors authenticate their texts in various ways. The publishers of *USA Today*, for example, know that its commercial success depends on the readers' faith in its honesty. When some of the newspaper's reporters were discovered to be fabricating and plagiarizing information, not only were reporters dismissed, but the editor also resigned because she felt responsible for maintaining the periodical's journalistic standards.

Of the many thousands of publications available, you may be personally familiar with the reputations of only a few. Yet before you put your faith in a source, you will want to discover something about the publisher. The tendency of a publication to publish certain views while excluding others is called *publication bias*. Some biases are political: *New Republic* is considered liberal, and *U.S. News and World Report* is considered conservative—yet both journals are respected for their intellectual content and journalistic standards. Journals published by professional organizations or religious groups may maintain high journalistic standards yet must be read in context: They represent the beliefs of a particular group, and those views will inevitably affect the use of evidence and the statement of claims. Other journals may be biased to the point of being distorted or dishonest, sources of propaganda and lies. Careful research should help you discover which publications to use and which to avoid. While the liberal bias of *The Humanist* should not cause you to dismiss it as a source, you should keep in mind its bias—its tendency to include certain views and exclude others—as you research and write.

You must be particularly careful when evaluating Web-based sources for their trustworthiness. While trustworthy Web sites are the result of dedicated teams of experts, it is also possible for a single individual to create a trustworthy site that contains erroneous information. Naturalnews.com is a very professional looking Web site notorious in the health care industry for its erroneous and misleading information. While a site's URL can give you some confidence—those ending in .edu and .gov are sponsored by educational institutions and government offices respectively—you should still follow up to be certain the information is reliable.

Coverage Even when you have found a publication and author who are authoritative and honest, you will still need to be concerned with the quality of the information. How current and how complete is it?

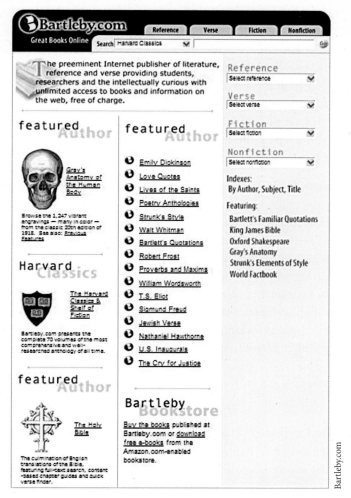

The Bartleby.com site is a reliable resource for electronic texts and reference materials.

How Current Is the Source? Some areas of knowledge change rapidly: Scientists make new discoveries, technology improves, elections and revolutions change governments, laws are passed or repealed, media stars rise and fall. Other areas of knowledge may change very little over long periods of time, such as historical records. Consequently, your sources may have a very long or very short "shelf life," depending on the subject. You will have to assess whether your source is current enough to remain meaningful.

Modes of publication have different speeds of production. For example, the Internet, television, and radio media are virtually instantaneous in making updates, followed closely by daily newspapers, and then by periodicals such as weeklies. Books, however, can take years to produce and more years to update. Most publications will provide a date of publication on the title page or somewhere near the beginning. The home page of a Web site usually will display the date of its most recent revision; some home pages, such as stock exchange Web sites, may even display the hour or minute. As a rule of thumb, use sources that are no more than five years old unless you are researching a historical issue. Keep in mind that some areas, such as technology, change very rapidly. Five years ago there were no 3-D TVs.

How In-depth Is the Source? You must determine whether a particular source provides enough information to support your claim. Secondary and tertiary sources can be useful for putting your primary sources in the kind of context you need to evaluate depth and quality of information. Even when you feel you have enough evidence, you should commit to not distorting an issue by omitting relevant facts. A half-truth often is a whole lie. When your research is not complete, you should either continue your research or qualify your results. For example, you can limit your conclusions by scope or by time: "My conclusions on language acquisition apply only to immigrants entering the United States from 1976 to 1988."

Rhetoric Rhetorical features can help you evaluate a text. You will want to consider the source's purpose, audience, structure, and style.

What Is the Purpose? The author may express a purpose directly in the text, often as part of the introduction, or the purpose may be implied by the text. Is the source intended to inform? To persuade? In some cases the author may have a hidden agenda, an ulterior motive that may not be directly detected by all members of an audience. For example, a scathing denunciation of one politician may actually be an endorsement of a competing politician or an attempt to stop a certain piece of legislation. Knowing the expressed, implied, and ulterior purposes of a source can help you determine how much trust to put in it.

Who Is the Audience? The intended audience for a source can reveal much about the quality of information contained in a source. Is the audience expert or novice, believer or skeptic, specific or general?

How Is it Structured? Is the source well or poorly organized? Does its organization affect the quality of the information? Is the structure appropriate to the purpose and audience? Does the author acknowledge alternative views?

PRACTICE 4.3   Evaluating Print Sources

Working individually or in groups, evaluate an article that you have obtained in your research. Use the following rubric:

Author: Is the author an expert? Do you trust and respect the author? Why or why not? What biases does the author appear to have?

Publication: How specialized is the publication? How trustworthy? What publication bias do you need to take into account when writing about the source?

Coverage: How current and in-depth is the source? Should you use it, or follow the bibliographic trail to seek better sources of information?

Rhetoric: How focused and appropriate is the purpose? Who is the intended audience? What structural weaknesses are evident? What gaps, if any, occur in the text? What, if anything, was confusing? Did the author acknowledge and refute contrary opinions? How effective is the style and tone of the piece? Select a representative paragraph and explain.

How Is the Style Used? The word choice, tone, and phrasings of a source can reveal an attitude and perhaps an ulterior motive. Is the tone reasonable? Sarcastic? When the author has discretion in choosing a word, is the choice biased or neutral? For example, a "battle" might be described as a "slaughter" or as a "peace-keeping exercise"—all of these word choices reveal something about the author's point of view.

Organizing with Other Texts

After you have read, annotated, and possibly summarized a number of sources, you will probably have a better idea of what shape your paper will eventually take. At this point, you may find it useful to rewrite your working thesis or research question, or you may decide that you need to obtain more information and refocus your research. Eventually, however, you will decide that you have all the information you need and will begin the process of organizing it. Careful organization at this stage can save a lot of headaches later when you are trying to draft your argument.

Some of your sources will inevitably agree with each other. In fact, some may share the same source material and build on one another. Other sources will disagree, and when they cite certain people, it will be to refute their views. Also, a few of your sources will likely address your topic directly, as if they were "made" for your paper. Others may scarcely mention your topic at all.

When you begin to organize your material, you will place your sources in categories that you create. Typically, you will place those sources that are in agreement together, and those that represent other viewpoints in other groups.

Ultimately, you will probably want to organize your research material according to how it will be used in your paper. Suppose you've found ten articles that you want to use in a research paper:

▶ **Literature review:** Three in support of your position and two against your position

▶ **Main argument:** Three as evidence to support claims

▶ **Refutation:** Two to represent a contrary view you plan to refute

Of course, this example is an oversimplification. You may reuse sources in your main argument that were introduced in your literature review. Nevertheless, having some kind of plan regarding where you will use your sources can be invaluable. One of the easiest ways to organize your sources is to paperclip the groups together in the order you will use them, and then to place adhesive notes on each of the groups. Some writers will benefit by creating a formal outline; others will work better with informal outlines and organized "stacks" of material.

When determining how to use the sources you have selected, ask whether source A agrees with B or whether source A has a different, even contrary thesis:

Similarity

▶ What would you gain from comparing A and B?

▶ Are A and B related strongly enough that they belong in the same section?

▶ Do they agree completely, or do they diverge on some points?

▶ Is one source more "extreme" than the other?

Difference

▶ Would you gain more from contrasting A and B?

▶ If two sources disagree, are they "polarized" or do they share some views in common?

Focus

▶ Do A and B address the same points, or is their "crossover" limited? (Unless one article directly responds to the other, most arguments will have limited crossover and will not "match up" claim to claim.)

▶ Is there enough crossover for you to discuss the articles together?

▶ Do A and B provide background information or engage in a current debate?

Sources

▶ Do A and B share sources in common?

▶ Does source A elaborate on or draw upon the sources represented in source B (and vice versa)?

▶ Would sources in their bibliographies be useful?

ANNOTATING, SUMMARIZING, AND PARAPHRASING

Three essential features of good critical reading practice are annotating, summarizing, and paraphrasing what you have read. *Annotating* refers to marking a text, whether on paper or electronically; *summarizing* refers to briefly stating the overall content of a source in your own words; *paraphrasing* refers to stating the specific meaning of a sentence or two from the source in your own words. Whereas summarizing abbreviates the original, paraphrasing maintains the same level of detail and does not attempt to represent the work as a whole. Annotating normally occurs during the responding phase as you work through a source for the first time, though it can occur later when you return to the source. (In fact, you will probably understand it better then and will want to revise or expand your annotations.) Summarizing and paraphrasing most commonly occur when you begin organizing with other texts, though they can be a part of your initial response to a reading (such as commenting on your reading in a two-entry journal).

Annotating the Text

Annotating a text can help you, as a reader, identify structural elements of the text (major claims, minor claims, topical headings, literature reviews, counterarguments, and the like) and document your initial responses to the reading. (See Chapter 3, Reading and Responding, for more about annotating.) Here are some ways to annotate the sources you have located (and photocopied or printed via computer):

▶ Circle unfamiliar words or phrases so that you can look them up and define them in the margins.

▶ Underline sentences that seem important. Often they contain major and minor claims. Alternatively, put stars or other indicators next to important information.

▶ Write comments in the margins—especially if you disagree with a point.

▶ Write questions. If the question is later answered, make a note of it.

▶ Make a note if the writer addresses a topic you have encountered in another source (this will help you synthesize information from your sources later).

▶ On a separate sheet of paper, summarize the essay immediately after you have read it.

▶ Avoid using a highlighter. It just "short-circuits" the annotating process.

Taking Notes There was a time when conducting research meant taking a stack of note cards to the library to write down every quotation and detail you expected to use in your argumentative paper. In more recent years, photocopying machines and the Internet have reduced much of the paperwork involved in taking notes. These days it is more likely than not that you will work from PDF files of articles as opposed to photocopies you make yourself from journals on a shelf. These copies almost always have the bibliographic information printed directly on the first page. Some PDF readers, as mentioned, allow you to annotate directly on the screen. Even if you are conducting your research exclusively on the Internet or working from a stack of photocopied articles, you should take careful notes. In addition to the critical reading practices outlined earlier, you should, at a minimum, create a record for every source you locate. If you are seriously considering using the material as a source, annotate it and create a record for it, whether that record is a traditional bibliography card or an electronic record created in a word processing program or electronic database.

Making Note Cards and Bibliography Cards Note cards and bibliography cards help keep your research organized and allow you to find a source if you need it later on. While it is possible to take notes by hand, as described below, you might consider using one of the many programs available for taking notes and organizing your research. Using programs like Evernote you can use your smartphone to take photos of sources, record audio notes, organize e-mail attachments, and even take notes by hand. Other word processing programs, such as Scrivener, actually have research and note-taking features embedded in the program so you can easily pause your writing, record a note, make an electronic note card, or access a PDF file of an article you've stored in your research database. While some of these programs are limited to text only, most allow you to create multimedia notes

PRACTICE 4.4   Creating Bibliography and Note Cards

Gather at least three of the sources you intend to use for a research project, or use sources as assigned by your instructor. After previewing, reading, and annotating the sources make bibliography cards for each one.
Begin by creating a bibliographic heading for the card, in MLA, APA, or
whatever style system your instructor has asked you to use. After you
have created the bibliography card, save it on your computer or set it
aside and begin making the note cards. If you are using a note-taking program or a word processor with a note-taking feature, you can organize
your cards in your research folder. Some programs allow you to hyperlink
electronic "cards" together to organize them.

If you work from notes on sheets of paper, or from photocopies directly,
paperclip the bibliography card to the notes or annotated copy. You may
choose to use your first note card to write a summary of the work (thesis
and main supporting points), and then record quotations and paraphrases
on subsequent cards. When you are finished, put the bibliography card
back on top of the pile and paperclip each source's cards together or bind
them with a rubber band. Binding each source's cards separately will help
you stay organized.

as well as to store and organize your research sources. If you are using a
note-taking program like Annotate that allows you to take notes and attach
them to a PDF of your research source, then all of this can be done
electronically. In some programs the notes and sources may be attached or
associated with each other, but that will vary depending on the particular
program you are using.

You may use two kinds of cards in your research: note cards and bibliography cards. Bibliography cards contain a complete bibliographic record of
the source. Sometimes a bibliography card may include a paragraph summary of the source (its thesis and main supporting points) or notes indicating its usefulness to you under several headings. For example, a bibliography
card could contain the following headings, plus a one- or two-sentence
comment under each heading:

- ▶ Purpose (what the source attempts to accomplish)
- ▶ Uses (why you are interested in the source)
- ▶ Limitations (how narrow or wide the scope of the work is)
- ▶ Weaknesses (where you see a flaw in the source)
- ▶ Additional features (what kind of extra elements it includes, such as
  bibliographies, appendices, or maps)

Gleick, James. "Have Meme, Will Travel." Smithsonian May 2011: 88–94.

Purpose: To convince the reader that popular ideas called "memes," named by scientist Richard Dawkins in his book The Selfish Gene, propagate themselves by the rules of natural selection.

Uses: Good introduction to concept. Examples from music and popular culture. Reputable author who writes frequently about science.

Limitations: Very brief and dated. Dawkins originally proposed the idea in 1976.

Weakness: Not enough detail here to be convincing. More data needed. Check Dawkins' original book and work of other scientists like Daniel Dennett, mentioned in the article.

Additional features: None.

When creating bibliography cards using this formula, you must distinguish between sources' limitations and weaknesses. Limitations concern only the depth and focus of the source. Weaknesses consider something that you think is wrong with the argument.

Note cards contain brief reference information at the top (author's name and title of the source), with quotations, paraphrases, and summaries being recorded along with their page number references. If you use note cards instead of working from notes on paper or photocopies, then it is important to put quotation marks around anything you copy directly from the source. Also, you should carefully record all of the features of the original, including spelling, punctuation, and the use of italics. Even if the source misspells a word or is grammatically incorrect, you should reproduce the errors in your quotation. You can acknowledge that the error is not yours by placing the abbreviation *sic* inside of brackets immediately after the error.

Gleick, "What Defines a Meme," Smithsonian May 2011.

p. 92: Emphasis on memes as "complex ideas" like belief in God (mentioned on p. 90), not simple ideas: "Memes emerge in brains and travel outward, establishing beachheads on paper and celluloid and silicon and anywhere else information can go. They are not to be thought of as elementary particles but as organisms. The number three is not a meme; nor is the color blue, nor any simple thought, any more than a single nucleotide can be a gene. Memes are complex units, distinct and memorable—units with staying power."

Summarizing

Some instructors may ask you to write summaries of your sources. For example, you may be asked to write an informal summary, a formal abstract, or a summary recorded on a note card. In some cases, you may wish to summarize a source in your research paper if it provides important background information, even though it does not contain information you plan to paraphrase or directly quote.

A summary may be written in one sentence, one paragraph, or several paragraphs; single-paragraph summaries are probably the most common method. In research writing, summaries are used to establish the context or provide background information where more specific information (such as that provided with a paraphrase or quotation) is not required. (For more on summaries, see Chapter 9, Arguing Visually.)

PRACTICE 4.5   Writing Summaries

Select an article from your research or use another source as directed by your instructor. After first carefully previewing and annotating the article, write three summaries: (1) one sentence long, (2) one paragraph long (about 100 words), and (3) one page long (about 250 words). Try this procedure for writing your summaries:

1. After you annotate, underline sentences that seem especially important. Try to identify the major and minor claims.
2. Paraphrase the underlined sections in your own words.
3. Compose your summary, introducing transition words to make it flow well.
4. Rewrite the summary, eliminating as many words as possible as long as the information is not compromised and the words flow well. Simplicity is the key to good summarizing.
5. If your summary doesn't seem to "flow," try rearranging, combining, or rewriting sentences.

Paraphrasing

Most of the information that eventually ends up in your researched argument will be paraphrased. This means that you do not summarize the material—it is a specific piece of information instead of a general idea—but rather put it in your own words. A summary is usually much shorter than the original source, whereas a paraphrase will be the same length as (if not longer than) the original.

Traditional Notes

▶ Make bibliographic entries on 3-inch by 5-inch cards.

▶ Copy quotations accurately.

▶ Indicate page numbers where information was found.

▶ Clip cards to your note sheets.

▶ Categorize notes, clip them together, label the stacks, and place them in the order you will discuss them before you write.

Electronic Notes

▶ Use a database to record electronic cards, or give each source its own word processing document.

▶ Group documents in folders and subfolders. This will help you categorize your research and make it easier to locate your sources once you are ready to write.

▶ Copy quotations accurately, and indicate the page numbers where the information was found.

Photocopies

▶ As soon as you copy a source, immediately write the complete bibliographic information at the top of the copy. If you wait, you may lose the information in the shuffle.

▶ Read and annotate the source soon after you copy it. Don't wait until later. Highlight or underline quotations you may wish to use.

▶ Write notes in the margins or on Post-it notes to indicate how and where you plan to use the information.

▶ Stack copies by category, clip stacks together, and label each pile. Arrange stacks in the order you will use them before you write.

Electronic Annotation of PDFs

▶ Check the document to see if it has complete bibliographic information. Make a bibliography card—handwritten or electronic—as a backup so you can find the source in case you lose the file.

▶ Read and annotate the source using electronic tools, including highlight, underline, and comment features. Include comments regarding where you plan to use the source.

▶ Organize documents in subfolders. If you reorganize your argument, you can move the folders around in the hierarchy. Opening only one folder at a time will keep you from getting confused as you write.

ELECTRONIC RESEARCH

These days, many students find it very tempting to conduct all of their secondary research on the Internet. Indeed, many instructors now allow their students to perform all of their research using the Internet and library databases without ever checking a physical book out of the library. So why not do all of your investigation in the privacy of your own home instead of taking a long trip to the library? While electronic research, whether carried out on the Internet or through databases and CD-ROMs that are available at your college library, seems easy at first, it can be as time-consuming as a trip to the library. In fact, research on the Internet, especially from home, can lead to many dead ends and unproductive hours of searching for the right information. Electronic research must be just as well-planned as traditional secondary research, and it requires the same evaluative steps as the less high-tech approach.

Just as traditional library research requires knowledge of the ways libraries organize information, some familiarity with the types of electronic resources that are available (and their limitations) can be helpful.

Research on the Internet

While no one will deny that the Internet's accessibility from any computer makes it convenient, its vastness (and its relative lack of organization) can make it difficult to find the kind of information you need. Information in libraries is neatly organized on shelves, where each item has its own special place and number. In contrast, the Internet is rather like a giant pile of books in the middle of the room. When you do a search on the Internet, you are rummaging through that pile (albeit very quickly). If you type the keyword "Shakespeare" into Yahoo!, for example, you will come up with millions of hits (who could ever look at them all?), including community theaters, costume shops, genealogy sites, and several breweries! Also, where these sites are positioned in your "results" has less to do with their quality and more to do with their willingness to pay the search engine company to list the site near the top. Be especially wary of "sponsored links." Usually they are commercial sites that have paid the search engine company to appear in a very prominent position at the top of the list. While these links may not look like "banner ads," they serve a similar purpose. If your Internet search is not carefully phrased and well planned, it can prove very difficult to find the sort of information you're looking for.

Another consideration when conducting an Internet search is the quality of the material that is published on the Internet. While book and magazine publishers are very careful to select only the best material for publication (largely because of the cash they must invest), anyone with an Internet

How Many Internet Sources Can I Use?

Just a few years ago, many professors would not allow their students to cite documents from the Internet. They deplored the poor quality of the resources their students found and believed using the Internet "short-circuited" the research process. Today, however, most professors encourage their students to cite information obtained on the Internet and even support students who create their own Web sites and blogs. It is becoming increasingly common for professors to require students to create at least one Web-based project. These days, some writing classes are even taught exclusively with "New Media" content with students composing—and publishing—directly to Web sites, wikis, and blogs. Many students use resources from the Internet exclusively in their papers, whereas others may find some of their sources in the library and other sources on the Internet or in their library's databases. Check with your professor to see what is permitted or required. Whenever you rely on Internet sources, they should be of the same quality as information obtained in the library, and they should be properly cited (see Chapters 12 and 13 for more information).

Yahoo! is one of the most popular search engines.

→ KEEP *PASS* IN MIND WHEN SELECTING AND USING ONLINE SOURCES

Purpose: Does the source adequately support the purpose of my argument? Does it contribute to my authority (*ethos*) as a writer? Is it substantive enough to strongly support the claims I am making?

Audience: Will the reader recognize or respect the author of the source? Does the Web site have a good reputation? Will this material help establish pathos with my audience by engaging the reader's concern and sympathy with the issue? Is it reasonably objective and free of excessive bias?

Structure: Does the source have a place in my argument or am I just trying to "squeeze it in" to get a certain number of sources? Is it the best document to support the claim where it is being placed? Is it substantive enough to support the claim? Does it represent an objection to my argument that I need to refute?

Style: Is the source written in a style that makes it appropriate for my purpose and audience? Do the media elements present—tables, graphs, illustrations, animations, and videos—reflect the seriousness of the issue, or do they appear trivial or amateurish? What effect might peripheral elements, like banner ads, have on the logos, ethos, and pathos of the site (and ultimately my argument)?

connection and a little know-how can place information on the Internet. While some of this information is indeed valuable, much of it is amateurish, short-sighted, poorly researched, horribly biased, or just plain wrong. When you obtain information on the Internet, you should evaluate the site carefully for knowledgeable authors, reputable publishers, fair content, and strong, balanced rhetoric.

Research Using Internet Search Engines Although the abundance of material available on the Internet presents a challenge when your goal is to find valuable, authoritative information, you should not ignore this resource. There are two keys to conducting successful Internet research: Use good research techniques, and evaluate Web information carefully for its quality. Poorly planned research can lead to legitimate-looking sites full of erroneous information. Try this: Search for Martin Luther King. One of the top "hits" is a site called *Martin Luther King, Jr.: A True Historical Examination*. While this site looks like a legitimate historical source at first glance, it is in fact full of inaccurate and untrue information with a white supremacist agenda. As with library research, you should formulate a working thesis or research question, create a research plan, and carefully read, annotate, and evaluate any information that you find.

Two of the most popular search engines on the Internet are Yahoo! and Google. Whereas Yahoo! is one of the oldest search engines and is famed for its huge collection of categories, Google is known for cataloging an enormous amount of material. These two options are not the only search engines available, however. Many specialized search engines exist, and one may deal specifically with your topic. Some Web sites even publish catalogs of hundreds of different search engines.

© Google, Inc.

An advanced search lets you limit your results to the specific types of information for which you are searching.

Basically, search engines list things in two ways. First, people submit their URLs to the engine, hoping they will be listed. Second, Internet "robots," sometimes called "spiders," search the Internet for things to list. Thus, even if you don't find success with one engine, you may have better luck using another engine.

How Do I Conduct an Internet Search?   If you are looking for something unusual, you may be able to find it using the general search function. More often, however, you will need to use the advanced search function. It allows you to filter your search using a specific sequence of words, determine where those words occur on the page, select sites with a particular type of suffix (such as .edu, .org, or .com), or even limit the search to a particular Web site (such as the massive Web MD site). Boolean operators—words like *and*, *or*, and *not*—can help you limit your search. Most of the time you can also put phrases in quotation marks if you want to return only pages with words in a particular order (for example, "building concrete dams" in that order, instead of all pages containing the words "building," "concrete," and "dams"). With a little experimentation, you may discover ways to limit your search so that you will have to wade through less irrelevant material. In general, limiting your search to sites that end in .edu (universities and colleges), .org (organizations), and .gov (the U.S. government) is a good idea. Searching on the .com suffix will often yield numerous commercial sites that provide little useful information. Web sites in other countries use suffixes with which you may be less familiar. For example, .co.uk designates commercial sites based in the United Kingdom.

How Do I Evaluate a Web Site?   A great deal of information exists on the Internet for evaluating Web sites. Most university and community college libraries provide some kind of advice for evaluating site content. Here are a few basic things to look for when you evaluate the quality of something you have found on the Web:

Author: Who wrote the piece? What else has he or she published on the Internet or in print (a quick search will help you with this question)? Is the author an authority in this subject area? Will your audience respect him or her? If no author is listed, is the Web site a reliable source of information?

Publication: Is the home site reputable and reliable? Is it easily recognized? How long has it been up? Does it update its content regularly? How biased is it? Are its writers reputable? Does it also publish in print? Where? If the source is an electronic magazine, how long has it existed? Does it co-publish in print?

Coverage: How current, complete, and in-depth is the information? Does it include illustrations? A bibliography? If the information is dated, would it make more sense to use a print source? Does the Web site offer links to other valuable sources of information?

Rhetoric: How focused and appropriate is the purpose? Who is the intended audience? What structural weaknesses are evident? What gaps, if any, occur in the text? What, if anything, was confusing? Did the author acknowledge and refute contrary opinions? How effective are the style and tone of the piece? Are logical fallacies evident?

Research on Subscription Databases Most libraries subscribe to specialized databases in a variety of disciplines. Many of these databases allow you to access them from your home computer using a password; others are kept on CD-ROMs that you can search using your library's computers. While some of these services will return only bibliographic references, others provide full-text versions of articles and books. These databases also have the advantage of being up-to-date, unlike the books found on your library's shelves.

Lexis Nexis and ProQuest are examples of general-purpose databases that are available through many college libraries. Additionally, your college library may subscribe to a number of specialized databases. For example, Project Muse provides access to articles published in a wide range of notable academic journals in the humanities, and ERIC lists conference presentations and articles in the field of education. A visit to your library will allow you to find out which sorts of databases are available in your particular area of research.

Electronic Searches for Articles, Books, and Government Documents Not too many years ago, a trip to the library meant spending hours paging through a cross-referenced "card catalog." In some libraries, these catalogs took up much of the first floor. These days, the space occupied by the paper-based catalogs has been largely usurped by desks and computers. These machines provide access to electronic "card catalogs" that allow you to search not only your own library's holdings, but often the holdings of libraries all over the country. At most schools you can access these databases from your personal computer by using your university ID and password. Usually a book requested will arrive in just a few days, instead of the two weeks or longer it used to take. Articles will usually arrive via e-mail as PDF files instead of as paper photocopies.

Boolean Operators

When you use a search engine to explore the Internet or a database like ProQuest, your results may include books, government documents, and articles from journals and popular magazines. Often, however, these searches will yield too many hits.

Narrowing a search: To narrow your search, you can use Boolean operators:

And will return items listing both words.

Or will return items listing one word or the other.

Not will not return items listing the word that follows it.

For example, if you typed:

childhood obesity epidemic

then you would return articles listing any of those words. If you typed:

childhood and obesity

or

obesity and epidemic

then you would more likely return the types of articles you were looking for.

Limiting a search: You can focus your search to have more hits and fewer misses by searching a phrase: a group of words together in a set order. Some search engines such as Google require quotation marks around the words to make a phrase: "child obesity epidemic" would omit sources that didn't have those three words together in that order. Other search engines such as EBSCO don't require quotations marks; they assume that any search terms typed together are a phrase.

Note: Different search engines may define Boolean searches in their own particular ways. Be sure to read the instructions for any Boolean or advanced search before typing in your search terms.

A FINAL WORD ON SOURCES: CURRENCY

So far, we have said only a little about the currency of sources. Most of the time, you want the sources you are relying on to formulate your argument to be as up-to-date as possible. While books usually contain the most detailed information, by the time they are published they are at least two years out of date. Articles contain less detailed information (although they may provide in-depth coverage of a limited topic) and tend to be several months out of date. Newspaper articles are very current, but usually offer only superficial coverage of a particular issue. Likewise, information obtained on the Internet or through your library's other electronic resources may be up-to-date, but may treat your subject in less detail than you need. When you evaluate your resources, you must balance these two issues—currency versus in-depth coverage. As the author of a research-based argument, you must be the judge about the appropriate balance in your particular case.

AVOIDING PLAGIARISM

Plagiarism is the act of presenting someone else's words as your own. It is both a form of academic dishonesty and a type of theft. When you commit plagiarism, you steal someone else's ideas and present them as being your own. Universities and colleges enforce strict penalties for plagiarism, including expelling students who commit this offense.

The ready access to the Internet has, unfortunately, increased instances of plagiarism in recent years. The most flagrant examples involve students who purchase papers over the Internet and turn them in as their own work. Some Web sites have even begun writing custom papers for students—for a hefty fee, of course. Other students have engaged in "cut and paste" plagiarism, in which they may "borrow" information from a Web site, paste it into their papers, and fail to give credit to the source. This epidemic has forced some professors to take desperate measures, including submitting papers through Internet services, such as turnitin.com, where they can be electronically checked for stolen material. Turning in work that is not your own cheats you of the education you deserve and is unfair to other students who have worked hard to produce their own papers.

Sometimes plagiarism may be accidental, but it still carries the same severe penalties as deliberate theft. One way students accidentally plagiarize is by improperly paraphrasing a borrowed source. Consider the following passage from page 74 of Richard Fortey's book *Life: A Natural History of the First Four Billion Years of Life on Earth:*

> So what are animals? In the first place, they feed: They feed upon plants, either directly, or by feeding upon some other animal that feeds upon plants. Animals are spongers on the hard work of photosynthesizers: They graze or hunt, or else they absorb nutrients from an organic soup which was ultimately brewed by plants.

If a paraphrase is poorly written, it may consist of groups of the same words used by the original source. This practice is a low-tech form of "cut and paste" plagiarism. In the example that follows, the underlined words were copied directly from the preceding passage:

> <u>Animals feed upon plants.</u> Sometimes they <u>feed upon other animals that feed on plants,</u> or they <u>sponge</u> off the <u>photosynthesizers. They graze, hunt,</u> and <u>absorb</u> nutrition <u>from</u> the <u>organic soup</u> made by the plants (Fortey 74).

Even though this passage has been rephrased, it contains so much of the original language that it constitutes plagiarism. While it is often not possible to avoid all of the language used in the original ("photosynthesizers" would be hard to replace without a long, awkward phrase because it is a technical term), groups of words and idiomatic language should not be duplicated. The following paraphrase attempts to capture the content of the original without duplicating the original language:

> According to Fortey, animals are organisms that feed upon plants either directly, by eating the plants themselves, or indirectly, by consuming creatures that feed upon plants. In some cases, animals feed upon the chemical by-products that plants produce (74).

In this paraphrase, most of the language is the writer's own. A few of the same words have been used, but not in the same way or in the same order as the original. While the word *directly* was used, it was utilized in a new way, and no other word could replace it without making the paraphrase awkward or changing the meaning of the passage. For example, the writer could have used the words *primarily* and *secondarily*, but they would have changed the meanings that "directly" and "indirectly" imply. In no case did the writer use the same groups of words as in the original, and the idiomatic expressions from the original quotation were left out as well. While it is important for a writer to use his or her own words in the paraphrase, it is equally important for the paraphrase to maintain the same length and emphasis of the original. Chapter 8 includes further guidelines for recognizing and avoiding plagiarism when you quote sources in your work.

PRACTICE 4.6   Paraphrasing a Challenging Passage

Read the following passage from Bill Joy's *Wired* article, "Why the Future Doesn't Need Us." Paraphrase all or part of the passage, being careful not to directly quote the original. If you do use groups of words, place them inside quotation marks.

"We are being propelled into this new century with no plan, no control, no brakes. Have we already gone too far down the path to alter course? I don't believe so, but we aren't trying yet, and the last chance to assert control—the failsafe point—is rapidly approaching. We have our first pet robots, as well as commercially available genetic engineering techniques, and our nanoscale techniques are advancing rapidly. While the development of these technologies proceeds through a number of steps, it isn't necessarily the case—as happened in the Manhattan Project and the Trinity test—that the last step in proving a technology is large and hard. The breakthrough to wild self-replication in robotics, genetic engineering, or nanotechnology could come suddenly, reprising the surprise we felt when we learned of the cloning of a mammal."*

PRACTICE 4.7   Before You Read

1. How concerned are you about the healthiness of the foods you eat?
2. Do you think that genetically modified foods are better, worse, or the same as natural foods?
3. Examine the essay's title. What does it suggest about the author's thesis?

STUDENT ESSAY

Anna Carling

Dr. Robert Lamm

Composition

24 January 2011

GMF: Genetically Modified Food, Generating a Moral Future

Genetically modified food (GMF), evocatively dubbed as "frankenfood," has fallen victim to the malice of propaganda. At the mere mention of GMFs, our brows drop and our lips purse as we fear the uprising of the killer bean, the vengeful lentil. We cling to our children and wonder when it is that the green pea will break down the door and complete its quest for world domination. The monstrous enemy, GMF, is out to get us and we are helpless.

The public perception of GMF has been heavily influenced by the damaging publicity it has received over the past decades. Sir Hans Kornberg, chair of the United Kingdom's Scientific Advisory Committee on Genetic Modification, and advocate for GMF, agrees, arguing that the mass anxiety regarding the controversial topic is partly the fault of the British tabloids, who coined the word "frankenfood" in the early 1990s—a "snappy word" guilty of "whipping up hysteria." This provocative term results in the inevitable analogy being drawn between the creation of Dr. Frankenstein's monster and GMFs, the insinuation being that to manipulate our food genetically is, like Dr. Frankenstein in Mary Shelley's novel, to create a monster, thousands of monsters in fact, all of which will be stacked on our shelves, ready to be taken to our homes where they can watch us from the comfort of the pantry.

Online forums reflect this mounting hysteria, witnessing people who argue that GMF is "inherently dangerous" and is "opening up a Pandora's box" (Moran). Others even fear that with the consumption of GMF, "we all may have a little Frankenstein in us" ("Frankenfoods..."). It is clear that hysteria governs the public's perception of GMF and blinds it to its great potential. This hysteria, however, the kind to which Kornberg refers, should not be the driving force when determining the future role of GMF. This decision should hinge around the moral and ethical values of what GMF has to offer.

Before condemning or imploring GMF, the process itself, as well as the motives behind it, needs to be understood. Food that has been genetically modified has undergone a process called genetic engineering, defined as:

> [T]he group of applied techniques of genetics and biotechnology used to cut up and join together genetic material and especially DNA from one or more species of organism and to introduce the result into an organism in order to change one or more of its characteristics. ("Genetic Engineering")

Simply, the DNA from one organism is transplanted into another, meaning that specific, precise characteristics can be adopted by the secondary species for a beneficial purpose. This may at first seem rather arbitrary or maybe, at best, novel. Such genetic modification, however, is subjected to heavy criticism and is considered by many to be immoral, particularly in the face of religion.

Calvin DeWitt, a respected environmental scientist and director of the *Au Sable Institute of Environmental Studies* for over 25 years, argues that "moving genes across species" is an "abuse of our knowledge of genetics" and is undergone without "respect for how creation operates" (qtd. in Popp). DeWitt would sympathize with Victor Frankenstein's belief of how "Supremely frightful would be the effect of any human endeavor to mock the stupendous Creator of the world." The theological argument here is that God's actions should not be mimicked by the inferior mankind.

Not only is GMF stripped of its deserved glory because of religious sentiments, but also because of its cynical labelling as an "unnatural technique," one that interferes with life's natural course. Mary Moran, a farmer from Vermont, is just one of many who consider GMO to be "futzing with nature," and is assured that "the outcome promises to be unpleasant." This interference of GMF with nature is an immediate rebuttal to its case, as is the condemning accusation of "playing God." These two phrases appear in many discussions with the ultimate assumption that committing one of these terrible felonies is criminal enough to entirely disregard any argument. They are terms that carry with them negative connotations so severe that no compromise can be made. The blasphemous undertones synonymous with "playing God," however, seem rather questionable, as do those associated with the abuse of nature. After all, many of life's greatest creations seem guilty of these sins. To disregard the use of GMFs on this basis would also call for the abolition of life support machines, anaesthesia, medicine, and many of life's other greatest inventions. "Playing God" is a term that drowns under a sea of negative assumptions. This, however, is a matter of definition: If "playing God" means doing what is best for mankind, this being the ambition of GMF, the title should be proudly worn.

Why else is GMF subjected to such controversy? Understandably, the relative unfamiliarity of GMF raises doubts with regards to its safety. Jeffrey Smith strongly opposes the industry, claiming that "eating genetically modified food is gambling with every bite" ("Genetic Roulette"). He is concerned for human health, stating that GMFs "could theoretically transform our intestinal flora into living pesticide factories" ("Genetically Engineered..."). Mike Adams, an editor of *NaturalNews.com* who crowns himself as "The Natural Ranger," shares similar concerns and, in an attempt to reach out to the younger population, raps in a YouTube video that "the side effects cause medical patients" and that, "the frankenseeds that they sow / They're gonna hurt us we know." Mike Adams is seen rapping his song "Just Say No to GMO," and the hysteria which is so eminent in today's society is encapsulated when later he preaches hyperbolically, "it's just poison stealing away your life, and that's what you eat with genetically modified."

Scientific evidence supporting these alarming claims, however, is absent. Kornberg serves as a reminder that these health risks are mere speculations, lacking any form of tangible, scientific evidence; as Chair of the Scientific Advisory Committee on Genetic Modification he knows of "no instance in which it [GMF] has caused any harm to any animal or human being."

Whitman writes that "with the exception of possible allerginicity, scientists believe that GM foods do not present a risk to human health" (7). Kaplan confesses that "there is not yet any overwhelming evidence that genetically engineered food is dangerous" (1).

The more cynical individual may well accuse genetically modifying food of being manipulative or abusive. The fearful will view the procedure

Carling 5

as dangerous or threatening. Cynics will insist that science is "asking for trouble," that mankind is walking "a slippery slope." It is, however, the innovative individual who will value this scientific feat, as it is he or she who can appreciate the incredible opportunities that come hand in hand with this practice, one which carries with it the potential to benefit the population worldwide.

Millions of people in the developing world are left hungry and malnourished. To address this problem is nothing more than a moral obligation. Vitamin A deficiency is just one of many threats facing developing nations. According to a global report published by an Interagency Steering Committee, nearly 670,000 children under the age of five die annually due to vitamin A deficiency (52).

Whitman states also that blindness resulting from vitamin A deficiency is "a common problem in third world countries" (3). With this knowledge, the Swiss Federal Institute of Technology, using its

© Neil Cooper / Alamy

Fig. 1 Starving children in Sudan, unable to grow their own crops and without any means of producing their own food.

understanding of genetic modification, developed a strain of rice known as "golden rice." This yellow-orange rice grain contains beta-carotene, an organic compound not found in naturally grown rice, which the human body converts into vitamin A. The International Rice Research Institute (IRRI) states that when combined with existing dietary sources, "golden rice is expected to have a significant impact in reducing malnutrition and premature death" (1). Genetically modifying food has the capacity to provide starving nations with vitamins and minerals to which they would otherwise not have access. To oppose a proposition such as the genetic engineering of food is tantamount to negligence.

Genetically modifying food is not immoral, but ethical. The process produces more resilient crops which yield healthier foods, not the disfigured "frankenfoods" as the masses like to assume. GMF is not the scheming work of the money maker, the business man, or indeed, Dr. Victor Frankenstein. Its emphasis is on progression and enhancement. Its ultimate goal is to cultivate crops of a better quality and to do so more efficiently. Its vision is to nourish the malnourished. The technology should, of course, be respected and treated with thorough caution and vigilance but when discoveries are made that have the potential to alleviate world hunger, such revolutionary successes should be fervently supported without delay. As Jonathan Swift writes in *Gulliver's Travels*, "whoever could make two ears of corn, or two blades of grass, to grow upon a spot of ground where only one grew before, would deserve better of mankind, and do more essential service to his country, than the whole race of politicians put together."

Carling 7

Works Cited

Adams, Mike. "Just Say No to GMO." *YouTube*. YouTube, 13 Oct. 2010.
Web. 30 March 2011.

"Frankenfoods: The Beginning of the End?" *The ME Moment*. The ME
Moment, 7 June 2010. Web. 29 March 2011.

"Genetic engineering." *Merriam Webster's Collegiate Dictionary*. 11th
ed. 2006. Print.

Interagency Steering Committee. *Investing in the Future: A United Call
to Action on Vitamin and Mineral Deficiencies*. Flour Fortification
(FFI), The Global Alliance for Improved Nutrition (GAIN), Micronutrient
Initiative (MI), The United Nations Children's Fund–UNICEF, United
States Agency for International Development (USAID), World Bank,
World Health Organization (WHO), 2009. Web. 10 Feb. 2011.

International Rice Research Institute (IRRI). *Golden Rice*. 2005. Web. 10
Feb. 2011.

Jamal, Farrukh, et al. "Genetically Modified (GM) Foods: A Brief
Perspective." *International Journal of Biotechnology and
Biochemistry* 6.1 (2010): 13–24. Web. 6 Feb. 2011.

Kaplan, David. M, Ph.D. "What's Wrong with Genetically Modified
Food?" *Ethical Issues of the 21st* Century (2004). Web. 8 Feb. 2011.

Kornberg, Hans. "Frankenfood: Monstrous or Misunderstood?" *BU
Today News and Events*. BU, 5 April. 2007. Web. 1 April 2011.

Moran, Mary. "Are GMOs dangerous? Farmers speak out." *Public Radio
Kitchen*. WBUR, 7 Feb. 2011. Web. 3 April 2011.

Popp, Trey. "Genetically Modified Organisms Are Generating a Good
Deal of Scientific and Economic Debate. How Organized Religion
Values This Technology Is Anyone's Guess." *AgBioWorld*. N.s. March
2006. Web. 24 March 2011.

Smith, Jeffrey M. "Genetically Engineered Foods May Pose National Health Risk." *News with Views*. N.s. 1 Aug. 2004. Web. 22 March 2011.

Smith, Jeffrey M. "Genetic Roulette: The Documented Health Risks of Genetically Engineered Foods." *Genetic Roulette*. Pure Zing. Web. 2 April 2011.

"Starving." *Counter Culture Conservative*. World Press, 3 June 2010. Web. 2 April 2011.

Whitman, Deborah B. "Genetically Modified Foods: Harmful or Helpful?" *CSA.com*. CSA Discoveries, 2000: 1–8. Web. 8 Feb. 2011.

PRACTICE 4.8   Responding to the Essay

1. Do you agree or disagree with the author's claim and supporting ideas? Did the author change your prior opinion in any way? How?
2. Where is the author's support stronger? Where is it weaker? Explain.
3. Does the author's treatment of other points of view affect your willingness to believe what he has to say? In what way?
4. What, if anything, would you change about the essay's organization and content? Is there anything missing that you would add?
5. Which of the appeals (logic, authority, emotion) do you think was strongest in this essay? Which was weakest? Why do you think so?
6. Name the essay's greatest strength and most significant weakness. Explain your answer.

Looking Back at Chapter 4

▶ Research is a three-stage process: *planning*, *exploring*, and *evaluating sources*.

▶ One of the best ways to find sources is to follow a "bibliographic trail."

▶ Research can involve either obtaining information in person (through *primary research*) or reading what others have written about a particular topic (through *secondary research*).

▶ Most libraries divide resources into five areas: books, periodicals, reference, government documents, and media.

► Librarians, instructors, and researchers often classify sources by their degree of originality, labeling them as different levels—*primary, secondary,* or *tertiary*—depending on the relative distance from "firsthand" information.

► Evaluate your sources by reading them *critically*: previewing, annotating, responding, and organizing.

► In research writing, summaries are used to establish the context or provide background information where more specific information (such as that provided with a paraphrase or quotation) is not required.

► You can evaluate a source by considering the particular strengths of the author, the reputation of the publication, the applicability to what you are researching, and the rhetorical strength of the text.

► Plagiarism—turning in work that is not your own—cheats you of the education you deserve and is unfair to other students who have worked hard to produce their own papers.

Suggestions for Writing

► Decide on a topic for research. Refine it into an issue first, and then a research question. Write a research plan for finding the answer to your question. Include strategies for physical library visits and online research. Include a description of types of sources you will use (books, professional journals, newspapers, online databases, Web sites) along with justification for using each source type.

► After conducting research, write a reflection essay about your research process. Explain the specific steps you followed, along with what worked and what didn't. Explain where you ran into dead ends, and what you did to revise your process to find the answer to your question. If you did not find the answer to your question, explain how you will revise your research strategy for your next attempt.

► Write a research plan for a project involving primary research. Explain what strategies you plan to use, and why you think these approaches will help you find the answer to your question. Write the questions you will ask in your interviews and/or focus groups.

5

Writing Process: Planning Arguments

> {
> A journey of a
> thousand miles
> begins with a
> single step.
> —Lao-Tzu
> (604–531 B.C.E.)
> }

A long journey can be intimidating, especially when it takes you into unknown territory. Completing the quest requires preparation, effort, a commitment of time, and solving problems both expected and unexpected. Ancient wisdom, however, reminds us that even the most arduous journey can be accomplished through a series of manageable steps.

Likewise, writing requires preparation, effort, a commitment of time, and plenty of problem solving. Fortunately, a number of techniques can make this process easier. Known as *planning* or *prewriting*, these techniques help you divide any assignment into a series of smaller, simpler tasks. Just as a journey of a thousand miles begins with a single step, so a book of a thousand pages begins with a single word. Planning can help you to make the first steps, to write the first words.

There are many planning techniques and many situations in which to apply those techniques. As you learn more about writing, you will not only expand your planning repertoire but also identify those methods that work best for you. To plan well, you'll need to (1) understand the assignment, (2) generate material, and (3) organize.

UNDERSTANDING THE ASSIGNMENT

Whether self-assigned, course-required, or job-related, writing assignments have elements that must be analyzed and understood early and reviewed throughout the writing process. Some of these elements are *task-specific* requirements dictated by an instructor, employer, or publisher: format, length, sources, and deadline. Other elements are based more on the *rhetorical context* that you can analyze with a kind of "tool kit" we call **PASS**: *purpose, audience, structure*, and *style*.

Task Specifications

A writing assignment usually has specifications regarding its format, length, sources, and deadline. Although these specifications are technical in nature, they are the first noticed and most easily assessed features of your finished product. By carefully following the task-specific requirements, you'll make a good initial impression on the reader and use your time efficiently throughout the writing process.

Format Formatting concerns the visual appearance of your text: margins, headings, pagination or headers, font type and size, bullets, indentations, cover sheets, tables, graphs, illustrations, and acknowledgment of sources. Instructors, employers, or publishers sometimes create their own formatting requirements. At other times, they defer to the formatting style prescribed by an authority such as a professional organization—for example, the style guides of the Modern Language Association (MLA) or the American Psychological Association (APA). Word processing programs have default (automatic) formats that can be changed by accessing the toolbar. (Chapters 12, MLA, and 13, APA, provide more information about formatting issues.)

Length Writing assignments usually have a prescribed length. Although planning can help with assignments of any length, with longer assignments planning may be indispensable, helping you conceive of the whole and organize its many parts. For your convenience, word processing programs indicate the number of pages automatically and will count the number of words and characters for you. Plan to stay comfortably within the constraints of any prescribed word or page count: Skimping on length usually looks like you are skimping on effort, while excessive length may indicate an inability to focus your thoughts and be concise. Tweaking the font size, margins, and line spacing to compensate for length problems won't fool anyone!

Sources Some writing assignments require sources; others may exclude their use. If you are using sources, you'll need to know how many, what kind, and how to find, evaluate, use, and acknowledge them. This chapter and most others in this book discuss using sources.

Deadline A deadline is a time limit for the completion and submission of a writing assignment. Also known as a due date, a deadline sometimes is self-imposed and flexible, especially when a project is self-assigned. Deadlines set by an instructor, employer, or publisher, by contrast, are usually beyond your control and firm (or at least regulated by a policy).

Scheduling When facing a firm deadline, you'll want to set up a personal schedule that breaks the assignment into subtasks, each with its own deadline. Scheduling can help you anticipate which parts of the process will take more time than others, such as ordering books or other research materials through interlibrary loan or from vendors, or working around the schedules of others to conduct interviews. You'll have a much better chance of producing quality material if you pace yourself and budget your time so you don't have to frantically write at the last minute. A schedule can be mapped out on a daily planner, calendar, or checklist.

PRACTICE 5.1   Making a Schedule

For a current assignment, make a schedule of stages and due dates. You could adapt the sample schedule shown earlier in this chapter.

PRACTICE 5.2 Formatting

1. Open this book to a pair of pages that include a photo. Without reading any of the words, observe and comment on any formatting features you can see: color, types of lettering, size of lettering, illustrations, white space, and how the parts are arranged.
2. Analyze the formatting of a paper you have completed in the past. Observe and comment on any formatting features you can see: color, typeface, size of type, use of headings, illustrations, white space, and the overall design—look and feel—of the document.
3. For a paper you are working on, consider your formatting options. Find out from your instructor how much formatting is permitted or desirable in that assignment.

→ SAMPLE SCHEDULE

Task	Date
Decide on a topic or subject	_____
Begin research	_____
Decide on an issue	_____
Decide on tentative thesis or major claim	_____
Complete rough first draft	_____
Complete polished draft for others to review	_____
Hold peer review or conference	_____
Complete final draft	_____
Submit (deadline)	_____

Rhetorical Context

Writers select a particular structure or form (for example, an essay or a letter) and adjust their style to fit a particular purpose and audience. Together, along with knowledge of the rhetorical situation occasioning the piece of writing, these considerations help the writer effectively respond to the rhetorical context. Don't forget PASS (purpose, audience, structure, and style).

Purpose You write to achieve a purpose, such as to inform, to entertain, to express yourself, or, of course, to argue. The general goal of argument is to change how an audience thinks and possibly how it acts in response to an issue. More specifically, argument focuses on making a case for particular claims: fact, identity, cause/effect, value, and proposal. (See Chapter 2, Claims and Support, for more information.)

Audience An audience is composed of your readers, listeners, or viewers. In a writing course you know your work is destined for an instructor's scrutiny—an audience of one—and this fact strongly influences how you write. However, instructors often expect you to write for a broader audience. When in doubt, assume your audience to be a reasonable but skeptical stranger who is moderately acquainted with the subject: Don't assume your reader already knows the same things you have read or discussed in class. Your instructor may even create a scenario, giving you a specific "imaginary" audience: expert or uninformed, friendly or hostile. You'll make adjustments in your writing for the audience, adapting your purpose, structure, and style to fit its characteristics. Indeed, some writers create a profile of the audience to help tailor their arguments to fit that particular group.

Structure Structure refers partly to the form, genre, or type of writing produced, and partly to the organization within a form. In professional writing, brochures, proposals, Web sites, and multimedia presentations all have their own specific rules for content, style, and layout. In academic settings, formal essays are commonly required in composition courses, but their internal features will vary with the techniques used to argue. Documents focusing on classification, definition, cause, and policy, for example, have distinctive organizational patterns. Also, arguments need not always be formal essays or even written documents. Editorials and editorial cartoons, letters to the editor, petitions, grant proposals, contract bids, debates, courtroom hearings, and advertisements—all are arguments. (Chapter 6, Drafting Arguments, contains more information on structure.)

Style Style refers to *how* something is said rather than *what* is said. It is conveyed by your attitude, tone, voice, sentence structure, and word choice. Think of style as a range of choices between formal and informal, serious and humorous, specialized and general purpose, familiar and distant. You'll want to use a style that fits your rhetorical context—that is, your purpose, audience, and structure. Document design is also a stylistic choice influenced by conventions of form and audience expectations.

Creating an Audience Profile The audience is a vitally important rhetorical consideration. Identifying the characteristics of your audience through an audience profile can help you understand the readers you wish to persuade and decide how you can adapt your argument to better fit them.

→ RANGE OF STYLES

Style in writing is analogous to style in dress, ranging from informal to formal. Research papers tend to be formal, written in an "academic style" that prefers third-person point of view and avoids contractions. In other words, you avoid the use of *I* or *you*, and you write out terms such as *should not* instead of using *shouldn't*. The rules are not hard and fast, however, and they depend upon the rhetorical context and the contract between the author and the audience.

> *Informal:* I think we should all work together so plagiarism doesn't mess up our school.

> *Formal:* Students, instructors, and administrators should cooperate in promoting a healthy atmosphere of academic honesty.

You have probably noticed that this textbook uses a less formal style, assuming a second-person point of view (POV) to address *you* directly. Second-person POV fits our purpose of acting as your mentor: We want to convey a tone that is friendlier than third-person POV will allow. Also, we would argue that the textbook itself is not a research paper—so cut us some slack, okay? (You wouldn't use slang phrases like "cut us some slack, okay" in a formal research paper.)

While there are no absolute cutoff points distinguishing degrees of formality in writing, you could think of your choices as a continuum, as displayed in the imaginary "formality meter":

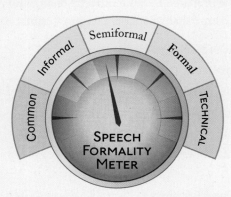

Style can range in degrees of formality.

Common Language is specific to the community where it is used. Incomplete sentences, alternative grammar, and idiomatic expressions are freely employed in some communities. Slang and other "unofficial" words may also be used.

> *Example of word choice expressing "amount":* a bunch.

Informal Language is used broadly outside of one's immediate family, neighborhood, or peer group to communicate with the world at large. Incomplete sentences and contractions are freely used, although alternative grammar, idiomatic speech, slang, and other expressions that might impede communication are avoided.

> *Example of word choice expressing "amount":* a lot.

Semiformal This language is commonly used to communicate, both in writing and speech, at work and in school. Incomplete sentences, alternative grammar, and idiomatic expressions are usually avoided. The writing in newspapers and magazines represents this level of formality.

> *Example of word choice expressing "amount":* many.

Formal This language is carefully written. Rules of punctuation and grammar are strictly followed. Contractions and other signs of informality are avoided. Words are carefully chosen to communicate specific ideas. Generally, a more complex vocabulary is employed.

> *Example of word choice expressing "amount":* an abundance.

Technical Sentences and paragraphs must follow a specific format. Words are often the jargon used by specialists and have very precise meanings. This language is typical of legal documents and technical manuals.

> *Example of word choice expressing "amount":* 6.74 liters.

PRACTICE 5.3   Applying Your Rhetorical Tool Kit

Evaluate the rhetorical features of the following excerpts. What are the apparent purpose, audience, structure, and style (PASS) of each? How would changing one rhetorical feature affect the other features?

> One of the oddest job offers I ever received came when a stranger telephoned to ask if I would be interested in researching and writing academic papers for university students. For the uninitiated, so-called "paper mills" sell term papers and essays to desperate students who hand them in as their own work. People picture the mills as a low-rent operation run out of someone's basement. Maybe in the days of bell-bottoms and peace symbols, but not anymore. Thanks to the Internet, email, and fax machines, academic plagiarism is easy—and big business.*

> Meta-analytic findings have suggested that individual differences are relatively weaker predictors of academic dishonesty than are situation factors. A robust literature on deviance correlates and workplace integrity testing, however, demonstrated that individual difference variables can be relatively strong predictors of a range of counterproductive work behaviors (CWBs).†

> _____
> *Rhonda Lauret Parkinson, *"Plagiarize at Your Peril"* McLeans, Canada, November 15, 2004. Reprinted by permission of the author.
> †Gale Lucas and James Friedrich, *"Individual Differences in Workplace Deviance and Integrity as Predictors of Academic Dishonesty"*

Below is the audience profile prepared by student Hetal Shah, who plans to write on the topic of plagiarism. (Shah's paper appears in Chapter 6.)

Audience Profile for the Topic of Plagiarism

  I. Rhetorical context (preliminary, tentative)
   A. **Purpose:** To persuade instructors to be more understanding of students who plagiarize and to be more lenient on plagiarists
   B. **Audience:** Instructors
   C. **Structure:** Argumentative essay based on research
   D. **Style:** Formal
 II. Profile of primary audience: Instructors
   A. **Audience's relevant demographics (e.g., profession, education, age, gender, race, religion):** The most important thing about instructors is

their <u>profession</u>: They are obliged to enforce codes of academic honesty. Also, their <u>education</u> level is important: They already know how to write well, so their standards about writing are high. Their <u>college preparation</u> may have been better than that of the students they now teach, so they may not understand the students' difficulties. <u>Age</u> is an issue because they may have forgotten what it's like to be a student.

B. **Audience's knowledge of the issue (ranging from expert to novice):** Instructors have an expert knowledge of how to use sources in writing. Their knowledge of teaching writing will vary: more with English instructors, less with other disciplines. Their knowledge of their own students' backgrounds and abilities will vary.

C. Audience's present attitude(s) toward the issue:

    1. **Audience's major concerns:** Students' learning of subject being taught, students' knowledge of writing, students' understanding of ethics

    2. **Audience's minor concerns:** Students' grades, stress, exhaustion, morale, future

III. Profile of secondary audience(s)

A. **Secondary audience 1**

    Audience: Administrators who influence policies affecting instruction and disciplinary policies

    Conflicts with primary audience: Probably few conflicts. Administrators and instructors probably will agree with one another and can be persuaded with the same arguments. Administrators might be more sympathetic to students, and might be more concerned with public relations and with a policy that is consistent and universal.

B. **Secondary audience 2**

    Audience: Students affected by instruction and by disciplinary procedures.

    Conflicts with primary audience: Most will already be sympathetic to claims that shift responsibility to instructors and administrators. Their concerns will focus less on ethics and knowledge, and more on grades and fair treatment. However, those who don't plagiarize will likely agree with instructors. They want a level playing field where students don't get high grades without doing the work.

IV. Arguments (claims and support) the audience(s) could accept

A. **Argument 1**

Claim: "When plagiarism is accidental, leniency should be shown."

Support: "It isn't an ethical weakness, only lack of knowledge."

"Students are in school to learn, not to be punished."

B. **Argument 2**

Claim: "Instruction about academic honesty could be improved. This would include ethical training and writing training aimed specifically at ways to avoid plagiarism."

Support: "Many educators, philosophers, and religious leaders believe ethics and morality <u>can be learned</u>; therefore, it <u>should be taught</u>."

"Students who haven't been taught how to use sources properly may be forced into making unethical choices."

V. **Rhetorical** context (revised after profiling the audience)

A. **Purpose:** To propose a fairer policy of academic honesty that clarifies the responsibilities of students, instructors, and administrators

B. **Audience:** Students, instructors, and administrators

C. **Structure:** Argumentative essay based on research

D. **Style:** Formal

As the student worked through the profile, she discovered that her preliminary purpose was unlikely to sway her intended audience: Instructors were unlikely to accept responsibility for the academic dishonesty of their students. Her revised purpose was a compromise claiming that students, instructors, and administrators share responsibility for the problem of plagiarism and that the remedy will require them to work together. Her audience was broadened, and her claim became more likely to change the way the audience thought and acted.

PRACTICE 5.4   Creating an Audience Profile

Use Hetal Shah's audience profile as a guide to create a profile of an audience for a topic or an issue you plan to write about.

> → AUDIENCE PROFILE
>
> I. Rhetorical context (preliminary, tentative)
>
>   A. Purpose:
>
>   B. Audience:
>
>   C. Structure:
>
>   D. Style:
>
> II. Profile of primary audience
>
>   A. Audience's relevant demographics (e.g., profession, education, age, gender, race, religion):
>
>   B. Audience's knowledge of the issue (ranging from expert to novice):
>
>   C. Audience's present attitude(s) toward the issue:
>
>   1. Audience's major concerns:
>
>   2. Audience's minor concerns:
>
> III. Profile of secondary audience(s)
>
>   A. Secondary audience 1
>   Audience:
>   Conflicts with primary audience:
>
>   B. [repeat as needed]
>
> IV. Arguments (claims and support) the audience(s) could accept
>
>   A. Argument 1
>   Claim:
>   Support:
>
>   B. [repeat as needed]
>
> V. Rhetorical considerations (revised after profiling the audience)
>
>   A. Purpose:
>
>   B. Audience:
>
>   C. Structure:
>
>   D. Style:

GENERATING MATERIAL

Much the same way that a carpenter gathers tools and materials before beginning to build a house, the process of generating material helps you gather claims and support before beginning to write a draft. Some scholars refer to this process of jotting notes and getting ideas down on paper as the "zero draft" in preparation for writing the first complete draft. On an intuitive level, you might think anything that keeps you from immediately starting your first draft is a waste of time; in practice, you'll find that generating materials makes drafting proceed more quickly and easily. Generating techniques include brainstorming, critical thinking, discussing, writing, sketching and scrapbooking, discovering, and researching.

Brainstorming

Brainstorming involves the rapid listing of ideas on a given topic. Its goal is quantity: Worries about quality are postponed until after the brainstorming

→ TECHNIQUES FOR GENERATING ARGUMENTS

Brainstorming: Rapid listing of ideas, words, or phrases suggested by a topic

Critical thinking: Interpretation, application, analysis, synthesis, and evaluation

Discussing: Vocal or Internet exchanges with others on a topic

Writing: Using prose to generate ideas, not necessarily to produce a draft
  ▶ Focused freewriting: Full-sentence rapid writing on a topic
  ▶ Journaling: Full-sentence reflective writing on a topic

▶ Blogging: Journal or log entries posted on the Web ("weblogging")

Sketching and scrapbooking: Collecting visual materials on a topic

Discovering: Using lists of points or questions as guidelines

Researching: Gathering information
  ▶ Primary research: Generating new information
  ▶ Secondary research: Finding information generated by others

---

Guidelines for Brainstorming

Brainstorming is the rapid listing of ideas, questions, and information about a topic. It produces a collection of words and phrases that later can be reflected upon, organized, and expanded.

- **Aim for quantity.** Don't stop for any reason. State (orally or in writing) as many ideas as possible in a given period of time.
- **Aim for speed.** Write as quickly as you can. Record your ideas in brief fashion—words, phrases, abbreviations. Don't let recording slow down your generation of ideas.
- **Build from the ideas already recorded.** When the initial stream of ideas starts to slow, expand on things you've already written.
- **Don't worry.** Suspend your inhibitions, never stopping to critique an idea. Write whatever comes to mind. Evaluate later.

session, when each idea is evaluated. Brainstorming is the most basic and versatile of all planning techniques.

Brainstorming can be performed individually or in any size group. When performed individually, it is a silent writing activity. In contrast, a group working collaboratively is highly vocal, with a designated person recording the ideas as words or phrases (not complete sentences) because speed is of the essence. Discussion of the ideas is suspended until the brainstorming session ends.

A typical brainstorming session lasts five to ten minutes, but it can be expanded or contracted to suit the situation. For a short writing assignment, a minute of brainstorming might suffice, whereas committees or think tanks may brainstorm for hours, days, or longer on major issues. For many writers, brainstorming recurs quite frequently: A writer may first brainstorm possible topics, then select an issue, and finally brainstorm terms, ideas, and claims specific to the selected issue.

Following is a list of terms and ideas that Hetal Shah produced during a two-minute brainstorming session on her topic of plagiarism:

writing is hard	paraphrasing	quoting	MLA
APA	punishment	flunking	Pressure
Deadlines	too many papers	ethics	Morality
tough teachers	Internet papers	Turnitin.com	paper mill
Footnotes	bibliography	works cited	Guilt
academic dishonesty	cheating	unfair	F

PRACTICE 5.5   Brainstorming

Choose a topic, perhaps one you may later argue. With a watch or clock in view, brainstorm and record a list of issues, terms, facts, ideas, and individuals associated with the topic. You are not limited to controversy: At this stage, simply list anything you know (or want to know) about the topic.

PRACTICE 5.6   Thinking Critically

Choose an issue, perhaps one that emerged from brainstorming or freewriting about a topic. Respond to the following questions and record your answers.

1. **Knowledge and clarification:** What facts do you know or perhaps need to know?
2. **Comprehension and interpretation:** What is its significance? What does it imply or *really* mean?
3. **Application:** What uses does it have to you or to others?
4. **Analysis:** What are its parts? How do they work together?
5. **Synthesis:** How does it relate to other things?
6. **Evaluation:** What is its importance? How good is it?

PRACTICE 5.7   Discussing

In a small or large group, discuss a controversial issue of your choice. Argue first as adversaries, taking opposite sides in a point-counterpoint fashion. Then change your approach, working collaboratively to solve the issue by finding common ground and making concessions.

Critical Thinking

Critical thinking involves "reading between the lines," looking beneath the surface meaning of a subject. A productive way to think critically is to ask and answer questions such as those modeled after Bloom's taxonomy. Questions can guide your brainstorming, freewriting, journaling, discussion, or research.

Here is a list of terms and ideas produced by Hetal Shah's ten-minute critical thinking session on the topic of plagiarism. These questions, which are derived from Bloom's taxonomy, also can be used to discover explanations for supporting evidence. (See the "Discovering" section later in this chapter.)

1. **Knowledge and clarification:** Plagiarism is considered cheating or theft. It's easy to plagiarize through Web sites—old student essays are there for the taking. Internet sources also sell customized essays. It's easy to take a published article and turn it into an essay. Penalties can be severe: failure, suspension, expulsion. Not sure what the school's policy is. Not sure how to completely avoid plagiarizing.

2. **Comprehension and interpretation:** Plagiarism can get you into trouble—a short-term fix that can backfire and end your education and maybe your future. But sometimes it's the last resort for desperate students out of time. Sometimes it's the only resort for students who don't know any other way to use sources.

3. **Application:** Plagiarism can get you out of trouble—a deadline or an overload of work. If you're not caught, it can get you a good grade. If you're caught, it's just the opposite: You're in trouble and you get a bad grade. Knowing how to use sources properly makes it possible to get the benefits and avoid penalties.

4. **Analysis:** The "parts" of plagiarism are materials taken from a source—a book or article—that you pretend you wrote yourself. Or it can be a whole essay someone else wrote, using articles and books legitimately. Or you can pretend you're paraphrasing, when you're really quoting without using quotation marks. Guilt and fear are parts of it—sometimes you're caught years after you plagiarized, so you're never in the clear. It's a decision made to go over to the dark side.

5. **Synthesis:** It's a form of cheating—"academic dishonesty." It's like stealing from someone (except the person may never miss what you've stolen!). It's also like a lifesaver for a drowning person—someone who might sink academically without it. It's similar to downloading music without paying royalties or copying answers from someone else's test.

6. **Evaluation:** It gets the job done, in a way. It's efficient—you get a grade without much work. It's scary but kind of a rush, like committing a crime and hoping no one knows it was you. Once you realize how bad some people think it is, you start feeling bad about yourself, like you're a fake. The worst thing is you never learn how to write your own stuff in a way that will help you in life.*

---

*From Benjamin S. Bloom et al., *Taxonomy of Educational Objectives*, Book 1, *Cognitive Domain* (Boston: Allyn & Bacon). Copyright © Pearson Education. Adapted by permission.

Guidelines for Critical Thinking (from Bloom's Taxonomy)*

1. Knowledge and clarification: What facts do you know or perhaps need to know?
2. Comprehension and interpretation: What is its significance? What does it imply or *really* mean?
3. Application: What uses does it have to you or to others?
4. Analysis: What are its parts? How do they work together?
5. Synthesis: How does it relate to other things?
6. Evaluation: What is its importance? How good is it?

Discussing

Talking about a subject can be a powerful method for discovering ideas. Interactive, focused discussions often reveal that you know more—or less—about a subject than expected. In either case, it can guide you to the next steps for planning. Discussion adds a social dimension to reading and writing, often making the process more enjoyable because it is interactive and sometimes dramatic. Sometimes discussion is structured around a prepared list of questions, such as those that guide critical thinking or audience profiling, but it can also be freewheeling and spontaneous.

Discussions can range from cooperative (a team effort to understand issues and solve problems) to adversarial (a debate that reveals points of contention, support, and rebuttals). They can occur in large groups, small groups, or pairs; before, during, or after reading or writing—whenever they are useful. Although discussions often occur in classroom settings, they may also take place through e-mail, chat rooms, and instant messaging.

> ## Guidelines for Discussing
>
> The following guidelines are adapted from the conflict resolution techniques introduced in Chapter 1. They can help make discussion more productive and civil.
> - Take turns introducing topics or issues.
> - Don't interrupt.
> - Respond positively.
> - Ask for clarifications.
> - Listen for omissions or evasions.

Writing

Writing can be used as a planning technique. This kind of writing is intended not so much to draft a text but rather to generate ideas before you begin putting the ideas into the form you want. Freewriting, journaling, and blogging are writing techniques used to generate ideas.

Freewriting *Freewriting*, also known as stream of consciousness writing or rambling, involves nonstop composing on a particular topic. Freewriters usually write in complete sentences, unlike the word-or-phrase listing of brainstorming. Freewriting sessions typically last five to ten minutes but can be expanded or contracted to fit the particular circumstances. Indeed, some essay tests may ask you to perform focused freewriting for an hour or more.

The most important goal while freewriting is to compose nonstop without worrying about anything except volume: The motto here is "The more, the better." To be able to write rapidly, freewriters suspend their "internal editor," ignoring concerns about errors, disorganization, poor word choice, or lack of ideas. Freewriting offers benefits that might not be achieved through other kinds of writing activities:

► Confidence that might otherwise be diminished by self-editing. If you burden yourself with concerns about saying something "just right," you may never get the idea on paper.

► Fluency through writing with a flow resembling conversation. When we speak, we seldom take long pauses and we almost never run to a dictionary to look up words. Freewriting can help a writer capitalize on the ease of oral communication.

► Freedom from "writer's block." You have no choice except to write. If you are stuck, write something like "I'm stuck, I'm stuck…" until you find something better to write.

PRACTICE 5.8   Focused Freewriting

Freewrite for a set amount of time on a subject or issue you plan to argue.

Focused freewriting takes the technique a little further, requiring that you write nonstop on a particular topic or issue. Focused freewriters attempt to make their writing coherent—logically flowing from sentence to sentence—but off-topic drifting is natural and acceptable. The following example is a five-minute focused freewrite on the topic of plagiarism by a student in Hetal Shah's collaborative learning group:

> I hope nobody reads this because I'm about to confess! I've plagiarized most of my life. In grade school, teachers would assign reports, and most of the time my report was copied straight out of an encyclopedia. It was never questioned, and I always got a good grade when I turned it in. LOL Book reports were a little harder, except sometimes you could copy a summary straight from the cover of the book! In high school they taught about citing sources and how to make a bibliography, but the English teacher was the only one watching how we used the sources. The biology teacher, the history teacher—I think they were more concerned with what we learned about their subjects and not so much about the actual writing. They never questioned how I came up with the wording while I just took the stuff straight from a book but dummied it down into my own style.

Journaling   A *journal* is your record of your experiences and reflections. Also known as a log and resembling a diary, journals can be freewritten. In this textbook, however, we distinguish between journaling and freewriting based on how the passage is produced. Journaling is more meditative, allowing you to pause as needed to think about what to write and even to revise what you have already written. Freewriting is nonstop writing and consequently more spontaneous.

Guidelines for Focused Freewriting

Focused freewriting involves writing nonstop about a topic or issue.

1. **Aim for quantity.** Don't stop for any reason.
2. **Aim for speed.** Write as quickly as you can. It's probably better (faster) if you use cursive rather than printing. If you can't think of something to write, then write something like "I'm stuck" until you're *not* stuck.
3. **Build from the ideas already recorded.** When the initial stream of ideas starts to slow, expand on things you've already written.
4. **Don't worry.** Suspend your inhibitions, never stopping to solve problems with spelling or word choice—settle for approximate spellings. Write whatever comes to mind about the topic or issue. Evaluate your writing later.

The rhetorical context of a journal is defined by its personal nature: for the purposes of reflection, exploration, and self-expression; for an audience of one (the author); through a freeform structure; and in a style that is precisely the voice of the writer. Although *journal* contains a root word from the French *jour* (meaning "day"), writers do not strictly have to write daily. They do need to write regularly, however.

PRACTICE 5.9   Journaling

Keep a journal for an extended period of time—days, weeks, or months. Focus the journal on an issue you plan to argue. You may wish to use free-writing as a means for writing the journal, or you may prefer to employ a slower, more reflective technique.

Blogging   A *blog* (a contraction of *Weblog*) is a personal journal made public by posting on a Web page. In the planning phase of writing, a blog may function like a journal while offering some additional benefits: It provides an audience that can respond, creating a community of learners that extends beyond the walls of a classroom to potentially anywhere on the planet. Anything that can be digitalized can be added to the blog—any form of writing, visuals, or music. The public nature of a blog changes the journal's rhetorical context.

> **Purpose:** While the purposes for writing a journal tend to be personal, exploratory, and tentative, a blog may have an effect on other readers, essentially becoming an argument.

> **Audience:** The audience of a journal initially is oneself, whereas the audience of a blog is, potentially, the world.

> **Structure:** Although a blog may retain the relaxed organization of a journal entry, a blogger often will rewrite for the sake of clarifying ideas for an audience.

> **Style:** A blog usually retains the voice of the author. However, because this writing is public, a blogger should observe certain conventions of public discourse, such as avoiding profanity and refraining from the expression of inflammatory ideas such as attacks based on race, culture, gender, or religion. Once a journal becomes public, the writer can be held ethically and legally responsible for its content.

→ BLOG: CHEATING AND COMMON KNOWLEDGE

I think the problem of cheating in schools is significant and important to address, and we must be aware of the ways that technologies can be used to facilitate cheating. But it would be wrong-headed to see either technologies or the commons as the source of cheating. Instead, we should try to understand the larger social context within which students live (a context that appears to reward cheating on a regular basis) and to develop ways of addressing those issues to encourage more ethical behavior. We should speak out against unethical behavior in all its guises. We should also develop processes within the academic sphere that reward creative behavior rather than promoting obsession with grades and similar phenomenal outputs.*

---
*Frederick Emrich, Blog: Cheating and Common Knowledge, Info-Commons.org. Reprinted by permission of the author.

PRACTICE 5.10 Blogging

Find a blogsite related to an issue you plan to argue. Read through the ongoing discussion and then join in if access is possible—in other words, post a response.

Sketching and Scrapbooking

Writers sometimes keep sketchbooks to help them remember experiences. Sketching often occurs as part of a journal entry, joining images with verbal reflections. Scrapbooks can include photos, clippings, and artifacts (such as a pressed flower or a ticket stub). Nonprint materials sometimes will be the object of your claims or the substance of your evidence. For example, if you were researching sexism in children's toys, you might clip images of Barbie dolls from magazines, photograph the doll or children playing, or download images from Web sources into a file. A scrapbook can be digital, consisting of pictures scanned or copied from Web sources. Digital materials can easily be integrated into a draft of an essay. (For more on visuals, see Chapter 9, Arguing Visually.)

PRACTICE 5.11 Visual Scrapbooking

Begin a scrapbook or sketchbook on an issue you wish to argue. Try to include examples from a variety of sources.

Discovering

Discovery techniques help you find ideas and facts that are accessible but unnoticed; they remind you where to direct your thoughts. Also known as *heuristics* (from the Greek *eureka*, meaning "I found it"), discovery techniques consist of routines or formulas, such as a list of questions.

Some discovery techniques are generic (all-purpose), such as the "reporter's formula," also known as the "five Ws and an H": who, what, when, where, why, and how. The leads of most news stories answer these questions. Other discovery techniques are geared toward a specific purpose, such as questions focused on an argument's claims, support, and rhetorical context.

Following are questions designed to help you discover claims, evidence, and rhetorical context. The student responses are focused on the topic of plagiarism.

Discovering Claims: What Are You Trying to Argue?

Fact: Is or was it real? Does or did it actually exist? The theft of ideas has been around for a long time. Copyrights and patents haven't always been part of the law and aren't respected everywhere in the world. Plagiarism may not be as one-sided as instructors think, though—it may be "factual" that instructors contribute to the problem.

Identity: What is it? Cheating. Theft. Borrowing. The sincerest form of flattery. An efficient way to get what you want. A misunderstanding. An epidemic.

Cause and effect: How does it work? Too much pressure on students. Unrealistic expectations. Poor instruction. Lack of ethics or morals.

Value: How is it judged? Harshly by instructors, with stiff penalties when formally investigated and tried. Lightly by students, many of whom don't see it as wrongful conduct.

Proposal: Should something be done? Better teaching not only about how to write but also about the policies that guide and procedures that enforce ethical conduct. Policies and pedagogy should be reviewed and revised.

> **Guidelines for Discovering Claims**
>
> **Fact:** Is or was it real?
> **Identity:** What is it?
> **Cause and effect:** How does it work?
> **Value:** How is it judged?
> **Proposal:** Should something be done?

Discovering Evidence: How Will You Support Your Argument?

Expert opinions: Research shows many experts, mostly instructors and school administrators, comment on the "epidemic" of academic dishonesty. Example: "When Academic Dishonesty Happens on Your Campus" by Karen L. Clos, Dean of Learning and Instructor at Barton County Community College.

Facts and statistics: Number of studies available on why students cheat. Many articles with figures on the increase in cheating, such as "A Culture of Copy-and-Paste" by Jessica Durkin.

> **Guidelines for Discovering Evidence**
>
> **Expert opinions:**
> **Facts and statistics:**
> **History:**
> **Personal experience:**
> **Scenarios:**
> **Specific examples:**

History: Apparently Shakespeare borrowed ideas from sources, and imitation has a long intellectual history. In "So, Is It the Real Thing?" Atul Prakash quotes Picasso as saying "a great artist steals."

Personal experience: Careful: I don't want to get into trouble for something I did a long time ago! Better to report what I know others have done or make up a scenario.

Scenarios: I can make up an example about a student under pressure who resorts to plagiarism. I can put a lot of sob-story elements that mitigate things: He wasn't taught properly, she'll lose her scholarship if she fails or if she's punished when caught, etc.

Specific examples: Brief interviews with other students; my observations of cheating by others; my observations of instructors; examples of policies and procedures related to cheating.

PRACTICE 5.12   Discovering Claims

For an issue you wish to argue, try to make each kind of claim: fact, identity, value, cause or effect, and proposal.

PRACTICE 5.13   Discovering Evidence

For a claim you wish to make, predict the kinds of evidence you might research or actually do this research.

PRACTICE 5.14   Discovering Rhetorical Context

For a particular assignment, determine the rhetorical context: purpose, audience, structure, and style.

Researching

Primary Research Evidence is considered primary when it comes not from other researchers but rather from your own activities: experiences or discoveries made through field work such as in a lab, an archaeological dig, a survey, or an interview. Sometimes the best source of evidence is actual experience, such as eating particular foods over a period of time to

PRACTICE 5.15 Experiencing

List experiences that are relevant to your argument. How practical are they in terms of your ability to attain them? Consider ways of acquiring and using personal experience to support an argument.

PRACTICE 5.16 Searching Databases and Libraries

Find an article, book, and Web source that are relevant to your issue or argument. Copy the bibliographic information, and write a brief summary of each source.

understand a popular diet. Field excursions may be useful to get a sense of the real world. Some experiences can be vicarious or simulated, as when you attend a realistic war movie to get a sense of real combat. (For more information on primary research, see Chapter 4, Researching Arguments.)

Secondary Research Secondary research involves gathering information from the experiences or studies of others. Print materials have long been the mainstay of researchers, but today researchers use a wide variety of sources, including audio recordings, visuals, and electronic texts. (For more information on secondary research see Chapter 4, Researching Arguments.)

ORGANIZING MATERIALS

Once you have generated materials to use in an argument, you'll want to organize them in some way that makes sense. This exercise can help with the drafting that comes afterward. Organizing also enhances other planning techniques, perhaps revealing the need for more brainstorming, discovery, or research. In fact, some organization techniques do double duty by helping to generate material. Charts, clusters, diagrams, and outlines are all useful guides for organizing.

Charting

Writers sometimes create columns and rows to clarify the connections between parts of their argument. Charts typically use columns to show categories of information and rows to show relationships. The intersection of each column and row forms a box called a cell. Here are some possible headings for charts:

CLAIMS AND SUPPORT CHART
Claim   *Evidence*   *Explanation*

PRO AND CON CHART
Reasons for   *Reasons against*

REBUTTAL CHART
Opposition   *Refutation*

A claims and support chart, for example, would state a claim in one cell. The supporting evidence would appear in an adjacent cell. A third cell could hold an explanation of the evidence. Because a claim may have more than one piece of supporting evidence, charts often need expansion or other modifications. Here is an example of a rebuttal chart:

Opposition	Refutation
Students are to blame for giving in to the temptation of an easy way to make a good grade.	Some students may not know how plagiarism is wrong. They haven't had adequate ethical education.
The instructor is to blame for not adequately training students in effective use of sources.	It is less a matter of training by teachers and more a matter of students not applying themselves.
The institution is to blame for not adequately informing students about policies against cheating.	Most students already know that they should give credit to their sources. They must take responsibility for knowing the policies.

Diagramming

Venn diagrams graphically depict how the elements of an argument are related. They show how much (or how little) two or more things (concepts, groups) have in common by depicting those elements as circles that are overlapping, enclosing each other, or separate. These diagrams often are used to explain logical syllogisms and are useful in conceptualizing a comparison and contrast argument. The following Venn diagram shows similarities and differences between plagiarism and theft.

Clustering

Clustering and similar techniques (webbing, mapping) also graphically depict the relationships between ideas. In these diagrams, the major claim (thesis)

PLAGIARISM
- Not really concrete: words and ideas
- Original author may never know, so no real harm is done.
- Plagiarizer may learn facts, which is why the original was written in the first place.

PLAGIARISM AS THEFT
- Words are a product; they took labor to produce and often have cash value.
- Laws and rules protect the owner of property, including words and ideas.

THEFT
- Concrete: physical possessions and money
- Victims usually know the theft has occurred.

The above Venn diagram shows the relationships between plagiarism and theft.

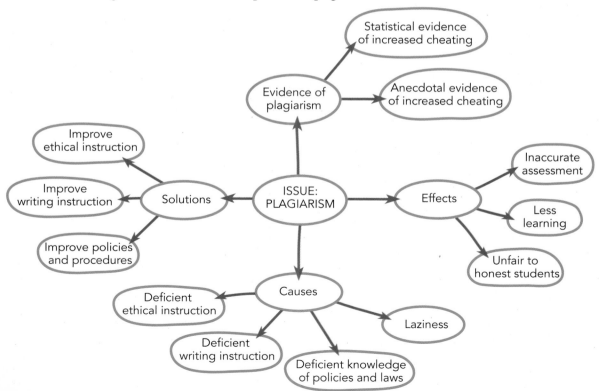

Clustering graphically organizes your supporting points.

is located in the center of the page, often inside a circle. Lines radiate from the center circle to secondary circles that represent supporting points or topics.

Clustering can be used to organize the information you already have and to reveal where your arguments may need more research. It requires no sequencing of major and minor points, so it is more flexible but less organized than an outline. Clusters, in fact, often are pre-outlines that later are sequenced formally. See the clustering template on the previous page.

Outlining

Like clustering, outlining shows the relationships among the various parts of an argument. However, outlining sequences the parts, often labeling them with Roman numbers, uppercase and lowercase letters, Arabic numerals, and so on. A combination of letters, numbers, and indentation can distinguish major and supporting evidence and explanations. Following is a template for a possible outline:

Title (tentative): Curing Plagiarism

  I. Introduction

    A. Problem: Increased plagiarism

      1. Anecdotal evidence of plagiarism (brief)

      2. Statistical evidence of plagiarism (brief)

    B. Current "solution" is ill informed and unfair.

      1. Places blame solely on students (brief statement)

      2. Present policies ignore some facts (brief statement)

    C. Thesis: A comprehensive and fair solution is needed

  II. A problem really does exist (fuller support than introduction).

    A. Statistical evidence of increase in plagiarism

    B. Anecdotal evidence of plagiarism

    C. Expert testimony about plagiarism

  III. Current views of the problem are one-sided.

    A. Places blame solely on students (fuller support)

    B. Present policies ignore some facts (fuller support)

  IV. A more balanced view of the causes of plagiarism

    A. Students' responsibility for problem

    B. Instructors' responsibility for problem

    C. Administrators' responsibility for problem

V. Conclusion

    A. Students' responsibility to change

    B. Instructors' responsibility to change

    C. Administrators' responsibility to change

PRACTICE 5.17	Organizing

Create a chart, cluster, diagram, or outline that organizes your claims, evidence, and explanations.

> **Framework for an Outline**
>
> I. First item
> II. Second item
>   A. Subitem
>   B. Subitem
>   1. Subsubitem
>   2. Subsubitem
> III. Third item

Looking Back at Chapter 5

▶ Planning helps you divide a large, complex writing task into a series of smaller, simpler tasks. To plan well, you'll need to (1) understand the assignment, (2) generate material, and (3) organize.

▶ Some task-specific requirements may be mandated by an instructor, employer, or publisher: length, format, sources, and deadline. Other elements are based on the rhetorical context: purpose, audience, structure, and style.

▶ Generating techniques that help you gather claims and support before beginning to write include brainstorming, critical thinking, discussing, writing (freewriting, journaling, blogging), sketching, discovering, and researching.

▶ Organization techniques facilitate writing the first draft and enhance other planning techniques, perhaps revealing the need for more brainstorming, discovery, or research. Charts, clusters, diagrams, and outlines are useful forms of organizing.

Suggestions for Writing

▶ Create one or more journal entries on your own use of planning. If you already use planning techniques, what works for you and what doesn't? If you don't use these techniques, reflect on why you don't and which ones you might try in the future.

▶ If you don't already use planning techniques, experiment with them. Then write one or more journal entries reflecting on the results.

▶ Use planning techniques as you prepare for a writing assignment.

6

Writing Process: Drafting Arguments

Brand X Pictures/Jupiterimages

The word *compose* comes from root words meaning to "place into position" or "put together." Perhaps you are familiar with composing in the musical sense, the process of a musician putting together notes to make a melody. *Composing* also is a synonym for *drafting*, the process of a writer putting together words and the ideas they represent into a unified text—a composition.

Drafting rarely is a straightforward process proceeding sequentially from the first sentence to the conclusion. Experienced writers instead prefer to draft the parts they're clearest about first, in hopes that the other parts will become clearer as the whole takes shape. Sometimes the introduction is written last, because only when the drafting process is complete does the writer fully realize the argument being made.

STRUCTURE OF AN ARGUMENT

An essay's overall structure consists of three major sections: (1) an introduction that provides a thesis statement or otherwise orients the reader toward a major claim, (2) a body consisting of paragraphs that break down the thesis into specific areas and treat each area in detail, and (3) a conclusion that provides closure. As you draft each section, you'll have to make a number of organizational decisions.

Drafting an Introduction

When you meet a stranger in a social situation, an introduction is usually needed before any productive conversation can follow. Most people need a little warming up first, such as sharing interesting personal details and general background information, and perhaps finding a purpose for further conversation. When a reader picks up a composition, there is a similar need for warming up—to pique the reader's interest, establish an issue, and make a claim. An introduction to a composition accomplishes these goals by providing a lead, background information, and a thesis or major claim.

→ CLASSICAL DIVISIONS OF AN ARGUMENT

Classical, as we use the term in this book, refers to rhetoric that originated with the public speakers (called *orators*) of ancient Greece and Rome. These arguments, on which modern arguments largely are based, assign specific duties to what we today call the introduction, body, and conclusion. Roman orators such as Cicero (106–43 B.C.E.) argued that good public speaking consisted of five canons: invention, arrangement, style, memory, and delivery. The second of these canons, *arrangement*, indicates that the parts of a speech should follow a particular order:

1. Exordium (in which the topic is introduced)
2. Narration (in which the central claims and background are given)
3. Partition (in which the parts of the argument are outlined)
4. Confirmation (in which the proof is offered)
5. Refutation (in which contrary arguments are answered)
6. Peroration (in which the matter is concluded, or wrapped up)

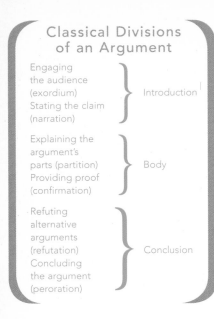

Classical Divisions
of an Argument

Engaging
the audience
(exordium)
Stating the claim
(narration)
} Introduction

Explaining the
argument's
parts (partition)
Providing proof
(confirmation)
} Body

Refuting
alternative
arguments
(refutation)
Concluding
the argument
(peroration)
} Conclusion

▶ A *lead* engages the reader's interest and establishes authority.

▶ *Background* information lets the reader understand the history, context, and importance of the claim.

▶ A major *claim* (an argumentative thesis) states or strongly implies what the author intends to argue.

These three components may vary in the order they are presented and in the emphasis each receives: more, less, or none at all, depending on the relevance to the overall composition.

It may help to think of the introduction as a "block of text" rather than as a paragraph. Even though it often lasts for only one paragraph, it can also be composed of two and occasionally even more paragraphs, depending on the length of each part. Introductions often are in proportion to the entire text. Very short writings might embed the introduction into the first body paragraph, often as the first sentence. For example, the one-sentence "lead" in a newspaper column or blog post often acts as the introduction. Longer compositions tend to have more substantive introductions. In fact, nonfiction books usually devote the entire first chapter to the introduction.

Drafting a Claim Regardless of which part of the composition you decide to draft, having the major claim written out and visible is essential to keeping yourself on the right track. As you draft your claim, test it by asking these questions:

▶ Is your claim really a claim? Does it take a position and argue a debatable issue within the "zone of reasonable skepticism"?

▶ Does your claim fit your audience?

▶ Is your claim focused?

Is your claim really a claim? Is it intended to change the audience's opinions and actions on an issue? Or are you unintentionally writing for another purpose: to inform, to entertain, or to express your feelings? Novice writers sometimes drift into other, nonargumentative purposes.

▶ **Sometimes an argument shifts into exploratory writing.** An author may think that the audience needs to be led "inductively"—that is, the audience is shown the evidence before being told a conclusion or claim. While exploratory arguments can be very convincing when well-executed, this method often leads to trouble for developing writers. Unfortunately, this practice often results in a rambling "for your information" download of loosely connected facts, with a brief concluding paragraph stating a claim more as an afterthought. Without the perspective of a claim, readers quickly begin to wonder, "What's the point?"

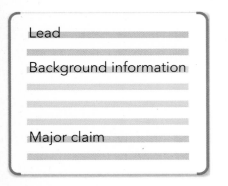

Lead

Background information

Major claim

A typical introduction contains a
lead, background information, and
major claim or thesis.

To decide whether to support stem-cell research, we should look at the facts.

This thesis statement leads to facts that lack the perspective of a claim.

▶ **Sometimes an argument shifts strongly into self-expression.** When an author has strong emotions about an issue, those feelings may erupt into prose that is strong but rings with the wrong "tone of voice"—a strident ranting or perhaps a fawning tribute. Although this kind of writing can be cathartic for the writer, it can be unintentionally amusing for the reader. Because of its charged emotions, the writer can lose the audience's respect (*ethos*) that allows the writer to persuade.

It's high time we threw those lying politicians in jail!

This thesis statement is more suggestive of mob violence than of reasoned action.

➜ THE MAJOR CLAIM

An argumentative thesis or major claim can be structured in varying degrees of detail.

▶ A claim can be stated in a simple form:

The university should show zero tolerance to plagiarists.

▶ It can be associated with a reason explaining the "why" or "because" of it:

The best way to stop the spread of plagiarism is to make examples of any offenders.

▶ Sometimes it may be accompanied by a forecasting statement that briefly announces the divisions of the topic to be covered:

A zero-tolerance anti-plagiarism policy offers three benefits: (1) plagiarists will no longer promote a climate of cheating, (2) more students will learn ethical behavior, and (3) all students will receive fair grades rather than grades they didn't earn.

AP Photo/Peter Morrison

Smokers have been banned from most interior spaces, including most restaurants and bars. Should smoking be banned in all places where people gather? Why or why not?

PRACTICE 6.1   Drafting Your Major Claim

Write out a major claim (thesis) for an argument. As you draft your claim, test it by asking these questions:

1. Is your claim really a claim?
2. Does your claim fit your audience?
3. Is your claim focused?

Does your claim fit your audience? Are you "preaching to the choir"—readers who already believe as you do—or are you "speaking a foreign language"—addressing readers whose beliefs are hopelessly different from yours? Adjust your claim to fit the audience, finding some practical goal worth arguing. Your audience should reside within what we have termed the "zone of reasonable skepticism"—it shouldn't believe your claim as yet, but should be willing to entertain the *possibility* that it *might* be valid.

▶ **Adjust your claim when you face overwhelming skepticism.** For example, although you might not be able to convince an audience of professors that they share responsibility for plagiarism by students, you might be able to convince them that some student plagiarism stems not from moral weakness but from a lack of knowledge about quoting, paraphrasing, and summarizing.

▶ **Adjust your claim to address a predisposition of acceptance.** If, for example, you and your audience were already in agreement about the need for improved instruction on using sources, you could argue for staff development to help instructors learn new techniques.

Is your claim focused? An overly broad claim weakens an argument. Novice writers understandably would rather deal with an excess of support rather than a shortage, but they often end up with a claim so broad the composition says very little and consequently is dull to read. Readers often prefer to learn "a lot about a little" rather than a "little about a lot." This goal can be achieved by (1) focusing on only part of a problem rather than many aspects of it or (2) being more specific about details. Consider the following examples:

BROAD, WITH SEVERAL PARTS
Plagiarism can be controlled by instituting an honor code that all students must sign, by strictly enforcing rules and penalties, and by ensuring that instruction on research skills is provided by all instructors.

Types of Claims

A major claim is an argument's thesis, the author's position on an issue. Below is a list of kinds of claims. (See Chapter 2, Claims and Support, for more information about claims.)

Fact: Is or was it real?
Identity: What is it?
Cause and effect: How and why does it work?
Value: How is it judged?
Proposal: Should something be done?

FOCUSED, WITH FEWER PARTS
The most effective way to curtail plagiarism is staff development to ensure instructors know how to teach research skills.

BROAD, WITH LESS-SPECIFIC DETAILS
There should be a clear policy on plagiarism.

FOCUSED, WITH MORE-SPECIFIC DETAILS
The Office of Student Affairs should articulate and publicize a plagiarism policy that considers not only the offense but also the knowledge and intent of the plagiarist.

Drafting the Background Information Rarely will a reader have all the prior knowledge needed to understand the issues at stake in your argument. In the introduction, your goal is to provide context, thereby helping the reader understand what the issue is, but without going into too much detail too early. The following suggestions and examples may help as you draft the background information for your introduction.

Emphasize the importance of an issue. By establishing the significance of the issue, the reader will be motivated to read on.

> Cheating in college is certainly not a new phenomenon. Underground paper mills, from which students can obtain previously prepared papers to be submitted as their own work, have existed for quite some time. However, with the growth of the Internet has come a concurrent and explosive growth in the number of online paper mills, drastically increasing the accessibility of previously prepared term papers.
> —C. R. Campbell, C. O. Swift, and L. T. Denton,
> "Cheating Goes Hi-Tech"

Present a quotation relevant to the topic. Quotations can be intriguing, can contribute authority, and can hint at the angle your argument will take.

> Picasso once said, "A good artist borrows, a great artist steals."…. Ask any writer, music composer, filmmaker, or designer and they'll tell you nothing is created in a vacuum, all ideas are drawn from outside inspiration. But the problem arises when you infringe on someone else's original work.
> —Atul Prakash, "So, Is It the Real Thing?"

Present one or more examples. Examples make the issue seem real.

> Last year, our college experienced a rash of cheating incidents that caused us to reevaluate how prepared we were to deal with academic dishonesty.

Within two weeks after a seemingly isolated incident in which one of our professors discovered a student cheating on a written assignment, four separate incidents of academic dishonesty were reported in our online program, in outreach and community education, and in on-campus programs as well.

—Karen Clos, "When Academic Dishonesty
Happens on Your Campus"

Present interesting facts or statistics. Information your reader does not know can sometimes whet the reader's appetite for more.

Academic dishonesty, which includes everything from wrongfully getting information by looking at a neighbor's test to plagiarizing information in a term paper, is a growing problem and concern for higher education. Several recent national surveys have found that more than half of all college students in the United States admit to some form of academic dishonesty, at least once during their college years. … Research shows a correlation between academic dishonesty and moral development (Barnett and Dalton 1981). That is, individuals with a higher level of moral development are less likely to be engaged in academic dishonesty because they consider that sort of behavior to be morally wrong.

—Mohammed Y. A. Rawwas, Jamal A. Al-Khatib, and
Scott J. Vitell, "Academic Dishonesty"

Pose a problem or a mystery. A problem or a mystery gives the issue significance while setting the stage for a solution.

For years, management educators have learned the tricks of the trade for avoiding academic dishonesty by students by changing assignments from semester to semester and even requiring in-class writing assignments that could be used as samples and compared to writing done outside of class. However, the enhanced opportunities for academic dishonesty presented by online term paper mills raise the bar for management educators in devising assignments that circumvent the offerings of such term paper services.

—Jeffrey Mello, "Commentary on
'Cheating Goes Hi-Tech'"

Briefly explain the issue's history. History can put an issue in context.

The Internet was still a toddler in the late 1990s. Today, it's a juggernaut. In the last five years, instances of plagiarism from webpages have grown perhaps just as rapidly as the Internet itself. In fact, some sites even boast "original" essays for sale.

—Jennifer Kabbany, "Educators:
Digital Plagiarism Rampant"

Dramatize. Make an issue come to life by providing a real-life story or example or by creating a believable scenario or hypothetical situation.

> Imagine a student who had never cheated before, who works hard and sincerely wants to learn and to better herself. This semester, however, she has taken on far too much work. She can't possibly write all the required research papers in the time by the end of the term. Her GPA hangs in the balance, as does her scholarship and her future. Panicking, she turns to what she sees as her last resort: an online paper mill that will provide what she needs—an instant essay.
>
> —Sam Nguyen, "The Temptation of Instant Essays"

Pose one or more questions. Questions that are related to your argument can pique readers' interest and help forecast the answers you will reveal.

> What is the relationship between academic dishonesty and workplace dishonesty? If a student is prone to cheating in college, will that same student be prone to cheating in the workplace?
>
> —Sarath Nonis and Cathy Swift, "An Examination of the Relationship Between Academic Dishonesty and Workplace Dishonesty"

Define a key concept. A definition can provide good background. However, opening with "According to *Webster's Dictionary*" is a very clichéd lead sentence.

> Indeed, there are many ways to misrepresent the truth. Part of the problem is that not everyone agrees on the definition of lying. Lying by omission, for example, is a form of passive deceit because a person is withholding information or not volunteering the truth…. Plagiarism is another form of lying. Plagiarism is a form of "literary theft," of which I would be guilty, if I didn't tell you that I copied that phrase from the *Merriam-Webster Dictionary*.
>
> —Michael Angelo Caruso, "There Are Many Types of Lies." From *National Driller*, March 1, 2005. Reprinted by permission of the author.

Present an analogy. An analogy helps a reader understand a new issue by comparing it to something more familiar.

> The 1960s gave us, among other mind-altering ideas, a revolutionary new metaphor for our physical and chemical surroundings: the biosphere. But an even more momentous change is coming. Emerging technologies are causing a shift in our mental ecology, one that will turn our culture into the plagiosphere, a closing frontier of ideas.
>
> —Ed Tenner, "Rise of the Plagiosphere"

Present various sides of the issue. Briefly citing several selected sources can show a range of opinions and the extent of differences.

> The ease of use of the Internet technology is the number one factor blamed for the increase in academic cheating (Decamp 2001). Another factor is an increasing number of digital paper mills mushrooming on the Internet such as Buyapapers.com…, Term Papers & Term Papers, … and Term Papers Amazon.
> —Apiwan D. Born, "How to Reduce Plagiarism" *Journal of Information Systems Education*, Vol. 14(3). Reprinted by permission of the *Journal of Information Systems Management.*

Begin creatively, with wit or word play. Begin with details that are humorous, or use a creative style. (See Chapter 11, Literary Arguments, for techniques.)

> Teachers do it, journalists do it, even educated priests do it. Cole Porter, composer of "Let's Do It, Let's Fall in Love," was accused of doing it, too—he was sued in 1946. "It," in this case, is not a matter of the heart, but the rather more cerebral issue of plagiarism.
> —Katherine Macklem, "Their Cheatin' Hearts"

PRACTICE 6.2 Drafting Your Background Information

With your major claim in mind, write an introduction that includes background information. You may wish to experiment with the models presented earlier in this chapter.

Drafting Your Lead Sentences When you write, keep in mind that you maintain your reader's interest only one sentence—if not one word—at a time. The first few words in your argument serve not only to engage your reader's interest, but also to give your reader a hint about the importance of the issue (and possibly even your stand on it). The lead sentence is not a "one off" like the verbal equivalent of the salesman sticking his foot in the door. It should be an integral, comprehensive part of the introduction that nudges the reader in the direction of the claim.

A cliché, such as Snoopy's "It was a dark and stormy night," makes a poor lead sentence.
(PEANUTS © 1969 Peanuts Worldwide LLC. Dist. By UNIVERSAL UCLICK. Reprinted with permission. All rights reserved.)

In some ways, the beginning of an essay is the most important part. If the audience members are not engaged immediately, they may never read the rest of the text. A lead can enable you to engage your reader's interest. Of course, the title itself is the first chance you have to catch a reader's attention. Once past the title, a reader will decide very soon whether the text is worth pursuing.

PRACTICE 6.3   Establishing Reader Interest with Leads

Below are the opening lines from the models of background information presented earlier in this chapter. How well would they motivate you to read on? Why do they work or not work?

1. "Cheating in college is certainly not a new phenomenon."
2. "Picasso once said, 'A good artist borrows, a great artist steals.'"
3. "Last year, our college experienced a rash of cheating incidents that caused us to reevaluate how prepared we were to deal with academic dishonesty."
4. "Academic dishonesty, which includes everything from wrongfully getting information by looking at a neighbor's test to plagiarizing information in a term paper, is a growing problem and concern for higher education."
5. "For years, management educators have learned the tricks of the trade for avoiding academic dishonesty by students by changing assignments from semester to semester and even requiring in-class writing assignments that could be used as samples and compared to writing done outside of class."
6. "The Internet was still a toddler in the late 1990s. Today, it's a juggernaut."
7. "Imagine a student who had never cheated before, who works hard and sincerely wants to learn and to better herself. This semester, however,..."
8. "What is the relationship between academic dishonesty and workplace dishonesty?"
9. "Indeed, there are many ways to misrepresent the truth."
10. "The 1960s gave us, among other mind-altering ideas, a revolutionary new metaphor for our physical and chemical surroundings: the biosphere."
11. "The ease of use of the Internet technology is the number one factor blamed for the increase in academic cheating."
12. "Teachers do it, journalists do it, even educated priests do it."

PRACTICE 6.4   Drafting Your Lead Sentence

Examine one of your own introductory paragraphs. Will it catch a reader's interest? Revise your writing, experimenting with alternative ways of engaging the reader's interest.

PRACTICE 6.5   Analyzing Introductions

Read the two introductory text blocks below, and locate their parts. Place brackets around the leads, and underline the claims. Which parts do you find the most compelling? Why? In what way(s) could they compel an audience to read the rest of the argument?

Excerpt A

Plagiarism has existed for hundreds of years, so it is not a new phenomenon, but we do hear about it much more nowadays than we ever have in the past. Indeed newspaper reports suggest that it is a £200 million industry that has grown up over the last few years supplying essays to students at all levels on any subject imaginable, some of them even tailored to the purchaser's express brief. Plagiarism has therefore become one of the issues of our times for our schools and universities. Why is that a problem for all learning officers and training managers, and all those in e-learning? Well think about it. If that is the culture from which employees and e-learning students come, how 'safe' is the work that they are submitting now for assessment? How concerned should you be? And what can you do about it?

—Will Murray, "The Plagiarism Phenomenon" from *E.learning Age*, October 1, 2006. Reprinted by permission of the author.

Excerpt B

The growth of academic dishonesty is discouraging to faculty, administrators, and ethical students. Faculty, in particular, are often wary of spending time and resources on educating college and university students about academic dishonesty. Administrators, too, are well aware of the costs imposed on the institution by dishonest behavior. And the ethical student knows that rampant cheating can devalue a college degree. But if institutions are to fully educate their students in honesty as well as in particular content areas, they should work to create an ethical campus climate where the rewards of ethical conduct may be as great as mastery of any program of study. Only when institutions treat ethics as an essential element of all conduct—at school, at work, and in personal lives—will students see the importance of infusing ethics in their academic conduct.

—Melanie Stallings Williams and William R. Hosek, *Strategies for Reducing Academic Dishonesty*

(continued)

Excerpt C

This spring, Jerry Ceppos, vice president for news at Knight Ridder, finished his term as president of the organization that accredits journalism schools. In a speech at the April 30 meeting of the Accrediting Council on Education in Journalism and Mass Communications, Ceppos ticked off a list of plagiarism cases that had cropped up at newspapers over the previous year. They ranged from student papers at the universities of Virginia and Kansas to the *Hartford Courant* and *Milwaukee Journal Sentinel* to *USA Today* and the *New York Times*. "If any outside poked his or her head in this room," Ceppos said, "the first question would obviously be, 'What are you doing about this epidemic of ethical problems in journalism?' "

—Jeff South, "Ethics in the Classroom"

PRACTICE 6.6   Drafting Introductions

For an issue that concerns you, draft an introduction that contains a lead, background information, and statement of your major claim.

→ SHOULD I WRITE MY INTRODUCTION FIRST?

The writing process is both situational and personal: You have your own habits and techniques that must be adapted to different kinds of assignments. You may be comfortable working from beginning to end, or you may prefer to move back and forth through the text as you draft. Here are a few pointers to help you craft your own individual style:

► After planning your argument, write your claim first. Put it on a piece of paper and tape it to the top of your computer screen or in some other visible position. Its presence may serve as a reminder to help you keep your essay focused and on task. (Some word processors will permit you to do this by keeping a window open for notes. You can keep an outline or your claim visible as you write.)

► Don't write your introduction first if you don't feel ready to do so. Jump into the body of the essay after you have figured out your basic organizational strategy.

► Decide how you want to organize your paper—what your main points will be, how you will refute the opposition's arguments, and so on—before you jump into your text. This will save you time reorganizing your text later on.

► If you are composing and the work just isn't moving along, you may need to return to the planning process, generating and organizing material. Do you need to construct a more detailed outline? Would writing out your supporting ideas help?

In a typical introduction to a college essay, the lead may or may not be distinguishable from the introduction as a whole, especially when the background information is interesting or when the claim is provocative. However, even in a short piece of writing, the first few sentences can be critical. Consider this opening line from David Glenn's article, "Judge or Judge Not?":

> In an ideal world, academe would respond to plagiarism allegations with a sure and swift machinery of justice.

This sentence conveys context—"academe," "plagiarism allegations"—while hinting at frightening, even harsh consequences—"sure and swift machinery of justice." A reader might read on purely for the information, but also might be enticed by the suspense of impending punishment or even by residual guilt from, shall we say, personal plagiaristic indiscretions.

Drafting the Body

The body of a composition consists of paragraphs that support the major claim with reasons in the form of evidence and explanations. Sometimes you can comfortably develop one reason per paragraph; at other times, you can devote several paragraphs to one reason or several reasons to one paragraph. This choice depends entirely on the volume of evidence and the amount of explanation it needs.

A paragraph has its own unity of purpose that may be either expressed as an explicitly stated main idea (topic sentence) or implied strongly by the evidence and explanations. As you draft the body, you'll have options about how to arrange the topic sentences and reasons within paragraphs.

Placing Main Ideas   Main ideas (also known as topic sentences) can appear anywhere within a paragraph. For the sake of illustration, we will highlight four paragraph structures:

▶ **Main idea at top:** You start with the supporting point and follow up by supplying the details that will convince the reader that the claim is valid.

▶ **Main idea at bottom:** You work through the details first, which allows the reader to accept the claim that is presented at the end as a sort of concluding sentence.

▶ **Main idea *delayed*:** You delay the claim by "easing into" a paragraph with a sentence or so of transitional material. Sometimes the main idea may not appear until the middle of the paragraph.

▶ **Main idea *implied*:** Sometimes you might choose to not state the purpose of a block of text, but leave it for the reader to figure out. This approach can be very effective if the block is well written, but can lead to confusion if it is not.

No method is superior to all of the others. In fact, the more you read, the more you will see that many writers mix all of these approaches to organization.

TOP **MAIN IDEA**	*BOTTOM* **MAIN IDEA**
Main idea Evidence Discussion	Evidence Discussion Main idea

DELAYED **MAIN IDEA**	*IMPLIED* **MAIN IDEA**
Transition Supporting claim Evidence Discussion	Evidence Discussion

A body paragraph's main idea (also known as topic sentence) can appear in different locations.

PRACTICE 6.7   Understanding Paragraphs

Read the paragraphs and then answer the following questions:

1. Does the paragraph have a stated or implied main idea? If stated, where is it located? If implied, what words hint at it?
2. Does the paragraph cohere, effectively supporting a stated or implied main idea? Explain.
3. Is the paragraph engaging? Why or why not?

Excerpt A

U.S. research conducted by Donald L. McCabe, a business professor at Rutgers University in New Jersey, comparing students in 1963 and 1993, shows the percentage of those admitting to copying from a classmate doubled to 52 per cent; those reporting having helped another student cheat jumped to 37 per cent from 23 per cent; and that the use of crib notes in test and exam settings increased to over a quarter from 16 per cent.

—Gulli, Köhler, and Patriquin,
"The Great University Cheating Scandal"

Excerpt B

Plagiarism is often unintentional, being the result of disorganisation, information overload, laziness, ignorance of citation rules or even fear of failure. Some people are blissfully unaware of the correct conventions for acknowledging other people's ideas and the need to express themselves in their own words. Ignorance of such conventions can and has led to accusations of plagiarism.

—Will Murray, "The Plagiarism Phenomenon"

→ EVIDENCE

Whenever you make a claim, a skeptical audience will require proof that it is true or reasons to accept it—in short, evidence. (For more on evidence, see Chapter 2, Claims and Support.) Evidence comes in the following forms:

Anecdotes: Narrate or describe real-life accounts of situations or events that have happened to you or to others.

Expert opinions: Quote, paraphrase, or summarize the opinion of an expert or experts on an issue.

Facts and statistics: Provide evidence that an audience will accept at face value.

History: Tell what happened in the past if it is relevant to the present or the future.

Scenario: Produce hypothetical or fictionalized accounts that dramatize typical or possible situations.

Specific examples: Offer a sampling of evidence to represent a larger body of evidence.

Organizing Evidence When you present evidence in an argument, it cannot stand alone. No bit of data is self-evident. It must be explained to establish its validation of the truth of the claim. The explanation of evidence within a block of text is typically organized in one of two ways:

▶ The *point-by-point method* discusses the evidence one piece at a time. This approach is useful when each piece of evidence needs its own explanation.

▶ The *block method* is used when either one piece of evidence is followed by several explanations or when several pieces of evidence can be lumped together and explained once.

POINT-BY-POINT METHOD

Claim

Evidence A

Explanation A

Evidence B

Explanation B

BLOCK METHOD

Claim

Evidence A
Evidence B
Evidence C

Explanation

Evidence and explanations can be presented point by point or separated into blocks.

→ EXPLAINING EVIDENCE

Evidence almost always needs some kind of explanation or discussion to strengthen its connection to the claim. The kinds of explanations below are based on a list of thought processes known as Bloom's Taxonomy.

Clarification (knowledge): Restate to make sure the evidence is understood. Paraphrase, summary, and emphasis help clarify evidence.

Interpretation (comprehension): Speculate on its significance. Evidence often requires an interpreter who can "read between the lines" and put it into perspective.

Application: Explain how the evidence applies. Application can show the connection between evidence and claim when the relationship isn't immediately clear.

Analysis: Explain the parts. Analysis divides a whole into its parts and explains how they work separately and in unison.

Synthesis: Relate it to other claims or other forms of evidence. Synthesis brings two or more arguments together, allowing for comparison/contrast, rebuttal, or an accumulation of mutually supporting points.

Evaluation: Explain its value. Evaluation is a kind of qualification, explaining how applicable the evidence is to the claim or how reliable and accurate it is.

PRACTICE 6.8   Understanding Evidence and Explanations

Read the excerpt from "The Great University Cheating Scandal" and then answer the following questions.

1. What is the major claim, and where is it located?
2. What statements could be considered "supporting claims?"
3. Does the paragraph support its claims with evidence and explanations? Where, and how well?
4. Some statements are presented as speculations rather than as facts. Does the evidence support the speculations?

"Whatever the policies implemented by universities, cheating is still rampant and getting worse. It would be easy to blame students for their transgressions. Yet it is the universities—the institutions issuing the degrees and guaranteeing educational quality—that must find solutions. Perhaps professors, charged with monitoring their students, don't make good cops. While instructors are 'required to report academic dishonesty,' says Christensen Hughes, 'some don't.' That may understate the problem. While the Guelph study notes that 75 per cent of professors and 80 per cent of teaching assistants thought a student had cheated in the previous year—almost half were absolutely sure of it—less than half said they believed that cheating is a serious problem. In a 2001 paper, U.S. business professors Sarath Nonis and Cathy Owens Swift cited research indicating that while '60 per cent of faculty members observed cheating in their classrooms … only 20 per cent of them actually met with the student and a higher authority.' Says Nonis, who teaches marketing at Arkansas State University: 'My gut feeling is that number might be even more now.'"

—Cathy Gulli, Nicholas Köhler, and Martin Patriquin,
"The Great University Cheating Scandal"

PRACTICE 6.9   Drafting Body Paragraphs

For an issue that concerns you, draft a body paragraph that contains a main idea, evidence, and explanation.

Opposition Arguments and Refutations   The body of an argument argues for a major claim not only by supporting it with reasons (evidence and explanations), but also by rebutting significant alternative arguments.

As your readers consider your argument, they may think of positions and claims that contradict the point you are seeking to prove. These positions, contrary to your own, are sometimes called *opposition arguments*

> **→ PROVIDING EVIDENCE**
>
> While drafting, you must decide what kind of evidence is needed and how much to use. (See Chapter 2, Claims and Support, for more about evidence.) As a rule, provide evidence that is sufficient, relevant, and appealing:
>
> **Sufficient:** Use only the minimum amount of information you need to establish the truth value of your claim, and no more.
>
> **Relevant:** Use only evidence that supports your claim; avoid anything that "sort of" or "might" support your claim. If the relationship between evidence and claim is blurry to you, it will be even more blurry to your readers.
>
> **Appealing:** Use evidence that will be received sympathetically by your readers. Avoid sources or types of evidence they might not respect or might find offensive.

or *alternative arguments*. The process of neutralizing them is called *refutation* or *rebuttal*. Although *refute* means "to prove something is false or in error," you can also advance your claim by showing yours to be better than the opposition's claim or by offering a compromise between your position and the opposition's position.

Refutation can be vital to a successful argument. There are four ways to organize the refutation of alternative arguments:

▶ *Early refutation* deals with alternative arguments shortly after the introduction or within the introduction.

▶ *Late refutation* deals with alternative arguments in a separate section near or in the conclusion.

▶ *Occasional refutation* deals with alternative arguments as they become relevant to topics within the body of the composition.

▶ *Complete refutation* deals with alternative arguments as the chief purpose of the composition. Typically, this approach entails a point-by-point organization.

Early Refutation Early refutation meets the opposition "head on," listing and usually discussing the alternative arguments in the early paragraphs and sometimes even in the introduction. Writers who opt for early refutation do so for several reasons:

▶ When an audience is clearly aware of opposing claims—perhaps even sympathetic to them—there is a danger that readers will resist your own claims until their doubts are allayed. Early acknowledgment of alternative arguments can remove these doubts or at least put your audience in a more receptive frame of mind.

▶ Acknowledging the opposition is a way to establish your own credibility, your *ethos*. You let the audience know not only that you have done your homework but also that your argument will not be one-sided. The audience will pick up clues from the tone of your writing style about how fairly you will treat the opposition.

▶ Introductions and early paragraphs often are used to establish the context of an issue, so identifying alternative arguments may be essential for clarifying the purpose and major claims of your composition.

Late Refutation   Sometimes writers postpone dealing with alternative arguments until the conclusion of the composition. This tactic has advantages for some purposes and some audiences:

▶ When an audience is unaware of the opposing arguments, the composition can become bogged down by introducing topics that have to then be dismissed before proceeding to your major claim.

▶ When an audience is aware of the opposing arguments but either is unconcerned by them or is sympathetic and receptive toward your claims, the refutation can be delayed.

Sometimes you cannot directly discredit or diminish the opposition. In fact, sometimes the opposition claim is not only valid but also appealing. In such cases, refutation does not prove error but rather offers your claim as being better than the rival claim. You offer the audience the greater of two goods; it is like concluding, "Now that you've seen my claim, isn't it better than my opposition's claim?"

Occasional Refutation   Sometimes you may decide that it is more advantageous to refute alternative arguments as the need arises. This method offers several advantages:

▶ Many arguments incorporate a number of claims, but not all of these claims have opposing claims needing refutation. Opposing arguments can occur anywhere in the body of your composition, whenever your rhetorical strategy calls for dealing with opposing views.

▶ Some arguments and opposing arguments have symmetry—for every pro, there is con; for every point, there is a counterpoint. A point-by-point organization can pair up each claim with an opposing claim, perhaps in the same paragraph or in juxtaposed paragraphs. For example, suppose that you have decided to argue in favor of the legalization of medical marijuana. Your opposing argument might line up with the opposition's argument something like this:

Opposition's Argument	Your Refutation
MAJOR CLAIM	
Students are responsible for their own acts of plagiarism.	Students are not solely to blame. Administrators and teachers are also responsible.
SUPPORT	
It is primarily an issue of character.	It is primarily an issue of ignorance of ways to correctly use sources.
SUPPORT	
Plagiarism can harm others in various ways.	Misunderstanding the cause of plagiarism can cause harm, also.
SUPPORT	
The solution is punishment.	The solution is a combination of ethical awareness, clear policy, and improved instruction.

Such a research paper would likely have the structure shown in the figure on the right.

Complete Refutation Your argument can be structured completely as a reaction to an opposing argument while not offering an alternative argument of your own. Sometimes it is important enough to expose a misconception or to advise against a course of action. Your argument would be saying, basically, "I don't know what the solution is to Problem X, but I know the opposition's solution is wrong." For example, you might give reasons why a policy against plagiarism is inadequate without offering a policy to replace it.

Drafting the Conclusion

Conclusions, like introductions, are specialized passages. They let the readers know that the essay is coming to an end and remind them of the main idea of the argument. A writer will often remind the readers of the thesis and sometimes summarize the main points of the essay. In arguments, the conclusion is usually the place to mention the major claim (thesis statement) again and to emphasize again some of the argument's most compelling claims that made up the body of the piece.

POINT / COUNTERPOINT

Introduction

Forecast (optional)

(1) Refutation

(1) Argument

(2) Refutation

(2) Argument

(3) Refutation

(3) Argument

Conclusion

Point and counterpoint organization.

If you have difficulty concluding your composition, consider these three techniques: (1) revisit the claim, (2) remind the reader of the argument's central ideas, and/or (3) offer a final parting statement. The first two techniques are relatively easy to understand. Sometimes the third is not. The parting statement may be thought of as the reverse of the lead that you used initially to gain the reader's attention and give some hint of the topic. Like the lead sentences used to pique the reader's interest, the parting statement casts a wide net, but is intended to "ease" the reader out of the argument while at the same time maintaining the reader's continued interest. It is like a train slowing down to let you off at your stop.

Here are some points to remember when writing a conclusion:

▶ Write the conclusion only after you know the final structure of your essay.

▶ Restate your claim, but don't quote it verbatim from the introduction. The claim can appear anywhere within the conclusion. When it appears at the bottom, it may serve as the parting statement.

▶ Summarize the most important supporting points, but don't make the conclusion read like a laundry list. Some writers will restate their response to an alternative argument before reintroducing their overall claim.

▶ Use transitional words and phrases.

▶ End with a general statement related to your topic. In most cases, it will be broader than your claim. Its purpose should be to maintain the reader's interest in the issue at hand.

▶ Don't undermine your efforts by being apologetic (e.g., "…but I'm not really an expert") or cute ("That's my story, and I'm stickin' with it").

→ OPTIONS FOR CONCLUSIONS

Summarize: Go over your major points, but don't simply repeat the introduction. Add some perspective and vary the phrasing.

Personalize: Explain how the issue affects you or the reader.

Focus: Emphasize a particular point over other points.

Quote: Revisit an earlier quotation in your text, or introduce another quotation that summarizes or provides perspective.

Question: Pose questions that may lead to action or further investigation.

Propose an action: Introduce a call for action, even though the text itself may be more about problems than solutions.

Warn: Caution about consequences.

Encourage: Offer some consolation.

Expand: Put the text in a larger context.

PRACTICE 6.10   Understanding Conclusions

Read the concluding paragraphs and then answer the following questions.

1. What technique of concluding does the author use: summarizing, personalizing, focusing, quoting, questioning, proposing, warning, encouraging, expanding, or some other method?
2. From the conclusion alone, can you guess the main idea of the essay as a whole? Speculate on some of the topics that could have been in the essay.
3. Which conclusion appeals to you most? Least? Explain.

Excerpt A

Educators are trying to upgrade their in-class tactics as well. Experts say teachers should make it more difficult for students to "cut and paste" by changing assignments every year and requiring more analysis than description. And they shouldn't assume that kids even know what plagiarism is, as many just aren't taught how to source or reference properly. Students aren't the only ones who need to work a little harder.

—Michael Hastings, "Cheater Beaters"*

Excerpt B

I never heard from the paper mill again. I'd like to think that our sting operation put a serious damper on their business, but I doubt it. Each year there is a new wave of stories about plagiarism running rampant on university campuses. Still, if my action makes even a few students think twice before passing off another person's words and ideas as their own, it will be worth it.

—Rhonda Lauret Parkinson, "Plagiarize at Your Peril"†

Excerpt C

I request every student to keep an electronic journal of how they complete a term paper from the beginning to the end. They need to

(continued)

---

*Michael Hastings, "Cheater Beaters." *From Newsweek*, September 8, 2003. © 2003 The Newsweek/Daily Beast Company LLC. All rights reserved. Used by permission and protected by the Copyright Laws of the United States. The printing, copying, redistribution, or retransmission of the Material without express written permission is prohibited. www.newsweek.com.
†Rhonda Lauret Parkinson, "Plagiarize at Your Peril" *McLeans*, Canada, November 15, 2004. Reprinted by permission of the author.

submit all articles they use in their papers along with highlighted areas from where they borrow ideas or concepts. Student electronic journals are recorded on a course management system called Blackboard where I can access and monitor student progress. One may find this activity very time consuming; however, I schedule my time to access each student's journal only once a week and set aside 15-20 minutes in every class to discuss with individuals about their paper. I believe that this on-going effort helps bring out the best in students.

—Apiwan D. Born, "How to Reduce Plagiarism"

Excerpt D

The Chinese people are eager to achieve a Western standard of living, and they deserve nothing less than to reap the benefits of their labor. But as long as authorities allow property rights and trademarks to be blithely ignored, and as long as academics treat original work as communal property to be pilfered at will, China's economic revolution will rest on a foundation of sand.

—Maclean's Canada Editors, "The China Syndrome: Corruption and Theft"*

Excerpt E

With the help of software like Turnitin, it should be relatively easy to distinguish intentional from unintentional plagiarism in most cases. As memory specialist Larry Jacoby of Washington University in St Louis points out, a person is unlikely to be able to regurgitate large chunks of text verbatim without remembering the source. When a general idea is being copied rather than actual words, intentionality becomes harder to determine. Then again, as Mark Twain pointed out..., all literature is plagiarized anyhow.

—New Scientist Staff, "Plagiarism"[†]

TYING IT ALL TOGETHER

Readers expect precision and unity in any kind of writing. In part, this is accomplished through a thesis and topic sentences. In addition, writers use qualifiers and transitions to smooth out the flow of words.

---

*Maclean's Canada Editors, "The China Syndrome: Corruption and Theft" May 15, 2005. Reprinted by permission.
[†]New Scientist Staff, "Plagiarism" December 16, 2006. www.newscientist.com.

Using Qualifiers

By their very nature, claims tend to be accompanied by a degree of uncertainty. Arguers often must qualify their claims by (1) explaining under which circumstances the claim is true or (2) estimating the probability that a claim is true.

Circumstantial Qualifiers Some claims apply only under certain circumstances. For example, you might claim that a plagiarist should be expelled only when the act was intended to cheat, not when the student simply didn't know how to use sources.

In the following excerpt, the qualifier is underlined:

> When stresses rise, the temptations of the internet and other ways of accessing answers make some students and delegates feel that plagiarism is a reasonably risk-free way out of difficulties.
> —Will Murray, "The Plagiarism Phenomenon"

Probability Qualifiers So many things in life are unknown, but decisions still must be made based on our "best guess." Sometimes you can find statistical data that will give you a numerical estimate of probability. At other times, you'll have to offer verbal qualifiers ranging from long explanations to simple adjectives such as *possibly, sometimes, potentially,* or *probably.*

In the following excerpt, the qualifier is underlined:

> If some graduates are competing for professional positions based upon dishonestly earned academic credentials, employers may suffer.
> —Will Murray, "The Plagiarism Phenomenon"

> If people understand what they have to gain from a learning exercise, they are less likely to consider plagiarism.
> —Will Murray, "The Plagiarism Phenomenon"

Using Transitions

Readers appreciate when you help them see how the parts of a composition relate to each other. You do this in part by directly stating the relationships in your thesis and topic sentences and in part by showing the relevance of

---

Qualifiers

Qualifiers describe the limits of a claim. Below are some examples:

absolutely	occasionally
probably	always
possibly	sometimes
most of the time	as a rule
seldom	typically
regularly	hardly ever
never	potentially
usually	tentatively
generally	often
least	frequently

your evidence. In addition, you can use transitions—that is, words or phrases that state how the parts are related. Without transitions, your reader may have to work harder to understand how sentences or whole paragraphs relate to each other and to the thesis.

Consider, for example, one of the most frequently used transitions in this book: "for example." It signals that something concrete will illustrate a generality. In addition, consider the transitional phrase "in addition." It signals that you are being given an additional example. You get the idea.

→ TRANSITIONS

Addition: again, also, and, as well, besides, in addition, furthermore, moreover

Cause and effect: accordingly, because, consequently, since, so, therefore, thus

Clarification: i.e., in other words, that is to say, to put it another way

Concession: granted that, naturally, of course, to be sure

Comparison: by the same token, comparably, in the same way, likewise, similarly

Contrast: but, conversely, however, in spite of, nevertheless, on the other hand

Emphasis: by all means, certainly, indeed, in fact, no doubt, of course, surely

Illustration: e.g., for example, for instance, specifically, to demonstrate

Purpose: in order that, in order to, intending to, so that

Sequence: finally, first (second, and so on), then, next, numbered list (1., 2., and so on)

Space: above, adjacent, adjoining, beyond, far, here, near, there

Summary: briefly, in conclusion, in the final analysis, to summarize, to sum up

Time: after, before, immediately, later, meanwhile, occasionally, soon

---

PRACTICE 6.11   Using Transitions to Achieve Coherence

Read the excerpts about plagiarism and respond to the following questions:

1. Locate each transition. Explain how they function in the paragraph. How do they vary in their functions?

2. Which transitions seems more sophisticated to you? Which type would you be inclined to use? How does the type of transition used affect the style of the piece?

3. Are there places where formal transitions are not needed to move effectively from one sentence to another? How is this effect achieved?

(continued)

Excerpt A

Plagiarism has existed for hundreds of years, so it is not a new phenomenon, but we do hear about it much more nowadays than we ever have in the past. Indeed newspaper reports suggest that it is a £200 million pound industry that has grown up over the last few years supplying essays to students at all levels on any subject imaginable, some of them even tailored to the purchaser's express brief. Plagiarism has therefore become one of the issues of our times for our schools and universities.

—Will Murray, "The Plagiarism Phenomenon"

Excerpt B

What was Dmitry Yemets thinking when he cloned Harry Potter to create his wizard Tanya Grotter—that they would meet and become friends? They did in fact meet, but it was in an Amsterdam courtroom, when British author J. K. Rowling asserted her plagiarism claim. True enough, the claim was not against Yemets but against the publisher, Byblos, who had set April 2003 as the release date for the first 7,000 copies of a Dutch translation of *Tanya Grotter and the Magic Contrabass.*

—Anna Dymkovets, "Cultural Clones"

Excerpt C

Such lapses of integrity are not unique to China, but poor peer-review mechanisms, misguided incentives and a lack of checks on academic behaviour all allow fraud to be more common. China may be susceptible, suggests Dr Cong Cao, a specialist on the sociology of science in China at the State University of New York, because academics expect to advance according to the number, not the quality, of their published works. Thus reward can come without academic rigour. Nor do senior scientists, who are rarely punished for fraud, set a decent example to their juniors.

—*Economist*, "Academic Fraud in China" July 22, 2010.
© The Economist Newspaper Limited, London (July 22, 2010).
Reprinted by permission.

PRACTICE 6.12   Using Transitions

Examine one of your own essays or one of a classmate. Circle all of the transitions. Insert (pencil in) additional transitions wherever a transition would help the flow.

Plagiarism is literary theft.

STUDENT ESSAY

As you read the following student essay, identify and evaluate its structural features: introduction (lead, background, major claim), supporting and rebutting body paragraphs (types of claims, evidence, and explanations; their organization), and conclusion. What does the author do well, and what could she improve?

Hetal Shah

EN 101

Dr. Everett

February 8, 2012

Curing Plagiarism

Academic dishonesty is spreading like an epidemic across colleges and universities. Its symptoms range from copying a friend's homework to looking at another student's answers during a test to turning in a term paper that is plagiarized. *Plagiarism*, which is *taking credit for someone else's words or ideas*, in particular has increased at an alarming rate. Schools and colleges seek to understand not only the causes for rampant plagiarism but also ways to treat it more effectively. The remedy lies in cooperation between instructors, administrators, and students: instructors should improve how they teach academic honesty, administrators should revise and publicize policies treating academic misconduct, and students should value ethics over grades.

Statistics show a tremendous increase in academic dishonesty across the nation. According to a study conducted by *Plagiarism.org* 58.3 percent of high school students in 1969 allowed others to copy their work. In 1989, about 97.3 percent allowed their work to be copied by other students. Even more students today are copying homework answers and cheating on tests to maintain high grades.

There are many causes of plagiarism. One reason is the pressure on students to achieve, varying from maintaining a high GPA in high school to get into a good college to keeping up grades while in college to hold on to scholarships (Durkin). A second reason is the competitive nature of grading: a student must be not just acceptable but better than others (Fanning 8). Plagiarism also occurs because it is socially acceptable: many students do not consider it to be cheating because all their friends are doing it. In addition, cheaters are convinced that they are not going to get caught (Gulli, Köhler, and Patriquin 34); 95 percent of high school students who cheated were never found out (Gomez 42). Finally, rigorous course loads have led many students, often those who are near the top of their classes, to cheat in an effort to keep up with the workload.

Acting as a kind of safety valve for the pressures on students, modern technology has contributed greatly to the rise of plagiarism. The Internet has broadened the horizons for those who plagiarize because it is easily accessible and its resources are huge. At least 305 "cheat sites" with names such as "schoolsucks.com" and "lazystudents.com" sell recycled and custom-made papers (Clos 2). A study performed by *Education Week* found that 54 percent of American students admitted using prewritten Internet essays as a source for completing assignments at least once (Durkin).

According to Apiwan D. Born, an educator who specializes in information systems, instructors tend to react to plagiarism after the fact, when instead they should be proactive, stopping it before it starts: "an instructor should focus on 'how to reduce and discourage cheating activities' rather than 'why students cheat and how they did it.'" Proactive measures include teaching writing as a process rather than as a product, using more group rather than solitary activities, conducting more writing activities in class rather than out of class, and educating students better about what plagiarism is and why it is wrong (Born 223).

Establishing a campuswide program for educating students about plagiarism and instructors about plagiarism prevention is an administrative task. Just as campuses provide seminars for faculty members to help them better serve students with handicaps or to avoid practices that might be taken as sexual harassment, training should take place to help faculty understand the causes of *and solutions* to academic dishonesty. Administrative policies regarding cheating should be not only judicial and punitive, as they are now, but also proactive and preventive: writing instruction and ethical instruction need to be highlighted, promoted, and practiced universally.

Finally, students should be held responsible. At present there is a culture of complicity, where honest students tolerate the cheating done by their peers: students who would without hesitation report the theft of physical property instead look the other way when intellectual property is stolen. Something like an honor code needs to be established. Without the support of the average student, any program that promotes academic honesty is doomed to failure.

The epidemic of cheating will continue to plague academia until instructors, administrators, and students work together to treat it. This means more than posting a policy statement in a syllabus or handbook. This means more than assigning the "avoid plagiarism" passage for students to read in their composition textbooks. This means more than using antiplagiarism websites and software to catch plagiarists and then punish them after the fact. It means, instead, a cooperative effort to <u>cure</u> plagiarism through improved instruction, improved administration, and improved student ethics.

Works Cited

Born, Apiwan D. "How to Reduce Plagiarism." *Journal of Information Systems Education* 14.3 (2003): 223–24. Print.

Clos, Karen. "When Academic Dishonesty Happens on Your Campus." *Innovation Abstracts* 24.26 (2002): 1–2. Print.

Durkin, Jessica. "A Culture of Copy-and-Paste." *Spiked Online*. Signet Group, 28 Apr. 2005. Web. 2 Feb. 2011.

Fanning, Karen. "Is Honesty Still the Best Policy?" *Junior Scholastic* 107.17 (2005): 8–9. Print.

Gomez, Dina S. "It's Just So Easy to Cheat." *NEA Today* 19.7 (2001): 42. Print.

Gulli, Cathy, Nicholas Köhler, and Martin Patriquin. "The Great
    University Cheating Scandal." *Maclean's.* 12 Feb. 2007: 32–36.
    ProQuest.Umi. Web. 8 Feb. 2011.

Plagiarism.org. iParadigms LLC. 2011. Web. 28 January 2011.

Looking Back at Chapter 6

▶ An essay's basic structure consists of three major sections: (1) an introduction that provides a thesis statement or otherwise orients the reader toward a major claim, (2) a body of paragraphs that break down the thesis into specific areas and treat each area in detail, and (3) a conclusion that provides closure.

▶ A basic introduction to a composition contains a lead, background information, and a thesis or major claim.

▶ The body of an argument argues for the major claim (1) by supporting it with reasons (evidence and explanations) and (2) by rebutting significant alternative arguments.

▶ A topic can be stated at the top of a text block or paragraph, at the bottom of a text block or paragraph, as a delayed topic (after a transition sentence), or as an implied topic (not directly stated).

▶ There are four ways to organize the refutation of alternative arguments: early, late, occasional, and complete.

▶ Arguers often must qualify their claims by explaining under which circumstances the claim is true or by estimating the probability that a claim is true.

▶ Conclusions can do many things: summarize, personalize, focus, quote, question, propose, warn, encourage, or expand.

▶ Transitions help maintain coherence within a composition.

Suggestions for Writing

▶ Write a journal entry about your own process of drafting.

▶ After choosing an issue that interests you, follow the suggestions in the chapter as you draft an argument.

Writing Process: Revising and Editing Arguments

7

© Steve Prezant/Blend Images/Corbis

Writing is a process of change. Through your efforts, a blank sheet of paper or a computer screen evolves into a text. As you then evaluate and rewrite what you've written, the text undergoes improvements in form and content. The latter changes are the result of revision and editing.

> There I am paying big money to you writers, and for what? All you do is change the words.
> —Samuel Goldwyn, Former CEO of MGM Studios

REVISING AN ARGUMENT

The word *revision* is derived from a prefix and root word that mean "see again." Revision is expressed as alterations of your words, phrases, and larger blocks of text. Yet these external, visible changes emerge from invisible thought processes within you. The greater part of "seeing again" is internal, growing with your understanding of the needs of people (an audience), your own needs (your purpose for writing), and the ways in which rhetoric and argument can satisfy those needs.

Looking at your own writing with fresh eyes can be tricky. Some authors find they benefit from putting their texts aside for a while, allowing a kind of "distancing" or perspective. Unfortunately, many writing assignments come with deadlines that rule out a prolonged cooling-off period for works in progress. Fortunately, writers have several methods they can use to quickly re-see and improve their work. For example, revision guides, checklists, and rubrics can all be used to evaluate your own writing. These three methods can also be used to gather and organize feedback from your peers and from your writing instructor, as well as to guide you in giving feedback to other writers in your class.

Revision Isn't Editing

Although the phrase "revision and editing" often is uttered in the same breath, as though the two are the same activity, they are actually fundamentally different processes. Revision is closely related to planning and drafting, in that these processes are primarily concerned with the content—the meaning or message—of a text. Like planning and drafting, revision is recursive, with the writer repeating this process as often as necessary until he or she is satisfied with what the text has to say. By contrast, editing is nonrecursive, a terminal phase that normally doesn't lead to the production of content. The primary concern of editing is the correctness of technical features—spelling, punctuation, usage, formatting, and other features that affect meaning only if they are performed incorrectly.

Efficient writers postpone editing as long as possible because it slows the writing process: You pause to look up a spelling or stop writing a particular thought because you can't figure out the punctuation or think of the right word. Inexperienced writers have difficulty turning off their "internal editor," the part of them that resists writing anything that isn't correct. If your writing has ever come to a screeching halt because of technical matters, your internal editor needs to take a break. To make matters worse, the technical changes that slow down your writing process may end up in the scrap heap later on as you revise.

Revision Guides, Checklists, and Rubrics

Revision guides, checklists, and rubrics all direct you to find and evaluate particular features (criteria) of your draft:

► They present the criteria (characteristics, descriptors) of good writing.

► They assume you can detect particular weaknesses and revise them once your attention is directed that way.

► They can be used to guide an evaluation of your own writings or the writings of others.

These three revision tools differ somewhat in how they are structured and used:

► The revision guide is long and detailed. It will help focus your attention on the many details to be considered while checking an early draft.

► The checklist is brief; a summary of the long revision guide. The checklist works best after you are familiar with the details of the revision guide.

► A rubric adds a grading scale to the criteria featured in both the revision guide and the checklist. Depending on how your instructor structures the activities in class, the rubric may or may not be useful.

Feedback from others also can be directed by a revision guide, checklist, or rubric. Feedback, which will be discussed later in this chapter, can occur in one-on-one discussion sessions (with an instructor or a peer such as another student) and group work or, less personally, through a reviewer's written or recorded comments.

Using a Revision Guide

Here are some suggestions for using a revision guide productively:

► **Consider every question.** Not all questions will be useful, but as a whole the guide should help pinpoint significant strengths and weaknesses or concerns.

► **Mark and annotate.** Show the locations of specific strengths and weaknesses.

► **Evaluate.** Finish by writing a brief statement about the strengths, your concerns, and your recommendations.

→ REVISION GUIDE

As you read the piece from start to finish, comment on the features of argument and rhetoric. Below are specific questions that might be useful. (A brief version of these features is presented later in this chapter as a Revision Checklist.)

ARGUMENT: Claims, Evidence, Explanations, Qualifications, and Refutations

Claims

▶ What is the major claim? Where is it stated or how is it implied?

▶ Is the major claim significant (worth arguing), clear, arguable, and relevant to an issue?

▶ What, if any, are the supporting claims? Where are they stated?

▶ Are the supporting claims clear, arguable, and relevant to the major claim?

▶ How could the claim(s) be improved?

Evidence

▶ What evidence supports the claim(s)? Where is it located?

▶ Is the evidence adequate, current, credible, and relevant to the claim(s) or supporting points (topic sentences)? Why or why not?

▶ How could the evidence be improved?

Explanations of Evidence

▶ What explanations are provided? Where are they located?

▶ Are the explanations clear, adequate, and relevant to claim(s) and evidence?

▶ How could the explanations be improved?

Qualifiers

▶ What qualifiers are provided? Where are they located?

▶ Are the qualifiers accurate and clearly phrased?

▶ How could the qualifiers be improved?

Refutations

▶ What are the opposition arguments? Are the opposition arguments refuted? Where are they stated and refuted?

▶ Are the opposition arguments presented and refuted fairly and adequately?

▶ How could the presentation and refutation of opposition arguments be improved?

RHETORIC: Purpose, Audience, Structure, and Style

Purpose

▶ What does the author want to accomplish? (The purpose may be identical to the major claim, or, more precisely, the change the author seeks in the reader.)

▶ In what ways could the intended purpose be reconceptualized (broadened, narrowed, redirected) by the author?

Audience

▶ Who is the audience? Where is the audience stated or how is it implied?

▶ Is the audience compatible with the other rhetorical features: purpose, structure, and style?

▶ In what ways could the intended audience be reconceptualized (broadened, narrowed, redirected) by the author?

Structure

▶ What form does this argument take (e.g., essay, letter, editorial)?

▶ Is the type of argument appropriate to the assignment and rhetorical context?

▶ Are the basic organizational features (introduction, body, conclusion, thesis and topic sentences, transitions, paragraphing) present and effective?

▶ If needed, are specialized organizational features (e.g., for definition, comparison/contrast, narration) present and effective?

▶ How could the structure be improved?

Style

▶ **Diction:** Are the word choices appropriate? Why or why not? What might be improved?

▶ **Voice:** Is the voice appropriately formal or informal? Do you have a sense of the personality of the author? What are the strongest and weakest examples of voice? What might be improved?

▶ **Tone:** Is the tone appropriate to the other rhetorical considerations: purpose, audience, and structure? Why or why not? What are the strongest and weakest examples of tone? What might be improved?

▶ **Point of view:** Is the point of view appropriate to the rhetorical context and task specifications? (For example, research papers tend to be written in the third-person perspective, whereas personal narratives such as anecdotes are typically written in the first-person perspective.) What might be improved?

▶ **Sentence variety:** Are the sentences appropriately varied in length and form (simple, compound, complex)? What might be improved?

PRACTICE 7.1   Using a Revision Guide

Use the revision guide on page 190 as you evaluate the following passage from the rough draft of James Southard's essay "P.S.I.: Plagiarism Scene Investigator." (The complete essay is presented later in this chapter.) Mark, annotate, and evaluate the passage. Focus on strengths, concerns, and suggestions about the claim, support, and technical features.

"The criminal justice system is not altogether cold hearted and can provide means of rehabilitation and redemption. For example, a first time shop-lifter is often given an opportunity to clear their name. Judges have the option to *divert* criminal proceedings under certain circumstances. Under a *diversion*, a judge will assign some sort of community service or class that the offender must attend. After completing this court assigned requirement, and after staying out of any more trouble, the court will expunge the defendant's record. With first time plagiarists, we could adopt a similar plan. It would involve actually charging the individual with theft of property and putting the offender in front of a judge. The judge could then assign a writing course to the plagiarist. Upon completion of the course and a verification that no further plagiarism has occurred, the student or writer could have their record cleared. Of course, if the plagiarist fails to fulfill the requirements of the diversion, he or she should be tried for theft of property and if found guilty, sentenced under the criminal code."

PRACTICE 7.2   Revising a Sample Paragraph

Revise the paragraph in Practice 7.1, using your evaluation of it as a guide.

PRACTICE 7.3   Using a Revision Guide on Another Writer's Paragraph

Choose a paragraph from another student's paper (or a paper of your own). Using the revision guide, evaluate the paragraph.

Using a Revision Checklist

A revision checklist contains criteria that are similar to those in a revision guide but presents them in a briefer form. Think of the revision guide as a training program: Using the guide is slow at first, but you eventually internalize the criteria. Once you become familiar with the guide, you can switch to the shorter, quicker checklist. The checklist is also useful for peer evaluation, as we will soon see.

→ REVISION AND EDITING CHECKLIST

This is a summary of key features of argument, rhetoric, and technique that we explained in the long "Revision Guide" earlier in the chapter and the "Editing Guide" later in the chapter.

Argument Claims, support (evidence and explanations), qualifications, and refutations are thorough, honest, and convincing.

- ▶ **Claim(s):** Clear, significant, arguable, and relevant to the issue.
- ▶ **Evidence:** Adequate, current, credible, and relevant to the claim(s).
- ▶ **Explanations:** Clear, adequate, and relevant to the claim(s) and evidence.
- ▶ **Qualifiers:** Clearly and accurately show to what extent a claim is applicable.
- ▶ **Refutation:** Opposition arguments are presented and refuted fairly and adequately.
- ▶ **Rhetoric:** Purpose, audience, structure, and style are effective.
- ▶ **Purpose:** Author's goal is clearly stated or strongly implied. (Purpose is the major claim plus the change the author seeks in the reader.)
- ▶ **Audience:** Appropriate for the purpose, structure, and style.

- ▶ **Structure:**
  - ▶ Basic organizational features (introduction, body, conclusion, thesis and topic sentences, transitions, paragraphing) are present and effective.
  - ▶ If needed, specialized organizational features (e.g., for definition, comparison/contrast, narration) are present and effective.
  - ▶ **Style:** Diction, voice, tone, point of view, and syntax are appropriate for the purpose, audience, and structure.

Technique Technical elements are correct.

- ▶ **Grammar and usage:** Sentences and their parts are formed according to accepted standards.
- ▶ **Mechanics:** Spelling, capitalization, punctuation, and formatting are correct.
- ▶ **Format:** The correct conventions of document design are followed, including such elements as line spacing, paragraphing, title page, heading styles, font, documentation style, and appropriate use of tables, graphs, illustrations, photos, and the like.
- ▶ **Task specifications:** Topic, deadline, length, sources, and referencing style are as required.

The checklist presented in this book includes criteria for argument and rhetoric. In addition, it includes criteria for technique, which encompasses grammar and usage, mechanics, and task specifications. Technique is a concern of editing. Editing and technique will be discussed more thoroughly later in this chapter.

Use a checklist much as you would a revision guide:

- ▶ **Consider every feature listed on the checklist.** Not all points will be useful, but as a whole the checklist should help pinpoint significant strengths and weaknesses or concerns.

- ▶ **Mark and annotate.** Show the locations of specific strengths and weaknesses.

- ▶ **Evaluate.** Finish by writing a brief statement about the strengths, your concerns, and your recommendations.

Using Rubrics

Checklists and revision/editing guides both present criteria that describe good writing. When you take criteria a step further and add a rating scale, the result is an evaluation tool known as a scoring guide or rubric. Letter grades are a traditional kind of rating scale: A, B, C, D, F. In recent years the trend has been to use a numeric scale—such as 0 to 3, 1 to 5, 1 to 6, or 0 to 9—for the convenience of calculating scores mathematically.

Instructors, institutions, and testing programs (such as AP and ACT) have developed their own rubrics. Although rubrics are most often used for assessments ("grading"), they also can be used by writers in much the same way they use checklists and revision/editing guides. In fact, knowing the value of criteria can be formative (instructional), not just summative (evaluative).

Students sometimes use rubrics (rather than revision guides or check-lists) to help them evaluate one another's essays or sample essays provided by instructors. Typically, the instructor will later reveal the actual rubric value for the writing sample, helping the students determine how well they do or do not understand the criteria. Professional evaluators call this kind of training *calibration*: the process of tuning one's ability to assess. Sample essays with established values are called *range finders*.

➔ RUBRIC FOR ARGUMENTS

This rubric features the same criteria featured in the Revision Guide and Revision and Editing Checklist; it adds a grading scale. The rubric is holistic: Each score evaluates all of the qualities as a whole.

Score 5: Essays meriting a score of 5 are of high quality, exhibiting advanced skill with argument, rhetoric, and technique:

▶ **Argument:** Claims, evidence, explanations, qualifications, and opposition arguments/refutations are presented in a thorough, honest, and convincing manner.

▶ **Rhetoric:** Purpose, audience, structure, and style consistently work in harmony to advance the argument.

▶ **Technique:** Grammar, usage, mechanics, and task specifications are nearly flawless.

Score 4: Essays meriting a score of 4 are of good quality, exhibiting proficient skill with argument, rhetoric, and technique. Minor lapses are evident in one category.

Score 3: Essays meriting a score of 3 are of adequate quality, exhibiting passable skill with argument, rhetoric, and technique. Minor lapses are evident in two or more categories.

Score 2: Essays meriting a score of 2 are of inconsistent quality, exhibiting developing skill with argument, rhetoric, and technique. Minor lapses in all categories or a major weakness in one area is evident.

Score 1: Essays meriting a score of 1 are of low quality. Major lapses in all categories are evident.

PRACTICE 7.4	Using a Rubric: "P.S.I.: Plagiarism Scene Investigator"

Using the Rubric for Arguments above, assess the complete draft of "P.S.I.: Plagiarism Scene Investigator" presented at the end of this chapter. In group discussion or a brief writing, justify your assessment.

→ TASK-SPECIFIC RUBRICS

Because all arguments are bound by rhetorical context—a specific situation framing a contract between a writer and a reader—rubrics can also be specific to a particular type of argument. For example, a rubric used to evaluate the argument made by a newspaper or online editorial would be very different from a rubric used to evaluate an argument made in a proposal to build a new campus student center.

GIVING AND RECEIVING FEEDBACK

Feedback is the advice you give to or receive from others. Advice can come from face-to-face exchanges, from written or recorded comments, or from a combination of these encounters. In a classroom setting, advice often comes from other students. This kind of feedback goes by many names, often including the word *peer* followed by another term: peer conferencing, peer response, peer review, or peer editing. *Peer evaluation* is the preferred term in this textbook.

When you evaluate the writing of others, additional guidelines should befollowed to ensure the advice is constructive: Be positive and be specific.

Be Positive

Even the best examples of writing likely will contain flaws, especially in earlier drafts, and sooner or later those flaws will have to be addressed. Nevertheless, it is vitally important to be constructive and considerate when giving feedback.

→ GIVING FEEDBACK

When giving advice to other writers, your major goals are to be positive and to be specific. One way to accomplish both these goals is to phrase advice as questions. This method also lets you indicate problems (being descriptive) without offering solutions (being prescriptive). In fact, it is better if the writer is the one who figures out the solution.

Below is a list of problems typically faced by writers and examples of questions that can lead to solutions. The list is not comprehensive; you'll have to react to other problems with questions (feedback) of your own creation.

Problem	*Question*
Thesis isn't a claim.	What kind of change in the reader do you want?
	Where do you state your major claim or thesis?
	Can you turn this thesis into a fact claim? Identity claim? Cause and effect claim? Value claim? Proposal claim?
Claim is too broad.	**Which part of the issue is most significant?**
	Are you arguing more than one major claim?
Evidence is insufficient.	What are some reasons you could give?
	Where do you give some support?
	Can you restate? Interpret? Apply? Analyze? Synthesize? Evaluate?
Evidence is irrelevant.	**How does that evidence fit your claim?**
	Could you delete part of that quotation?
Evidence is excessive.	Do you need all that information to support your claim?
Quotations need work.	**Who is the source, and why is he or she worth quoting?**
	Could you paraphrase some of these quotations?
	Could some of the quotation be deleted?
Evidence needs explaining.	How does the evidence fit your claim?
	What does this statement mean?
Explanation isn't clear.	**How could you make this clearer?**
	Should you restate? Interpret? Apply? Analyze? Synthesize? Evaluate?
Style is inappropriate.	How will a reader react to your tone?
	Is your word choice appropriate to the reader?
	Is a first-person point of view appropriate for this writing?
Writing is disorganized.	**What is the main idea of this paragraph? Does that point fit?**
	Would a forecast statement in the introduction help show your organization?
	How does this idea or sentence lead to the next one?
Wording is repetitive.	Could you eliminate some repeated phrases or ideas?
	Could you combine some related sentences?
	Could you vary the way you say this?

Working Effectively with Others

When you work with other students in groups, whether to create an original project (such as a group presentation) or to receive feedback about something you bring to the group (such as a rough draft of a paper you have written), this activity is often termed collaborative learning or cooperative learning. Such activities give students an opportunity to learn from one another in a way that is not possible in a whole-class activity. You should take advantage of this time by doing the following:

- **Come prepared to your group meeting.** When you come unprepared, you affect the performance of the entire group.
- **Be an active participant.** Passive group members hinder the learning of everyone involved.
- **Avoid dominating the group.** When one person dominates the conversation, others do not have as much of a chance to contribute.
- **Respect other group members.** Treating others with respect contributes to group cohesion and makes the experience more pleasant for everyone involved.

Any writer who has made a serious attempt at producing a piece of writing will be sensitive about its reception. It is unrealistic to expect complete emotional "detachment" of an author from a work.

Unfortunately, evaluators tend to have a keener eye for flaws than for virtues: *Error marking* traditionally is synonymous with *paper grading*. Fortunately, there are several ways to make criticism more constructive:

> ► **Limit the number of critical "summary" remarks.** Few people are able to assimilate more than three or four new concepts in a feedback session. Also, you don't want to make the person despair.

> ► **Balance the negative with the positive.** Always find positive traits in the writing: People tend to learn very well from positive feedback.

> ► **Soften criticism by phrasing an observed weakness as a question.** For example, instead of saying "Your evidence is outdated," you could ask, "Have you looked for more recent data?"

Be Specific

Broad, generic feedback is quick and easy to give and receive, but it has little constructive value. For example, labeling an entire piece of writing as "good" or "I don't like it" seldom tells the author enough to lead to better writing. A writer needs to know very specifically *what* is effective or ineffective: a particular word, a particular example, or a particular sequence of sentences. It is even more useful if the writer knows *why* something works or fails.

Learning to evaluate writing may be one of the best ways to grow as a writer: *Identifying* quality can take you most of the way toward *producing* quality. At first it may be easier to evaluate others' writing than to evaluate your own work, probably because you are "too close" to your own material. As you learn to spot the best and worst qualities of other people's writings, you begin to "internalize" those criteria and to understand them better in your own work.

James Southard shared an early draft of his essay "P.S.I.: Plagiarism Scene Investigator" with a peer-evaluation group in his writing class. Here is the introduction to his essay, with annotations James made during discussion of his draft. (The complete version of the rough draft is presented later in this chapter.)

Plagiarism is <u>defined</u> as "stealing somebody's work or idea: the process of copying another person's idea or written work and claiming it as original." (Bing/Encarta) This is a simple definition. So, let's be a little more specific. When a person copies and pastes from an internet or written source without giving the original author credit for the work, they are committing plagiarism. When a person recycles <u>an old</u> essay and calls it an original work, they are committing plagiarism. When a person directly quotes the words of a speech or interview without crediting the speaker, they are committing plagiarism. Any college student <u>knows</u> about plagiarism and the possible consequences of committing the offense, but is plagiarism really that serious? What's the big <u>deal? When</u> committing plagiarism, that person is committing a <u>crime.</u>

Good to define key terms. Sometimes better to postpone the definition until you've established the issue or hooked the reader's attention.

Check MLA

Interesting parallel structure in three consecutive sentences.

Do you mean someone else's essay?

This is a fact claim. Support and document here or later in the essay.

Unclear how "big deal" leads to the crime claim. If crime is your thesis, re-organize to lead up to it.

Literally or figuratively? Perhaps compare to other theories or metaphors.

James's writing teacher reviewed a very rough draft of "P.S.I.: Plagiarism Scene Investigator" and sent him an e-mail with the following suggestions about his introduction.

FROM: Rob Lamm
TO: James Southard
DATE: 4/26/2012 09:22 AM
CC:
BCC:
SUBJECT: Your essay draft

Dear James,

I've read the rough draft of your essay, "P.S.I.: Plagiarism Scene Investigator."

It's coming along nicely. Below are some suggestions to help you make it even better.

Strengths
• Your intro displays some elements of a good introduction: It establishes an issue—a problem to be solved.

- The issue or problem has significance and a sense of urgency.
- Stylistically, it uses a technique of parallelism called symploce: you repeat the beginnings and endings of a series of sentences for emphasis and intensification: "When a person ... they are committing."

Concerns

- Can you think of a better opening than the definition? A definition is useful, but other leading sentences can hook a reader's interest more effectively.
- Your thesis seems to be that plagiarism is a crime. Do you mean literally or figuratively? Perhaps the intro could contrast the crime metaphor with other ways that scholars view plagiarism, such as a form of ignorance or as a disease.
- Consider also using transitions. What transitional word, phrase, or sentence can show the connection between the last two sentences: "What's the big deal? When committing plagiarism, that person is committing a crime."

After reflecting on the feedback from his classmates and instructor, James revised the introduction to his essay:

Educators often speak of plagiarism as if it were a disease: "The whole world ... is worried about what is often regarded as 'the plagiarism epidemic'" (Howard). The same educators seem to think the vaccine is as simple as educating students concerning the rules of how to properly document works and the consequences of failing to follow these rules. Indeed, many plagiarists plead ignorance (Shafer). Yet it's hard to believe that college students have had no prior education about plagiarism. The health metaphor is flawed and thus is unlikely to lead to a "cure" or any other kind of solution. Instead of using a disease metaphor, I propose that educators and students use a crime metaphor.

PRACTICE 7.5	Using a Revision Guide or Checklist to Give Feedback

Using the revision guide or checklist discussed earlier in the chapter, evaluate the complete rough draft of James Southard's essay, starting on page 206. Mark, annotate, and evaluate, focusing on strengths, concerns, and suggestions. Phrase some suggestions in the form of questions. Share your comments and suggestions with your classmates. What are the most useful and constructive ways to deliver feedback? At what points does it become challenging to evaluate someone else's writing?

EDITING AN ARGUMENT

Editing is a process of tidying up the technical and mechanical features of a piece of writing—that is, "dotting the 'Is' and crossing the 'Ts.'" Known sometimes as proofreading, most editing can be postponed until a draft is completed, although fastidious people may have trouble ignoring errors even temporarily. Whether sooner or later, eventually the editing must be done.

Over the years you probably have been taught many rules about spelling, punctuation, grammar/usage, and formatting. As you edit, your personal storehouse of knowledge is your primary resource. However, so many rules exist that you'll probably supplement your own body of knowledge with reference books—a dictionary, a thesaurus, and a writer's handbook (for usage and mechanics). If you use a word processor, these resources may be part of your software package.

A final aspect of editing involves formatting and document design. This means that your final document has the correct appearance—the title page, pagination, paragraph spacing, font choice, headings, and so on conform to the documentation style you are following (such as MLA or APA). Formatting can also involve the correct placement and formatting of photos, illustrations, maps, and more.

Editing on a Word Processor

Electronic versions of dictionaries, thesauruses, and handbooks often are integrated into word processors. These tools alert you to potential errors as you write, highlighting misspelled words or faulty sentences. Clicking on a highlighted passage summons a menu of suggestions and additional tools. At other times, you may choose to activate proofreading and editing software by clicking on typed words or a toolbar. You can also use the document map to help you view the structure of the essay as a whole and move sections around. Some specialized word processors like Scrivener also have note-taking and research functions you might find useful.

Commands and Functions   Word processors allow you to issue commands and perform functions important in editing and proofreading: copy, count (words, pages), find and replace, delete, move, search. A person who is skilled in the use of a word processor can apply these functions to great advantage, making changes much more rapidly than is possible with pen and paper. You should always check the checker, because it will accept any correctly spelled word, regardless of meaning.

Spelling Checker   A checker can spot possible problems and enable you to choose from a menu of suggested spellings or add new spellings to its list. Auto-correct is an option that will empower your word processor to make some changes automatically. A spelling checker, however, can make mistakes. Its lexicon may be limited, omitting some words that are acceptable: The words *prewrite* and *freewrite,* for example, are accepted in the English profession but are not recognized by many spelling checkers. Also, a checker will accept a properly spelled word even when it is the wrong word. If, for example, you mistyped "spell" as "spiel," the spelling checker would not catch the error because "spiel" is the correct spelling for another word.

→ CANDIDATE FOR A PULLET SURPRISE *JERROLD H. ZAR*

This poem was originally published in the January–February 1994 issue of the *Journal of Irreproducible Results.* By the author's count, 127 of the 225 words in the poem are incorrect (although all words are correctly spelled).

I have a spelling checker, It came with my PC.

It plane lee marks four my revue Miss steaks aye can knot sea.

Eye ran this poem threw it, Your sure reel glad two no.

Its vary polished in it's weigh.

My checker tolled me sew.

A checker is a bless sing, It freeze yew lodes of thyme.

It helps me right awl stiles two reed, And aides me when eye rime.

Each frays come posed up on my screen Eye trussed too bee a joule.

The checker pours o'er every word To cheque sum spelling rule.

Bee fore a veiling checker's Hour spelling mite decline, And if we're lacks oar have a laps, We wood bee maid too wine.

Butt now bee cause my spelling Is checked with such grate flare, Their are know fault's with in my cite, Of nun eye am a wear.

Now spelling does knot phase me, It does knot bring a tier.

My pay purrs awl due glad den With wrapped word's fare as hear.

To rite with care is quite a feet Of witch won should bee proud, And wee mussed dew the best wee can, Sew flaw's are knot aloud.

Sow ewe can sea why aye dew prays Such soft wear four pea seas, And why eye brake in two averse Buy righting want too pleas.

Jerry Zar, "Candidate for a Pullet Suprise." From *Journal of Irreproducible Results*, Jan–Feb, 1994. Reprinted by permission.

Grammar Checker A word processor can check for lapses in accepted grammar and usage. A grammar checker can also give you short lessons in style, explaining why some things are incorrect and offering alternatives. Like spelling checkers, grammar checkers have limitations and sometimes must be ignored or overruled.

Dictionary This resource can be activated by clicking on a word in your text or by clicking onto an icon displayed on a toolbar. Although useful, these dictionaries may be less complete than hardcover collegiate dictionaries.

Synonyms (Thesaurus) Highlighting a word and clicking will activate this resource. The list of synonyms may be useful yet less complete than a print version of a thesaurus.

Translator Some software provides English-to-foreign language translations. Also, a number of Web sites provide this service. While these programs are useful for gaining an understanding of basic information from a foreign-language Web site or other source, they are notorious for making mistakes in their translations. Don't trust the accuracy of the translation unless it has been checked by someone fluent in the language.

Evaluator Some software programs will "grade" your writing. This kind of evaluation is not a substitute for a human editor, but it can give you feedback by evaluating features such as sentence and paragraph length and the average words per sentence or paragraph and can highlight words that might be used improperly.

    Note: It is important to note that none of these programs can "read" your writing or make contextual decisions about your prose. It is unwise to assume that a grammar checker or other device can "fix" your writing for you. If you use any of these tools, remember that you, as a writer, have to make the final decision.

Ironic Rules for Writing

1. Don't abbrev.
2. No sentence fragments.
3. Implement the vernacular.
4. Dump the slang. It sucks.
5. Avoid clichés like the plague.
6. Try to never split an infinitive.
7. Don't never use double negatives.
8. Passive voice should be made active.
9. Avoid redundant punctuation!!! Okay???
10. And do not start sentences with conjunctions.
11. Prepositions are words you shouldn't end with.
12. Use parallelism when you speak and in writing.
13. Fix comma splices, use a conjunction or semicolon..
14. Each of the pronouns should agree with their antecedent.
15. Mixed metaphors are like a disease that must be ironed out.

PRACTICE 7.6 Revising "Candidate for a Pullet Surprise"

Revise the humorous poem "Candidate for a Pullet Surprise" by replacing all the incorrect words and phrases with ones that are correct.

PRACTICE 7.7   Using Word Processing Tools

While working with a word processor, practice using its commands and tools: copy, count (words, pages), find and replace, insert, format, delete, move, navigate (scroll), search, spelling checker (use it to automatically correct misspellings), grammar checker (use it to automatically correct grammatical errors), synonyms, translation (to or from a foreign language).

→ EDITING GUIDE: TECHNIQUE

Grammar and Usage

Sentences: Are the sentences formed correctly? Are there any "fused sentences" (comma splices or run-ons) or fragments?

Words: Are the forms of words correct? Are there incorrect singular or plural nouns or verbs? Do all of the pronouns have antecedents? Do all verbs agree with their subjects?

Meaning of words: Do the words mean what they are intended to mean? Are there errors in diction, "wrong words"?

Positions of words: Are words arranged in correct order? Are any modifiers placed in a way that could be misread (dangling, squinting, misplaced)? Are instances of "parallelism" correct or faulty?

Mechanics: Are spelling, capitalization, punctuation, and formatting correct?

Task Specifications: Did you use the required topic, deadline, length, sources, and referencing style?

The eraser's comment is a good reminder that first drafts can usually be improved.

Editing Guides

An editing guide, like a revision guide, directs you to find and evaluate particular features of your draft. It aims specifically at correctness: grammar/usage, mechanics, and task specifications. This kind of guide often is joined with a revision guide, forming a dual-purpose "revision and editing guide."

Editing Marks

Professional editors use a variety of symbols and abbreviations to show where and how a text should be corrected. Known as *editing marks* or *proofreading marks,* they are fairly easy to learn and very handy for shortening the time it takes to mark a paper.

The passage below is a paragraph from a student essay. Errors have been added to help illustrate the use of editing marks.

(¶) Statistics support the claim of a tremendous increase in academic dishonesty across the nation. For example, according to a study conducted by The State of Americans: This Generation and the Next, 5.3 percent of high school students in 1969 allow (Tense) others to copy their work. In 1989, about 97.3 percent. (Frag) Copyright their homework (Dgl mod), high grades are all that students seem to care about. Bassed (SP) on these disturbing statistics, it is relevant that (Wdy) pressures are negatively affecting (Awk) the maintenance of Academic (lc) Integrity (lc) in the many schools. Plagiarism and cheating are also on the rise in schools because many students do not think, or rather do not even understand, that such acts are illegal. A student don't (SVA) feel that copying someone else's work is socially inacceptible (SP), all (CS) their friends are going it. They (Ref?) are convinced that they are not going to get caught (Lincoln 47). Ninety-five percent of high school students who cheat admitted (Tense) that they do not get caught (Gomez 42).

→ EDITING AND PROOFREADING MARKS

Can you think of a way to correct each of the examples?

Symbol	Meaning	Example
Abr	Abbreviation problem	(Abr) Doct. Peterson is the best pharmacy professor on campus.
Agr	Agreement problem	(Agr) Salar and Won Ho is going to Law Vegas next month for a seminar.
Ante? or Ref?	Pronoun antecedent missing or unclear	My friends Phil and Dave painted (Ante?) his apartment last weekend.
Awk	Awkward language	The earthquake was a (Awk) really awful bad disaster.
Cap (X̲)	Faulty capitalization	Next year I'm going to study at the university of london. (Caps)
C/S	Comma splice	(C/S) I'm going to the store, I'm going to buy bread.
Delete (˜)	Problem word or phrase	Next month five students are going before the̶ the (Del) academic discipline board for plagiarism incidents.
Dic	Diction problem (word choice)	I performed really (Dic) good on the test.
Dgl mod	Dangling or misplaced modifier	(Dgl mod) Lying beside the street in a drainage ditch, I discovered a wallet walking home.
-ed	Problem with -ed verb ending	If you had (-ed) jog with Fred every morning like you had planned, you would be in better shape these days.
Frag	Sentence fragment	Dealing with angry people on a daily basis at my job at the police department. (Frag)
F/S	Fused sentence or run-on	I'm going to the store (F/S) I'm going to buy bread.
Insert (∧)	Missing word or phrase	Next month five students are going before _the_ ∧academic discipline board for plagiarism incidents.
lc	Improper capitalization	One of the most important influences on modern life is M̶arket C̶apitalism. (lc)
//	Problem with parallelism	In college, I'm planning on majoring in English and (//) to play football.
P/A	Pronoun agreement problem	(P/A) The average student gets their chance at success if he studies hard.
Para (¶)	Make a new paragraph	My supervisor said, "I'll have to let you go if you don't lose weight. It's bad for the company's image." (¶) "Try it," I said. "Try it, and I'll sue."
Rep.	Repeated word or phrase	Technically, I'm having trouble understanding technical technology. (Rep)
SP	Spelling error	My favorite (SP) professer is Dr. Roberts.
-s	Problem with -s ending	Dr. Stephens plan (s) to run for public office.

(continued)

→ EDITING AND PROOFREADING MARKS *(continued)*

Symbol	Meaning	Example
SVA	Subject and verb agreement problem	*(SVA)* The <u>committee</u>, which includes Aditi and Kareem, <u>are</u> voting in favor of the amendment.
Tense	Verb tense problem	In Shakespeare's Hamlet, the title character <u>will lecture</u> his mother on morality after he <u>killed</u> Polonius. *(Tense)*
Wdy	Wordy phrase needs to be simplified	One of the <u>really major</u> problems <u>with not only American, but the society of the world in general</u> today is the lack of civility <u>and the tendency to be curt and impolite to others</u>. *(Wdy)*
WW	Wrong word	*(WW)* One <u>affect</u> of higher gas prices is that some people get more exercise.

PRACTICE 7.8   Using an Editing Guide and Editing Marks: "P.S.I.: Plagiarism Scene Investigator"

Using the editing guide and editing marks, annotate the errors in the following passage from James Southard's rough draft. (Errors have been added to the original draft.)

"What plagiarism fighting tips can we gains from the criminal justice system. First, their must be penalties to fit the crimes, colleges and universities usually meet out justice in terms of grade reductions, suspensions, and expulsions. Ignoring their conscience, punishments such as fines, community service, permanent records, and embarrassing publicity (such as as releasing names to the press) may be appropriate for plagiarists. For a thief, it often is the deterrent of severe punishment that makes them think twice. And follow the straight and narrow."

PRACTICE 7.9   Before You Read

Working individually or in a group, consider the problem of plagiarism.

1. If you were given a job to prevent plagiarism, what actions would you take?
2. How severely should plagiarists be punished?
3. Examine the essay's title. What does it suggest about the author's thesis?

STUDENT ESSAY

James Southard

Dr. Lamm

Composition

25 April 2012

P.S.I.: Plagiarism Scene Investigator

Educators often speak of plagiarism as if it were a disease: "The whole world . . . is worried about what is often regarded as 'the plagiarism epidemic'" (Howard). The same educators seem to think the vaccine is as simple as educating students concerning the rules of how to properly document works and the consequences of failing to follow these rules. Indeed, many plagiarists plead ignorance (Shafer). Yet it's hard to believe that college students have had no prior education about plagiarism. The health metaphor is flawed and thus is unlikely to lead to a "cure" or any other kind of solution. Instead of using a disease metaphor, I propose that educators and students use a crime metaphor.

Specifically, I propose that we look to the criminal justice system as a model for ways to understand and to combat plagiarism. A plagiarist is more like shoplifter stealing a candy bar or a car thief stealing a car: some people will break the rules even though they know stealing is wrong and even though they know how *not* to steal.

Plagiarism is defined as "stealing somebody's work or idea: the process of copying another person's idea or written work and claiming it as original" (Bing/Encarta). When a person copies and pastes from an internet or written source without giving the original author credit for the work, they are committing plagiarism. When a person recycles an old essay and calls it an original work, they are committing plagiarism. When a person directly quotes the words of a speech or interview without

Southard 2

crediting the speaker, they are committing plagiarism but more specifically, they are stealing.

Proverbial wisdom and probably many plagiarists say "no harm, no foul." Is plagiarism really that serious? Ideas aren't physical objects, so what's the big deal? This question is answered in criminal codes across the country. Take for example Arkansas' theft of property statute:

> A person commits theft of property if he or she knowingly takes or exercises unauthorized control over or makes an unauthorized transfer of interest in, the property of another person, with the purpose of depriving the owner of the property. (A.C.A. 5-36-103)

This statute covers more than stealing physical items. It includes theft of property that "has inherent, subjective or idiosyncratic value to the owner or possessor even if the property has not market value or replacement cost" (A.C.A. 131). This offense is considered a Class A misdemeanor and carries with it a possible punishment of a year in jail with up to a $1000.00 fine. However, if the offense is repeated against the same individual, the crime can be raised to the status of a Class D felony. This level of felony carries the possibility of a prison sentence with up to a $10,000.00 fine. The law doesn't exclude the possibility of a civil suit being brought against a person for this type of theft.

Stealing intellectual property can cost a person a lot. Just ask the people that have stolen music online and been caught. Ask the people who have been caught making illegal copies of movies. Individuals who have been convicted of these crimes have been forced to pay thousands for the offenses. Depending on what is plagiarized, the cost can be high. Even though the people stealing music and movies aren't necessarily calling the works their own, the theft is similar in nature.

Southard 3

What plagiarism-fighting tips can we gain from the criminal justice system? First, there must be penalties to fit the crimes. Colleges and universities usually mete out justice in terms of grade reductions, suspensions, and expulsions, but perhaps that is not enough. Fines, community service, permanent records, and embarrassing publicity (such as releasing names to the press) may be appropriate. For thieves, it often is the deterrent of severe punishment that makes them think twice and follow the straight and narrow.

The criminal justice system is not altogether cold hearted and can provide means of rehabilitation and redemption. For example, a first time shoplifter is often given an opportunity to clear their name. Judges have the option to *divert* criminal proceedings under certain circumstances. Under a *diversion*, a judge will assign some sort of community service or class that the offender must attend. After completing this court assigned requirement, and after staying out of any more trouble, the court will expunge the defendant's record. With first time plagiarists, we could adopt a similar plan. It would involve actually charging the individual with theft of property and putting the offender in front of a judge. The judge could then assign a writing course to the plagiarist. Upon completion of the course and a verification that no further plagiarism has occurred, the student or writer could have their record cleared. Of course, if the plagiarist fails to fulfill the requirements of the diversion, he or she should be tried for theft of property and if found guilty, sentenced under the criminal code.

By the strict enforcement of rules and laws against plagiarism, educators can make a real difference. Students will be motivated to pay attention when they are taught the ways to properly use sources, and would-be plagiarists will become upright intellectual citizens. Above all, fewer victims will be shouting, "Call the Police, I've been plagiarized!"

Southard 4

Works Cited

Devine, Joseph. "Fighting Back Against Intellectual Property Theft."
EzineMark.com, 19 Apr. 2010. Web. 19 Apr. 2011.

Howard, Rebecca Moore. "The Search for a Cure: Understanding the
'Plagiarism Epidemic.'" McGrawHillHigherEducation.com, 2003. Web.
22 Apr. 2011.

Kohn, Alfie. "Standardized Testing and Its Victims" *Education Week*,
27 Sep. 2000. Web. 15 Apr. 2011.

Plagiarism defined. *Bing/Encarta Dictionary*. Web. 20 April. 2011.

Shafer, Jack. "Why Plagiarists Do It." *Slate*, 26, April 2006. Web.
23 Apr. 2011.

"Theft of Property." A.C.A. 5-36-103 (2010). Print.

PRACTICE 7.10   Responding to the Essay

1. Do you agree or disagree with the author's claim and supporting ideas? Did the author change your prior opinion in any way? How?
2. Where is the author's support stronger? Where is it weaker? Explain.
3. Does the author's treatment of other points of view affect your willingness to believe what he has to say? In what way?
4. What, if anything, would you change about the essay's organization and content? Is there anything missing that you would add?
5. Which of the appeals (logic, authority, emotion) do you think was strongest in this essay? Which was weakest? Why do you think so?
6. Name the essay's greatest strength and most significant weakness. Explain your answer.

Looking Back at Chapter 7

- ▶ Revising is "re-seeing." One way to re-see is to understand the qualities that characterize good writing.

- ▶ Checklists, revision guides, and rubrics can not only help you re-see and revise but also can help you advise others.

- ▶ Postpone editing until you are satisfied with the rhetorical and argumentative features of your draft.

- ▶ Use the tools of the trade. A dictionary and thesaurus are basic resources that are typically available as books or as word processing software.

- ▶ Word processors offer many tools and commands that facilitate revision.

- ▶ Rubrics can help you understand which qualities characterize good writing and how those qualities are evaluated.

Suggestions for Writing

- ▶ In both your current and later writing assignments, use a revision/editing guide, checklist, or rubric as you critically read and revise your work.

- ▶ In both your current and later writing assignments, use a revision/editing guide, checklist, or rubric as you give feedback to other writers.

8

Using Sources, Avoiding Plagiarism

© Mike Baldwin / Cornered

"It's not the same. I was caught stealing office supplies. You, on the other hand, got caught stealing ideas."

(© Original Artist Reproduction rights obtainable from www.CartoonStock.com.)

Isn't plagiarism wonderful? For a few dollars a student can buy a recycled essay from an online paper mill (or splurge for a custom-written version), deliver it to the instructor, and then nervously await the grade, hoping not to get caught. What could go wrong?

> Copy from one, it's plagiarism; copy from two, it's research.
> —Wilson Mizner, American screenwriter (1876–1933)

Derived from the Latin word *plagiarius*, "kidnapper" or "plunderer," *plagiarism* is intellectual theft. It is the unauthorized use or imitation of someone else's writing.

To answer that question, check your institution's regulations on "academic misconduct." If caught, a plagiarist may suffer any one of a range of penalties: a failure on a paper, a failure in a course, or possibly expulsion from school. Whether caught or not, the plagiarist fails to gain practical knowledge essential to success in life and work.

Though plagiarism is sometimes intentional, it is more often caused by a failure to understand how to cite properly. Through this chapter, you'll learn the skills that will help you avoid plagiarism: quoting, paraphrasing, summarizing, and synthesizing.

▶ **Quote:** Use the ideas and the wording of a source, unchanged from the original.

▶ **Paraphrase:** Use the ideas of a source unchanged, but express them in your own writing style.

▶ **Summarize:** Use the ideas of a source in briefer form and in your own writing style.

▶ **Synthesize**: Use two or more sources to make a point, quote, paraphrase, summarize, or blend.

QUOTING

A quotation is an exact repetition of words written or spoken by someone else, usually enclosed by a pair of quotation marks. Quotations have many uses in writing, but along with their application comes responsibilities.

"When you quote a Presidential candidate, Gorman, you do not—I repeat—do not roll your eyes."

Quotations often are followed by commentary.
(James Stevenson/all rights reserved http://www.thecartoonbank.com)

Why Quote?

Quotations perform important functions in argumentative writing: They appeal to authority, provide evidence, reveal issues, hook interest, dramatize, and add eloquence.

Appeal to Authority: Use Experts for Support
When you quote the words of an expert, it is as if you brought that person to speak personally to your reader. The following example introduces the source by name and credentials and then lets him speak to the reader:

> According to Matt Zimmerman, attorney for the Electronic Frontier Foundation, "The First Amendment protects individuals' right to speak anonymously and forces litigants to justify any attempts to unmask anonymous critics."

Provide Evidence
A quotation can provide evidence. For example, if you are arguing about gun control, you might quote Article II of the Bill of Rights:

> Although the Second Amendment protects the right to bear arms, it also requires regulation: "A *well regulated* [emphasis mine] Militia, being necessary to the security of a free State, the right of the people to keep and bear Arms, shall not be infringed."

Reveal Issues
A quotation can help establish the nature, history, or extent of an issue:

> According to attorney Alison Virginia, King, "The heart-wrenching suicide of Missouri teenager Megan Meir in 2006 directed national attention to the devastating effects of online harassment and cyberbullying."

Capture Interest
A controversial or outrageous statement may provide an "interest-catching lead":

> Paris Hilton uses animal puns to explain her philosophy: "Every woman should have four pets in her life. A mink in her closet, a jaguar in her garage, a tiger in her bed, and a jackass who pays for everything."

Dramatize: Use Dialogue to Make an Issue Come Alive
Because readers respond more readily to real people rather than to abstractions and concepts, your writing can be enlivened with dialogue, perhaps coupled with narration and description:

> "You lie!" shouted Representative Joe Wilson, jabbing his finger toward President Obama.

Chip Somodevilla/Getty Images

South Carolina Representative Joe Wilson interrupted President Obama's health reform speech by shouting "You lie!"

Add Eloquence: Display Skillful Phrasing   Sometimes you may wish to preserve the original wording because its rhetorical style is striking. In the following quotation, John F. Kennedy skillfully uses a technique known as inversion or **chiasmus,** reversing the order of the terms *you* and *your country* in two parallel, contrasting clauses:

> Kennedy reminds us of the selflessness of patriotism: "Ask not what your country can do for you; ask what you can do for your country."

How to Quote

To quote effectively, practice these skills:

- ▶ **Be Honest:** Provide Context and Interpretation
- ▶ **Be Concise:** Quote Sparingly
- ▶ **Give Credit:** Name Your Sources
- ▶ **Tag:** Attach Your Words to the Quotation
- ▶ **Change:** Add, Delete, Alter

> → THE QUOTING PROCESS
>
> **Plan**
> - ▶ **Read critically and annotate.** Look for passages that can enhance your argument. Such passages can be used to support your argument or to represent opposition arguments.
> - ▶ **Make choices.** Determine how much of the source you wish to delete, quote, paraphrase, or summarize.
>
> **Draft**
> - ▶ **Integrate.** Connect the quotation to your text with an introductory lead-in.
> - ▶ **Explain.** Restate, interpret, apply, analyze, synthesize, and evaluate the quotation as needed.
>
> **Revise**
> - ▶ **Check major features:** Honesty, conciseness, credit, tags, and changes.

Be Honest: Provide Context and Interpretation A quotation doesn't always speak for itself. It probably was preceded or followed by other statements that reveal the source's true meaning—such remarks are the "context" of a statement. Out-of-context quoting can distort the truth. To present another person's ideas honestly, (1) provide context when needed and (2) interpret fairly.

The following example corrects a misinterpretation by providing additional context and interpretation:

> During the 2008 presidential race, Obama conceded "that John McCain has not talked about my Muslim faith." Immediately, some of Obama's detractors misinterpreted this statement as an admission that Islam was his true religion. Obama—a practicing Christian—actually was acknowledging that McCain showed integrity by not exploiting the wide-spread confusion about Obama's beliefs.

Be Concise: Quote Sparingly You may be tempted to quote excessively—too often and at too great a length, especially when you are struggling to meet a deadline or to satisfy a word count. The result seems like a string of oversized pearls of other people's wisdom, with you providing only the string. However, your reader primarily wants to hear your voice, your argument. You can own the argument by doing the following:

- ▶ Shorten each quotation to only the relevant parts
- ▶ Quote only when it clearly works better than alternatives
- ▶ Use alternatives such as paraphrasing and summarizing

The following example shows how to shorten by deleting unnecessary points, paraphrasing one point, and quoting a memorable phrase.

> **ORIGINAL, FULL-LENGTH QUOTATION** Kushner defines WikiLeaks as follows: "Designed as a digital drop box, the site is a place where anyone can anonymously submit sensitive or secret materials to be disseminated and downloaded around the globe" (63).
>
> **SHORTENED QUOTATION** Kushner calls WikiLeaks a "digital drop box" for anonymous whistleblowers (63).

Give Credit: Name Your Sources When you quote, give credit to the source with an attribution known as a reference or citation. This credit can be *in-text* (within your text but attached externally to the main body of the sentence) or *in-sentence* (grammatically part of your own sentence).

In-text Citations Often you will give credit to your source in a standardized, formal method known as a *bibliographic style.* Style guidelines are issued by professional organizations such as the Modern Language Association (MLA) and the American Psychological Association (APA). A style dictates the following:

► What kind of reference information must be given

► Where it should be displayed, and

► How it should be displayed.

> **MLA IN-TEXT CITATION: Source and page number are given in parentheses.**
>
> Although WikiLeaks demands transparency from governments and businesses, ironically this "next-generation whistleblowing machine can also be maddeningly opaque" about its own management (Kushner 63).

In-sentence Citations You can place credit for your source within your own sentence. In-sentence citation is especially advisable when the name of the source gives the quotation more authority. The simplest way to integrate a citation is by including a tag naming the source: "According to Jones...." or "Smith states that...." To emphasize the credentials of the authority, add brief biographical information.

> **MLA IN-SENTENCE CITATION: Source and credential are named in-sentence, while the page number is in parentheses.**

Amy Chua, author of *Battle Hymn of the Tiger Mother*, asserts that "What Chinese parents understand is that nothing is fun until you're good at it" (27).

Tag: Attach Your Words to the Quotation When you quote, attach your own words to the quotation. This extra wording goes by various names: "tag," "lead in," "attribution," or "signal phrase." Whatever you call it, tagging is useful and standard: it can tell something important about the source, and it helps the reader see how the quotation connects to the rest of your text. Less convincing is a tag that names a title of a book or article: the real authority is the person who wrote or spoke the quotation.

Standard Practice The most common way to tag a quotation is to name the source. If you add a credential, such as the person's expertise (title, profession, training), you'll make the quotation more convincing.

Dropped Quotations Quoted sources that lack a tag are known variously as dropped, floating, free-floating, freestanding, or dumped quotations. Even when dropped quotations follow the logical flow of a paragraph, you are still obliged by convention and common sense to integrate them with a tag of your own words.

Following is an example of the same quotation in both "dropped" and "tagged" forms.

> **DROPPED QUOTATION (The absence of a tag makes the quotation's relevance unclear.)**
>
> "Everything has changed: the nature of threat, the sources of information, the technology use" (Treverton 40).
>
> **TAGGED QUOTATION (The tag relates the quotation to an issue and also provides a credential for the source.)**
>
> Gregory Treverton, former vice chairman of the National Security Council, underscores the 9/11 effect: "Everything has changed: the nature of threat, the sources of information, the technology use" (40).

Vary Your Tag's Location Although it makes sense to provide introductory material at the beginning a quotation, readers also prefer varied sentence patterns. Minor changes in punctuation will enable you to locate your tags at the beginning, middle, or end:

Examples of Varied Tag Locations with Additional Information

Beginning Tag—naming source and giving a credential

House Majority Leader John Boehner stated, "Our spending has caught up with us, and our debt soon will eclipse the entire size of our national economy."

Middle Tag—using a verb that conveys the tone of the source

"The American people spoke pretty loudly," exclaimed Boehner. "They said stop all the looming tax hikes."

Ending Tag—providing commentary about the quotation

"Over the last two years since President Obama has taken office, the federal government has added 200,000 new federal jobs," alleged Boehner, but that number conflicts with the Bureau of Labor Statistics' estimate of 58,000.

Vary Your Tag's Wording Some verbs and phrases are neutral, including little or no information to influence the reading of a quotation. "Jones writes…." or "In the words of Smith…." leads a reader into a quotation without revealing how the source is related to the issue or how you feel about the source.

However, you have the option of including non-generic tag verbs or modifiers that can add useful information: "Jones agrees that…." or "Smith disputes the fact that…." provides not only variety but also interpretation.

Follow up the Tags' Quotations with Explanations Experienced writers rarely move past a quotation without discussing it, instead "milking it for all it's worth." Inexperienced writers overlook a quotation's potential for

---

→ VARY YOUR TAG'S WORDING

When introducing a quotation, you can vary your tags. Some tags are neutral in the way they influence your reader, but others can guide the reader's interpretation or evaluation of the quotation.

▶ **No influence:** Some tags have little influence on the reader: for example, "states," "says," or "writes."

Patrick Henry states, "Give me liberty, or give me death!"

▶ **Interpretive influence:** Some tags suggest the attitude that a source or quotation takes toward an issue. For example, "agrees," "protests," or "questions."

Bravely, Patrick Henry exhorts his fellow legislators, proclaiming, "Give me liberty, or give me death!"

▶ **Evaluative influence:** Some tags suggest the attitude that you take toward the source or quoted information.

Bravely, Patrick Henry placed his life on the line: "Give me liberty, or give me death!"

→ ADD MORE INFORMATION TO TAGS

You can go beyond the minimal requirements of a tag, expanding it to include many kinds of relevant information.

▶ **Reveal the credentials of the source:** J. R. R. Tolkien, author of *Lord of the Rings*, defines fantasy as....

▶ **Clarify the relevance of a quotation to an issue:** Jones refutes Smith, saying....

▶ **Share an attitude of a source toward an issue:** Smith blusters....

▶ **Share your estimate of the value of the source:** Jones is mistaken when she states....

▶ **Comment on the content of the quotation:** Plagiarism can actually be encouraged by policies that seek to discourage it: "We had been operating on an outdated and semi-relevant policy that clearly affected the punishment that could be meted out" (Clos).

---

initiating discussion and consequently find themselves in desperate need of quotations to meet a required word count. See Chapter 2, Claims and Support, for more on how to explain.

Example of a quotation with follow-up explanation:

> *The Sun* ran a story with the interesting headline: "72,000 stimulus payments went to dead people." In fact about 7,000 people die every day in the United States, so every single day the number of people who would have qualified for a payment changed enormously. The headline could have as easily read: "Government agency did a very good job implementing congressionally mandated stimulus payments."
>
> —Letter to the Editor, *The Lowell Sun*

PRACTICE 8.1   Vary Your Tag's Wording

a. For the following quotation, write tags that (1) do not influence the reader, (2) help the reader interpret the source's attitude, and (3) inform the reader of your attitude toward either the quotation or the source.

> No, no, no, not God Bless America. God damn America for killing innocent people.
>
> —Reverend Jeremiah Wright, from his sermon "Confusing God and Government"

b. For your own writing project, select quotations and then write tags that vary their influence: neutral, interpretive, and evaluative.

PRACTICE 8.2   Vary Your Tag's Locations

a. For the following quotation, write tags that attach at the beginning, middle, and end.

You have to be unique, and different, and shine in your own way.

—Lady Gaga

b. For your own writing project, select quotations and then vary your tag placements: beginning, middle, and end.

→ PUNCTUATING QUOTATIONS

Following are rules for quotation marks and examples of how they interact with other punctuation.

1. **A comma follows a partial-sentence introduction to a quotation.**

Hamlet ponders, "To be, or not to be?"

2. **A colon follows a complete-sentence introduction to a quotation.**

Hamlet poses an existential question: "To be, or not to be?"

3. **A comma or period goes inside the final quotation mark, unless a parenthetical reference follows it.**

"I was a veteran," Michael Jackson said, "before I was a teenager."

"I was a veteran, before I was a teenager" (Jackson).

4. **A period is the only kind of "end punctuation" following a parenthetical reference.**

The novel *A Tale of Two Cities* begins, "It was the best of times. It was the worst of times" (Dickens 1).

5. **Exclamation marks or question marks remain with the quotation, even if a final period comes after a parenthetical reference.**

"Families, I hate you!" (Gide 38).

6. **A question mark or exclamation mark is placed according to its relation to the quotation.**

Nixon proclaimed, "I am not a crook!"

Did Nixon proclaim, "I am not a crook!"?

7. **A semicolon or a colon goes outside the final quotation mark.**

Before *Star Wars* premiered, George Lucas thought it was "too wacky for the general public": to his surprise, it resulted in a multi-billion dollar business empire.

8. **Two square brackets indicate additions or alterations.**

► Use brackets to add a comment or correction: Sarah Palin tweeted, "Ground Zero Mosque supporters: doesn't it stab you in the heart, as it does ours throughout the heartland? Peaceful Muslims, pls refudiate [*sic*]." (Palin accidentally coined a new word by merging *refute* and *repudiate*.)

► Use brackets to show changes such as capitalizing a lowercase letter in the original quotation: "[C]ome on up and see me sometime," West suggested.

► Do not use brackets to indicate changing a period to a comma at the end of a quotation:

ORIGINAL

"It ain't over 'til it's over."

CHANGED

"It ain't over 'til it's over," said Yogi Berra.

9. **An ellipsis indicates a deletion.**

► Type three periods to create an ellipsis:

► "I have a dream that... this nation will rise up and live out the true meaning of its creed."

► To show a deletion at the end of a quoted sentence, place the ellipsis (three periods) at the end of the sentence followed by the final period followed by quotation marks:

(continued)

King proclaimed, "I have a dream that one day this nation will rise up...."

10. **An ellipsis is not necessary for a deletion at the beginning of a quotation, but bracket a change in capitalization.**

"[A]n A-minus is a bad grade" to a tiger mom (Chua 5).

11. **A pair of single quotation marks is placed inside a pair of double quotation marks to show a quotation within a quotation.**

"Yogi Berra-isms include 'It ain't over 'til it's over.'"

12. **A block quotation uses indentation to replace a pair of quotation marks.**

  ▶ MLA: Use block quotations when the quotation is more than four lines of prose or three lines of verse. Indent the entire blocked quotation one inch from the left margin only, not from the right.

▶ APA: Use block quotations when the quotation is more than forty words. Indent five spaces or one return.

▶ Place parenthetical references after the block quotation's end punctuation.

The energy, the faith, the devotion which we bring to this endeavor will light our country.... And so, my fellow Americans: ask not what your country can do for you; ask what you can do for your country. My fellow citizens of the world: ask not what America will do for you, but what together we can do for the freedom of man.

(Kennedy)

Change a Quotation: Add, Delete, Alter Quotation marks make a serious (and sometimes legal) promise to the reader: "Everything inside these boundaries are exactly the way the original was written or spoken." However, under certain circumstances you may change a quotation by (1) adding necessary information, (2) deleting unneeded parts, or (3) altering grammatical or mechanical elements. Specialized punctuation marks are used to signal these changes—a pair of square brackets [ ] for each addition and an ellipsis . . . for each deletion.

Add to a Quotation Sometimes quotations need additional material to make them function smoothly in your text. You can add material if you enclose it in square brackets. Brackets create a zone within a quotation where you momentarily suspend the obligation to quote verbatim. Using brackets, you can include a number of your own additions to a quotation:

▶ **Changes in the original forms of the words:** To blend or integrate a quotation with your own writing, you may need to change the capitalization of an initial letter, the tense or number of a verb, the person or number of a pronoun, or other features.

  ▶ **Original:** "The Chinese mother believes that: schoolwork always comes first; an A-minus is a bad grade; your children must be two years ahead of their classmates in math..." (Chua 5).

  ▶ **Changed:** "[A]n A-minus is a bad grade" to a tiger mom (Chua 5).

► **Clarifications:** Because quotations often are taken out of context, you may need to add words to clarify a name, a pronoun reference, or an event.
"Kate [Middleton] married Prince William on April 29 [2011]."

► **Explanations:** Sometimes you may highlight (underscore, italicize, bold) a portion of the quotation to emphasize something. Brackets allow you to explain that you added the highlighting, using phrases such as "emphasis mine" or "italics added."
"Ask *not* [emphasis mine] what your country can do for you."

► **Corrections:** A quotation may contain a factual error that you can correct if it doesn't substantially change the meaning of the quotation.
"Easter is calculated by the 1528 [1582] Gregorian calendar."

► **Disclaimers:** A misspelling or error in typing, grammar, or fact could create confusion about whether you or the source is the origin of the error. Writers traditionally bracket and italicize the Latin word *sic* (which means "thus" or "as such") to indicate that the error comes from the original source.
'The sign painter wrote, "I learned to spell in shcool [*sic*]."'

AP Photo/News & Record, Joseph Rodriguez

When you quote a misspelled word such as "shcool" you can use [sic] to inform the reader that the misspelling was in the original source.

PRACTICE 8.3   Add to a Quotation

a. For the following quotation, use brackets to add some information (such as converting British pounds to $322 million and clarifying that "it" refers to "plagiarism").

It is a £200 million industry that has grown up over the last few years supplying essays to students at all levels on any subject imaginable.*

—William Murray, "The Plagiarism Phenomenon"

b. For your own writing project, select quotations and then add words to integrate them into your own sentences. Use brackets, as needed.

Delete from a quotation. If you can remove unneeded information from a quotation without distorting the meaning, the result will be clearer and more concise. To indicate a deletion, insert an ellipsis where the deletion occurred. Make an ellipsis by typing three periods in a row (...).

Although an ellipsis technically is an addition to a quotation, MLA style does not require it to be enclosed in square brackets. However, MLA does recommend using square brackets around your own inserted ellipsis dots in the rare situation where you're quoting a passage that itself contains an ellipsis. For example, in the following quotation from *To Kill a Mockingbird*, the two unbracketed ellipses were written by author Harper Lee to represent speech pauses; the bracketed ellipsis shows where the student writer deleted a part of Scout's speech.

> Scout seems unaware that she had softened the hearts of the lynch mob: "Well, Atticus, I was just sayin' to Mr. Cunningham that entailments are bad an' all, but [...] it takes a long time sometimes ... that you all'd ride it out together..." (Lee 154).

Several other rules guide your use of ellipses. Which rules apply depends on (1) where the deletions occur within a sentence and (2) how the ellipsis interacts with other punctuation marks.

► **A deletion at the beginning of a sentence:** An ellipsis is not required when the deletion occurs at the beginning of a sentence, as long as the remainder of the quotation preserves the source's meaning. When the introductory deletion causes a sentence to begin with a lowercase letter, use brackets to insert a capital letter.

---

*William Murray, "The Plagiarism Phenomenon." From E.learning Age, October 1 2006. Reprinted by permission of the author.

ORIGINAL

"I have a dream that one day this nation will rise up and live out the true meaning of its creed."

CHANGED

"[T]his nation will rise up and live out the true meaning of its creed."

▶ **A deletion within a quoted sentence:** Use the standard ellipsis with a space before and after each ellipsis point.

"I have a dream that . . . this nation will rise up and live out the true meaning of its creed."

Martin Luther King, Jr.'s, speeches and writings are frequently quoted.

▶ **A deletion at the end of a quoted sentence ending with a period:**
Placement of the final period depends on whether a parenthetical reference concludes your sentence.

> *Without a parenthetical reference:* When your sentence ends with an ellipsis, the period goes after the last word in the sentence.

> King proclaimed, "I have a dream that one day this nation will rise up...."

> *With a parenthetical reference:* When your sentence ends with a parenthetical reference, use an ellipsis after the last word of the quotation, and then close the quotation. Place the period after the parenthetical reference.

> "I have a dream that one day this nation will rise up..." (King).

PRACTICE 8.4   Delete from a Quotation

a. For the following quotation, use ellipsis marks to delete unneeded words (such as the middle section).

If companies are hiring people who are fundamentally not honest, but have rationalized their dishonesty and they're cheating, then companies are going to be dealing with fraud.
—Stephen Cover, *The Speed of Trust*

b. For your own writing project, select quotations and then delete unneeded words. Use ellipsis marks as needed.

Alter grammatical or mechanical elements in a quotation. When part of a quotation is blended grammatically with part of your sentence, sometimes the forms of some words need to be changed.

You can change the forms of function words. In the following example, the verb tense changes from present to past:

ORIGINAL

"If you are lucky enough to live in Paris as a young man, then wherever you go for the rest of your life it stays with you, for Paris is a moveable feast" (Hemingway).

ALTERED

Hemingway believed that Paris was a "moveable feast" and that "wherever you [went] for the rest of your life, it [would stay] with you."

Under certain circumstances, you can make changes in punctuation without bracketing the change. For example, you may change a period to a comma at the end of a quotation.

ORIGINAL

Sometimes a cigar is only a cigar.

ALTERED

"Sometimes a cigar is only a cigar," admitted Freud.

You can change double quotation marks to single quotation marks for a quotation within a quotation.

ORIGINAL

What does she mean by "glom"?

ALTERED

"What does she mean by 'glom'?"

PRACTICE 8.5   Change a Quotation: Add, Delete, Alter

a. Use brackets and ellipsis marks to change the following quotation, doing all of the following:
   1. Delete some information (such as "The fact is")
   2. Add some information (such as "Barack Obama" after "he")
   3. Alter the grammar and/or mechanics so the two quoted sentences become one sentence, and
   4. Add your tag (neutral or interpretive).

   Why doesn't he show his birth certificate? The fact is, if he wasn't born in this country, he shouldn't be the president of the United States.

   —Donald Trump, businessman and political hopeful

b. For your own writing project, select quotations and then change them. Use ellipsis marks or brackets, as needed.

> **→ INCLUSIONS FOR BRACKETS**
>
> You can add anything to a quotation that you think is necessary. Good manners suggest that you not embarrass your source by calling excess attention to errors. Also, you should not overuse the brackets: opt for paraphrasing when many changes are needed.
>
> Below are words and phrases typically placed in brackets.
> ► Error noted but not corrected: "shcool [*sic*]..."
> ► Error corrected: "shcool [school]..."
> ► Error replaced: "[school]..."
> ► Altered mechanics: "[A]sk what you..."
> ► Added formatting: "To be *or* [italics mine]..."
> ► Clarification: "they [plagiarists]..."
> ► Censorship: "I'm so [expletive] sorry..."

PARAPHRASING

Paraphrasing is expressing someone else's ideas not merely in your own words but in your own style—that is, using your own word choice, sentence structure, and organization of ideas.

Why Paraphrase?

Use paraphrasing to make yourself the main speaker, to clarify the source, to add zest to the original, or to extract key points without the problem of excessive ellipses.

Make Yourself the Main Speaker Your readers primarily want to read your words—to "hear" what you have to say, even when you are using the ideas of others.

Clarify When the Original Source Is Difficult to Understand
Clarification may be necessary to explain difficult concepts or terminology, antiquated language, or unusual phrasing.

Add Stylistic Zest When the Original Source Is Worded Blandly You probably wouldn't paraphrase famous quotations, such as Kennedy's "Ask not what your country can do for you; ask what you can do for your country." In many other communications, however, it is the meaning—not the means of expression—that is memorable.

→ THE PARAPHRASING PROCESS

Plan Read, annotate, and make choices.

▶ **Read critically and annotate.** Identify the major claim and the important supporting points.

▶ **Make choices.** Determine how much of the source you wish to delete, to quote, to paraphrase, or to summarize. For a paraphrase, list synonyms for keywords and phrases. List major ideas to be expressed in the paraphrase. If sequence is important, organize the ideas by sequence. If not, consider presenting the ideas in an order that differs from the original.

Draft Write in your own style: re-word, re-sentence, and re-paragraph.

▶ **Avoid looking at the original.** If you work from memory and notes, you'll be less likely to mimic the original.

▶ **Don't editorialize.** Be as objective as possible. A paraphrase is not a review: Refrain from evaluating the quality of the information or from reacting personally. Don't distort the meaning of the original.

▶ **Integrate.** Connect the paraphrase to your text with an introductory lead-in.

Revise Cross-reference with the original source.

▶ Are the wordings, sentence structures, and organization **distinctly** your own?

▶ Is the length about the same as the original? (This is a matter of practicality—it will usually take approximately the same length to convey the same meaning.)

▶ Is the original meaning complete and undistorted?

▶ Did you give credit to your source?

The original source may contain additional points that are not relevant to your discussion. Irrelevant content in a quotation can mislead or confuse a reader. Of course, you can delete unwanted materials from a direct quotation, but overuse of ellipsis marks can render a passage difficult to read.

How to Paraphrase

To paraphrase correctly, be true to the source's meaning, state the meaning in your own style, suspend the use of quotation marks, and give credit to the source. An effective paraphrase is true to the original and in your own style, without quotation marks and with due credit to the original source.

Guidelines for Paraphrasing

Be True to the Original Don't add facts, opinions, or interpretations unless you are clear that these are your own. The length of the paraphrase usually is similar to the original, unless you have also summarized some parts and/or deleted unnecessary information.

Use Your Own Style The wording is your own, except for words that cannot be changed without losing the original meaning. The sentence structure is your own. When paraphrasing paragraphs, the sequence of ideas is your own.

Omit the Quotation Marks Use quotation marks only with direct quotations—when you have not changed the original source at all. Of course, you'll place quotation marks around any unchanged portions of the original that you might include in the paraphrase.

Give Credit Give credit to your source as a tag or as a parenthetical reference following MLA, APA, or other style guidelines. Giving credit is also known as attributing credit, or attribution.

Methods for Paraphrasing Paraphrasing shares some techniques with quoting: be honest, be concise, give credit. However, paraphrasing has unique methods of its own. Three major techniques are **re-wording, re-sentencing**, and **re-paragraphing**. Employing any one of them in isolation may still result in plagiarism, but using them together will help ensure the writing style is your own.

- ▶ Re-word: Use synonyms for words or phrases.
- ▶ Re-sentence: Use different sentence patterns.
- ▶ Re-paragraph: Use a different paragraph organization.

Re-word: Replace words or phrases with synonyms.

- ▶ You don't have to change all the words, but your goal is to re-state the passage in your own words.
- ▶ If an important word has no equivalent, keep the original word.
- ▶ If the original passage contains an important phrase that is the "intellectual property" of the writer, you can quote that phrase. For example, Stephen Colbert invented the word "truthiness" so you would quote that word if you paraphrased something from Colbert.

Original: "And most hip-hop, whatever its 'message,' is delivered in a cocky, confrontational cadence" (McWhorter).

Re-worded: According to McWhorter, the majority of rap, regardless of its meaning, is performed in a self-confident, combative style.

Re-sentence Change sentence patterns.

- ▶ Change parts of speech: Turn a noun into a verb or vice versa: this usually forces a significant change in sentence structure.
- ▶ Change the order the information emerges in the sentence, as in sentence inversion.
- ▶ Change the modification: adjectives, adverbs, various phrases can be added, subtracted, or moved around.

Original: "The 'in your face' element is as essential to the genre as vibrato to opera, reinforced as rappers press their faces close to the camera lens in videos, throwing their arms about in poses suggesting imminent battle" (McWhorter).

Re-sentenced, with new subject and predicate that cause other changes:
McWhorter describes the performance as aggressive yet as basic to the art form as brush strokes are to painting, with hip-hoppers—thrusting their faces toward the lens of the camera—waving their arms and striking poses like battling warriors.

Re-paragraph   Re-arrange the content of multi-sentence paraphrases.

► Re-locate parts of paraphrased sentences by placing them earlier or later in the paragraph.

► Combine two or more sentences into one sentence.

► Split a long sentence into two or more sentences.

Original

And most hip-hop, whatever its "message," is delivered in a cocky, confrontational cadence. The "in your face" element is as essential to the genre as vibrato to opera, reinforced as rappers press their faces close to the camera lens in videos, throwing their arms about in poses suggesting imminent battle. The smug tone expresses a sense that hip-hop is sounding a wake-up call, from below, to a white America too benighted to listen. I can count on hearing about a "hip-hop revolution" from at least one questioner at every talk I give these days.

—Dr. John McWhorter, linguist, and author of "Mean Street Theater"

Re-paragraphed (with re-ordered details and sentence combining):
Professor John McWhorter, a linguist who speaks on African-American culture, notes that out-of-touch Caucasians are alarmed by the aggression they see in hip-hop: violent posturing and angry facial expressions backed by a driving rhythm. At presentations given by McWhorter, the concerned citizens invariably ask him if a revolution is on the way.

PRACTICE 8.6   Paraphrase a Sentence: Re-Word and Re-Sentence

a. Paraphrase the following sentence: re-word, re-sentence, and tag.

"Reducing plastics, consuming less energy, walking more, traveling more by bus and train, and finding other ways to create value are some steps toward sustainability" (Gupta 18).

b. For your own writing project, select a sentence to paraphrase: re-word, re-sentence, and tag.

PRACTICE 8.7   Evaluate Paraphrased Sentences

For each of the following quotation-paraphrase pairs, evaluate the quality. Has the original meaning been preserved? Is the style of the paraphrase different enough? Which techniques were used to change the style?

1. **ORIGINAL:** "Nearly four million Americans are tipping the scales at more than 300 pounds" (Koontz).

   PARAPHRASE: Americans today are more overweight than ever: there are about four million people who weigh more than 300 pounds (Koontz).

2. **ORIGINAL:** "A study in *Obesity Research* found that newlyweds gain an average of six to eight pounds in the first two years of marriage" (Koontz).

   PARAPHRASE: According to Koontz, research indicates that typical newlyweds gain six to eight pounds within two years.

3. **ORIGINAL:** "At the heart of this obesity epidemic is a debate over whether obesity is a biological 'disease'" (Koontz).

   PARAPHRASE: The obesity problem has people arguing about whether it should be called a disease (Koontz).

4. **ORIGINAL:** "The causes of epilepsy are varied, and one seizure alone doth not an epileptic make" (Koontz).

   PARAPHRASE: Epilepsy has varied causes, and one seizure does not make an epileptic (Koontz).

5. **ORIGINAL:** "Both sunlight and tanning beds increase the risk of skin cancer" (Koontz).

   PARAPHRASE: Tanning beds and sunlight pose a threat to skin health by increasing a person's chances of getting skin cancer (Koontz).

PRACTICE 8.8   Paraphrase a Paragraph: Re-Word, Re-Sentence, and Re-Paragraph

a. Paraphrase the following passage: re-word, re-sentence, and re-paragraph.

   "One of the best innovations of mankind—the car—is anti-green in every way possible. Just imagine if we had not innovated the car, how much healthier our environment would be. We are talking about sustainability after killing the environment. It is like praying for life after the patient is dead" (Gupta 18).*

   —Praveen Gupta, *Manufacturing Excellence*

b. For your own writing project, select a multi-sentence passage to paraphrase: re-word, re-sentence, and re-paragraph.

---

*Manufacturing Excellence: Can Sustainability be Sustained? by Praveen Gupta, October 28, 2009, *Quality Magazine*. Copyright © 2009, BNP Media. Reprinted by permission of BNP Media.

SUMMARIZING

A summary is a reduction of a longer text into a condensed form. Also know as a précis, brief, or abstract, and figuratively described as "the bottom line," it is shorter than the original text, presenting only the essential information. A summary may be written as a single sentence, as a single paragraph, or in a much longer form, depending on the length of the original and on how much information you wish to convey.

Why Summarize?

You will encounter summaries in virtually every field that uses information. Although they lack the elaboration found in full-text documents, they are valued for their conciseness.

▶ Article databases (such as ABI Inform, Biological Abstracts, and hundreds of others) offer summaries (abstracts) to full-text articles so that researchers can preview longer works, deciding whether the longer readings will be useful before accessing the original versions.

▶ To cope with information overload, researchers sometimes read summaries almost exclusively, thereby gleaning the main ideas of the original writings.

"My platform can be summarized in a single word: Leadership!"

A summary is a brief statement of a longer text. (Robert Mankoff/all rights reserved http://www.thecartoonbank.com)

> **THE SUMMARIZING PROCESS**

Plan

▶ **Read critically and annotate.** Identify the major claim and the important supporting points. As you read, watch for topic sentences—the author may have already identified important points for you.

▶ **Make choices.** Decide which information to present fully, which to condense, and which to omit.

Draft Write in your own style.

▶ **Don't editorialize.** Be as objective as possible. A summary is not a review, so refrain from evaluating the quality of the information or reacting personally. Don't distort the meaning of the original.

▶ **Integrate.** Connect the quotation to your text with an introductory lead-in.

Revise Check your summary by cross-referencing it with the original source.

▶ Are the wordings, sentence structures, and organization **distinctly your** own?

▶ Is the length shorter than the original?

▶ Is the original meaning complete and undistorted?

▶ Did you give credit to your source?

▶ Writers present summaries in their writings (1) to be concise and (2) to focus on the relevant points of a source without presenting irrelevant points. If your purpose in a summary is to make a point and not to produce an abstract of a source, you can pick and choose what you will include.

How to Summarize

Summarizing shares some techniques with quoting and paraphrasing: be honest and give credit. However, summarizing has techniques of its own: Present main ideas, condense major support, and omit minor support.

▶ **Present Main Ideas.** Present major claims in enough detail that the information is clear.

▶ **Condense Major Support.** Reduce some major supporting evidence and explanations from paragraphs to sentences or from sentences to phrases.

▶ **Omit Minor Support.** Disregard most of the supporting evidence and explanations.

Sometimes when you summarize, your major goal is to provide a brief yet balanced view of an entire text. An annotated bibliography and an abstract of a journal article, for example, are intended to be read by wide audiences and must be written so that anyone can get an overview. When you summarize to make an argument, however, you can target what you present—as long as you don't distort the meaning of the original text.

You'll have to decide which points you wish to make and how much depth to give those ideas. Sometimes you can summarize a huge amount of information in a few words. Darwin's *The Origin of the Species,* for example, can be reduced to "all organisms change over time through a combination of variation and adaptation"; a summary that brief may be adequate to make a point in an argument about intelligent design. At other times, however, you may need to provide more information about the original source.

Following is an excerpt from an argument made by Dr. Gregory Stock on the topic of human longevity. It will help illustrate how to summarize.

> We've developed many ways of trying to accept not only these ravages, but death itself. The first is to ignore descent: We can simply pretend it isn't happening. This works when we're young, but becomes ever less effective as the years march by and our strength seeps from us. The second way is to deny death: We can assert that the soul is eternal, that our memory will live on, that we are young at heart, that we are not older but better. A third way is to battle the process like Ponce de Leon did slogging through Florida, Dorian Gray, or those engaged in anti-aging research because, in the backs of their minds, they hope to extend their own future. Or we can accept this descent as sad but inevitable, and say that it's natural and can't be avoided, or even tell ourselves that it's the best thing and claim, like Leon Kass, the chair of the President's Bioethics Advisory Commission, that death gives meaning.*
>
> —Dr. Gregory Stock

To summarize Dr. Stock's passage, you must decide what to present fully, what to condense, and what to omit.

▶ **Present main ideas:** The key point seems to be contained in the first sentence: "We've developed many ways of trying to accept not only these ravages, but death itself." It may be difficult to shorten this statement.

▶ **Condense major support:** Dr. Stock has signaled the major supporting points with transitions: *first, second, third, or.* The main point of each sentence could be shortened at all these points and placed in a single sentence.

▶ **Omit minor support:** Specific examples—references to Ponce de Leon or Leon Kass—probably can be left out of the summary.

*Debates: Point-Counterpoint: Would Doubling the Human Life Span Be a Net Positive or Negative for Us Either as Individuals or as a Society? Gregory Stock, Daniel Callahan, *Journals of Gerontology - Series A: Biological Sciences and Medical Sciences,* Oxford University Press June 1, 2004. Copyright © 2004, Oxford University Press. Reprinted by permission

PRACTICE 8.9　Summarize a Paragraph

a.　Write a thirty-five-word summary of the following paragraph, an excerpt from "Cyberbullying: Identification, Prevention, and Response" by Sameer Hinduja, Ph.D., and Justin W. Patchin, Ph.D., of the Cyberbullying Prevention Center.

There are many detrimental outcomes associated with cyberbullying that reach into the real world. First, many targets of cyberbullying report feeling depressed, sad, angry, and frustrated. As one teenager stated: "It makes me hurt both physically and mentally. It scares me and takes away all my confidence. It makes me feel sick and worthless." Victims who experience cyberbullying also reveal that are were afraid or embarrassed to go to school. In addition, research has revealed a link between cyberbullying and low self-esteem, family problems, academic problems, school violence, and delinquent behavior. Finally, cyberbullied youth also report having suicidal thoughts, and there have been a number of examples in the United States where youth who were victimized ended up taking their own lives.

b.　For your own writing project, locate a passage and then summarize it.

→ SYNTHESIS VS. PLAGIARISM

This chapter opened with an epigraph that quoted these words from Wilson Mizner, a screenwriter: "Copy from one, it's plagiarism; copy from two, it's research." In what ways might Mizner be correct?

If you have only one source, you are limited not only in the depth and breadth of information, but also in the way the information is expressed. Multiple sources let you know the range of ideas and the range of expressions.

Consider, for example, a definition. A word's meaning is essentially "common knowledge" and "public domain," but the wording of the definition is "intellectual property." So, if you look up the definition of a word such as plagiarism from only one dictionary, you may be obliged to quote that dictionary:

▶ Encarta: Plagiarism is "stealing somebody's work or idea: the process of copying another person's idea or written work and claiming it as original."

However, if you check other dictionaries, your personal knowledge of the word grows:

▶ Dictionary.com: Plagiarism is "the unauthorized use or close imitation of *the* language and thoughts of another author and the representation of them as one's own original work."

As you research multiple sources, the range and depth of information becomes clear to you. For example, the differences between Encarta's and Dictionary.com's definitions of plagiarism are easy to detect: Encarta uses "stealing" and "copying" to describe the action, while Dictionary.com uses "unauthorized use" and "close imitation." Dictionary.com uses the words "language and thoughts" to represent the object involved, while Encarta uses "idea or written work."

So, is Wilson Mizner correct? Could you synthesize these two sources to coin your own definition of plagiarism…without plagiarizing?

Below is a 39-word summary of Stock's 166-word passage:

According to Dr. Gregory Stock, humankind copes with aging and death in several ways: denial of physical effects, the consolation of eternal afterlife, the development and use of anti-aging treatments, and philosophical resignation to the natural scheme of life.

SYNTHESIZING

Synthesis is the use of two or more sources to make a point. As you synthesize, you can use any or all of the techniques we've practiced in this chapter: quoting, paraphrasing, and summarizing. The key is not to feature a single source in isolation but rather to reveal similarities and differences across multiple sources.

Why Synthesize?

In a research paper, you synthesize whenever you use more than one source for one purpose. Derived from a Greek prefix word meaning "put together," synthesis is exactly that: you put together the pieces of others' works into a new whole that serves your argument.

Synthesis strengthens your claims, support, and authority.

▶ Stronger authority: When you cite one expert, your reader begins to trust that your claim in valid, that you are not alone in your opinion. When you cite several experts or sources, trust becomes stronger because you are seeking a consensus among experts. More research also makes you more of an expert, less of a novice.

→ THE SYNTHESIZING PROCESS

Plan Read, annotate, and make choices.

▶ **Read critically and annotate.** Identify the similar or contrasting claims and their supporting evidence. Make margin notes about the similarities and differences between them as well as your response to them.

▶ **Make choices.** Determine how much of each source you wish to delete, to quote, to paraphrase, or to summarize. If sequence is important, organize the ideas by sequence.

Draft

▶ Use juxtaposition and transitions to bring the sources together.

▶ Provide explanations as needed.

Revise Cross-reference with the original sources.

▶ Are the original meanings clear?

▶ Is the relationship among the sources clear?

▶ Did you give credit when the information is the intellectual properties of others?

► Better claims and support: Using multiple sources, you are better equipped to make valid claims supported by appropriate evidence. Your sources may reveal areas where people agree or disagree, areas that are worthy of argument. You can use synthesis to reveal consensus or variety.

How to Synthesize

► **Through research, locate materials that focus on a specific part of an issue.**

► **Look for agreements and disagreements:** Multiple sources can reveal areas of consensus or opposition.
  ► *Agreement:* If your research reveals consensus, the result can be a "band wagon" effect: agreement among several sources can be stronger evidence than from a single source. Sometimes these make complementary rather than identical points.
  ► *Disagreement:* If your research reveals that one source supports a claim while another does not support it, your argument can examine the disagreement, weigh the contrasting evidence, and reach a conclusion. Sometimes these are alternative rather than opposite points.

► **Create sentences and paragraphs that bring the materials together.**
  ► Juxtapose (put close together) the materials. You can discuss them in the same sentence, adjacent sentences, or adjacent paragraphs.
  ► Use transitions and explanations to highlight the points of agreement or disagreement.

Single-sentence example of synthesis of several poems, taken from a student's literary argument:

Poets disagree on how selfless love should be: Emerson exhorts, "Give all to love: Obey thy heart"; Yeats cautions, "O never give the heart outright"; and Housman forbids, "Give not your heart away."

Paragraph example of synthesis of several sources, excerpted from a student's paper on plagiarism:

There are many causes of plagiarism. One reason is the pressure on students to achieve, varying from maintaining a high GPA in high school to get into a good college to keeping up grades while in college to hold on to scholarships (Durkin). A second reason is the competitive nature of grading: a student must be not just acceptable but better than others (Fanning 8). Plagiarism also occurs because it is socially acceptable: many students do not consider it to be cheating because all their friends are doing it. In addition, cheaters are convinced that they are not going to get caught (Gulli, Köhler, and Patriquin 34); 95 percent of high school students who cheated were never found out (Gomez 42).

PRACTICE 8.10   Synthesize Sources that Agree

a. Synthesize the following to showcase their points of agreement.
    "We can accept as a given, that the formal education system is now making great strides in educating students about the internet and about good research practice, as well as rewarding students for using the internet to find good quality content" (Murray 23).*

    —William Murray, "The Plagiarism Phenomemon"

    "While 10 per cent of U.S. students surveyed in 1999 confessed to yanking whole passages from the Web to write their papers, almost 40 per cent admitted to the practice six years later, according to McCabe's research" (Gulli, Köhler, and Patriquin 32).

b. For your own writing project, locate two or more sources that are in agreement and then synthesize them.

PRACTICE 8.11   Synthesize Sources that Disagree

a. Synthesize the following to showcase their points of disagreement.
    "Cheating is the result of the desire to get ahead while taking shortcuts" (Eerkes, qtd. in Gulli, Köhler, and Patriquin 32).

    "Plagiarism is often unintentional, being the result of disorganisation, information overload, laziness, ignorance of citation rules or even fear of failure" (Yaccino 74).

b. For your own writing project, locate two or more sources that are in disagreement and then synthesize them.

Looking Back at Chapter 8

► Plagiarism is intellectual theft. It is the unauthorized use or imitation of someone's literary or artistic work.

► Research skills empower you to avoid plagiarism: quoting, paraphrasing, summarizing, and synthesizing.

---

*William Murray, "The Plagiarism Phenomenon." From E.learning Age, October 1 2006. Reprinted by permission of the author.

▶ A quotation is an exact repetition of words written or spoken by someone else, usually enclosed by a pair of quotation marks.

▶ Quotations perform important functions in argumentative writing: They appeal to authority, provide evidence, reveal issues, capture interest, dramatize, and add eloquence.

▶ To quote, be honest, be concise, give credit, tag, and edit without distorting the meaning of the original.

▶ Paraphrasing is expressing someone else's ideas not merely in your own words but in your own style—that is, using your own word choice, sentence structure, and organization of ideas.

▶ Use paraphrasing to make yourself the main speaker, to clarify the source, to add zest to the original, or to extract key points without the problem of excessive ellipses.

▶ To paraphrase, re-word, re-sentence, and re-paragraph as needed.

▶ A summary is a reduction of a longer text into a condensed form.

▶ To summarize, present main ideas, condense major support, and **o**mit minor support.

▶ Synthesis is the use of two or more sources to make a point.

▶ To synthesize, locate related materials, look for agreements and disagreements, and write passages that bring the materials together.

Suggestions for Writing

▶ Revise the quotations in one of your essays.

   1. Improve your integration and explanations.

   2. Change some quotations into paraphrases or summaries.

▶ Paraphrase something you have read; include it in an essay you are writing.

▶ Write a summary for an article you have researched; include it in an essay you are writing.

▶ Write a synthesis essay that focuses on agreements and disagreements on an issue.

9

Arguing Visually

Corbis

T he proverb "A picture is worth a thousand words" may not be mathematically accurate, but its meaning is undeniable. A visual image can convey a sizable amount of information. Visuals have always been valued in communication, but within the past generation, technology has made it possible for nonprofessionals to include images in their texts. Current technology—including computers, scanners, e-mail, the Web, facsimile machines, and software for generating images and processing photographs—can allow you to combine your words with visual images to make more powerful arguments.

Images that can be used to supplement a text may include photographs, drawings, charts, and graphs. In some cases—such as in advertisements—text

Physicians Against Land Mines
Member of the International Campaign to Ban Land Mines

www.banmines.org

This is a PSA—a public service announcement—that uses its visual power to make an argumentative point. What claim is this composition trying to make? How do the *words, shapes, colors*, and *images* work together to drive the point home? (Copyright 1998–2003 by Center for International Rehabilitation. All Rights Reserved.)

may be combined with pictures to create an argument complete with a claim, supporting evidence (provided through both words and images), and sometimes even a hint of refutation. At other times, an image such as a carefully composed photograph or a statistical graph can imply an argument without fully articulating a claim or presenting evidence. In this case, the claim can usually be figured out and the evidence is often the subject matter of the image itself. Because images may suggest various elements of argumentation rather than state them directly, understanding visual arguments requires taking a fresh approach to the material. In other words, you have to "read" visual arguments differently. In addition to looking for claims, support, and refutation, you should consider the effect that the overall design of the image has on the reader.

ELEMENTS OF DESIGN

Document design in professional writing can be very complex. Designers consider not only the interaction of text, pictures, and color schemes, but the "viewing order" on a page, the proximity of different items on the same page, enclosure of text and images in boxes, and alignment of page elements, just to name a few common features. For our purposes, however, we will focus primarily on four basic concepts: *text*, *image*, *color*, and *overall design*.

Text

In conventional written texts like those your produce with a word processor, words provide most of the raw material for building arguments. You may support an argument with a photograph, bar chart, or political cartoon, but on the whole you will argue through words. In other cases—for example, on Web sites or in print advertisements—the textual part of the argument is brief and takes on a graphical dimension. A bit of text can be enclosed in a box, put to one side of the main text in a different color, and the reader understands that this material is supplemental to the text it sits next to. (This is the principle of *proximity*.) Text can become an image in its own right by using different fonts, sizes, margins, and color schemes. The text that makes up Emina's leg is both a written message and a phantom limb that emphasizes the fact that the leg is missing. Moreover, when the text is very concise (as in a PowerPoint presentation), it becomes extremely important for it to be well written, clear in purpose, and supported by images or, in the case of the Internet, linked to other pages where more supporting information can be found.

Elements of Text You can change the visual impression that a text makes on a reader by changing the style—that is, the appearance—of the letters and symbols that make up a particular argument. Particular textual styles are grouped into categories called typefaces. The appearance of a typeface can vary in terms of its font size, style, color, emphasis, and artistic effects.

Size A typeface is called a *font* when it is reproduced in a particular size. The smaller the number of the font, the smaller the size of the text. One of the most common fonts used in word-processed documents is 12-point Times New Roman. Although fonts as small as 8 points are sometimes used, typefaces smaller than 12 points can cause eyestrain for some people and are best avoided.

Style Typeface styles are classified into two broad categories: serif and sans serif. Serif typefaces feature flattened "tails" on most of the letters. These tails are especially prevalent on capital letters. The Times New Roman typeface, which is a default setting on many word processors, is a serif font. Another commonly used font, Arial, is a sans serif font. Sans serif typefaces are "plain" in the sense that they do not feature flattened tails.

Special styles In addition to the general categories of serif and sans serif, a number of typefaces are notable because they simulate handwriting, are particularly elaborate, or are especially artistic. For example, handwriting typefaces may simulate crude children's handwriting (Crayon), flowing calligraphy, or ordinary cursive script. Elaborate type styles may consist of elegant letters that, although beautiful, can be difficult or irritating to read; these typefaces should be used sparingly. For example, fancy styles such as Edwardian Script are best reserved for special documents (e.g., wedding announcements) where elegant, flowing script is required. Reading long passages set in such a type style can be very difficult. Artistic styles—in which the forms of the letters are works of art in themselves—can be useful (if employed with caution) to create a desired impression.

PRACTICE 9.1	Emotions and Typefaces

What is your emotional reaction to each of the typefaces featured in the Artistic Typefaces sidebar? The statement, "War is not healthy for children or other living things," is the same in each example. How does the typeface influence your reaction to it?

Color Although we will consider color in more depth shortly, this typeface characteristic is worth mentioning briefly here. The color in which text is presented is part of the overall visual impression that you wish your argument to make. As such, it should be considered carefully. A conventional written argument should usually be presented in black in a standard

---

Typefaces

Examples of Serif Typefaces
Book Antiqua
Courier New
Bembo
Palatino Linotype
Times New Roman

Examples of Sans Serif Typefaces
Arial
Futura Book
Impact
Lucida Sans Unicode
Clearface Gothic

Artistic Typefaces

War is not healthy for children or other living things. (Dissonant)

War is not healthy for children or other living things. (Edwardian Script)

War is not healthy for children or other living things. (Woodcut)

War is not healthy for children or other living things. (Gigi)

War is not healthy for children or other living things. (Old English Text MT)

WAR IS NOT HEALTHY FOR CHILDREN OR OTHER LIVING THINGS. (STENCIL)

War is not healthy for children or other living things. (Crayon)

PRACTICE 9.2   Text as Image

Working individually or in groups, study this advertisement and then answer the questions below the advertisement.

WOMEN OF BRITAIN
**COME INTO
THE FACTORIES**
ASK AT ANY EMPLOYMENT EXCHANGE FOR ADVICE AND FULL DETAILS

© Lordprice Collection / Alamy

1. Where is your eye drawn when you first glance at the image? Where does your eye go next?

2. What audience does this poster target? What makes you think this?

3. Why does the audience look up at the figure? Why are her arms outstretched? Why do the planes overhead pass between her hands? What do you think she is offering to the audience?

4. How does the poster employ pathos—particularly the idea of female empowerment—to achieve its aim? What role do ethos and logos play in the ad?

5. Explain how text, image, color, and design work together to accomplish the poster's goal.

font such as Times New Roman 12. When text is employed as part of an image (or as a visual effect within a written text), its color should be selected for both ease of reading and desired effect. In most cases, the text should contrast sharply with the background (which is why black letters are usually printed on white paper). In addition, you should consider the difference in impact between various colors. Red is an "alarm" color, associated with stoplights, warning signs, and blood. Green is associated with "go" and also with growth, gardens, and nature in general. Purple is often thought of as rich and royal, whereas yellow and orange are associated with warmth.

PRACTICE 9.3   Images that Argue

Working individually or in groups, consider the following cartoon, which comments on rising gas prices, and then answer the following questions.

Arcadio Esquivel, Cagle Cartoons, La Prensa, Panama

1. What claim is being made here? How do you know?

2. What does the gas pump represent in this picture? Why do you think so?

3. This image makes an argument by analogy when it compares the gas pump to a robber. Is this comparison valid? Why or why not?

Images

In visual arguments, images work with text to persuade the audience. In some cases the image by itself can be the argument. Consider the photograph below taken in Appalachia in the 1930s. How does the photo by itself, and without a caption, make an argument about poverty or child neglect? More often, images, whether they are photographs, artwork, or graphs depicting data, often function rhetorically as a type of evidence to support the writer's claim. The types of images we will consider in this chapter include advertisements, photographs, artwork (including political cartoons), graphs (which often represent complex numerical data as pictures), and Web pages (which are organized visually).

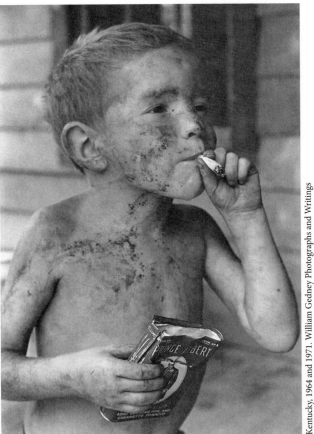

Kentucky, 1964 and 1971. William Gedney Photographs and Writings

Elements of Images In most arguments, visuals serve as a kind of evidence to help support a claim. Sometimes a claim may be part of the overall visual argument. In many ads, the text will provide (or imply) the claim and the artwork that accompanies it will serve as the evidence to support it. The ad below uses a compelling visual image to convince young people to think twice before taking Meth. The bloody rag on the girl's stomach suggests she has been a victim of a stabbing or other violent crime. This creates a disturbing image of the horrors of methamphetamine addiction that words alone could not convey. The *pathos* of this unsettling image underscores the *logos* present in the ad's text. The text and image work together to persuade the reader.

Using Images in Your Own Arguments When you use images in your arguments, it is important to think about the role the image plays in successfully making its case to the target audience. Images should not be used as mere decoration or dropped into the argument with the assumption that the reader will understand why they are there. Just as textual evidence should be integrated into the overall argument and discussed in order to validate the central claim, so should images be explained and discussed in the body of the text.

When you consider using images in your arguments, think carefully about the appropriateness of your selection. Follow the guidelines for using images to help you decide when, where, and how to place an image. When selecting images, you should consider first and foremost the rhetorical context of the document, and what role the image will play

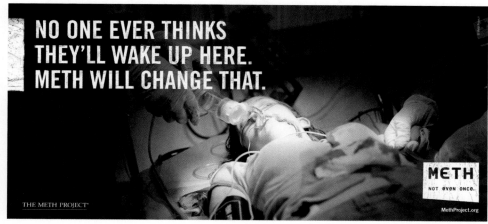

→ TIPS FOR EVALUATING IMAGES IN ARGUMENTS

When you evaluate an image that is used to support another argument (or even one that implies an argument of its own), let your eye explore the image for a moment before you try to analyze it. Normally, texts with strong visual features are read in a "Z" pattern, left to right, diagonally, then left to right again. Often the logo or message is placed in the lower right corner. However, the orientation of text and image can alter this pattern, so you should pay careful attention to how you work your way through a visual argument at first glance. A visual argument can also be linear (tracking from top to bottom) or circular or follow some other pattern. Consider the following when studying a visual argument:

► Where does your eye fall when you first observe the image? Where does it wander next? Where does it end up?

► Is the claim—what the advertisement is trying to get you to do—stated directly or implied? Is the visual argument "text heavy" or "text light," and what does this design decision contribute to the document's argumentative purpose? If text is not present, can you supply words to accompany the image? What sort of argument does the image imply?

► How does the style (overall design, the "look and feel") of the visual argument help persuade the audience? When considering overall design, think about how all of the elements—text, image, and color—work together. For example, the infamous Joe Camel cigarette ads used cartoons aimed at adults to communicate the overall "smoking is cool" message of their ads. What about a particular visual text appears to work well? What doesn't seem to work? Why do you think this?

► If the text is a part of a larger argument (such as an image on a Web page or a graph in a magazine article), how does it serve to support the overall argument? How does the writer integrate it into the larger argument? Does it complement the argument or distract from it?

► How does the image relate to other images included in the argument? (*Note:* Multiple images can support the text of a written argument, or several images could be presented together to imply an argument. Sometimes a series of paintings or a collection of sculptures might imply an argument in this way.)

► Is the image effective in its context (either within the supporting text or as part of another setting)? What are the strengths and weaknesses of the image?

► Does anything about the image work against the point it is trying to make? Is it inappropriate or offensive in some way? Why do you think so?

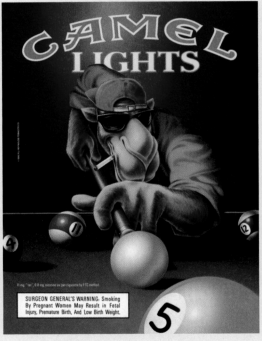

Image Courtesy of The Advertising Archives

in supporting your argument. Keep PASS (Purpose, Audience, Structure, and Style) in mind:

► How does the image support the document's persuasive purpose?

► How effectively does it help communicate that purpose to the target audience?

→ TIPS FOR USING IMAGES IN YOUR ARGUMENTS

Think about the following questions before you decide to add a cartoon, photograph, or other visual element to your argument:

▶ *What essential role will the image play in supporting my argument?* Add an image to an argument only if it supports what you have to say without distracting your audience from your primary purpose. Adding a carefully selected graph, for example, can make numerical data more viable for the reader by presenting it in a visual format.

▶ *How will I integrate it into the overall argument?* An image should not be dropped into a text unless it plays an essential role in the argument. A frequent mistake beginning writers make is to drop in a graph without bothering to explain what the data means and how the data validates what is being argued in the text. Always discuss the graph, photo, or illustration and explain how it supports your argument. Don't leave your reader to wonder about it. This will only weaken your argument.

▶ *How many images should I add?* Be selective. Treat images—and quotations—like hand grenades: Use them sparingly, and only when absolutely necessary. It is very easy to overpower an academic paper with too many images. One image every three pages or so should be more than sufficient. If you insert more, you probably aren't integrating them properly into your discussion. Some types of documents, such a brochures, wikis, or Web sites, rely more heavily on images than academic papers. You should follow the conventions of the genres for other types of text in selecting images, placing them, and determining the appropriate balance between text and image.

▶ *Where should I put the image?* Normally, an image will go close to the information with which it is associated. This is the rule of *proximity* mentioned earlier in this chapter. However, you should also consider the layout of the page—its overall balance—especially if multiple images appear on the same page. Positioning too much material on one side of the page or the other can make it seem lopsided. Consider the likely reading order when the image is added to the page. If you use two images on the same page, place one on the upper right and the second on the lower left. This will work well with the natural reading order ("Z") and will help balance the page.

▶ *How big should the image be?* First and foremost, don't let the image overpower the rest of the text. It should enhance what is being said, not distract the reader from your argument. Use your own judgment, realizing that the image should be big enough to be easily seen without eyestrain, but not so big that it takes over the page. Again, follow standard conventions for other document types by studying samples from other disciplines.

▶ *Should I select images of a particular style?* Sometimes drawings or cartoons provide the most effective support; at other times color photographs work best. You should avoid selecting images that clash when they appear together, especially if they are positioned on the same page. As a rule of thumb, avoid clip art. It will make your document look like the work of an amateur.

▶ *Do I cite my image or use a caption?* Cite your image in the bibliography (Works Cited in MLA style, References in APA style) just like any other source that you borrow from someone else. Captions are essential because they help identify the image and place it in the appropriate context. Be sure to integrate your image into the discussion. Don't count on the caption to do the work for you.

▶ *Do I need to obtain someone's permission before using the image?* If your text will be published on the Internet or in another public format, you need to obtain permission from the image's creator. If you are just using it for a class assignment, then you don't have to obtain permission.

▶ Where should it be placed in the overall structure of the argument, and how should it be integrated into the argument so that it is a functional part of the text and not merely decoration?

▶ How does it fit the style—what Web designers like to call the "look and feel" of the document—in a way that helps it communicate its purpose to the target audience?

It is just as inappropriate to add an out-of-place image to your document as it is to drop a quotation into your paper that does not support what you are trying to say. Likewise, the inclusion of too many images—even when they are carefully selected—can overpower your document and cause your reader to forget about your argument.

Visual Representations of Data   In academic papers, particularly in areas like engineering, mathematics, health care, and the social sciences, you may need to include breakdowns of statistical data in a fashion that is easy to digest at a glance. Visual representations of data generally come in two common forms: *tables* and *graphs*.

Tables are nongraphical layouts of figures in columns and rows that make it easy to see relationships between numerical information in a way that would be awkward or difficult to understand if it were only discussed in the text. Consider the table below, which comes from the government report *Are They Ready to Work?* The reader can quickly determine at a glance that the top three skills demanded by employers in three educational categories were related to reading and writing ability.

The data in this table would take many pages of text to discuss on their own, and they would not be as effective as they are when presented in table

---

A majority of employer respondents view *Reading Comprehension and English Language* as "very important" basic skills for job success for new workforce entrants at all education levels.

High School Graduates

Rank	Basic Knowledge/Skills	
1	Reading Comprehension	62.5%
2	English Language	61.8
3	Writing in English	49.4
4	Mathematics	30.4
5	Foreign Languages	11.0
6	Science	9.0
7	Government/Economics	3.5
8	History/Geography	2.1
9	Humanities/Arts	1.8

Basic knowledge/skills rank ordered by percent rating as "very important."
Number of respondents varied for each question, ranging from 336 to 361.

Two-Year College Graduates

Rank	Basic Knowledge/Skills	
1	Reading Comprehension	71.6%
2	English Language	70.6
3	Writing in English	64.9
4	Mathematics	44.0
5	Science	21.2
6	Foreign Languages	14.1
7	Government/Economics	6.7
8	Humanities/Arts	4.4
9	History/Geography	3.6

Basic knowledge/skills rank ordered by percent rating as "very important."
Number of respondents varied for each question, ranging from 334 to 360.

Four-Year College Graduates

Rank	Basic Knowledge/Skills	
1	Writing in English	89.7%
2	English Language	88.0
3	Reading Comprehension	87.0
4	Mathematics	64.2
5	Science	33.4
6	Foreign Languages	21.0
7	Government/Economics	19.8
8	History/Geography	14.1
9	Humanities/Arts	13.2

Basic knowledge/skills rank ordered by percent rating as "very important."
Number of respondents varied for each question, ranging from 382 to 409.

format. This does not mean that the table should be dropped into the main text and allowed to stand independently. The table should be integrated into the text by first being introduced and then by having its conclusions discussed. Keep the rule of *proximity* in mind when considering where to place your table. In this report, for example, the table appears at the bottom of the page, under the text where it is discussed, making it easy for the reader to glance down to access the information.

Graphs are visual depictions of data. (Though graphs and charts are distinguished from each other in technical writing, for simplicity's sake we will use the term graphs to refer to any visual depiction of numerical data.) You are probably already familiar with *circle graphs*, often called *pie charts*, which displays how the percentage of a total number is divided. A glance at the pie chart below shows how the 2009 budget of the United States is divided. The protruding slice emphasizes that 10 percent of the total budget is spent on interest alone, which implies the argument that this may be

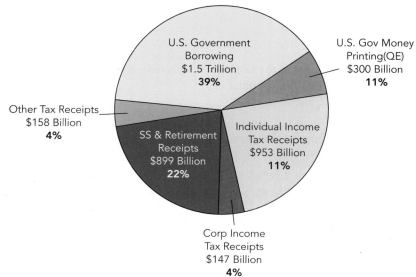

**U.S. Government Sources of Funds
(Fiscal Year 2009-Approximately $4 Trillion Total)**

U.S. Government Borrowing $1.5 Trillion **39%**

U.S. Gov Money Printing(QE) $300 Billion **11%**

Other Tax Receipts $158 Billion **4%**

SS & Retirement Receipts $899 Billion **22%**

Individual Income Tax Receipts $953 Billion **11%**

Corp Income Tax Receipts $147 Billion **4%**

Note: Fiscal year runs from Oct 2008 through Sep 2009

a problem. When deciding whether to use a pie chart as opposed to another type of graph, it is important to consider the number of categories represented. A circle graph with too many categories—a lot of tiny "slices"—can be difficult to read.

Another common visual representation of numerical data is a *bar graph*. This type of graph shows numerical data relative to each other. It differs from pie charts in that the different values do not have to add up to 100, though they can. The chart below from page 31 of *Are They Ready to Work?* makes it possible for the reader to see at a glance that college graduates are much better prepared for work overall than are high school graduates, though fewer than a quarter of college graduates fall into the "excellent" category.

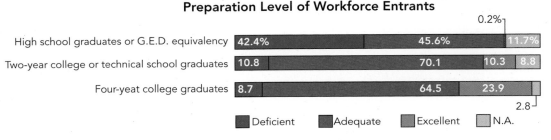

Preparation Level of Workforce Entrants

		0.2%
High school graduates or G.E.D. equivalency	42.4%	45.6%	11.7%
Two-year college or technical school graduates	10.8	70.1	10.3	8.8
Four-yeat college graduates	8.7	64.5	23.9	2.8

◼ Deficient   ◼ Adequate   ◼ Excellent   ◻ N.A.

Number of respondents varied for each question, ranging from 401 to 423. N.A. selected when company does not hire in selected category. percentages may not add to 100% due to rounding.

Number of respondents varied for each question, ranging 401 to 423. N.A. selected when company does not hire in selected category. Percentages not add to 100% due to rounding.

Yet another type of visual representation that you may encounter in your research is a *line graph*. This type of graph is used to represent the changes in a value over a range, usually time. (Although line graphs are probably most frequently used to show trends over time, such as changes in the president's popularity over the course of his presidency, they can be used for other purposes. In a scientific study, a line graph might be used to show the structural weakness of a metal as the temperature increases, for instance.) The following line graph, from the World Meteorological Association, charts the rise in world temperatures as the result of greenhouse gases.

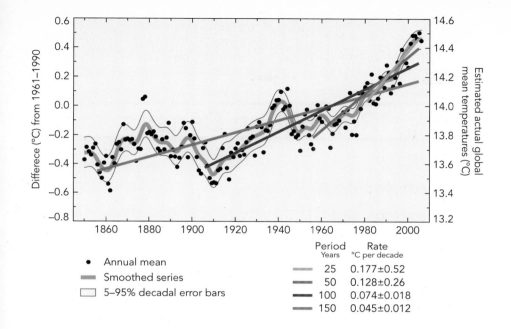

Period	Rate
Years	°C per decade
25	0.177±0.52
50	0.128±0.26
100	0.074±0.018
150	0.045±0.012

- Annual mean
- Smoothed series
- 5–95% decadal error bars

To sum up, tables and graphs are efficient ways of displaying complex numerical data in a small space. They have the advantage of letting the reader understand at a glance complex relationships between data that might take many pages of text to explain. However, they should not be dropped into a text, but rather be fully integrated into the discussion in order to be effective.

Color

Color, whether within your printed text or as part of your images, can be a powerful asset if used properly, but may be a disaster if misused. On a black-and-white page, color usually attracts the eye. If you want the eye to go to a particular place—to look at an image or to identify a section heading, for instance—then color can help you organize your page. By contrast, excessive use of color or selection of difficult-to-read hues will lead to trouble. Read the text in the boxes on the right.

The text in the top box is easily readable; the text in the bottom box is not. Similarly, light text on a dark background can strain the eyes.

> **Purple text on yellow is easily readable.**

> However, purple on blue is a completely different matter.

Working individually or in groups, critique the presentation slide for its use of color.

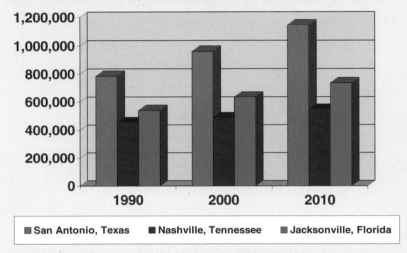

This population chart comes from a student PowerPoint presentation. It would be more difficult to read if the bars were presented in differing shades of gray.

1. Where does your eye travel when you look at the image? Is this a good thing or a bad thing?

2. How does the slide take advantage of the colors in the photograph for selecting background and text colors?

3. Overall, how well does the color scheme work? Indicate one feature you like and one you would change.

4. How does this slide use visual cues to summarize complex information? What knowledge are you able to glean from the graphic presented here?

Color and Rhetorical Context: PASS When you think about using colors in slide presentations or other documents consider the purpose, audience, structure, and style of your rhetorical context:

Purpose: What color schemes would work best to support my topic? If you are making a presentation about environmental damage to the oceans, you might choose blues and greens to suggest water.

Audience: What color schemes would my audience find most appealing? Perhaps a bold red might be too jarring, or you are afraid it might signal "stop!" to your audience. On the other hand, it might communicate passion and power.

Structure: How can I use color to pull my presentation or document together? If you are using headings in a longer document, headings of a uniform color can help create structure. Similarly, a slide presentation can be unified by using similar color palettes on all slides. If you use photographs, you can "pull" colors from the photos into the surrounding page or slide background.

Style: What overall "feel" do I want the presentation or document to have? Your choice of color palette can affect how the audience responds to the document emotionally. By combining fonts with images and color, you can create a style that is subdued and serious or lighthearted and whimsical.

A final word of advice: Test your color schemes against different backgrounds. Colors look different when contrasted against light or dark backgrounds.

Overall Design

When people respond to visuals within the context of larger arguments, or respond to stand-alone visual arguments such as magazine advertisements, they do not react to independent elements such as text, image, and color. Instead, the composition as a whole affects them. But how do you "read" visual arguments?

▶ Slow down your process of looking at the visual. Notice where your eyes go. Does the image draw them to a particular place? Keep in mind the "Z" structure common in many visual documents.

▶ After taking in the visual as a whole, note your initial reaction. Do you find the visual persuasive or otherwise appealing? Why or why not?

▶ Now consider the parts. Study the text, the images, and the colors in turn. How does each function independently, and how does each serve to support the others?

▶ Do any of the images seem to hold multiple meanings? What might those meanings be?

▶ How do the parts work together to communicate purpose, audience, structure, and style?

Using Color

Use color in the following situations:

- To draw attention to important headings in a text
- To enliven an illustration, photograph, or chart
- To emphasize only the most important elements on a page (don't overdo it)

Hint: If you use a chart with several variables, colors are easier to read than different shades of gray.

Don't use color in the following circumstances:

- For the main text of your typescript
- For too many design elements (reserve it for important headings and illustrations)
- If it causes excessive eyestrain (avoid using similar colors together, and avoid light text on a dark background)

PRACTICE 9.5   Responding to the Overall Design

Working individually or in groups, examine this advertisement.
Note your initial reaction to the image, and then answer the following
questions.

Compassion Over Killing/Erica Meier

(continued)

(continued)

1. What is your initial reaction to this ad? Would your reaction be different if the image in the girl's eye were a fish? Why?

2. What is the ad's purpose? Who is the target audience? How do you know?

3. Where is your eye led when you look at the image? Why is this important?

4. In what way might the phrase, "See her as more than a meal," have more than one meaning? Explain.

5. What do the images of the eye and the cow symbolize? Why is the girl looking at the cow? What is she about to do?

6. What unstated message is the ad trying to relate? How do you know?

7. How effective is the ad in accomplishing its goal? State one weakness and one strength of the ad.

UNDERSTANDING VISUAL ARGUMENTS

Although it may not seem possible at first glance, visual arguments can be "read" just as written arguments are read. Written arguments operate on the basis of rhetoric. That is, they have a logic—a system of codes and rules—that they follow and that the audience understands. By presenting claims and evidence, written arguments convince their audience of the legitimacy of their claims. Similarly, visual rhetoric operates by a system of rules that the "reader" understands. Type style, images, color, and overall design all contribute to how a visual argument persuades the reader through the presentation of claims and evidence—sometimes explicitly, but most often implied—in a visual format.

When you prepare to evaluate a written argument, you preview the argument first by trying to make sense of its basic parts and any other clues you can glean from the text: its author, its publication site, its main divisions, any subtitles it contains, and so on. Next, you read the argument and try to understand how its parts work together. Finally, you evaluate the argument as a whole. In similar fashion, understanding visual arguments requires you to preview, examine, and respond to the visual text.

Tips for Presentations that Stand Out

If you present your argument or other research in your class, take the following points into consideration if you want to avoid "death by PowerPoint"!

- *Don't treat your presentation like a paper.* Slides are not documents, but visual enhancements of your talk. Don't put so many words on your slides that the audience will just read them, or worse, you will turn around and read them. Keep the focus on you.

- *Rehearse your talk.* Practice your presentation until you know it by heart, and keep within the allotted time. Nothing damages the *ethos* of a presenter more than a poorly rehearsed talk.

- *Limit the number of slides.* For most presentations, five or six slides should be more than adequate. The more slides you have to prepare the poorer will be the quality of each slide.

- *Plan your slides on paper.* Brainstorm just like you would to write a paper by sketching out your slides. Try several designs until you hit on one you like. Make a "test slide" and run it by your friends before settling on a final design.

- *Keep PASS in mind.* Design your slides so that your purpose is clear, your audience is attentive, the structure of the presentation (and individual slides!) makes sense, and the style of the presentation suits purpose, audience, and structure.

- *Focus on overall design.* Use text, image, and color together so the slides are balanced and pleasing to the eye. Make sure they eye goes where you want it to. Use the rules of proximity, enclosure, and balance to your advantage.

- *Just because you can doesn't mean you should.* Don't clutter your slides with unnecessary details. Avoid silly animations and transitions at all costs.

- *Avoid clip art.* It just makes your presentation look amateurish.

Evaluating Visual Arguments: Previewing, Examining, and Responding

As with arguments constructed solely of text, it is important to preview, study, and respond to visual texts. Whether the text is a television commercial or a political poster, you bring your own preconceptions with you. Your attitude toward designer jeans (are they a coveted status symbol or a waste of money?) will affect how you might approach a Calvin Klein advertisement. Further, the *rhetorical context* of the visual text—where you see it—can inform and affect how you respond to it. The rhetorical context brings with it both the texts that surround it and the assumptions you make on where you find it. Commercials viewed during the Superbowl— where the rhetorical context consists of the other commercials, the game itself, and the cultural significance of the game—might cause you to respond differently to a commercial than if viewed on YouTube or in the middle of the evening news.

Previewing As with a conventional text, you can preview a visual argument. This means that you take a few moments to think about your opinions prior to responding to the argument and the context in which it is presented. However, unlike a written argument, which requires you to turn pages to get an initial sense of how the argument is organized, what its major sections are, and what its thesis is, a visual argument is previewed in a flash. If you don't take a moment to slow yourself down and think about your opinion of the topic and the context in which it appears, you might leap to the responding stage without considering how you got there. Slowing down your response to a visual argument will allow you to take note of your point of view, to think about the context in which the argument appears, and to consider how the various elements work together to persuade an audience.

Here are some pointers for previewing a visual argument:

1. Glance at the advertisement, poster, billboard, or Web page. Then STOP.

2. Before offering an opinion or analysis of the ad, television commercial, or photograph, think about the following:

   ▶ Do you have an opinion regarding the topic at hand? What is it? Is your opinion positive, negative, or neutral? Take a moment to write that opinion in the form of an argumentative claim.

   ▶ *Rhetorical Context:* How does the place where the visual text appears affect what you think about it? Is it in a magazine? On television? In Facebook? On a bulletin board in your dorm hallway? Although billboards, magazine advertisements, television commercials, and the like may seem random, they usually are not. Magazines for teenage girls rarely advertise 4 × 4s, and commercials during sporting events usually do not sell lipstick.

▶ *Purpose:* If its claim is stated in words, what is it? If it is not, what do you believe it to be? How do you know? What is your opinion of the issue being addressed? (If you are a vegetarian, how would you respond to a Web site promoting the beef industry?)

▶ *Audience:* Who do you believe the target audience to be? Are you a member of that group? What assumptions, expectations, or attitudes might affect how you approach the visual text? (If you believe that luxury cars are frivolous status symbols, would this affect how you might approach an ad for a Lexus?)

▶ *Structure:* At a glance, what are the structural features of the argument? Is it composed of text, image, and color, or only a few of these elements?

▶ *Style:* What "feel" does the visual text project, even before you think about what it has to say, and how do you react to this?

Examining After you have considered your own opinion of the topic, take a moment to examine how the various elements of the visual argument work together to persuade the target audience. To do so, think about how each piece of the argument—be it text, image, or color—contributes to the overall persuasive purpose.

Text Use the following guidelines to understand how the elements of a visual argument work together:

▶ How much text is included? Some visual arguments have none, while others may contain several paragraphs.

▶ Why is a particular typeface or text color used? For instance, why would an ad for wine employ flowing script instead of a more practical type style like Arial? Similarly, why would the voice-over on a television commercial promoting a political candidate speak in a deep formal voice with patriotic music playing in the background? Why not use a child's voice?

▶ Can you put the claim or other accompanying text into your own words?

▶ Why do you think the text that is present was used? Why not more? Less? How does it appeal to the target audience?

Images What kinds of images does the composition include? Why do you think those particular images were selected? How do those images appeal to the target audience? Are they persuasive? How so?

Color When considering color, think not only about vibrant colors, but also about the shades of black and white used in certain compositions. With particular types of compositions (e.g., editorial cartoons), convention, rather than the argumentative purpose, may dictate if and what kinds of colors are used. Why do you think particular colors were used? What effect—emotional or otherwise—does the color scheme have on you? Would you have responded differently to another color scheme? If text is present and appears in color, why do you think those colors were selected? Is the color intended merely to draw attention to the text, or does it also serve another purpose?

Responding Once you have thought about the various pieces that make up a visual argument, consider how those elements work together to construct the whole and frame your response to the overall design:

- ► How do the different elements of type style, image, and color work to create an overall persuasive piece? Do these elements complement one another, or do they have a more contrastive relationship?

- ► Do you find the overall visual argument persuasive? Why or why not?

- ► Are there elements of the design that you would change? How? Why would you make these changes?

- ► What would you consider the greatest strength and the greatest weakness of the overall design?

- ► How does the design work to accomplish its purpose? Will it persuade its target audience? How do you know?

- ► How does the visual argument fit into its imediate context (its placement as a graph in an article or as an advertisement in a subway train, for example)? Does the same text include other visual arguments (such as other illustrations within the same article or book)? How do these visual arguments complement one another in an effort to accomplish a larger goal?

PRACTICE 9.6

Previewing, Examining, and Responding to Visual Arguments

Working individually or in groups, preview, examine, and respond to the visual argument that appears in the domestic violence ad below. Write one or more paragraphs explaining the argument's purpose and describing its target audience. Discuss the argument's use of text, images, and color. Finally, explain the argument's primary strengths and weaknesses. Do you find it persuasive? Why or why not?

IN THE REAL WORLD 1 IN 4 UK WOMEN WILL SUFFER

DOMESTIC VIOLENCE

AT SOME TIME IN THEIR LIVES

Say no to the violent abuse of women, visit womankind.org.uk | WOMANKIND WORLDWIDE

Join the White Ribbon Campaign

WOMANKIND Worldwide

This ad for Womenkind Worldwide, an organization that educates people about domestic violence issues, has styled this ad so that it resembles popular Calvin Klein ads. How effective is this approach?

Types of Visual Arguments

This chapter has mentioned many types of visual arguments, but many others exist as well. It would be impossible for this chapter to list every type of visual text found in today's media-rich culture. In the pages that follow, you will have the opportunity to work with a few types of visual texts that commonly present arguments and that you probably see almost every day:

- ► Print advertisements
- ► Political posters and propaganda
- ► Political cartoons
- ► Photographs
- ► Web pages

Of course, these are not the only types of visual arguments that exist, nor are they even the most important ones. (While tables, graphs, and charts are extremely important, we have dealt with them separately in this chapter so they are not included in this list.)

Print Advertisements   Along with television commercials and roadside billboards, print ads are probably the form of visual argument that you are most familiar with. In addition to being strikingly visual, magazine ads are particularly useful for studying visual argumentation because they are placed in context with other forms of persuasion. Magazines typically contain many ads and feature numerous articles. By studying these other "texts" within the magazine, it is relatively easy to get a clear idea of what the readership is like and who the target audience for a particular ad might be. With print ads in particular, it is a good idea to study not only the ad itself, but also other ads in the magazine, along with articles, editorials, regular columns, or other features.

Some scholars define "op-ads" as advertisements that promote ideas rather than products. Most of the ads in this book can be classified as op-ads (opinion advertisements). Much like an op-ed ("opposite the editorial page," a.k.a. opinion editorial) in a newspaper, where an editor writes an opinion—usually in the form of an argument—on a particular subject, an op-ad argues a position on a particular issue of relevance to the target audience.

Political Posters and Propaganda   It is not easy to state definitively where political posters, print ads, or television commercials end and propaganda begins. Generally speaking, propaganda is often the product of a government or other political organization, and it usually consists of a whole campaign as opposed to a single occurrence. For example, the U.S. government's "war on drugs" may be thought of as a propaganda campaign, whereas a few months of ads, commercials, and posters during a candidate's run for public office would not be thought of in quite the same way. Furthermore, propaganda seeks to promote a particular ideology or way of thinking, and it attempts to persuade a mass audience—often an entire population—to adopt this point of view.

Editorial Cartoons The cartoons that appear on the editorial pages of most newspapers are political in nature. They generally present arguments or other commentary through drawings accompanied by a small amount of text. Because editorial cartoons are timely and often reflect current events in the news, many can be difficult to appreciate if you are not familiar with the events they comment on. While many of these cartoons critique particular personalities (many of whom are quickly forgotten), some touch on individuals and themes that are nearly universal, so they are easily understood generations later. Thus, the key to understanding political cartoons is having some familiarity with the issues they treat. In some situations, this knowledge may require research on your part, especially if the cartoons are several years old.

Popular Culture Arguments can be made in media other than written arguments and print advertisements. For example, a variety of media within popular culture are used to convey or imply arguments. Radio ads, songs, television commercials, music videos, graphic novels, and entire motion pictures are used to present positions on issues. For example, singer Sinead O'Connor once famously tore up a picture of Pope John Paul II on *Saturday Night Live* to punctuate her views on traditional Catholicism. (In 1997, the singer asked the pope's forgiveness and was ordained a priest by a breakaway Irish congregation in a move John Paul II labeled as "bizarre.") The rock group U2 is also well known for taking a stand on numerous issues. Concert venues have been used to promote awareness of global issues. For example, the Live 8 concert tackled the issue of poverty (which allowed a number of individuals to pick up the microphone to make specific arguments of their own). Even comic books have been employed to make argumentative statements.

Arguments that employ not only static visual images, but also voices, music, and motion, can add to the complexity of the argument being made. In addition to considering the argument's text, color, image, and

AP Photo/Rene Macura

Celebrities, such as Brad Pitt, Djimon Hounsou, and Bono, frequently take a stand on social issues.

composition in such cases, you might take into account the authoritative and emotional effects that the choice of music (classical versus grunge rock), voice (not only what is said, but who says it and how the words are conveyed), and motion (cigarette smoke that turns into a skeleton) may have on the target audience. Music videos and op-ad television commercials are particularly good examples of visual arguments that take advantage of these additional features.

Photographs Some individuals might say that photographs do not "argue" but rather merely depict reality. Although this might be a reasonable statement in some cases, professional photographs—especially those taken by photographers who carefully select their subjects, frame them in specific ways, and try to use color, light, and shadow to their advantage— can imply arguments.

These arguments can be difficult to interpret because their claims are rarely stated explicitly. Instead, a person who looks at a photograph that seems to promote a point of view should supply the claim and be able to explain how the image suggests that particular viewpoint. In other situations, photographs may function as a form of evidence to support a text-based argument. For example, "before and after" photos of a trash-filled slum that has been transformed into a pristine neighborhood could be used to support an argument centered on revitalization projects for urban neighborhoods. If such photos are particularly powerful, they may serve a dual function: they may make an argument on their own and serve as evidence to support a larger argument. In the context of a text-based argument, it is important to consider what role the photos play in validating the overall argument.

Web pages Web pages are complex documents. They combine text, images, color, and overall design to draw in viewers to sell a product or promote a particular idea. While many Web sites appear to be purely informational, most are not. Even Aunt Mandy's photos of her grandchildren on the family Web site promote a particular point of view. At the very least, Aunt Mandy is projecting a particular idea of her family that she hopes her viewers will accept.

When examining a Web page, you should consider how the visual elements work in concert with the text to persuade the viewer. Web pages often do not present evidence directly in their arguments but rather link to other sites or pages containing that evidence. Also, Web documents, like print ads, tend to argue in sentence fragments and bulleted points as opposed to carefully crafted paragraphs and whole essays. When evaluating these documents, it is important to note that Web pages are a relatively new genre and are still evolving. They operate by different rules of discourse than, say, editorials in newspapers or lengthy articles in magazines. When evaluating arguments presented on the Web, keep in mind these considerations and the fluid, multiple-authored nature of the Web.

AP Images

This photo makes an implied argument about the treatment of prisoners in Iraq.

ANALYZING VISUAL ARGUMENTS

Take a few minutes to study the advertisement on page 267. The Union of Concerned Scientists published this ad as a response to an earlier ad from the Auto Alliance claiming that "Today's cars are virtually emission free."

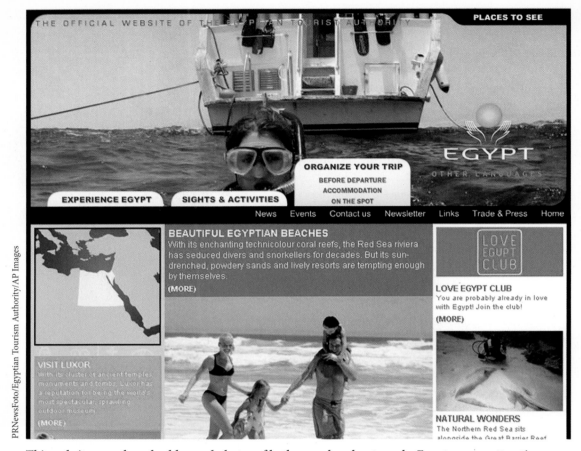

PRNewsFoto/Egyptian Tourism Authority/AP Images

This website uses the color blue and photos of bathers on beaches to make Egypt a more attractive vacation destination. The site uses proximity by placing relevant links in sidebars that will draw viewers further into the site and persuade them to (hopefully) vacation in Egypt.

The Auto Alliance ad was similar to this one in that it featured a toddler in a safety seat getting chocolate all over the car with the slogan "Your car may never be spotless but it's 99% cleaner than you think." Preview, examine, and respond to the ad by completing the practices that follow.

CREATING YOUR OWN VISUAL ARGUMENT

Although professional advertisements and other visual arguments are complex compositions put together with very expensive software, you can create compelling visual arguments of your own using a standard word processor. Begin just like you would for a written argument—determine your purpose, define your audience, and conduct your research. The more you know about

IF TODAY'S CARS ARE 'VIRTUALLY EMISSION-FREE'...

...THEN SO IS THIS CIGARETTE.

AUTOMAKERS ARE TRYING TO DECEIVE YOU ABOUT VEHICLE POLLUTION,
claiming that, "Autos manufactured today are virtually emission-free."*

Seems they're ignoring the fact that new vehicles actually produce **more** global warming emissions than they did 20 years ago. In fact, only four nations on earth produce more heat-trapping carbon dioxide than U.S. autos do alone. And even under tighter government standards, autos will still emit 500,000 tons of smog-forming pollutants and 350,000 tons of toxics linked to cancer.†

Does that sound "virtually emission-free" to you?

Rather than using their lobbyists—the Alliance of Automobile Manufacturers—to spread disinformation, automakers should put their talented engineers to work in support of federal and state initiatives that clean our air and protect our kids.

To find out more, visit www.ucsusa.org

Union of Concerned Scientists
Citizens and Scientists for Environmental Solutions

Warning: Global warming pollution from automobiles is projected to lead to worsening smog, an increase in asthma-triggering pollen and molds, and a substantial rise in heat-related illness and death.

Union of Concerned Scientists

(continued)

(continued)

1. **Previewing:** First, glance at the advertisement to preview it. What does the purpose of the op-ad appear to be? Who is the target audience? Guess as many details about the target audience as you can. Be prepared to defend your answer, either verbally or in writing.

2. **Examining:** Working individually or in groups, now consider the following questions:

   a. Is the claim clearly stated or is it implied? Write the claim down. If it is implied, write the claim in your own words. On a scale of 1 to 10, how confident are you that your rendering of the claim is accurate? If you are working in groups, is there disagreement about the argument's claim? Why?

   b. What does the argument imply in the way of evidence? Text? Image? What role does color play? How does the overall design contribute to presenting the claim and its accompanying evidence to the audience in a convincing fashion?

3. **Responding:** Take a few moments to respond to the ad.

   a. Do you agree with the ad's claim? Why or why not?

   b. Did you find the ad convincing? Why or why not? (Analyze the effectiveness of the ad in terms of connecting claims and evidence regardless of whether you agree with the claim.)

   c. Analyze the ad in terms of text, image, color, and overall design. What is the strongest feature of the ad? What is the weakest? Why do you say this?

   d. Would this argument be stronger if situated within the context of a traditional written argument? Why?

your audience the better you will be able to design a visual text that will be persuasive. Next, brainstorm by sketching your argument out on paper. Determine what kinds of text, image, and color you want your overall composition to have. Then obtain images (remember to credit your sources!), take photographs, draw, use design software, or other means to create the pieces for your design. (In the two student examples that follow, one student took her own photos while the other student drew the images.) Finally, put your composition together in a way that creates structure and underscores your message. Study the two images and answer the questions in the practice that follows.

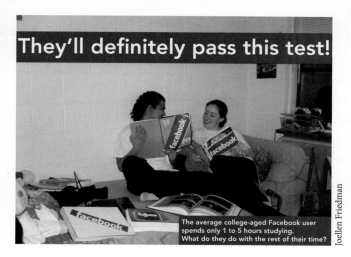

They'll definitely pass this test!

The average college-aged Facebook user spends only 1 to 5 hours studying. What do they do with the rest of their time?

Joellen Friedman

85% of college students have adopted their college network on Facebook. Using Facebook correlates to **academic success** by improving student-teacher interactions.

Take a bite out of technology to build an online learning community.

Priya Panchal

PRACTICE 9.8   Comparing Student Visual Arguments

Study the student visual arguments above, and answer the questions that follow.

1. What claim is each student visual argument trying to make? If you were to state a claim for each, what would it be?

2. Which of the two do you agree with most? Which do you find most convincing? Why?

3. Who do you think the intended audience for each composition might be? Why do you say this?

4. How do text, color, and image work together to create an overall argument?

5. What would you change about each visual argument? Why?

Looking Back at Chapter 9

- ► Visual presentations serve to present arguments, sometimes with little or no accompanying text.
- ► Visual texts typically consist of four elements: text, images, color, and overall design.
- ► The style of a typeface can be varied by font size, style, color, emphasis, and artistic effects.
- ► Images include photographs, drawings, graphs, and Web pages.
- ► Tables, pie charts, bar charts, and line graphs should be carefully selected and integrated into the discussion rather than just "dropped in."
- ► Like written texts, visual arguments can be "read" rhetorically and logically.
- ► Visual arguments include print advertisements, political posters and propaganda, political cartoons, photographs, Web pages, and graphs and charts.
- ► Visual arguments either can stand alone or can be used as an element of a larger argument.

Suggestions for Writing

- ► Locate two op-ads that present different opinions on the same topic. Compare the strengths and weakness of the two advertisements. Which one is better, and why?
- ► Select one of the photos in this chapter (or another you have found on your own) and explain how effectively it implies a particular point of view. What sort of written argument might it be used to support?
- ► Select a popular television commercial and explain how it uses visual elements to persuade its audience.
- ► Choose a music video that seems to make an argument (both explicitly and implicitly). What argument is being made, and how effective is the presentation?
- ► Choose a graphic novel that makes an argument. In a written analysis explain how novel's text and images work together to make

the argument. In what way does the artwork make the argument more compelling?

▶ Choose a topic of your own and create a PowerPoint-based argument that includes both visual and textual elements. Present your argument to your class.

▶ Create a Web page for presenting an argument. Include textual and visual elements.

▶ Write a new argument (or expand one you have already written for this class) using three separate visual elements. Two of those visual elements should be of different types (e.g., photograph, political cartoon, graph, drawing, or illustration).

▶ Write a paper explaining when not to use visuals in your written arguments.

▶ Select two Web sites to compare. Choose one that presents a well-designed, convincing argument and another that does not. Explain why one Web site succeeds and the other fails to convince its viewers.

***The Center for International Rehabilitation (formerly known as Physicians Against Land Mines),** Emina's Story. Although used primarily for military purposes, land mines exact a horrifying toll on civilian populations, primarily in developing nations. It is estimated that more than 80 percent of all land mine victims are civilians. Of these, 30 to 40 percent are children under age fifteen. In 1999, 137 countries signed a treaty prohibiting the use, stockpiling, and production of land mines, but the United States, along with Russia and China, refused to sign. In 1996 Dr. William Kennedy Smith founded Physicians against Land Mines (PALM), which describes itself as a non-governmental organization whose mission is to end the death, dismemberment and disability caused by land mines. It sponsored public information initiatives, advocated reforms in international law and ran numerous disability programs. PALM educated the public through advertisements such as the one reprinted here, designed by advertising company Leo Burnett, for use in magazines, in bus shelters, and inside buses and trains. Several magazines—including Harper's, Atlantic Monthly, Bomb and People—have donated space for this ad campaign. In 1998 PALM became the Chicago-based, not-for-profit organization "Center for International Rehabilitation" (CIR) and initiated its Rehabilitation Engineering Research Center on Landmine Victim Assistance. Today the CIR conducts research, raises awareness, and promotes action to improve the quality and advancement of medical and rehabilitation services in remote and medically underserved areas. The CIR describes its work as "empowering individuals and communities across the globe to improve the lives of people with disabilities and expanding treatment options, for those who otherwise would not have access to specialty care, through innovative engineering projects, capacity-building education programs, interactive online tools, and human rights advocacy."

10 Using Logic

> It is a capital mistake to theorize before one has data. Insensibly one begins to twist facts to suit theories, instead of theories to suit facts.
> —Sir Arthur Conan Doyle's Sherlock Holmes, *A Scandal in Bohemia*

When the fictional detective Sherlock Holmes would come upon a crime scene, he often solved the case by observing clues that others had overlooked or misinterpreted. Holmes had a keenly developed ability to think *logically*, analyzing and interpreting beyond the surface facts. As you encounter arguments in everyday life (and particularly in this book), you will find logic to be indispensable.

In this book we have spent a great deal of time talking about purposes and audiences, structure and style, planning and revision, claims and support. Equally important is the thinking that lies beneath the surface of the argument itself: the logic that causes the words to make sense and persuade an audience. Because of the central role it plays in making your argument both sound and persuasive, it should be attended to at all steps of the writing process.

This chapter begins by defining logic. Next we'll see how a logical statement known as a syllogism forms the basis of an argumentative claim. Then we'll work through the elements of practical logic as defined by Stephen Toulmin to understand how the various components of argumentation work together to persuade an audience of a claim's believability. In doing this, we will consider two kinds of audiences: those that are open-minded but yet undecided about your position and those that are resistant to the viewpoint you are putting forward. Finally, we'll expose "logical fallacies": faulty logic or substitutes for logic. Along the way, we'll review logic-related concepts that are discussed earlier in this book: persuasive appeals and a method of conflict resolution developed by psychologist Carl Rogers.

WHAT IS LOGIC?

Logic describes the processes we use to reach conclusions. In technical terms, it is the science of valid inference and correct reasoning. An **inference** is the process of arriving at a conclusion from an examination of known facts or examples. **Reasoning** may be considered the mental process by which such conclusions are determined.

Logic traditionally is categorized as two kinds: **inductive reasoning** and **deductive reasoning**.

▶ **Induction:** Discovering a general principle by observing many specific occurrences. This is how scientific theories and laws are formed: "Every apple that I've thrown in the air always falls back to the ground; therefore, a force such as gravity must pull them downward."

▶ **Deduction:** Reaching a conclusion by applying a principle (known as a *premise* or *warrant*) to a specific fact: "I already accept the premise that there is a force of gravity; therefore, if I throw an apple into the air, I'm sure that it will fall back to the ground."

If the reasoning process is followed according to logic's rules, then the conclusion is considered **valid**. However, when a fact or premise is erroneous, the conclusion can be both valid and false.

▶ **Valid yet false conclusion through induction:** "Every politician I have observed is a liar; therefore, all politicians are liars." (You haven't observed enough politicians.)

Context

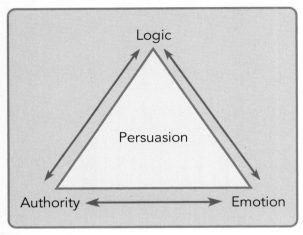

Authority, emotion, and logic are three methods used to persuade people. Rhetorical context helps you determine the best balance between these appeals that will be most persuasive to your audience. To learn more about the inter-connectedness of these" persuasive appeals," see Chapter 1, Introduction. Later in this chapter, the power of emotion is demonstrated. Advertising and propagarida both offer emotion as a substitute for logic.

Remember PASS

- **Purpose:** What you want the reader to do or believe
- **Audience:** The individuals who you want to take this action
- **Structure:** The best organization and content to accomplish your purpose
- **Style:** The appropriate language your audience is likely to respect and respond to positively

▶ **Valid yet false conclusion through deduction:** "That person is a politician; since all politicians are liars, that person must be a liar." (You've applied a false premise to the specific fact.)

DEDUCTIVE LOGIC

Aristotle's Formal Logic

The origins of deductive logic can be traced back to ancient Athens, and Aristotle (384–322 B.C.E.) was one of the first to record its techniques in his book *Rhetoric*. But Greek orators probably used this reasoning to prepare their persuasive speeches for many generations before Aristotle. Literacy was only a few generations old at the time of Aristotle, and little is known of the preliterate, oral practices of rhetoric.

Aristotle presented argument in the form of a word equation called a *syllogism*. In its most basic form, a syllogism presents an argument divided into three parts:

▶ The **major premise** is a general concept that the audience can accept as being true.

▶ The **minor premise** is a specific concept that the audience can accept as true.

▶ The **conclusion** is an assertion that emerges from the relationship between the two premises.

The major and minor premises, if accepted by the audience, lead to an inescapable conclusion. For example, if you agree with (1) the major premise that all humans eventually die and with (2) the minor premise that a particular being is human, then you must agree with (3) the conclusion: the particular being will eventually die.

The following syllogism is a classical example of Aristotle's formal logic:

Major premise: All men are mortal.

Minor premise: Socrates is a man.

Conclusion: Socrates is mortal.

The order in which the major premise, minor premise, and conclusion are presented is traditional. As a sentence, the syllogism might read like this:

If all men are mortal, and if Socrates is a man, then Socrates is mortal.

Syllogisms often are phrased as *If..., then ...* or end with *therefore, consequently,* or *thus*. However, the parts of the syllogism could easily be inverted, leading to a sentence like this:

Socrates is mortal because he's a man and all men are mortal.

The problem with syllogistic reasoning, as already mentioned, is that it is very easy to construct a false, or even ludicrous, syllogism, as the penguin cartoon illustrates. However, if the audience is willing to accept the major and minor premises, then accepting the conclusion is inevitable.

Toulmin's Practical Logic

In 1958, philosopher Stephen Toulmin published a book titled *The Uses of Argument*, which ultimately changed the way modern rhetoricians think about the elements of argumentation. Toulmin challenged the classical view of argument (which was based largely on Aristotle's *Rhetoric* and other works) and sought to create a more practical way of understanding argumentation.

According to Toulmin, arguments are won and lost at the sentence level. For that reason, in this chapter we concern ourselves not with the overall structure of a protracted argument but rather with the very practical business of making claims and convincing an audience that those claims are believable. (For more extensive discussions of organizing an overall argument, see Chapter 5, Planning Arguments, and Chapter 6, Drafting Arguments.)

Toulmin maintained that the certainty required to make Aristotle's logic functional was seldom found in real-life situations. In practice, decision makers usually work with incomplete evidence and unsure or contradictory facts. In a courtroom, for example, the prosecution and the defense present very different versions of the truth to the judge and jury. Today, Toulmin's logic is sometimes called "practical" or "informal" in contrast to Aristotle's logic.

Toulmin's syllogisms function much like those of Aristotle but conceptually his practical logic is based on probable, not assured, conclusions. His terminology also parallels that of Aristotle:

▶ **Warrant:** Toulmin's warrant functions like Aristotle's major premise by guaranteeing (like a product's warranty) that the evidence leads to the claim by providing the relevant principle, belief, or law.

▶ **Reason:** Toulmin's reason (grounds, data, or evidence) functions like Aristotle's minor premise by supporting the claim with specific reasons and evidence.

▶ **Claim:** Toulmin's claim functions like Aristotle's conclusion, offering an assertion.

The following syllogism is an example of Toulmin's practical logic:

Warrant: Unhealthy practices should be outlawed.

Reason: Smoking is unhealthy.

Claim: Tobacco smoking should be outlawed.

Toulmin's approach to logic is used throughout this chapter as a means of analyzing and evaluating the arguments. However, it should be remembered that Toulmin's system contains the same basic weakness as Aristotle's. Just as the audience must accept Aristotle's major premise in order for the conclusion to be accepted, in Toulmin's system the warrant must be accepted as true by the audience in order for the claim to be perceived as true. Both approaches require that the argument be approached as a sort of social contract between the writer and the audience. As long as the underlying assumption (or assumptions) made by the writer are accepted as true, there is a reasonable chance that the audience will perceive the claim as true.

THE LOGICAL STRUCTURE OF AN ARGUMENT
True, Valid, and Sound

In logic, the terms *true, valid*, and *sound* have specialized uses. "True" and "false" can be applied to each statement in a syllogism: warrant, reason, and claim (as well as backing, rebuttal, and qualifier). For example, you could say that a warrant is false, but you wouldn't describe it as valid. *Validity* is applied specifically to the logical form of the syllogism and is used in phrases such as "valid argument" or "invalid argument." A syllogism can contain false (even absurd) statements yet be a valid argument, as in the following example:

Claim: President Washington is a Martian.

Reason: Because President Washington is a horse.

Warrant: All horses are Martians.

> ### Claim, Reason, and Warrant
> - **A claim:** Something that the writer wants the audience to believe
> - **A reason:** A statement that explains why the assertion should be believed
> - **A warrant:** An unstated assumption that is shared by the writer and the audience and that makes it possible to see a valid logical connection between the assertion and the reason

---

→ UNDERSTANDING SYLLOGISMS AND ENTHYMEMES

Aristotelian Syllogism As we have already said, in the language of formal Aristotelian logic, a syllogism is a complete logical statement that consists of a major premise, a minor premise, and a conclusion. The argumentative thesis statements discussed in this section are based on this basic logical structure.

> **Major premise:** All fish live underwater.
> **Minor premise:** All trout are fish.
> **Conclusion:** All trout live underwater.

Toulmin Syllogism In the language of practical Toulmin logic, a syllogism is a complete logical statement that consists of a warrant, a reason, and a claim. A Toulmin syllogism functions like an Aristotelian syllogism. The warrant acts like a major premise, the reason acts like a minor premise, and the claim acts like a conclusion. However, Toulmin logic is considered to be the more practical of the two and is applied to real-life situations where warrants and reasons lack certainty.

> **Warrant:** We should take every opportunity to learn about life.
> **Reason:** The elderly have much to teach us about life.
> **Claim:** We should learn what we can from the elderly.

Enthymemes An enthymeme is an incomplete syllogism consisting of a claim (conclusion) but missing one or both of the other parts. Enthymemes typically omit the warrant (major premise) when the audience already is aware of the general principle, belief, or law.

> **Enthymeme:** We should learn everything we can from the elderly because of what they can teach us of life.

This enthymeme assumes the audience values knowledge. Sometimes the reason (minor premise) also can be omitted.

> **Enthymeme:** Learn from your elders!

A *sound* argument is structurally valid <u>and</u> contains only true statements. An audience will judge a claim to be false if it judges either the reason or warrant to be false:

> **Claim:** You should paint this bike pink.
>
> **Reason:** Because it will be more attractive.
>
> **Warrant:** Pink bikes are attractive.

Although this example is trite, it serves to illustrate the principle: If an individual does not share the warrant that pink bikes are attractive, then no logical connection between claim and reason is made. If you have any doubt that your audience will accept your warrant as reasonable (if not flatly true), then you should rewrite your argumentative thesis to better "reach" the audience with a warrant it will accept.

The Basics

A complete syllogistic sentence consists of three elements:

> **Claim + Reason + Warrant:** We should not allow racial profiling to be used to search passengers at airports because that is a form of racism, and, as everybody knows, racism is bad.

This sentence is unnecessarily long and complex because it states the obvious. We are making certain assumptions about the audience here: Who is the audience? If your audience is likely to believe your warrant, then you can delete it:

> **Claim + Reason + ~~Warrant:~~** We should not allow racial profiling to be used to search passengers at airports because that is a form of racism. ~~and, as everybody knows, racism is bad~~.

Then the thesis can look like this:

> **Thesis:** We should not allow racial profiling to be used to search passengers at airports because that is a form of racism.

Multiple Reasons

Argumentative thesis statements can have more than one associated reason. Using multiple reasons should be done with care, because the more reasons you give, the more complex the argument becomes:

> **Claim:** Responsible owners will neuter their cats.
>
> **Reasons:** Neutering prevents pets from wandering, helps control the population of feral cats, and prevents males from spraying.

Warrant: Actions that control cat behavior and overpopulation are desirable.

The advantage of listing several reasons is that they help you structure your argument. If a series of reasons appears in an argumentative thesis, they also provide the reader with a mini-outline of what may appear later in the text of the argument. However, this strategy also limits you somewhat, because you should address everything mentioned in the paper's thesis within the body of the full argument. In addition, the argumentative claim can become very long and unwieldy.

Multiple Warrants

Even if only one reason is stated, certain ideas may be "loaded" with multiple warrants:

Claim: Stem-cell research should be banned.

Reason: Stem-cell research is murder.

Warrants: Stem cells count as human life and to end human life is wrong.

Social and ethical issues rendered as claims tend to have multiple warrants behind them. It may be valuable to list as many of these assumptions as you can think of. If the audience finds some of them questionable, you may need to address this skepticism directly as part of your extended argument.

Problem Claims

There are a number of problems you might encounter while formulating a claim. Fortunately, most of them are easy to avoid.

The Audience Doesn't Share Your Assumption Because not all audiences are the same, sometimes your readers may not share your underlying warrant.

Claim: Gasoline automobiles should be made illegal.

Reason: Auto emissions promote global warming.

Warrant: Things that promote global warming should be avoided.

Problem: The audience might not believe that global warming is a reality.

One solution to this problem is to address the concern by rewriting the claim. By changing either the claim or the reason, the shared assumption will be changed as well:

Claim: Gasoline automobiles should be replaced with hybrids.

Reason: They pollute less and save gas.

Warrant: Polluting the air is bad, and saving money is good.

In modifying the claim, the warrant—the underlying belief or assumption—was also changed (and ideally will now be accepted by the target audience).

The Language of the Claim Can Be Interpreted in Various Ways If your language is not specific enough, you may leave your claim open to multiple interpretations.

Claim: Dr. Flanagan is an excellent professor.

Reason: Because she knows her subject so well.

Warrant: Excellent professors know their subjects.

Problem: The audience may have a different understanding of "excellent." Would an "excellent" professor also have to be an outstanding teacher or an engaging speaker?

Solution (Make the language more specific): Dr. Flanagan is an excellent professor because she is not only a knowledgeable person, but also a dynamic, engaging teacher.

In this case, excellent could have been replaced with informative, but that would create another problem: a circular claim (see below). By expanding the single reason to two reasons, the writer addresses the reader's assumptions. The underlying assumption would now become multiple as well: excellent professors are both knowledgeable and engaging.

The Claim Is Circular The assertion and the reason must make different statements. A claim is thought of as circular if the reason merely rephrases the claim. (See "Circular Reasoning" and "Begging the Question" in the Logical Fallacies section of this chapter.)

▶ **Claim:** Illegal drugs should be avoided.

▶ **Reason:** Because they are against the law.

▶ **Warrant:** All illegal things should be avoided.

▶ **Problem:** The assertion, reason, and warrant are almost identical.

▶ **Solution (Rewrite the reason to make a different statement):** Illegal drugs should be avoided because they are bad for your health.

→ CLAIM WORKSHEET

The questions below can help you develop your claim.

1. Which debatable issue is being argued? Example: Should Americans be allowed to buy inexpensive drugs from Canada via Internet pharmacies?

2. What is your opinion regarding this issue? It will become your claim. Example: Americans should be able to buy drugs from Canadian Internet pharmacies.

3. Now state a reason that your audience should perceive your claim as true. (Use to get your reason started, although you may rephrase your argumentative claim later.) Example: Americans should be allowed to buy drugs from Canadian Internet pharmacies because the prohibition is based on corporate greed.

4. What assumption are you making? Example: Things that are done purely for profit motives are not legitimate reasons to make something illegal.

5. Who is your audience? Example: Pharmacists who work for large pharmaceutical firms and (1) have high standards regarding drug control and quality and (2) stand to profit from higher drug sales in the United States.

6. Is your audience likely to agree with your warrant? Example: No, because it believes that lax regulations in Canada may result in the availability of drugs that might not meet U.S. standards.

7. If your audience does not accept your claim, how will you attempt to convince it that the warrant is believable? Example: By arguing that Canadian standards are as good as, and sometimes exceed, U.S. standards.

The assumption that things that are bad for your health should be avoided is general enough to be accepted by a wide audience.

One could suggest that this point is not actually arguable because it is a commonly accepted belief and does not address a debatable issue. However, that point turns on the values and beliefs of the target audience. Certain audiences might argue that the right to enjoy the effects of illegal drugs outweighs the health concerns: People should have the right to enjoy illegal drugs regardless of health concerns because individuals, not governments, should bear responsibility for their own health.

The Syllogism Is Stated as an Argumentative Claim In the text of an argument, the syllogism will rarely be written in a formal format as presented in this chapter, but rather will typically be rendered in the form of a claim. The claim may consist of one or two sentences (or even more) and usually will not include the warrant (unless the arguer believes the audience will not accept it, in which case the warrant has to be argued and proven). Sometimes the reason will be stated before the claim. At other times it will follow the claim.

Claim: Pit bulls should not be bred for profit.

Reason: Because they present a danger to society.

Warrant: Things that present a danger to society should not be allowed.

► Using a "because" clause:

Pit bulls should not be bred for profit because they present a danger to society.

► As two separate sentences:

Pit bulls should not be bred for profit. The reason is that they present a danger to society.

► With the reason and the claim reversed:

Because they present a danger to society, pit bulls should not be bred for profit. Pit bulls present a danger to society. As a result, they should not be bred for profit.

This claim could be written in a variety of ways, employing various transition words, as one or two sentences.

PRACTICE 10.1   Transforming a Syllogism into an Argumentative Thesis

Working individually or in groups, select one of the issues listed below or come up with a topic on your own. Identify a target audience for that issue, and then write a syllogism for it. Decide whether your audience is likely to agree with your warrant (and which strategy you must employ to convince the audience that it is true). Finally, write an argumentative thesis (Claim + Reason) in at least three different ways.

1. Should the government pay to clean up pollution caused by corporations? (Assume that the corporations were following all government regulations when the pollution occurred.)
2. Should the president of the United States be allowed to serve more than two terms in office?
3. What should be done (if anything) to deal with illegal immigration from south of the border?
4. Does the use of "politically correct" language, sometimes called "speech codes," foster more equality in the United States (or elsewhere in the world, for that matter)?
5. If delinquent children commit crimes, should their parents be held accountable for their bad parenting?
6. What should your community do to increase employment and/or reduce crime in poverty-stricken areas?

A.J. SISCO/UPI/Newscom

Who is responsible for cleaning up environmental hazards? If the company responsible can't—or won't—deal with the damage, should the taxpayers have to foot the bill?

Grounds, Backing, Qualifiers, and Rebuttals

As we have noted, the core of an argument is its claim, reason, and warrant. However, other elements of an argument—backing, grounds, qualifiers, and rebuttals—often are required to make it convincing:

▶ **Grounds**: Reasons, which tend to be stated in generalities or abstractions, often need support in the form of concrete evidence known as grounds, data, or evidence. For example, if your stated reason for banning smoking is "because it is unhealthy," your grounds might reveal the kinds, frequency, and severity of health problems suffered by smokers.

▶ **Backing:** Underlying assumptions—warrants—sometimes need to be supported with their own evidence and explanations, which are known as backing. For example, if you claim that smoking should be banned and your warrant is that personal health is a public issue, your backing might include evidence showing (1) the health expenses of smokers and (2) the effects of those health expenses on overall insurance rates.

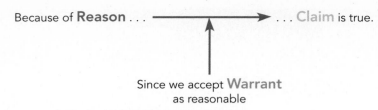

Figure 10.1   A Simple Three-Part Toulmin Model

> **What's the difference between *grounds* and *backing*?**
>
> *Grounds* and *backing* consist of extended arguments—presentation and discussion of evidence—used to validate either a reason (usually stated as a part of the claim) or a warrant. Grounds consists of primary argument used to reinforce the claim + reason; backing consists of additional arguments that sometimes have to be made if the audience might doubt the truth of the unexpressed assumption, or warrant. In such a case, the warrant would need to be expressed and supported with additional argument or *backing*.

► **Qualifiers:** Sometimes you must specify under what conditions a claim is true—by using qualifiers such as always, sometimes, usually, or never.

► **Rebuttals:** Sometimes you must refute or rebut one or more opposition arguments.

The simple syllogism shown in Figure 10.1 above maps how these elements work together.

The essential meaning of this schematic is this:

Because of the reason and the warrant, it is possible for the audience to accept the claim.

To make this schematic more concrete, let's put it in sentence form:

Handguns are used more often in the execution of violent crimes than anywhere else. Because of this reason, they should be made illegal.

Although *because* is attached to the claim here, it refers back to the reason stated in the previous sentence. This handgun example is mapped out in Figure 10.2 below.

The example presented here works well if the audience shares the underlying warrant. In the real world, of course, logic is rarely a simple matter of

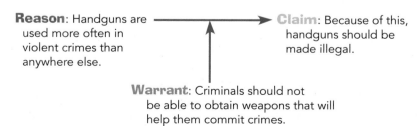

Figure 10.2   An Example Using a Three-Part Toulin Model

writing an argumentative claim that will allow the unexpressed assumption to be shared by the author and the audience. Indeed, in most cases, some measure of disagreement will occur between the assumptions made by the author and the beliefs of the audience. Typically, a number of related warrants may influence the way an audience responds to a claim. This likelihood requires us to consider two ways of looking at evidence.

Approaches to Evidence

When you present an argument, even one as brief as the two sentences outlined above, you can support it in two ways:

▶ If the audience is likely to see the warrant (W) as possibly true, then you should present evidence called grounds (G) to support your reason (R). The assumptions that you are making are that the warrant will be accepted by the audience and that you need only to convince the audience of the truth value of R.

▶ If the audience is likely to see W as probably false, then—in addition to providing G to support R—you should present evidence called backing (B) to convince the audience that W is believable.

Gun control continues to be hotly debated in the United States.

PRACTICE 10.2 Identifying When Backing Is Needed

Working individually or in groups, determine which warrants connect the claim(s) to the reason(s) in the following brief arguments. Identify an audience that would likely accept the warrant as well as an audience that would doubt the warrant. Explain how you would present the argument to a skeptical audience.

1. Persons convicted of felonies should have to wear tracking devices even after they have served their sentences. It is important for the government to be able to keep track of these criminals so they will be prevented from committing new crimes.

2. Children today have an inability to control their emotions. One reason for this is that many of them do not receive discipline at home, and the law prevents children from being properly disciplined at school. It is my opinion that schools should have the option of punishing children for misbehavior. Such punishment options should include spankings because a little bit of pain and humiliation can be an effective teacher.

3. Various women's groups have argued for equal opportunities for women. In the military, women are allowed to perform most jobs except those involving direct front-line combat. If women are to be truly equal, then all jobs in the military should be open to them. In addition, they should be assigned to such jobs in exactly the same way that men are. If they are going to serve in the military, they should not be able to "opt out" of combat positions.

4. In certain states, Native American tribes are allowed to run "bingo halls" that effectively amount to casinos. Because of treaties that were put in place many years ago, different rules apply to businesses that operate on Native American–owned land than apply to businesses that are operated by the rest of the population. Because gambling is a dangerous addiction that attracts crime, these casinos should be closed.

Figure 10.3   A Three-Part Toulmin Model Plus Grounds and Backing

Let's clarify these types of evidence by expanding the schematic a little bit, as is shown in Figure 10.3 above.

Now let's get specific. If you assume—rightly or wrongly—that your audience shares your warrant that "Criminals should not be able to obtain weapons that will help them commit crimes," then your argument may look a bit like the one shown in Figure 10.4 below.

Conversely, if you are aware that your audience either (1) may not share your warrant or (2) may entertain, or otherwise be aware, of multiple warrants, then you must state your warrant in the course of the argument. Recall that if the warrant is shared by author and audience, then it usually remains unstated. However, if it is likely to be the subject of disagreement, then this assumption must be stated directly and supported with appropriate evidence—ideally with

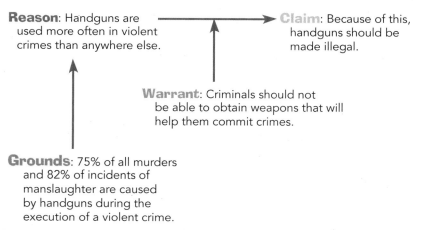

Figure 10.4   An Example Using a Three-Part Toulin Model Plus Grounds

Reason: Handguns are used more often in violent crimes than anywhere else.

Claim: Because of this, handguns should be made illegal.

Warrant: Criminals should not be able to obtain weapons that will help them commit crimes.

Grounds: Only 13% of handguns held in American homes are fired for self-defense. During the twentieth century, 350,000 people were murdered with handguns.

Backing: In England and Wales, where handguns are illegal, only 0.11% of the population has been murdered with firearms, whereas in the United States, where 39% of households own handguns, the handgun murder rate is 5.70%.

Figure 10.5   An Example Using a Three-Part Toulmin Model Plus Grounds and Backing

the result of at least causing the audience to entertain the possibility of the truth value of your claim (see Figure 10.5 above).

In this example, evidence in the form of grounds is not enough to convince the audience, which doubts the truth of the warrant. Therefore, further evidence in the form of backing must be provided with the hope that the audience will entertain the possibility that the assumption is correct. Only after the audience accepts this warrant will it be compelled by grounds in support of the reason. Remember, it is the warrant that allows a connection to be made between the claim and its reason.

The Qualifier

A qualifier is a word or phrase that is employed within an argumentative claim or the supporting reason and that serves to limit—to qualify—the claim for specific kinds of cases. Qualifiers can help you avoid making erroneous absolute statements that may cause your audience to reject your claim out of hand. Absolute statements can come off as jarring and dogmatic, and they can put your audience in a defensive state of mind. What would you think if you encountered the following statement on a professor's syllabus?

NOTICE: ABSENCES ARE NOT ALLOWED. If you miss class FOR ANY REASON, you will receive a FAILING GRADE!

PRACTICE 10.3	Rewriting with Qualifiers

Working individually or in groups, rewrite the following argumentative thesis statements. Consider whether qualifiers should be used in each case. Be prepared to explain your purpose and target audience to your group, your instructor, or the rest of the class.

1. The first time someone is arrested for a drug offense, that person should be locked up for twenty years with no chance of parole.
2. Gay couples should always be allowed to adopt children.
3. Because automobile emissions contribute to global warming, all gasoline-powered automobiles should be replaced with gas/electric hybrids or with hydrogen fuel-cell cars.
4. Children lose a portion of what they learned in the preceding school year during summer vacation. For this reason, a twelve-month school term should become mandatory.
5. In lieu of prison sentences, convicted felons should be required to perform labor for their victims. The dollar equivalent of their crime should be set by a jury.

Now how about this:

> NOTICE: Attending class is extremely important. Missing more than three classes will result in a lower grade, although you will be excused for documented illnesses and school-sponsored activities as appropriate.

Most likely you see the second statement as "friendlier" and "more reasonable." The first statement is absolute and lacks qualifiers. The second statement contains qualifiers that limit its application to specific circumstances. Now read the following statement without a qualifier:

> Because the military is required to operate efficiently, civilian employees of military bases should be required to work Monday through Friday without exception.

Now with a qualifier:

> Because the military is required to operate efficiently, with the exception of Muslims who attend prayers on Friday, civilian employees of military bases should be required to work Monday through Friday without exception.

A qualifier limits the application of a claim and thus avoids a potential objection. In the preceding example, a Muslim employee might contend he should be able to trade working on Friday in exchange for working on

Sunday. If a qualifier is placed in the claim, then the objection is avoided. Here is another example:

> Video games may desensitize impressionable young people to violence. Therefore, all video games should be banned.

Now here it is with a qualifier:

> Certain video games that reproduce murderous rampages, like *Grand Theft Auto,* may desensitize impressionable young people to violence. While some games are innocent fun, those that realistically simulate murder should be banned.

A qualifier usually makes a claim more acceptable to a potential audience and limits the claim's application to specific cases so it will not be seen as dogmatic or absolute. The qualifier limits the claim so that the warrant connecting the claim and the reason may have an exception applied to it. In the first of the two video game examples, the warrant might be stated as follows:

> Things that might incite violence should be banned because they will make society safer.

Most people, however, are not likely to accept the idea that all video games (or other forms of popular entertainment, for that matter) are likely to incite violence. By qualifying the claim and limiting it only to games that simulate murder, a more reasonable claim is made that the audience may be more likely to accept.

Objection and Rebuttal

All audiences (even friendly ones) will inevitably raise questions about your argument. These questions are **objections**—specific counterclaims that the reader generates or that recur as the reader ponders your argument. The best thing you can do in the course of making your argument is to anticipate potential objections (although you will probably not think of all possibilities) and respond to them. A **rebuttal** is an argument you make in response to a specific objection. An objection may be stated in the form of a question, or it may be a fully developed argument complete with claim(s), reason(s), warrant(s), and supporting evidence in the form of grounds and backing. Likewise, your rebuttal will generally take the form of a fully developed argument. You must (1) summarize the opposing argument, (2) recognize its strengths (this will help you establish authority and build sympathy with your audience), and (3) argue against its weaknesses.

If we return briefly to the gun control example from earlier in this chapter, you can see how this might work:

Your claim: Handguns should be made illegal because they cause thousands of deaths as the result of accidents and their use in violent crimes.

Audience objection: Most handguns are owned by responsible citizens who keep them in their homes for self-defense. Besides, there is a constitutional right to bear arms.

Your rebuttal: Only 13 percent of handguns have ever been used by Americans to protect themselves from criminals. It stands to reason, then, that the majority of these weapons are fired either accidentally or to commit a crime such as murder. Furthermore, 67 percent of all murders in the United States are committed with handguns. In England and Wales, where handguns are illegal, only one-tenth of 1 percent of the population has been killed with firearms, whereas in the United States, almost 6 percent of the population has been murdered with firearms. In the United States, handguns are present in 39 percent of homes. This would seem to suggest that the presence of so many handguns in the United States has led to more murders.

It is even possible for an entire argument to take the form of rebuttal. An argument's purpose can be to summarize and respond to positions that differ from the writer's own position. This technique works rather like an inverted pyramid. The author first outlines a series of objections to a particular point of view, then summarizes each one in turn, and finally refutes each one in turn. By the end of the argument, only one alternative remains; this—generally the author's thesis—is the one the writer endorses.

PRACTICE 10.4	Identifying the Elements of a Refutation Argument

A refutation is an argument replete with all of the elements—claim, reason, warrant, evidence (grounds and backing), and qualifiers. Working individually or in groups, reread the preceding refutation, and identify or reconstruct the following:

1. The original argument's thesis, complete with claim, reason(s), and warrant(s).
2. The claim, reason(s), and warrant(s) of the objection.
3. The claim, reason(s), and warrant(s) of the rebuttal. Also, identify how the evidence functions as grounds (supporting a reason) and backing (validating a warrant).

Does the refutation contain more than one claim?

ROGERIAN ARGUMENT: THE CONFLICT RESOLUTION APPROACH

In some cases, you may be faced with an audience that is strongly opposed to your position. Such audiences might be perceived as so strongly skeptical—unwilling to even consider the evidence and claims you present— that even if you articulate your underlying assumptions and present evidence to back them up, they are likely to reject what you have to say out of hand. As a rhetor you want to "reel in" your audiences and bring them within the "zone" so they are at least willing to listen. One way to do this is to employ the Rogerian method of dealing with strong objections. The idea is to get your audience to see your argument from your point of view.

Psychologist Carl Rogers developed an approach to dealing with objections and rebuttals that (at least in theory) has the effect of reducing just this type of resistance. When Rogers was working with groups of patients,

---

PRACTICE 10.5   Identifying Objections and Preparing a Rebuttal

Working individually or in groups, read the following claims carefully. Identify one or more objections to each, and write a claim/reason statement that rebuts the objection.

1. A private company should have the right to scrutinize the health habits of its employees and to fire those who live unhealthy lifestyles and may cause the company's insurance rate to rise.
2. Because children are especially impressionable, advertising should be banned during children's television shows.
3. If a college athlete is found to have used steroids to enhance his or her performance, then the athlete should have to repay the institution for the cost of his or her education. The athlete has defrauded the institution and has defrauded the public that has paid to see him or her perform.
4. The United States needs a government-subsidized health care program. Health care and drug costs in this country have skyrocketed out of control.
5. Male scientists outnumber female scientists because evolution has given women better social skills and men better spatial acumen. This makes men better mathematicians, and mathematics is the basis of science.
6. If a person dies but some of his or her organs are still functional, the person should be able to put a provision in his or her will allowing the family to sell the functional organs.

before he would allow a patient to rebut someone else's opinion about a subject, he required the patient to acknowledge the other person's argument to the second patient's satisfaction. This method, whether used in a live setting such as a therapy session or in writing, forces an individual not only to summarize, but also to recognize the legitimacy of another argument before proceeding. This strategy is very useful for rebutting arguments: If the alternative argument is summarized with care, you will become more aware of its claims, reasons, warrants, and forms of support than you might otherwise. Further, in carefully summarizing the opposing position you are in a sense respecting members of your audience who may strongly disagree with you. In doing this, in satisfying them that you are treating their position fairly, they may be more willing to consider what you have to say. (For more on Rogers' techniques, see "Conflict Resolution" in Chapter 1 of this book.)

USING EMOTION TO REINFORCE LOGIC

Emotion sometimes is viewed suspiciously as a rival to logic. In practice, argument often blends feelings with reasons. The following is a discussion of how writers sometimes use emotion inappropriately as well as how it can be used appropriately to reinforce a claim.

Invoking Emotion Inappropriately

While it is important—even unavoidable—to utilize emotion to convince your audience of your argumentative purpose, this tactic should not be the primary means for moving your audience to action. An argument employs logic—presenting claims and supporting them with evidence—as the primary means of convincing an audience. Other forms of persuasion may use emotion as a primary tool. For example, works of art commonly use emotion as the major way of convincing an audience to hold a particular opinion. When was the last time you went to a particularly memorable movie and said, "That film was certainly persuasive. Its presentation of claims and evidence was flawless!"? More likely you were moved emotionally by the film. You sympathized with the major characters and with their point of view.

Likewise, emotion can be used as the primary means of persuasion in messages such as political propaganda. In such cases, the logic is often overshadowed by the strong emotional element. Look at the following propaganda posters from the 1930s. How do these posters inappropriately use emotion to convince the audience of their claims?

The poster reads, "The Jew; Inciter of War, Prolonger of War."

This American propaganda poster from World War II uses fear as its primary means of persuasion.

PRACTICE 10.6   Evaluating Propaganda

Study the propaganda posters above. Working individually or in groups, answer the following questions.

1. Examine the German poster. What is the purpose of the curtain? What does it imply? Does the face behind the curtain look friendly or threatening? How so? What might the raised fists represent?
2. Now consider the American poster. Why does the globe display North America? Explain.
3. In each case, who is the intended audience? How do you know?
4. How do the images in the posters attempt to incite the emotions of the audience?
5. Is logic employed in any way (to validate the claims)? Explain.

Using Emotion Appropriately

While emotion is sometimes used inappropriately to motivate an audience (such as using images of attractive women to sell cars), when balanced appropriately with authority and logic, it can cause your audience to view your argument sympathetically. Appealing to emotion is "inappropriate" when it replaces claims and evidence; appealing to emotion is "appropriate" when it reinforces the logic of your argument. Emotion should never be substituted for logic when your goal is to persuade an audience. An advertisement that uses a supermodel to sell beer is persuasive, but it is not argumentative. When using emotion within an argument, it is important to keep this distinction in mind.

Consider the following paragraph from Ann Coulter's article, "Not Crazy Horse, Just Crazy," in which she criticizes the academic practice of professorial tenure:

> Tenure was supposed to create an atmosphere of open debate and inquiry, but instead has created havens for talentless cowards who want to be insulated from life. Rather than fostering a climate of open inquiry, college campuses have become fascist colonies of anti-American hate speech, hypersensitivity, speech codes, banned words, and prohibited scientific inquiry.

Coulter's carefully chosen words—"talentless cowards," "fascist colonies," "anti-American hate speech"—serve to evoke the emotions of her readership. Other audiences may not be equally receptive to her message, however. The paragraph's point may be reasonable, but its presentation is so emotionally charged that Coulter's passion effectively buries the effect that her claim and associated evidence might otherwise have.

Victor Hanson makes a similar point in his *National Review* article, "Topsy-Turvy," albeit without the same level of emotional intensity:

> There are many explanations for this disturbing picture, both institutional and generational. Lifelong employment through tenure can breed complacency, ensure mediocrity, and foster insularity. Underachieving but tenured academics, despite dismal teaching evaluations and nonexistent scholarship, are virtually immune from meaningful censure—docked pay or dismissal—from their peers. Instead, they are like Brahmins from their seventh year to retirement— essentially three decades and more of institutional unaccountability.

This passage is more successful not only because emotion is not used as the primary means of persuasion, but also because the more balanced tone helps the author create a reasonable, authoritative voice to which the audience may be more likely to respond. The lesson here is clear: An argument that

PRACTICE 10.7   Evaluating "Got Milk?"

Study the "Got Milk?" poster. Working individually or in groups, answer the following questions.

1. In what ways is it appropriate or inappropriate to use the image of a model to sell milk?
2. Is the caption "Model Behavior" effective? Appropriate?
3. Is the text persuasive? Explain.
4. This ad is one of a series. What other images have been used? Were they appropriate?
5. If you created your own "Got Milk" ad, what image, slogan, and text might you use?

What is argumentative about this image? What is emotionally persuasive? What is the difference?

carefully balances authority, emotion, and logic is more likely to be considered sympathetically by a potential audience.

LOGICAL FALLACIES

From time to time, you may encounter arguments that either don't make sense or only seem to make sense until closer inspection reveals them to be false. Such arguments probably contain logical fallacies. Although fallacies often are accidental, sometimes they may indicate a deliberate attempt to deceive. Learning more about fallacies will help you form your own arguments and understand those of others.

This section examines a few of the many kinds of fallacies, grouping them by their effect on an audience: substitutions, distractions, and distortions.

Substitutions (Nonlogical Appeals)

Sometimes, the fallacies are substitutes for logic: Ethos and pathos sometimes are valued to the exclusion of logos. Nonlogical appeals may be based on authority, faith, fear, popularity, pity, and an assortment of other substitutes for logic.

PRACTICE 10.8   Substitutions

Identify each of the following nonlogical appeals.

1. "If you do that, your soul will be condemned to hell."
2. "Please give me a passing grade; otherwise, I'll lose my scholarship."
3. "If you use this cologne, people will be attracted to you."
4. "If you're so smart, why ain't you rich?"
5. "One billion Chinamen can't be wrong."

Authority (argumentum ad verecundiam) Under many circumstances, an appeal to authority can be legitimate. It has roots in the reality that we cannot be experts in everything, so we must trust the opinions of others: We accept the claim of a respected expert as factual without demanding full logical proof. Michael Jordan, for example, is a good spokesperson for athletic equipment but perhaps less credible if he endorses hair care products. Appeals to authority are fallacious when (1) the "authority" is not actually an expert, (2) authorities are in disagreement, or (3) the arguer misrepresents authority's opinion.

Faith (fiatism or blind faith) This appeal holds that some matters (spiritualism, loyalty) supersede personal judgment and logic. Faith is a hallmark of many religious believers and ideologues (those who hold unquestioning beliefs in particular causes or political leaders). Appeals to faith work only when you "preach to the choir"—that is, you present your argument to someone with identical beliefs who already accepts your claims.

Fear (argumentum in terrorem, argumentum ad metum) This appeal uses apprehension and dread to achieve a desired result. In spiritual terms, this fear may be the consequence of eternal damnation, while governments may threaten with legal repercussions. This fallacy is similar to the appeal to force (*argumentum ad baculum*), which goes beyond intimidation into physical coercion.

Pity (argumentum ad misericordiam) Known also as *special pleading*, this emotional appeal depends on making the audience understand and sympathize with the feelings of someone else. For example, when hardships of a personal nature affect job or school performance, employees or students sometimes plead for special consideration.

Other Appeals **Ignorance (argumentum ad ignorantiam):** If it hasn't been proven false, it must be true; or if it hasn't been proven true, it must be false.

Force (argumentum ad baculum): Might makes right.

Novelty (argumentum ad novitatem): Newer is better.

Numbers (argumentum ad numerum): More of something is better.

Popularity (argumentum ad populum): Many followers is a reason to follow. Known also as the bandwagon, mob appeal, and appeal to the masses.

Poverty (argumentum ad lazarum): Avoidance of wealth indicates virtue.

Tradition (argumentum ad antiquitatem): Older is better.

Wealth (argumentum ad crumenam): Wealth is validating.

Distractions

Sometimes the argument shifts to a related issue or even to something unrelated.

Attacking the Person (argumentum ad hominem, "argument against the person") Attacking the credibility *(ethos)* of the arguer shifts attention from the merits of the argument. The fallacy lies in the perception

PRACTICE 10.9 Distractions

Identify each of the following distractions.

1. "Sure, I know smoking causes cancer. But hey, bird flu could kill me tomorrow."
2. "Newt Gingrich cheated on his wife. You can't trust him on anything."
3. "Socialists want universal health care, and so do you. You're like the Socialists."
4. "If you don't like being called a 'Femi-Nazi,' perhaps you would prefer 'idiot.'" –Rush Limbaugh

that a disreputable person cannot be trusted regardless of his or her claims and evidence. Name calling or hurling epithets is an *ad hominem* attack that attempts to discredit opponents by associating them with a label that the audience considers negative: racist, nazi, commie. Ad hominem attacks are related to guilt by association and poisoning the well, discussed below.

Guilt by association This diverts attention away from the issues at hand and toward the reputations of others who support a particular claim. For example, Barack Obama felt he had to distance himself from his controversial former pastor Jeremiah Wright.

Poisoning the well The tactic of poisoning the well discredits opponents before an audience receives their arguments. The opponents become, figuratively, like a toxic water source that no one will use in the future.

Red Herring (ignoratio elenchi, irrelevant conclusion) A red herring is an issue that distracts an audience from the main discussion. Metaphorically, it is like using a smelly fish to throw hunting dogs off the scent. Also known as the *run-around*, a *wild goose chase*, and a *smokescreen*, a red herring is introduced as though it is relevant to the main issue but causes discussion to shift to the red herring. For example, opponents of Obama's health plan shifted the argument toward "death panels" that they said would be a by-product of the legislation.

Distortions

Analogy An analogy highlights a similarity between otherwise dissimilar concepts, people, objects, or events. Analogies are often used to make an abstraction more concrete. If the similarity isn't relevant to the argument or if the differences between the two subjects are significant, it is a fallacy. For example, economists have spoken of "trickle-down" economics, which advocates making the wealthy become wealthier, based on the hypothesis that they will in turn make purchases and investments that stimulate the economy—metaphorically "raining money" on those employed by the well-to-do. This analogy doesn't prove that tax cuts for the rich actually benefit the poor.

Anecdotal Evidence   Anecdotes are short stories that illustrate a point. They can be very useful in making an abstract concept more concrete and in adding pathos to an argument by connecting issues with real-life events, people, and emotions. Anecdotal evidence is fallacious when it is nonrepresentative, misleading the audience to overgeneralize the point being made. In such a case, the anecdote purports to represent a common occurrence but actually depicts "an exception to the rule."

Begging the Question (petitio principii)   Begging the question is a deductive fallacy that uses the conclusion as one of the premises. For example, Chief Justice William Rehnquist detected this fallacy in *Cruzan v. Director, Missouri Department of Health*:

> If the question is, Is Nancy Cruzan capable of making her own decision regarding the continuation or termination of life support, then to say that "Nancy Cruzan is incompetent"—without further argument, evidence, reasons, etc.—is to assume the question at hand. "Incompetent" is, in this context, simply a synonym for "incapable of making an informed decision."
>
> —William Rehnquist

Sometimes the phrase "begs the question" is used in a context that has nothing to do with an argument or logical fallacy. In this alternative sense, it means "raises interest in further discussion." For example, someone might say, "This early freeze begs the question, 'Is global warming a reality?' "

Cherry Picking (card stacking)   Cherry picking or card stacking occurs when an arguer is assumed to be presenting all major aspects—both pro and con—of an issue, but, in fact, has overrepresented one side and underrepresented the opposition. Figuratively, this practice is like cheating in a card game by making sure you get the best cards as they are dealt, or like selecting bits of evidence as one might pick and serve the best cherries while bypassing the rotten, worm-eaten ones. Prosecutors cherry-pick damaging evidence while defense attorneys cherry-pick exonerating evidence.

Circular Reasoning (circulus in demonstando) This form of begging the question occurs when the conclusion is used as a part of the evidence. Such a fallacy often is accidental, occurring when a slight rewording of the conclusion disguises it enough that it looks like evidence. For example, consider the statement "Brad Pitt is handsome because he is good looking." *Handsome* and *good looking* are synonyms, so the evidence is the same as the claim.

Equivocation Based on root words meaning "equal voice," equivocation is based on ambiguity: one word with two or more meanings. The equivocator allows the audience to think an obvious (more agreeable) meaning when, in fact, a secret (less agreeable) meaning is intended. If a parent asks "Did you break this window," a child might respond "I didn't touch it": the child's body may not have been in contact with the glass, but the ball he threw did the damage.

False Cause False cause is known also as a *post hoc fallacy*, from the Latin *post hoc ergo propter hoc*, meaning "after this, therefore because of this." When two events occur in close succession, such as a power outage that happens immediately after you switch on an appliance, we tend to think of the two events as being related. Sometimes the cause-and-effect relationship is actual, but other times it is just coincidence and thus is a fallacy. A simple example is that a crowing rooster doesn't cause the sun to rise. A more complex example is whether violent metaphors in political rhetoric ("Second Amendment Correction," "reload") cause actual violence, as in the 2011 shooting of Arizona representative Gabby Giffords.

False Dilemma In this situation, the arguer presents an incomplete set of choices. Aggressive salespeople often use this tactic: "Would you rather risk an asthma attack or purchase this deluxe air purifier?"

Hasty Generalization When a claim is based on too few examples, it may be in error. For example, if the first few students you met on campus were smoking cigarettes, you could be premature in assuming that most or all students smoke. Anecdotal evidence in particular can lead to hasty generalization. To minimize the risk of errors in generalization, statisticians follow guidelines concerning sample sizes and random selection.

Loaded Question Also known as a complex question, a loaded question combines two or more propositions into a single statement. If the responder answers one half without debating the other half, he or she makes a concession. The classic example is, "Have you stopped beating your wife?" This question implies that a simple answer is possible, but in reality any simple answer—yes or no—is an admission that one is or was a wife-beater.

Non Sequitur A *non sequitur* is a faulty or irrelevant conclusion. This term literally means "doesn't follow," in the sense that the conclusion doesn't follow from the evidence and explanations. One kind of non sequitur arises when the arguer claims that contradictory statements are both true. Non sequiturs can be understood more clearly by examining the logic as a syllogism. Two kinds of syllogistic non sequiturs exist: affirming the consequent and denying the subsequent.

The following is an example of affirming the consequent:

Major premise: All men are mortal.

Minor premise: I am mortal.

Conclusion: Therefore, I am all men.

The second example involves denying the subsequent:

Major premise: If I'm in Dallas, I'm in the United States.

Minor premise: I'm not in Dallas.

Conclusion: Therefore, I'm not in the United States.

Quoting out of Context Removing a quotation from its context can distort the original meaning. For example, the apparent winner of a debate might say of the opposition, "They would like to declare the contest was a draw." Spin doctors for the opposition might quote the apparent winner as saying, "The contest was a draw."

Slippery Slope This type of distortion assumes that if you make an exception to a rule, the rule will become open to other challenges and continually weakened. A slippery slope is a particular instance of analogy, arguing that your present position is like standing atop a steep, slick hill. If you descend from the top, the force of gravity begins to pull you downward, making it much easier to go lower than to return to the top. In truth, the slope slips both ways: it can be viewed as an "uphill climb" to a better way of doing things. The issue of same-sex marriage, for example, slips the slope in both directions. Some see it as a descent from morality, whereas others view it as an ascent toward civil rights.

Straw Man With a straw man argument, the arguer portrays the opposition's argument in a way that is easy to discredit—much the same way that a scarecrow is defenseless and easy to knock over. This can be accomplished by restating or simplifying the opposition's position, thereby making it undesirable or indefensible. If, for example, an arguer portrayed environmentalists as being concerned only with some philosophical opposition to progress but failed to mention concerns over the ecological balance of the planet, this argument would be a straw man.

Through the straw man fallacy, an arguer over-simplifies the opposition to make his or her claims easier to rebut.

PRACTICE.10.10   Distortions

Identify each of the following distortions.

1. "Southeast Asian countries are like dominoes. If one falls to communism, its neighbors will fall as well."
2. "Republicans care only about the rich, Democrats only about poor, and Libertarians only about themselves. Vote Green!"
3. "If we don't allow gays to marry, interracial marriage may become illegal."
4. "You said that nothing is better than barbecue, so I figured you wanted nothing for dinner."
5. "People who live near foul-smelling swamps get malaria, so it is probably the odor that causes the disease." (*Malaria* literally means "bad air.")

Looking Back at Chapter 10

► Logic is a study of establishing a relationship between ideas. It describes the processes we use to reach conclusions. In technical terms, it is the science of valid inference and correct reasoning.

► Deductive logic, the hallmark of argument, begins with a general point of agreement (a law, shared-belief, scientific principle) and applies it to a specific point of agreement (evidence, reason) to convince an audience to accept a point of disagreement.

► Aristotle presented argument in the form of a word equation called a syllogism, which is composed of the major premise, the minor premise, and the conclusion.

► Stephen Toulmin's logic functions like that of Aristotle, with the conceptual difference that it is practical and based on probable, not assured, conclusions.

► Toulmin's terminology parallels that of Aristotle: Toulmin's *warrant* resembles major premise, his *reason* resembles minor premise, and his *claim* resembles conclusion.

   ○ A *claim* is an idea that the rhetor wants the audience to accept as true; a *reason* is a statement explaining why the audience should believe the claim is true, and a *warrant* is an unexpressed assumption that the writer believes he holds in common with the audience.

   ○ Reasons are supported with primary evidence and discussion known as *grounds*; if the audience does not share the underlying assumption (*warrant*), then the warrant has to be expressed and supported with additional argument known as *backing*.

   ○ *Qualifiers* are statements that limit the application of a claim in order to overcome potential objections from an audience; *rebuttals* are specific arguments made against opposing claims.

► Rogerian arguments attempt to reduce the resistance in an audience by first carefully stating and acknowledging the legitimacy of the opposing view.

► Appealing to emotion is inappropriate when it is used in the place of claims and evidence; it is appropriate when it is used to reinforce the logic of your argument.

► Logical fallacies can be grouped by how they are perceived by an audience: substitutions, distractions, and distortions.

Suggestions for Writing

Select an argumentative topic for an essay. Before beginning to draft the essay, write the argumentative thesis and the supporting claims of the essay in the form of syllogisms. Anticipate any objections and prepare a rebuttal for each objection. Here are some questions to consider:

▶ Should uniforms be required in public schools? Why or why not? What are some advantages of uniforms? Some drawbacks?

▶ Are television commercials partly to blame for increases in childhood obesity? How about the Internet? What responsibility do corporations that advertise unhealthy lifestyles bear for children who end up with diabetes and other diseases?

▶ Should any form of "shame" punishments become legal? For example, should a judge be able to sentence someone who is convicted of public intoxication to several hours of wearing a sign in public reading, "I was drunk in public"?

▶ Should people of certain ethnicities be allowed to receive special education in their ethnic group? For instance, should Native Americans receive education in their particular ethnic history? Should this be done in the public schools, and should taxpayers have to foot the bill?

▶ Should children be allowed to pray in school? When both religious children (who want to pray) and nonreligious children (whose parents do not want them exposed to religion in any form) are present, who has the dominant right? The religious children? The nonreligious children? Why?

▶ Given that the U.S. divorce rate is close to 50 percent, should state governments be able to require premarriage counseling prior to issuing a marriage certificate? Should state governments be able to require a waiting period (six weeks, for example) before issuing a marriage certificate so that a hasty decision is not made?

▶ Should persons on welfare be able to undergo plastic surgery? What if the surgery is reconstructive and not cosmetic? Should welfare recipients have access to lifestyle-enhancing drugs such as Viagra, which may not be medically necessary?

▶ If a university discovers that a tenured professor had been convicted of, and served a sentence for, a serious crime such as murder, should that professor be fired? What if the crime happened thirty years ago and the professor has been a model citizen since then?

11

Literary Arguments

Jemal Countess/WireImage/Getty Images

{
Words mean more than what is set down on paper. It takes the human voice to infuse them with deeper meaning.

—Maya Angelou, poet and best-selling author
}

We begin this chapter with a quotation from Maya Angelou, famous for her poetry, plays, novels, and histories and notable as an actress, civil-rights activist, and teacher. Dr. Angelou reminds us that words do not always speak for themselves, that "It takes the human voice to infuse them with deeper meaning."

When you write an argument about a story, poem, play, novel, or speech, you look for deeper meaning—you *interpret*: You make claims that require support—evidence and explanations—for them to be accepted by your readers. The support takes various forms: quotations from the work you analyze, research on what others say about it, and your interpretation of the work and its meaning.

In this chapter you'll find examples of ways to argue your claims about literature: guidelines, an analytical paragraph, a student review, and a student essay. You'll also find the tools necessary for revealing the deeper meaning of literature: literary terminology.

The literary terms presented in this chapter are divided among five forms of literature: *poetry*, *fiction*, *drama*, *speech*, and *humor*. Often you'll find that the same literary terms apply to many forms of literature, seldom to one form. For example, terms listed as *poetic* overlap into *fiction* and *speech*, just as terms used in *fiction* overlap into *drama*, and so on. Look to your instructor for hints about which terms are relevant to your writing assignment.

POETRY

Poetry is difficult to define, but probably you have your own sense of it and can distinguish poetry from other forms of literature such as a novel, essay, or drama. To one great American poet, emotion is its distinguishing characteristic:

> A poem begins with a lump in the throat; a home-sickness or a love-sickness. It is a reaching-out toward expression; an effort to find fulfillment. A complete poem is one where an emotion has found its thought and the thought has found the words.
>
> —Robert Frost

To many, poetry is defined by its conventions. Poetry traditionally has been distinguished from prose by its patterns of rhyme and rhythm as well as its specific forms such as a sonnet, ballad, haiku, dramatic monologue, or sestina. However, modern poetry tends to be freer in structure and style.

Glossary for Poetry

Below is a glossary to help you explain your literary arguments about poetry.

alliteration: Repetition of a consonant sound beginning or within one word or among adjacent words. Excessive use creates a **tongue twister**.

> He clasps the crag with crooked hands.
>
> —Alfred, Lord Tennyson

> She sells sea shells by the sea shore.

allusion: A brief reference to a person, event, or other work of literature.

> In T. S. Eliot's poem "The Love Song of J. Alfred Prufrock" the narrator states "I am not Prince Hamlet," an allusion to Shakespeare's play.

ambiguity: Double meaning, making it possible to interpret a word or larger portion of writing in more than one way.

> Robert Frost's poem "Stopping by Woods on a Snowy Evening" mentions "the darkest evening of year," which literally means the winter solstice but figuratively can mean a time of sadness.

> The witches tell Shakespeare's Macbeth that "none of woman born" can harm him, which he interprets as saying that he is invulnerable. The other meaning is that Macduff, born by caesarean section, will kill Macbeth.

apostrophe: Direct address to an abstraction or to a person that is not present.

> Death, be not proud, though some have called thee/Mighty and dreadful, for thou art not so.
>
> —John Donne, "Sonnet X"

assonance: Repetition of a vowel sound in one word or among adjacent words.

> Hear the mellow wedding bells. . . .
>
> —Edgar Allan Poe, "The Bells"

blank verse: Verse without a pattern of rhyme but usually with a rhythm such as iambic pentameter.

> Something there is that doesn't love a wall,
> That sends the frozen-ground-swell under it,
> And spills the upper boulders in the sun.
>
> —Robert Frost, "The Mending Wall"

connotation: The implied, subjective, or associative meaning of a word, distinct from the **denotation** of its dictionary definition. For example, the term *capitalism* **denotes** an economic systems based on free trade (its dictionary definition), but **connotes** positive meanings to some people (freedom, prosperity) and negative meanings to others (greed, a lack of compassion for the poor).

consonance: Repetition of a consonant sounds (but not intervening vowels) at the ends of adjacent words, as in struts/frets:

> Life's but a walking shadow, a poor player, that struts and frets his hour upon the stage and then is heard no more.
>
> —Shakespeare, *Macbeth*

concrete poetry: The formatting of the poem into a shape relevant to the meaning. For example, a poem about a star would arrange its words in the shape of a star.

free verse: Verse without a pattern of rhyme or rhythm.

> I celebrate myself, and sing myself,
> And what I assume you shall assume,
> For every atom belonging to me as good belongs to you.
> I loaf and invite my soul,
> I lean and loaf at my ease observing a spear of summer grass.
>
> —Walt Whitman, "Song of Myself"

➔ FIGURATIVE LANGUAGE

"A rose is a rose is a rose." Often enough, the word *rose* does refer to a shrub having a prickly stem, compound leaves, and fragrant flowers. Yet Gertrude Stein, author of that famous quotation, would be the first to tell you that the word *rose* is not always literally a plant but sometimes a symbol of love, beauty, or spring. She might even tell you that in her poem the meaning of *rose* changes with each repetition.

Figurative language refers to ways that words can be used to mean something other than their literal, denotative meanings. *Figures* are the ways in which the language is crafted. When the order or arrangement of words affects the meaning of the writing, they are called *figures of form*, also known as *schemes*. When the words themselves mean something other than the literal definition, they are called *figures of speech*, also known as *tropes*. As you learn more about schemes and tropes, your own writing may bloom . . . like a rose.

THE RESEARCHERS HAD NO CHOICE BUT TO CHANGE THE STANDARD OF MEASURE TO "HAPPY AS DOUG"

OFF THE MARK ©(2005) Mark Parisi. Reprinted with permission of UNIVERSAL

Some similes continue to be used long after their original meanings are lost. "Happy as a clam" may have originated from the longer simile "Happy as a clam at high tide," referring to a time when clams are most safe from predators.

figures of speech: Language used in a non-literal way. Examples include simile, metaphor, personification, and synethesia. (Also **hyperbole,** defined in humor glossary.)

▶ **simile:** Comparison using *like* or *as.*

> He's welly like a cock as thinks the sun's rose o' purpose to hear him crow.
> —George Eliot, *Adam Bede*

▶ **metaphor:** Comparison not using *like* or *as.*

> Life for me ain't been no crystal stair.
> —Langston Hughes, "Mother to Son"

▶ **personification:** Giving human qualities to inanimate objects or abstractions.

> [The survivors] came through the jaws of death/Back from the mouth of Hell.
> —Alfred, Lord Tennyson,
> "The Charge of the Light Brigade"

▶ **synesthesia** ("joined feelings"): Describing a sensation using terms from another sense. Examples include *sharp taste, loud color, bitter cold,* and *resounding defeat.*

> There interposed a fly/With blue, uncertain, stumbling buzz.
> —Emily Dickinson,
> "I Heard a Fly Buzz When I Died"

foot: Repeating metrical unit, usually of two or three syllables. A foot is pattern of unstressed and stressed syllables: types of feet are listed below. A foot is part of the way we describe meter, the rhythmic pattern of a line of poetry. The foot is joined as an adjective in front of another term that expresses number of feet, as in "trochaic tetrameter." (See **meter,** below.)

▶ **iamb** (iambic): two syllables, one unstressed then one stressed: *Example:* Ren-ée

▶ **trochee** (trochaic): two syllables, one stressed, then one unstressed: *Example:* Mar´-y

▶ **spondee** (spondaic): two syllables, both stressed: *Example:* Mi´-mi´

▶ **anapest** (anapestic): three syllables, two unstressed, then one stressed: *Example:* Ga-bri-elle´

▶ **dactyl** (dactylic): three syllables, one stressed, then two unstressed: *Example:* Jenn´-i-fer

▶ **amphibrach** (amphibrachic): three syllables, unstressed, stressed, then unstressed: *Example:* A-man´-da

image: Descriptive or figurative language. Sometimes called a "mental picture," an image can appeal to any of the five senses. Writers sometimes use images as symbols or to establish a theme or mood. The author's use of images is called **imagery**. Poet Edgar Allan Poe was known for death imagery and author Henry David Thoreau for nature imagery.

meter: Pattern and frequency of stressed and unstressed syllables in a line of poetry. Meter is described by a number of "feet" (repeating units) in a line. (See **foot**.)

▶ **iambic pentameter:**

> I saw the sky descending black and white.
>
> —Robert Lowell

▶ **monometer:** one foot in each line (example is trochaic monometer)

> Adam
> Had 'em
>
> —Shel Silverstein, "Fleas"

▶ **dimeter:** two feet in each line (example is trochaic dimeter)

> Simple Simon
> Met a pieman
>
> —Nursery rhyme

▶ **trimeter:** three feet in each line (example is trochaic trimester)

> Little lamb, who made thee?
> Dost thou know who made thee?
>
> —William Blake,
> "The Lamb," *Songs of Innocence*

▶ **tetrameter:** four feet in each line (example is iambic tetrameter)

> I think that I shall never see
> A poem lovely as a tree.
>
> —Joyce Kilmer, "Trees"

▶ **pentameter:** five feet in each line (example is iambic pentameter)

> Two households, both alike in dignity,
> In fair Verona, where we lay our scene
>
> —Shakespeare,
> Prologue of *Romeo and Juliet*

▶ **hexameter:** six feet in each line (example is dactylic hexameter, typical of Greek and Latin epic poems; also known as *heroic meter)*

> Goddess, please sing of the wrath of Achilles, the son of good Peleus.
> —Homer, first line of *The Iliad*

onomatopoeia: Word that mimics a sound. Also called an **echo word**. *Examples: bang, beep, buzz, ring, splat, woof, cri-itch* (biting a potato chip), *spohlap* (dripping water).

oxymoron: A phrase composed of terms that are opposites. *Examples: virtual reality, jumbo shrimp, head butt, pretty ugly,* and *tight slacks.*

refrain: A phrase, line, or group of lines that repeat at intervals, often at the end of a stanza.

> Jingle Bells! Jingle Bells!
> Jingle all the way!
> Oh, what fun it is to ride
> In an one-horse open sleigh!
>
> —John Pierpont (1785–1866),
> refrain from "Jingle Bells"

rhyme: Words with a similar sound.

▶ **end rhyme:** Similar-sounding words at the ends of lines

> I think that I shall never see
> A poem as lovely as a tree
>
> —Joyce Kilmer (1886–1918)

▶ **internal rhyme:** Similar-sounding words within a line (the example has internal rhymes of dreary/weary and napping, tapping, and rapping)

> Once upon a midnight dreary, while I pondered weak and weary,
> Over many a quaint and curious volume of forgotten lore,
> While I nodded, nearly napping, suddenly there came a tapping,
> As of some one gently rapping, rapping at my chamber door.
> —Edgar Allen Poe, "The Raven"

▶ **single rhyme:** Last syllables rhyme. *Example:* fine/wine

▶ **double rhyme:** Two syllables rhyme. *Example:* poet/know it

▶ **triple rhyme:** Three syllables rhyme. *Example:* phenomenal/
  abdominal

▶ **sight rhyme:** Words of similar spelling but different sound. Also called
  eye rhyme. *Examples:* dead/bead, ranger/anger

▶ **slant rhyme:** Close but not perfect rhyme, with slight variation in the
  vowel or consonant. Also called *near-, half-, off-, family-,* or
  oblique-rhyme. Can be an eye rhyme. *Examples:* fine/rhyme, soul/all

rhyme scheme: Pattern of rhyming words at the end of lines of poetry. To
help describe the scheme, the first instance of a rhyme sound is labeled "A"
and each new rhyme sound takes the next letter of the alphabet. Some types
of poems required specific rhyme schemes:

▶ **couplet:** two consecutive lines: AA, often followed by other couplets:
  BB, CC, etc.

> So long as men can breathe or eyes can see,
> So long lives this, and this gives life to thee.

> —Shakespeare,
> concluding couplet of "Sonnet 18"

▶ **triplet:** three consecutive lines: AAA. If the triplet makes a **stanza**
  (see below), it is also a **tercet.**

> A still small voice spake unto me,
> "Thou art so full of misery,
> Were it not better not to be?"
> Then to the still small voice I said;
> 'Let me not cast in endless shade
> What is so wonderfully made.'

> —Alfred, Lord Tennyson (1809–1892),
> "The Two Voices"

▶ **interlocking four-line:** ABAB

> Shall I compare thee to a summer's day?
> Thou art more lovely and more temperate:
> Rough winds do shake the darling buds of May,
> And summer's lease hath all too short a date,

> —Shakespeare,
> first quatrain of "Sonnet 18"

▶ **limerick:** AABBA

> I sat next to the Duchess at tea,
> Distressed as a person could be.
>> Her rumblings abdominal
>> Were simply phenomenal—
> And everyone thought it was me!

—Woodrow Wilson (1856–1924)

▶ **Shakespearian or English sonnet:** ABAB CDCD EFEF GG

> Shall I compare thee to a summer's day?
> Thou art more lovely and more temperate:
> Rough winds do shake the darling buds of May,
> And summer's lease hath all too short a date,
> Sometime too hot the eye of heaven shines,
> And often is his gold complexion dimmed,
> And every fair from fair sometime declines,
> By chance, or nature's changing course, untrimmed.
> But thy eternal summer shall not fade,
> Nor lose possession of that fair thou ow'st,
> Nor shall death brag thou wander'st in his shade,
> When in eternal lines to time thou grow'st.
> So long as men can breathe or eyes can see,
> So long lives this, and this gives life to thee.

—Shakespeare, "Sonnet 18"

rhythm: Pattern of stressed and unstressed syllables in a line. Stress refers to the way some parts of words are spoken with more emphasis, expressed slightly more loudly or with more breath. This is also called "accent." Rhythm sometimes is synonymous with **meter** (see above for definitions and examples), but other times is used to express cadence impressionistically (e.g., "syncopated" or "driving") rather than in the numerical beat-counting terminology of meter. For example, examine the first line of Poe's "The Raven." The stressed syllables have been bolded:

Once upon a **mid**night **drear**y, **while** I **pon**dered **weak** and **weary**

The rhythmic pattern begins with a stressed syllable followed by an unstressed syllable, and this pattern continues through the line. Some poets vocalize the rhythm by using the sound "DUM" for stressed syllables and "da" for unstressed syllables. Using this method, the Poe's first line has this rhythm:

DUM-da-DUM-da-DUM-da-DUM-da/ DUM-da-DUM-da-DUM-da-DUM-da

stanza: Unit of lines that form a pattern throughout a poem. A stanza often is named by the number of lines it contains: See **rhyme scheme** for examples.

▶ **couplet:** two lines

▶ **tercet:** three lines

- ▶ **quatrain:** four lines

- ▶ **cinquain:** five lines (also quintain or quintet)

- ▶ **sestet:** six lines

- ▶ **septet:** seven lines

- ▶ **octave:** eight lines (also octet)

symbol: Something that stands for something else.

In *The Great Gatsby,* the giant billboard eyes of T. J. Eckleburg stand for God.

Hester Prynne's scarlet *A* begins as a symbol of her adultery but changes to a symbol of her charity.

theme: A major idea, motif, or "thread" that runs through a literary work. The theme may be directly stated, such as the opening line "Good fences make good neighbors" in Robert Frost's poem "Mending Wall," or instead may be a matter of interpretation based on the evidence within the literary work. Many literary arguments are based on claims about theme.

PRACTICE 11.1   Literary Argument about Poetry

Read the poem "Phenomenal Woman" on page 316 for understanding and interpretation. Consider the following questions:

1. Define *phenomenal*. To you, what makes a woman "phenomenal"?

2. How typical is your definition of a "phenomenal woman"? What other opinions are typical? Who holds those opinions? Do you believe those opinions are acceptable?

3. What do lines 1–4 tell you about the speaker's physical appearance? Why does she begin with facts that seem to undercut her claim of being "phenomenal"? In what way is she making an argument? Is she rebutting the counter arguments?

4. In the poem, what personal features does the speaker offer as evidence of her phenomenal nature? Are they convincing? Do these examples fit your definition?

5. Whom do you think the speaker is addressing in this poem? Explain.

6. Do you believe that the speaker is as popular with men as she claims to be? For example, "Then they swarm around me." Explain. You may need to infer, using your experiences that come from outside the evidence of the poem.

7. Near the end of the poem, why does the speaker say "Now you understand/Just why my head's not bowed"? Why does she assume the audience would expect her to bow her head?

8. How do you interpret the poem? If your interpretation requires evidence and explanations to convince a reasonably skeptical audience, then you're making a literary argument.

(continued)

(continued)

"Phenomenal Woman" by Maya Angelou

Pretty women wonder where my secret lies.
I'm not cute or built to suit a fashion model's size
But when I start to tell them,
They think I'm telling lies.
I say,
It's in the reach of my arms
The span of my hips,
The stride of my step,
The curl of my lips.
I'm a woman
Phenomenally.
Phenomenal woman,
That's me.

I walk into a room
Just as cool as you please,
And to a man,
The fellows stand or
Fall down on their knees.
Then they swarm around me,
A hive of honey bees.
I say,
It's the fire in my eyes,
And the flash of my teeth,
The swing in my waist,
And the joy in my feet.
I'm a woman
Phenomenally.
Phenomenal woman,
That's me.

Men themselves have wondered
What they see in me.
They try so much But they can't touch
My inner mystery.
When I try to show them
They say they still can't see.
I say,
It's in the arch of my back,
The sun of my smile,
The ride of my breasts,
The grace of my style.
I'm a woman

Phenomenally.
Phenomenal woman,
That's me.
Now you understand
Just why my head's not bowed.
I don't shout or jump about
Or have to talk real loud.
When you see me passing
It ought to make you proud.
I say,
It's in the click of my heels,
The bend of my hair,
the palm of my hand,
The need of my care,
'Cause I'm a woman
Phenomenally.
Phenomenal woman,
That's me.

→ EXAMPLE OF A LITERARY ARGUMENT ABOUT A POEM

The paragraph below is an excerpt from Vitaliy Kotyakov's "Analysis of 'Phenom-enal Woman.'" The first sentence goes beyond a restatement of the poem to argue an interpretation. Note how Kotyakov quotes evidence from the poem and then explains the evidence in terms of her literary argument. In what ways do you agree with her analysis? In what ways do you disagree? Why?

> Attractive personality is much more powerful than attractive genetics or any ability to fill in an impossible role. The speaker [in "Phenomenal Woman"] then explains to these women, and rightly to all women, that it is her own attractive personality that is the reason men "stand or fall down on their knees" before her. It does not mean that she does not try to be her best, but she does not see conformity as justifiable and therefore the reason why "[her] head's not bowed". She then goes on to explain in detail her own reasons and her own aims in attractiveness. She measures her own achievement by measurable decisions she can make such as her "smile," "style," and "stride," not impossible standards.*

*Vitaliy Kotyakov's "Analysis of 'Phenomenal Woman.'" Associated Content online Copyright 2009 by Associated Content. Reproduced with permission of Associated Content in the format Textbook and Other Book via Copyright Clearance Center.

PRACTICE 11.2   Writing about Poetry

For a poem you are reading, you may be required to write an essay, review, or some other document. Following are some guidelines:

1. Discuss the poem's words. These words work together to establish the poem's "voice." Circle the most significant words in the poem, and explain why you think they might be important in explaining the poem's overall meaning. (You don't have to make your final judgment about the poem's meaning just yet.)

2. Identify the poem's figurative language and other literary devices. How do they contribute to the poem's extended meaning to you? How might they affect a different reader?

3. Comment on the poem's form. Is it a lyric, narrative, or dramatic poem? Why is this form appropriate to the meaning you have identified?

4. Now working from the meaning you have identified, develop a claim about the poem. Connect one of the poem's elements you have identified (words, voice, literary devices, form) to the meaning or theme you have identified. In some cases, you may be more

(continued)

(continued)

concerned with the writer's techniques than with your interpretation. (For an example, see the Student Essay at the end of this chapter.)

5. Cite a specific passage as *evidence* to support your *claim* from the poem. *Explain* this passage in terms of your claim.

FICTION

Fiction is a broad category that may include any work of imaginative prose. Novels, literary short stories, and popular fiction of many genres (kinds of literature) such as romance, detective stories, and science fiction are included in this category. Fiction is distinguished by narration (organization through time: the "voice" that tells the story), description (organization through space: vivid, "life-like" word pictures), and dialogue (character speech, usually enclosed in quotation marks).

Glossary for Fiction

Below is a glossary to help you explain your literary arguments about fiction.

allegory: An extended metaphor in which the characters, events, and/or objects symbolize something else. For example, in John Bunyan's *Pilgrim's Progress*, the protagonist named Christian meets Mr. Worldly Wisdom on his way to the Celestial City: The characters and events represent the moral challenges of the faithful. George Orwell's *Animal Farm* allegorically critiques the Russian Revolution through a story of animals that rebel against their farmer.

antagonist: An adversary who opposes the protagonist or hero in a drama or narrative. *Example:* Iago in Shakespeare's *Othello*. Also known as *villain*, *nemesis*, or *bad guy*.

character: A fictional person.

▶ **static character:** does not change during the story

▶ **dynamic character:** changes during the story

▶ **flat character:** has one or few characteristics

▶ **round character:** has several characteristics

characterization: How the author reveals the nature of the character. Authors characterize through the manner in which the character speaks (**dialogue**), through description of the character's appearance, and through narration of the character's actions.

conflict: A struggle between opposing forces that is resolved in a **climax**. (See **plot**.) Conflicts can be categorized by the forces in opposition: person against person, person against nature, person against self, person against society, person against technology.

dialogue: The words spoken by a character to another. A character can reveal thoughts through **internal dialogue**. English convention encloses dialogue in quotation marks.

fable: A brief tale in a style suitable for a very young audience, typically featuring animals as characters. A fable usually concludes with a clearly stated moral.

mood: A dominant feeling suggested by a work, such as "sad," "light," or "chaotic."

narrator The teller of the story. In a work of fiction, the narrator also is fictional, distinct from the author. The narrator can be first person (see **persona**) or third person. (See **point of view.**)

narrative devices: Ways in which the author alters the sequence of events in a story.

▶ **foreshadowing:** Early hints about something that happens later in a story.

▶ **flashback:** A momentary interruption in a story to narrate an event that happened at an earlier time.

▶ *in media res:* Beginning a story in its middle. Literally, "into the middle of things."

persona: A first-person narrator who is distinctly different from the author: The author uses a character as a kind of mask. *Persona* is derived from the Latin *per sonare*, meaning "to speak through." The term originates in early drama, when actors wore masks that amplified their volume. *Example:* The narrator of Jonathan Swift's "A Modest Proposal" proposes cannibalism as a solution to starvation, while Swift actually wants a humane solution to the problem.

plot: A story's sequence of events in the order presented by the author. Many plots follow a sequence that includes distinct parts or **acts**, beginning with an **exposition** and progressing through an **inciting moment, climbing action, climax,** and **falling action** until reaching a **resolution**. These plot elements are defined below, with examples from the main plot of J. R. R. Tolkien's *The Lord of the Rings*. (*LOTR* also has subplots, each with its own sequence of acts.)

▶ **exposition:** The introductory segment that provides background information and introduces elements such as setting, characters, and something about the conflict or inciting moment. At first the characters are relaxed, feeling little tension or anxiety. In *LOTR*, readers are introduced to the peaceful life of Hobbiton, to some aspects of Middle Earth, and to the protagonists Frodo and his Uncle Bilbo. The readers learn that Bilbo has a magic ring, foreshadowing the *inciting moment*.

▶ **inciting moment:** The element (issue, event, or object) that makes the story possible, setting events in motion, and elevating the tension felt by characters and audience, a.k.a. the **conflict** (struggle between forces) or **story question**. In *LOTR*, the wizard Gandalf discovers that Bilbo's ring possesses evil powers that could destroy Middle Earth.

▶ **rising action:** Secondary conflicts or complications that the protagonists must confront before resolving the main conflict. Tension increases. In *LOTR*, the protagonists engage in a quest to destroy the ring. The complications include obstacles and battles. The ring becomes heavier and more treacherous as it nears Mt. Doom.

▶ **climax:** The turning point at which the main conflict is resolved. The audience feels the greatest tension at this point. In *LOTR*, the ring is destroyed by Frodo and Sam despite the complications of the protagonists' exhaustion, the ring's power over Frodo, the attack by Gollum, and the raging battle between Sauron's forces and the armies of Gondor and Rohan.

▶ **falling action:** The events that immediately follow the climax and that lead to the resolution. The climax may not immediately release all the tension felt by the audience. Parts of the story may remain to be completed, especially subplots or complications of the main conflict.

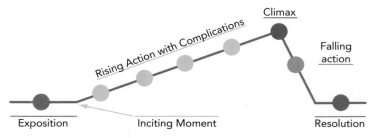

Gustav Freytag, a 19th century German novelist, noticed a pattern in the plots of prose fiction and drama. He diagrammed the plot as a curve that represents changing levels of tension felt by the audience during a story. His diagram, called *Freytag's Pyramid*, often is taught in literature courses.

This plot diagram shows how the main events in a story are organized. A plot follows a sequence of events, sometimes called "acts": exposition, inciting moment, rising action, climax, falling action, and resolution. The diagram shows the changing levels of tension or anxiety felt by the protagonists and sympathetically by the audience.

In *LOTR*, the evil of Sauron dissipates, the orcs flee, and Sam and Frodo are rescued from an erupting Mt. Doom by the Eagles.

- ▶ **resolution:** The return to a state of low tension. Conflict ceases and characters relax. Also called **denouement**, or "untying." In *LOTR*, the protagonists recuperate and celebrate; various plot twists are untied and concluded.

point of view: Describes how a narrator knows the content of the story. The narrator can be inside the story (first person POV) or outside the story (third person POV). POV also is defined by the amount of information known or provided by the narrator: omniscient, limited omniscient, or objective. Further, a narrator can be reliable or unreliable.

- ▶ **first person POV:** The narrator is part of the action. This kind of narration usually is limited to the observations and reflections of the narrator. The narrator at times seems to speak directly to the reader while using personal pronouns such as "I," "me," "my," etc.

- ▶ **third person POV:** The narrator is not part of the action, using third-person pronouns to describe what the characters do: "he," "she," "they," etc.

- ▶ **omniscient POV:** The narrator knows everything, including the thoughts of the characters.

- ▶ **limited omniscient POV:** the narrator doesn't know everything, or at least doesn't reveal everything. This allows for some suspense and surprises for the audience.

- ▶ **objective POV:** The narrator is limited to things that can be observed. This is sometimes called the "fly on the wall" technique.

- ▶ **reliable narrator:** The narrator tells the truth. The reader is able to trust the narrator's perspective.

- ▶ **unreliable narrator:** The narrator intentionally deceives, leaves information out, or doesn't understand the story as well as the reader. The reader has to work to "read between the lines" and interpret the story.

setting: The time and place of a story.

style: An author's distinctive manner of expression. In part, style emerges from word choice and sentence structure. Style emerges also from imagery and the kinds of comments made by the author.

subplot: A secondary story within a story.

PRACTICE 11.3   Writing about Fiction

For a story you are reading, you may be required to write an essay, review, or some other document. Following are some guidelines:

1. Mark the literary devices you recognize. How do they contribute to your interpretation?

2. Develop a claim about the story. Your claim probably will focus on your interpretation and be supported by your discussion of specific literary devices. In some cases, you may be more concerned with the writer's techniques than with your interpretation. (For an example, see the Student Essay at the end of this chapter.)

3. Cite specific passages from the story. Explain them in terms of your thesis or topic sentence.

4. Organize your literary argument around the specifications provided by your instructor.

5. If research is part of the assignment's specifications, use your sources two ways: (1) to discover claims worth arguing and (2) to discover support for your own arguments.

A LITERARY REVIEW

A review makes a value claim. It rates something, based on qualities that the reviewer believes to be important. Anything can be reviewed—any product (cars, refrigerators, literary works) and any performance (a politician's record, an athlete's abilities, an actor's skills). Since this chapter focuses on literary arguments, you might be asked to write a literary review.

The purpose of a literary review is to provide information for potential audiences so they can decide whether to partake in a literary experience: read a book or attend a drama. The literary terms found in this chapter's glossaries can help you express your evaluation to your readers.

Following are guidelines for writing a review and an example of a book review written by a student.

Writing a Literary Review

Writing a review, you'll go through a familiar process: planning, drafting, and revising.

PLANNING   Prewriting activities will make your process productive.

▶ **Know the genre**: Regardless of what you review—prose, poetry, film, drama, music, restaurant—you should know techniques and the terminology. Do a little research in advance if you lack the knowledge.

▶ **Know your readers:** What do they need to know from your review? What is their level of knowledge about the genre?

▶ **Experience the work:** If possible, more than one experience can help you to assess and explain better. Repeated experiences are easy for short works such as poems, songs (which are like poems), or short stories. For a book, you can re-read selected parts.

▶ **Take notes:** Write down your impressions. Identify details that will help you explain your claims. Notes are especially useful when repeated experiences are impractical, such as a life performance of a drama.

▶ **Decide on your claim:** A review may contain a variety of claims about the various qualities of the genre, but ultimately it is a holistic evaluation: thumbs up/down or perhaps a rating based on a range of numbers, such as four out of five stars.

▶ **Organize:** What major supporting points will you cover? In what order will you present your points? What kind of evidence and explanations will you provide?

DRAFTING A review has an introduction, body paragraphs, and a conclusion.

▶ **Title:** Reviews usually have titles that reveal the name of what is being reviewed but also may hint at the reviewer's opinion.

▶ **Introduction:** A review often begins with an interest-catching sentence: a lead or "hook." The introduction of a review provides essential information: names (e.g., title, author, actor) and contextual information (e.g., subject, historical background of a work). If the review is negative, the introduction may begin with a few positive remarks before transitioning to an unfavorable evaluation-claim.

▶ **Body paragraphs:** The body paragraphs will cover various supporting points. For a book, this may be characterization, plot, or writing style. For music, the points may involve lyrics, vocalization, instrumentation, or arrangement. If conciliatory remarks are needed but not mentioned in the introduction, the first or last body paragraphs can offer concessions.

▶ **Conclusion:** The last part of the review makes clear your evaluation and recommendations. Some brief summarizing of early points may be helpful.

▶ **Follow conventions.** Below are some tips to help you write.

1. **Organize around points.** A literary review doesn't have to be a re-telling of a whole story. Instead, pick out the elements that best support your claims.

2. **Don't over-summarize.** If your review involves a literary work, you'll be obliged to convey something about the overall story. You could write a paragraph that summarizes, but summarizing might work better as you reveal the specific points you wish to make.

3. **Don't over-quote.** You can choose a few outstanding quotations, but these usually are few and brief.

4. **Don't spoil.** If you review a literary work, don't reveal so much that you spoil the suspense or surprises intended for the audience.

5. **Be clever.** Brighten a review with your wit. Readers like reviews to be entertaining.

6. **Be fair.** If your review is positive, you can still concede some weaknesses of the work. If your review is negative, you can still mention some redeeming characteristics. Don't be cruel.

REVISING   Does the review accomplish your goals and follow conventions?

▶ Is your evaluation claim clearly stated?

▶ Have you offered examples with explanations without spoiling the experience for future audiences?

▶ Have you been fair?

→ TITLING YOUR REVIEW

Review titles usually announce to a prospective reader the name of the work and of the author. Sometimes the title hints at the reviewer's opinion and perhaps provides an interest-catching hook such as wordplay. Consider the titles of these reviews of the novel *Sing You Home*: What does each do?

▶ "Jodi Picoult's *Sing You Home*." Review by Susan Salter Reynolds, *Los Angeles Times*

▶ "Picoult Takes on Another Family Issue in *Sing You Home*." Review by Amanda St. Amand, *St. Louis Post-Dispatch*

▶ "Jodi Picoult's *Sing* Homes in on Gay Rights." Review by Jocelyn McClurg, *USA Today*

→ INTRODUCING YOUR REVIEW

Choose a strategy to introduce your review: Give background on the subject or theme of the work. Or provide background on the author. Or launch into a specific feature of the work. Or let your reader know something about your overall evaluation of the work. Consider the opening lines to these reviews of the novel *Sing You Home*: What does each do?

► "Jodi Picoult's novels do not gather dust on the bedside table. They are gobbled up quickly and the readers want more."

—Susan Salter Reynolds, *Los Angeles Times*

► "Jodi Picoult has evolved into the 'issues' writer for popular fiction, and she tackles another thorny one in *Sing You Home*, her latest tale of someone's personal tragedy."

—Amanda St. Amand, *St. Louis Post-Dispatch*

► "Did President Obama get his hands on an early copy of *Sing You Home*? Or does best-selling novelist Jodi Picoult, as usual, have an uncanny sense of good timing?"

—Jocelyn McClurg, *USA Today*

→ CONCLUDING YOUR REVIEW

Your reader will use your evaluation to decide whether to become an audience for the work. State your conclusion, along with any qualifications needed for fairness. Consider these concluding lines from reviews of the novel *Sing You Home*: What does each do?

► "Overall, I liked *Sing You Home* more than Picoult's other releases over the past few years. Still, I would not label *Sing You Home* a 'must read' for 2011."

—Review by Erin Collazo Miller, *About.com Guide*

► "Vanessa's confessional remarks read as if they're from a high school health textbook with a chapter on 'Understanding Your Gay or Lesbian Loved One.' Nothing much is risked; nothing fresh is illuminated—that's the feel of much of *Sing You Home*. It's a lightly entertaining melodrama, which skims through and then wraps up some messy dilemmas. But this 'song' is flat."

—Review by Maureen Corrigan, *Washington Post*

PRACTICE 11.4   Before You Read the Student Review

1. Have you read a review before? What purpose does a review serve? What are some features of reviews that you expect?

2. Examine the title. What information does it provide? Does it attract your attention?

STUDENT REVIEW

Brittany Einhorn

Professor Everett

Composition

March 16, 2011

Review: In Tune with *Sing You Home*

Covering topics from suicide and school shootings to medical tragedies and sexual assault, Jodi Picoult is well-known for making her readers see issues like these in a new light. *Sing You Home*, a novel that was number one on both the *New York Times* and *USA Today* book lists, is no different, portraying the story of a woman who falls for someone who is not the typical prince charming.

In an America where people still look twice when seeing two men holding hands, you have to give Jodi Picoult a bit of credit for her courage in telling a story of a woman's love for another woman. Zoe, a music therapist and atheist, falls in love with Vanessa, a school counselor. She loves Vanessa not because she is a woman; rather, she just loves who she is. Their love is conveyed in a very natural way: Picoult describes it as the way that any two human beings would fall in love. Through their relationship, Picoult attempts to portray the social struggles of gay couples.

Picoult always presents both sides to a story and allows the reader to be sympathetic toward two conflicting outlooks. In *Sing You Home* Max, Zoe's former husband, goes from being an alcoholic to a devout Christian member of Eternal Glory Church. Because of Zoe and Max's difference in beliefs they must settle in court a dispute on who will possess their frozen embryos. While Picoult does indeed make both characters sympathetic, it is very clear which side she favors. As a result of the outrageous character-smearing tactics by Max's pastor and by his lawyer, the readers soon favor Zoe.

The story starts with Zoe and Max married and expecting. It progresses to a legal battle with the same man, now her ex-husband, over their frozen embryos. Zoe and her new wife Vanessa want custody. Much happens between page 1 and the conclusion on page 466.

I had reservations about some of the many social issues that Jodi Picoult presents. Gay marriage, frozen embryos ("pre-born children?"), divorce, adultery, abortion, teen suicide, and religion all come up in this novel. Some of these issues are introduced but never concluded. For example, the fate of the character Lucy, a suicidal teen that Zoe meets during music therapy, is left a mystery. Near the end of the court case, Pastor Clive comes in the courtroom claiming he "can sink [Zoe]" with scandalous evidence, but that, too, is never resolved.

Picoult's style of writing leaves her readers with quotations about life that they'll want to write down and hang up on their refrigerators or post on Facebook immediately. For example, Picoult writes, "Anxiety's like a rocking chair. It gives you something to do, but it doesn't get you very far." She provokes emotions, smiles, and remembrances.

One last and remarkable thing about Jodi Picoult's style is that readers never know the ending until the very final pages. You should tune in to *Sing You Home* until the last bittersweet notes. For this thrilling and unique page-turner, Jodi Picoult deserves four out of five stars.

PRACTICE 11.5   Responding to the Student Review

1. Examine the introduction. What does the reviewer do to draw the reader into the review? Is the introduction effective?

2. Examine the body paragraphs. Are they well organized? Do they provide useful information?

(continued)

(continued)

3. At what point do you know whether the review is positive or negative? At what point does the reviewer reveal some shortcomings of the novel? Was that location effective?

4. Examine the conclusion. Is it convincing? Does it display wit?

5. Identify a major strength and a major weakness of the review. What could the reviewer have done to improve the review?

DRAMA

A drama is a literary work designed to be performed by actors on a stage. The term *drama* can be generic for any kind of on-stage performance or can be specific for serious (non-comedic) works such as tragedies. A drama also is known as a play or stage play. The written text of a drama, known as a script, consists primarily of dialogue assigned to specific characters. The script may also contain stage directions.

Below is a glossary to help you explain your literary arguments about drama.

Glossary for Drama

catharsis: Emotional cleansing through experiencing the strong emotions stimulated by a drama. A tragedy arouses emotions of fear or pity that Aristotle theorized left the audience cleansed or refreshed.

comedy: A drama with a positive "reversal of fortune"—a happy ending. Comedy can be part of a romance that ends happily, but also can be part of satire. Satire tends to be pessimistic as it ridicules folly. (For more on satire, see **Humor** later in this chapter.)

comic relief: A scene or character that interrupts the intensity of action, typically in a tragedy. For example, in Act 2 of Shakespeare's *Macbeth*, the monologue of a drunken porter provides comic relief after the murder of Duncan.

conventions: Ways of doing things in a creative work that are unrealistic yet accepted by the audience. In a drama, conventions include the aside, a chorus, *deus ex machina,* monologue, and soliloquy.

▶ **aside:** Words spoken directly to the audience but not heard by the other actors on stage. Conventionally, the actor would turn his/her head "aside" (away from the other actors) momentarily and comment to the audience.

▶ **chorus:** A group of actors in Greek tragedy who speak in unison to comment on the action.

▶ **deus ex machina:** An improbable solution to a conflict or complication in the plot. The phrase comes from a Greek phrase meaning "god from a machine." Greek drama sometimes climaxed with a character representing a god being lowered by pulleys onto the stage. In modern drama, it refers to any unlikely occurrence or character that resolves the plot.

▶ **monologue:** Words spoken by a single character without other characters responding.

▶ **soliloquy:** Longer than an aside, words directed by an actor to the audience but not heard by the other actors. Hamlet's "To be or not to be" speech is a soliloquy.

costumes: The clothing worn by actors on stage.

gestures: The facial expressions and bodily movements of an actor.

pathos: The emotional elements of a tragedy that result in pity for a character.

props: Objects used on stage for setting (e.g., furniture, plants) or for handling by actors (e.g., dishes, swords). The word is short for stage properties. Props are distinct from costumes.

recognition: The moment of realization. In cases of dramatic irony, it is the point at which the protagonist learns the truth that the audience already knew. (See **Humor** later in this chapter for more about dramatic irony.) In *Star Wars*, recognition occurs the moment that Luke learns that Darth Vader is his father.

reversal: The moment that the plot shifts into a new, unexpected direction, often in an opposite direction: victory becomes defeat, order becomes chaos.

scenery: The way the stage is decorated to simulate a real location. Examples include a shabby apartment for *A Raisin in the Sun* or a cornfield for *Oklahoma!*

script: The written text of the drama, containing dialogue and stage directions.

stage direction: In the script, the playwright's notes on action and setting. Directions often include suggestions to the actor on how to interpret or deliver lines of dialogue or to the stage manger on how to arrange the scenery.

tragedy: A drama in which characters suffer catastrophe and possibly death. The misfortunes may be a consequence of a tragic flaw possessed by the protagonist. Examples include Shakespeare's *Macbeth* and Arthur Miller's *Death of a Salesman*.

tragic flaw: A weakness of character, such as the pride of Oedipus, that leads to tragic consequences.

tragic hero: The protagonist of a tragedy. The character possesses a tragic flaw that causes a reversal of his or her fortune.

PRACTICE 11.6   Writing about Drama

For a drama you have read or viewed, you may be required to write an essay, review, or some other document. Following are some guidelines:

1. Mark the literary devices you recognize or take notes. How do they contribute to your interpretation?
2. Develop a claim about the drama. Your claim probably will focus on your interpretation and be supported by your discussion of specific literary devices. In some cases, you may be more concerned with the writer's techniques than with your interpretation. (For an example, see the Student Essay at the end of this chapter.)
3. Cite specific passages from the drama. Explain them in terms of your thesis or topic sentence.
4. If you have watched the drama, discuss the visual elements of the scene you have chosen to analyze—actors on stage, set features, costumes, lighting.
5. Organize your literary argument around the specifications provided by your instructor.
6. If research is part of the assignment's specifications, use your sources two ways: (1) to discover claims worth arguing and (2) to discover support for your own arguments.

SPEECH

A speech is a literary work designed to be spoken. It shares many of the features found in other literary works: It usually is non-fiction prose and in some respects is like an oral essay. A speech also resembles drama in that delivery skills are important: volume and gestures. A speech can be "flowery," embellished with poetic figures of speech. Often, a speech includes humorous elements such as jokes as "ice breakers" or witty observations.

This part of our "Literary Arguments" chapter highlights two elements of speech: figures of form and rhetorical questions. These add power and style to writing and speaking.

Glossary for Speech

Below is a glossary to help you explain your literary arguments about speech.

Figures of Form **Figures of form**, also known as *schemes*, are ways of organizing the parts of a sentence—words, phrases, and clauses—to add variety and beauty and to enhance the audience's interest and understanding. From your experiences with writing, you know that a sentence can be formed in many ways. The examples in this section should help you expand your knowledge of the basic figures of form and their effects on style. We have grouped them by how they affect sentence structure: unusual word order, omission, repetition, and substitution.

Unusual Word Order Interrupt or invert the expected flow of words.

anastrophe: Transpose (invert) words—for example, by placing a predicate before a subject or an adjective after a noun.

> Let me not to the marriage of true minds/Admit impediments.
> —Shakespeare, Sonnet 116

> Into exile I must go. Failed have I.
> —Yoda,
> *Star Wars Episode III: Revenge of the Sith*

parentheses: Interrupt the flow of a complete sentence by inserting a word, phrase, or clause. The insertions—parenthetical statements—can be encapsulated within pairs of punctuation marks: Dashes and parentheses are standard, but ellipsis marks and commas are sometimes used.

> She had a heart . . . how shall I say . . . too soon made glad. . . .
> —Robert Browning, "My Last Duchess"

Omission Omit words not needed to complete the meaning. Be careful, however, not to make the sentence too difficult to understand or too different from the style of your other sentences.

ellipsis: Delete words that normally would be repeated in a sentence if the reader knows what they would be.

> To err is human, to forgive divine.
> —Alexander Pope

zeugma: Omit to make a kind of **pun**. Write a sentence that normally would use the same word but with two meanings. Phrase the sentence so you can omit one of the two words. This practice is known as zeugma (Greek for *yoking)*, joining two meanings in one verb.

> Oh, flowers are as common here, Miss Fairfax, as people are in London.
>
> —Oscar Wilde,
> *The Importance of Being Earnest*

> You held your breath and the door for me.
>
> —Alanis Morisette, "Head Over Feet"

Repetition Repeat words, phrases, and clauses to clarify, emphasize, and make memorable. Recurrence in the form of a refrain is a standard feature of songs and poetry, but repetition can have powerful effects in prose as well. Parallelism—a repetition of grammatical structures—naturally accompanies the repetition of parts of speech.

anadiplosis: "Doubling back." Repeat the end words of a previous phrase, clause, or sentence at the beginning of the next phrase, clause, or sentence.

> A word is a group of letters/Letters strategically placed to make a sound/A sound that creates an image.
>
> —Lynnie Lowe, "Anadiplosis"

> Fear is the path to the dark side. Fear leads to anger. Anger leads to hate. Hate leads to suffering. I sense much fear in you.
>
> —Yoda,
> *Star Wars Episode I: The Phantom Menace*

anaphora: Use the same words at the beginning of each phrase, clause, or sentence in a series.

> I have a dream that one day this nation will rise up....
> I have a dream that one day on the red hills of Georgia...
> I have a dream that one day even the state of Mississippi....
> I have a dream that my four little children....
> I have a dream today.
>
> —Dr. Martin Luther King, Address to civil rights marchers, Washington, D.C.
> Aug. 28, 1963.

> To do two things at once is to do neither.
>
> —Publilius Syrus, circa 100 B.C.E.

> I came, I saw, I conquered.
>
> —Julius Caesar,
> Message to Roman Senate, 47 B.C.E.

chiasmus: Repeat two words or phrases but in reversed order, often to negate the first half (**antithesis**) or to reveal irony.

> And so, my fellow Americans: ask not what your country can do for you; ask what you can do for your country.
>
> —John F. Kennedy,
> Inaugural Address, 1961

> Nowadays all the married men live like bachelors and all the bachelors live like married men.
>
> —Oscar Wilde,
> *The Picture of Dorian Gray*

climax: Repeat parallel structure with increasing intensity or importance.

> In the beginning was the Word, and the Word was with God, and the Word was God.
> —John 1:1-2 (King James bible)

> One equal temper of heroic hearts/Made weak by time and fate, but strong in will/To strive, to seek, to find, and not to yield.
> —Alfred, Lord Tennyson, "Ulysses"

epistrophe: Repeat at the end of each phrase, clause, or sentence in a series. Also known as **antistrophe** and **epiphora**.

> The time for the healing of the wounds has come. The moment to bridge the chasm that divides us has come.
>
> —Nelson Mandela,
> South Africa Presidential Inaugural Address, 1994*

isocolon: Repeat parts of speech (nouns, verbs, adjectives, and so on) and patterns of phrases and clauses, but not the identical words. The Greek word *isocolon* means "equal member": The repeated parts usually are the same length and parallel in structure. The effect is stronger is the rhythm is similar. **Anaphora**, **antistrophe**, and **symploce** (defined below) are forms of isocolon that repeat specific words.

> Marry in haste, repent at leisure.
>
> —Scots proverb

> An envious heart makes a treacherous ear.
>
> —Zora Neale Hurston,
> *Their Eyes Were Watching God*

---

symploce: Repeat words at both the beginning and at the end of a series of phrases, clauses, or sentences. *Symploce* combines *anaphora* and *antistrophe*.

> When I was a child, I spoke like a child, I thought like a child, I reasoned like a child; when I become a man, I gave up childish ways.
>
> —Corinthians 13.11

> When there is talk of hatred, let us stand up against it. When there is talk of violence, let us stand up and talk against it.
>
> —Bill Clinton

synonymy: Restate in equivalent words for emphasis or clarification. The synonyms often are equivalent terms but sometimes are metaphorical. When overdone, this technique creates humor.

> My truest friend, my buddy, my pal, my Rock of Gibraltar, my guiding star.
>
> —Trebor Malm

> You're the top!
> You're the Coliseum.
> You're the top!
> You're the Lovre Museum
>
> —Cole Porter (1891–1964), "You're the Top"

Substitution A subject can be represented by another word or phrase that is part of it or associated with it.

metonymy: Identify a subject using something associated with it.

> The White House announced a new tax plan. (*The White House* = "executive branch")

> The world will little note nor long remember what we say here, but it can never forget what they did here. (*The world* = "people")
>
> —Abraham Lincoln, "The Gettysburg Address"

synecdoche: Identify a whole by naming a part.

> The rancher owns a thousand head. (*head* = cattle)
> All hands on deck! (*hands* = sailors)

PRACTICE 11.7 Scheme in "I Have a Dream"

Scheme in Martin Luther King, JR.'s "I Have a Dream" Speech

Read the excerpt of Martin Luther King, Jr.'s "I Have a Dream" speech and answer the questions that follow.

"I have a dream that one day this nation will rise up and live out the true meaning of its creed: 'We hold these truths to be self-evident, that all men are created equal.'

I have a dream that one day on the red hills of Georgia, the sons of former slaves and the sons of former slave owners will be able to sit down together at the table of brotherhood.

I have a dream that one day even the state of Mississippi, a state sweltering with the heat of injustice, sweltering with the heat of oppression, will be transformed into an oasis of freedom and justice.

I have a dream that my four little children will one day live in a nation where they will not be judged by the color of their skin but by the content of their character.

I have a *dream* today!"*

1. **Understanding "I Have a Dream":** The excerpt from Martin Luther King, Jr.'s speech uses repetition (anaphora) at the beginning of each sentence. In what ways is this effective? Does it matter which words are repeated?

2. **Imitating "I Have a Dream":** Write an imitation of the "I Have a Dream" excerpt, substituting your own dream for King's or using a repeated phrase of your own invention.

*Martin Luther King, "I Have a Dream." Reprinted by arrangement with The Heirs to the Estate of Martin Luther King Jr., c/o Writers House as agent for the proprietor New York, NY. Copyright 1963 Dr. Martin Luther King Jr.; copyright renewed 1991 Coretta Scott King.

PRACTICE 11.8 Figures of Form

1. **Discovering figures of form:** Look for figures of form as you read. Formal speeches are a rich source of schemes, as are other literary works such as poetry. The figures you find can be recorded in a journal or writer's scrapbook. The figures may also prove useful if you write a literary argument about a particular work.

2. **Drafting and revising figures of form:** As you draft or revise one of your own arguments, consider using figures of form to add eloquence.

PRACTICE 11.9   Writing about a Speech

For a speech you have heard or read, you may be required to write an essay, review, or some other document. Following are some guidelines:

1. Take notes on the literary devices you recognize. How do they contribute to your interpretation?

2. Develop a claim about the speech. Your claim probably will focus on your interpretation and be supported by your discussion of specific literary devices. In some cases, you may be more concerned with the writer's techniques than with your interpretation. (For an example, see the Student Essay at the end of this chapter.)

3. Cite specific passages from the speech. Explain them in terms of your thesis or topic sentence.

4. Organize your literary argument around the specifications provided by your instructor.

5. If research is part of the assignment's specifications, use your sources two ways: (1) to discover claims worth arguing and (2) to discover support for your own arguments.

Rhetorical Questions   Rhetorical questions are asked for a purpose other than to receive information in return. They make statements implicitly, not explicitly. Rhetorical questions can create a bond with the audience, as if an actual conversation is taking place between writer and reader or speaker and listener. Avoid using questions to cover up a lack of a strong claim or evidence, and avoid tiring the reader with too many questions. Speakers and writers use rhetorical questions for a number of purposes:

▶ **To scold:** "What on earth do you think you are doing?"

▶ **To express emotion such as rage or grief:** "Why me, Lord?"

▶ **To rouse others' emotions:** "Are we going to put up with this?"

▶ **To reason aloud:** "What would motivate someone to do such a thing?"

▶ **To engage the audience:** "What would you do in this situation?"

▶ **To be cautious, considerate, or subtle:** "Do you have a non-plaid necktie that might go with that plaid shirt?"

▶ **To imply evidence:** "Could we offer a free trial of Extenze Male Enhancement if it didn't really work?"

—Television advertisement

▶ **To imply a controversial claim rather than stating it directly:** "What can be done about religious extremism?"

▶ **To be poetic:** "Shall I compare thee to a summer's day?"

—Shakespeare, "Sonnet 18"

PRACTICE 11.10 Rhetorical Questions

1. **Analyzing rhetorical questions:** The following passage is from a humorous article—not a speech—by Emily Prager about the cultural impact of Mattel's Barbie and Ken dolls. Many of Prager's points are phrased as rhetorical questions. For each question, speculate on (1) why she chose a question over a direct statement, (2) which claim or support is implied, and (3) how persuasive it is.

> I used to look at Barbie and wonder, What's wrong with this picture? . . . There are millions of women who are subliminally sure that a thirty-nine-inch bust and a twenty-three-inch waist are the epitome of lovability. Could this account for the popularity of breast implant surgery? . . . Why, I wondered, was Barbie designed with such obvious sexual equipment and Ken not? Why was his treated as if it were more mysterious than hers? Did the fact that it was treated as such indicate that somehow his equipment, his essential maleness, was considered more powerful than hers, more worthy of the dignity of concealment?*

2. **Writing rhetorical questions:** For an issue that interests you, write rhetorical questions for each of the purposes discussed. After you write, consider whether each question would be more effective or less effective than a direct (declarative or exclamatory) statement.

---

*Emily Prager, *"Our Barbies, Ourselves."* Copyright © 1991 by Emily Prager, reprinted with permission of The Wylie Agency, Inc.

HUMOR

Humor consists of anything that amuses people. It can range from a short "one liner" joke to full-length novels, plays, or films. In addition to making an audience smile or laugh, humor has a number of practical uses: It can support a claim or discredit the opposition, make you aware of strategies used by others, hook your audience's interest, make an argument memorable, and form a bond between you and the audience. Conversely, it can be abused as a means of attack or as a distortion of the truth.

A caricature exaggerates characteristics, sometimes making an identity claim about a person's true nature. (Kaladhar Bapu)

Glossary for Humor

Below is a glossary to help you explain your literary arguments about humor.

caricature: Exaggerate a person's physical or behavioral characteristics. In writing, this is accomplished through description and/or dialogue.

> As President Bush so eloquently put it, "Mathematics are one of the fundamentaries of educationalizing our youths."
>
> —Dave Barry

exaggeration: Overstatement or understatement. Exaggeration can be ironic.

▶ **overstatement**: Exaggerate something as though it were larger or more significant than it really is, as in "big as a house." Also known as **hyperbole**.

> And meaner than a junkyard dog.
>
> —Jim Croce, "Bad, Bad Leroy Brown"*

understatement: Portray something as smaller or less significant than it really is, as in "small as a mouse."

Last week I saw a woman flayed, and you will hardly believe how much it altered her appearance for the worse.

—Jonathan Swift. *A Tale of the Tub*

▶ **litotes:** Understate the affirmative by stating the negative: "not too shabby" means "pretty good."

We made a difference. We made the city stronger, we made the city freer, and we left her in good hands. All in all, not bad, not bad at all.

—Ronald Reagan, "Shining City on a Hill" Farewell Address

insult: Harsh language can be intended to offend or show disrespect. Insults can be amusing, even though attacking a person rather than an idea is considered an unfair way to argue (see *ad hominem attacks* in the "Logic" chapter's section on fallacies.) Also called **invective.**

[Katherine Hepburn] ran the whole gamut of emotions from A to B.

—Dorothy Parker

To those she [Dorothy Parker] did not like, she was a stiletto made of sugar.

—John Mason Brown

Thou poisonous bunch-back'd toad!

—Shakespeare, *Richard III*

Ya cheese-eatin' surrender monkeys!

—Groundskeeper Willie of *The Simpsons*, insulting the French

---

➡ SHAKESPEARE INSULT KIT

Insult (invective) is a form of humor. To create a Shakespearean insult, begin with "Thou," and follow with one word from each of the three columns below. For example: "Thou beslubbering, toad-spotted harpy!" The words below were collected from Shakespeare's dialogue.

Column 1	Column 2	Column 3
beslubbering	beef-witted	codpiece
goatish	beetle-headed	harpy
ruttish	flap-mouthed	lewdster
saucy	ill-breeding	maggot-pie
villainous	toad-spotted	strumpet

irony: The contrast between the expected and the actual. Other forms of humor—satire or ridicule, for example—may take inspiration from the ironic gap between the ideal and the real, between expectation and realization, between what is stated and what is meant. Irony can be classified into several categories, such as dramatic, situational, and verbal.

> ▶ **dramatic irony:** Characters know less about the truth than the audience does. Fate may be important to the plot, and the tragic end is inescapable once a choice is made. For example, Sophocles' King Oedipus searches for his father's killer, not knowing that *he* is the killer. In comedy, the audience may foresee a blunder or comeuppance before the protagonist experiences it.

> ▶ **situational irony:** A contrast between what is expected to be true and what is actually true. This type of irony often inspires satire, a form of ridicule with an implied claim that the situation should be improved. Examples include medicines that actually make people sick; policies that cause the problems they are meant to prevent; and hypocrites such as police officers who are crooks, religious leaders who are sinners, and experts who are ill informed.

> ▶ **verbal irony:** A contrast between what is stated and what the speaker or writer really means. Sarcasm is one form of verbal irony. In Shakespeare's *Julius Caesar*, Mark Anthony refers sarcastically to assassins as "honorable men." In popular culture, statements such as "What could go wrong?" ironically imply that something will *definitely* go wrong.

parody: Imitates a form or style, often for the purpose of satire. Sometimes a parody makes use of a familiar form as a way to make fun of something else, much the way that JibJab uses familiar tunes to convey lyrics that satirize politicians. Sometimes a parody makes fun of the genre it imitates, such as movie parodies: *Young Frankenstein* (horror conventions), *Kung Fu Hustle* (martial arts conventions), or the many parodies of *Star Wars*.

satire: Ridiculing foolish practices and debunking silly ideas. Satiric style can be genial (a.k.a., *Horatian*) such as a monologue by Jay Leno, or harsh (a.k.a., *Juvenalian*) such as Swift's "A Modest Proposal," a mock-serious essay that proposes cannibalism as a solution to poverty and a food shortage.

How does this cartoon use allusion and wordplay together?

Satire is perhaps more a goal than a technique; toward that goal, it enlists techniques such as **exaggeration**, **insult**, **irony**, and **parody**. It can range from sentence-length to an entire book, play, or movie.

wordplay: Verbal humor based on identical or similar sounds presented with two meanings. Also know by the Greek name *paronomasia*, it can take the form of **double entendre**, which is a **pun** with a naughty second meaning. GEICO, an insurance company, is sometimes represented by a pun-inspired cartoon gecko. Examples:

A pun is the lowest form of wit, therefore the foundation of all wit.

—Henry Erskine

I used to be Snow White, but I drifted.

—Mae West

Nothing runs like a Deere.

—Slogan for John Deere tractors*

PRACTICE 11.11   Insults

Understanding insults: In a brief writing or in a group discussion, reflect on insults.

1. Where have you witnessed insults being hurled? What were they like?
2. Why do people insult each other?
3. Are insults ever justifiable? Explain.
4. In what ways do insults help or hurt an argument?

PRACTICE 11.12   Understanding Satire

In a short writing or a group discussion, respond to the following questions about the following passage from Jonathan Swift's "A Modest Proposal." Remember that Swift is the author, but the narrator is a fictional persona, different from Swift.

An Excerpt from Swift's "A Modest Proposal"

The following passage is from an essay written by Dr. Jonathan Swift (of *Gulliver's Travels* fame) and circulated in Dublin as a mock political-tract in 1729. Considered a satirical masterpiece, the full title is "A Modest Proposal for preventing the children of poor people in Ireland, from being a burden on their parents or country, and for making them beneficial to the publick." Alarmed by the numbers of starving poor people in Ireland, Swift also was frustrated by the lack of any serious plan to feed them. "A Modest Proposal" is narrated by a *persona*—a fictional narrator whose views are different from those of the author. The persona/proposer claims to have a reasonable, effective solution to the problem of poverty and starvation.

> "I have been assured by a very knowing American of my acquaintance in London, that a young healthy child well nursed, is, at a year old, a most delicious nourishing and wholesome food, whether stewed, roasted, baked, or boiled; and I make no doubt that it will equally serve in a fricasie, or a ragout. I do therefore humbly offer it to publick consideration, that [Irish children] at a year old, be offered in sale to the persons of quality and fortune, through the kingdom, always advising the mother to let them suck plentifully in the last month, so as to render them plump, and fat for a good table. A child will make two dishes at an entertainment for friends, and when the family dines alone, the fore or hind quarter will make a reasonable dish, and seasoned with a little pepper or salt, will be very good boiled on the fourth day, especially in winter."
>
> —Jonathan Swift

1. What is the narrator proposing? Would the solution be effective at reducing poverty and hunger? Who might object and for what reasons?

2. Does the narrator seem to have a reasonable tone of voice? What evidence is there to support your assessment of the tone? Does the tone contrast with the proposal? What technique of humor involves such a contrast?

3. A logical argument consists of a claim and support. What kinds of support are offered by the narrator? If the narrator is logical, what might Swift be saying about logic?

4. What do you think Swift's true purpose was in writing "A Modest Proposal"?

→ WRITING YOUR OWN "MODEST PROPOSAL"

Jonathan Swift's "A Modest Proposal" is a satiric classic, and his methods still work well. After reading his essay, consider using his style to satirize a modern issue. (Note: The full text of this reading can be found in Part 2 if you are using this text with a reader. If not, you can find the reading online.)

Planning

▶ Select a real issue, one that needs to be solved but that society seems incapable of dealing with. Examples include the national debt, pollution, the energy crisis, a deadlocked Congress, racism, sexism, or any other issue that is serious.

▶ Brainstorm solutions. Invent one that is outrageous. However, be aware that "political correctness" has boundaries that even satirists must respect. For example, avoid any proposal that could be interpreted as a hate speech.

▶ Research or brainstorm the context of the problem: How bad is it, really? Who is suffering? What will happen if nothing improves the situation?

▶ Brainstorm details for your solution. How will it be implemented? What are its benefits?

Drafting

Introduction

▶ Begin your proposal by identifying the problem. You can devote the introduction and perhaps the first body paragraph to this task. Since the problem is real, you could use real sources to document it. However, don't overdo this part: a reader may lose interest before realizing that you are writing a satire.

▶ Adopt a serious, humane tone. Assure the reader that your heart is in the right place. Avoid ranting. Instead, be calm and reasonable.

Body

▶ Transition into your proposal. Your tone should be oblivious to any real objections that might be raised. Be enthusiastic. Emphasize how reasonable people certainly will see the value of your proposal.

▶ In a series of paragraphs, reveal the details of how your proposal will be implemented and who will benefit.

▶ If possible, use sources to support your proposal. Swift invented authorities, and you could also. However, you may find real sources that seem to support your proposal. Such sources may be ripe for being satirized.

Conclusion

▶ If you follow Swift's model, your conclusion will mention all the failed or neglected proposals. Swift concludes that readers shouldn't reject his proposal if they already have failed to follow any reasonable proposal.

Revising

▶ Did you introduce a significant issue?

▶ Is your proposal outrageous yet not dangerously offensive?

▶ Did you maintain your reasonable tone?

▶ Did you explain the details of how your proposal will work and how it will be beneficial?

▶ Did you conclude by reminding the audience of how other proposals have either failed or have not been taken seriously?

PRACTICE 11.13   Writing about Humor

For a humorous work you are reading, you may be required to write an essay, review, or some other document. Following are some guidelines:

1. Mark the literary devices you recognize. How do they contribute to your interpretation?

(continued)

(continued)

2. Develop a claim about the humorous work. Your claim probably will focus on your interpretation and be supported by your discussion of specific literary devices. In some cases, you may be more concerned with the writer's techniques than with your interpretation. (For an example, see the Student Essay at the end of this chapter.)

3. Cite specific passages from the humorous work. Explain them in terms of your thesis or topic sentence.

4. Organize your literary argument around the specifications provided by your instructor.

5. If research is part of the assignment's specifications, use your sources two ways: (1) to discover claims worth arguing and (2) to discover support for your own arguments.

PRACTICE 11.14   Before You Read the Student Essay

1. How concerned are you about issues such as poverty or hunger? To what degree are these issues relevant today?

2. Do you enjoy satire? What kinds of satire have you enjoyed? Do you think it appropriate to find humor in serious issues?

3. Preview the title of the student essay. Does it reveal the likely content? Does it create interest?

STUDENT ESSAY

Einhorn 1

Brittany Einhorn

Professor Everett

Composition

2 March 2011

   Persona, Irony, and Twisted Logic in Swift's "A Modest Proposal"

In Jonathan Swift's essay "A Modest Proposal," a concerned citizen whom we shall call the "proposer" advances a rather unique proposition to solve the problem of poverty and hunger in 18th century Ireland:

"[A] young healthy child well nursed, is, at a year old, a most delicious nourishing and wholesome food, whether stewed, roasted, baked, or boiled; and I make no doubt that it will equally serve in a fricasie or a ragoust" (par. 9). In other words, the proposer recommends cannibalism, presenting children as culinary delights. Of course, this proposal is made satirically, not seriously. In order to bring the hardships of Ireland to the attention of the world, Swift writes this outrageous proposal, ridiculing leaders and citizens who through inaction and callousness have condemned the Irish commoners to poverty, ignorance, crime, and starvation. Swift accomplishes his satiric goal through techniques of persona, verbal irony, and twisted logic.

Swift's essay is narrated by a *persona*, a kind of alter ego who doesn't necessarily represent the views of the author. Swift's persona is a very serious, educated, logical Irish man who probably holds a position of money and authority in Dublin society. This persona "misleads readers by emphasizing the humble and selfless intentions of his proposal" (Porter). The persona/proposer begins the essay by reasonably presenting the problem of poverty as "a melancholy object" (par. 1). After describing the dire problem, he springs on the reader an impossible solution, cannibalism. From then on, his persona is "notable for his vanity, his cold-heartedness, and the ruthlessness of his logic" ("'A Modest Proposal': Study Questions"). In using this persona, Swift strips the Irish gentry—landowners with the power to make changes—of the pretence of being decent human beings. He does so to make them aware of how their negligence and callousness have contributed to the plight of the poor.

Swift's persona enables him to express his views through a form of verbal irony: his meaning is the opposite of the statements made by the proposer. This verbal irony is evident in the title of the essay, in the tone of the proposer's words, and in every aspect of the proposed solution.

The title "A Modest Proposal" is ironic because the proposal is anything but modest: it is bold and outrageous. The proposer's matter-of-fact tone of voice is ironic in part because he is suggesting something inhumane, but also because he first sets himself up as having humane intentions worthy of public praise:

> I think it is agreed by all parties, that this prodigious number of children in the arms, or on the backs, or at the heels of their mothers, and frequently of their fathers, is in the present deplorable state of the kingdom, a very great additional grievance; and therefore whoever could find out a fair, cheap and easy method of making these children sound and useful members of the common-wealth would deserve so well of the publick, as to have his statue set up for a preserver of the nation. (par. 2)

Note the tone of compassion as he describes the current conditions as "deplorable" and how he promises to make the poor children into "useful members." Although a reader at first may assume the children will be "useful" by becoming productive citizens, in reality the proposer intends to use them as food.

Verbal irony is evident as the proposer reveals the details of his proposal. For example, he offers recipes in the same helpful tone of voice that a modern chef would use to describe ways to prepare a turkey or a ham:

> A child will make two dishes at an entertainment for friends, and when the family dines alone, the fore or hind quarter will make a reasonable dish, and seasoned with a little pepper or salt, will be very good boiled on the fourth day, especially in winter. (par. 10)

The verbal irony continues throughout the essay as the proposer speaks of ways of breeding and butchering children as one might speak of livestock: "I rather recommend buying the children alive, and dressing them hot from the knife, as we do roasting pigs" (par. 16). The irony is stark when the same sentence juxtaposes horrific words such as "carcass" with genteel words such as "persons of quality" and "dainty": "[He] sold the carcass to persons of quality, as a prime dainty" (par. 18).

Another satiric method of Swift is his exposé of twisted *logic*. The proposer "can coldly discuss the economic and social benefits of killing and eating children without ever giving much thought to the moral problems" (Smith). How does one support an argumentative claim? One way is through *ethos*, the authoritarian appeal of expert testimony. One expert cited by the proposer is "a very knowing American of my acquaintance" who assures him "that a young healthy child well nursed, is, at a year old, a most delicious nourishing and wholesome food" (par. 9). As a comic bonus, this satiric appeal to authority implies that the "very knowing" American had previously engaged in cannibalism.

Another way to logically support a claim is to argue through cost-benefit analysis. For example, the proposer explains the benefits of cannibalism: "Thus the squire will learn to be a good landlord, and grow popular among his tenants, the mother will have eight shillings neat profit, and be fit for work till she produces another child" (par. 14). The proposer admits that for the consumer, the cost of a delicious child may be high: "I grant this food will be somewhat dear, and therefore very proper for landlords, who, as they have already devoured most of the parents, seem to have the best title to the children." In this statement, the proposer does not mean literally that the landlords have eaten the Irish. Rather, it "illuminates how the absentee landlords have already drained the peasants of all they have, and may as well take and eat their children" ("'A Modest Proposal' P.5: 5").

In "A Modest Proposal" Jonathan Swift skillfully uses persona, verbal irony, and twisted logic "to point out problems in society" (Smith).

In doing so, he helped raise the consciousness of those who might have the power to improve the economic situation of the Irish. Swift created a satiric masterpiece that to this day entertains readers and inspires the methods of comedians and social reformers.

Works Cited

"'A Modest Proposal' P.5: 5." *AVHS AP Lang and Comp*, 2011. Web. 27 Feb. 2011.

"'A Modest Proposal': Study Questions." *Sparknotes.com*. Sparknotes, 2011. Web. 1 Mar. 2011.

Porter, Jane. "Swift's Ironies in 'A Modest Proposal'" *Victorianweb.org*. The Victorian Web, 8 Sept. 2003. Web. 26 Feb. 2011.

Smith, Nicole. "Comparison of the Use of Irony and Satire in 'A Modest Proposal' and *Gulliver's Travels* by Jonathan Swift." *Articlemyriad. com*. Article Myriad, 2010. Web. 27 Feb. 2011.

Swift, Jonathan. "A Modest Proposal." *Gutenberg.org*, 27 July 2008. Web. 24 Feb. 2011.

PRACTICE 11.15   Responding to the Student Essay

1. Do you think the student essayist explains Swift's techniques effectively?
2. Is the organization effective? Point out examples.
3. Does the essay support its point well? Are quotations explained? Point out examples.
4. What, if anything, would you change about the essay's organization and content?

Looking Back at Chapter 11

▶ Your literary argument is a claim that requires support—evidence and explanations—for it to be accepted by your readers. The support takes various forms: quotations from the work, research on what others say about the work, and your analyses of the work and of your research.

▶ Poetry is distinguished from prose by its patterns of rhyme and rhythm as well as its specific forms such as a sonnet, ballad, haiku, dramatic monologue, or sestina. Modern poetry tends to be freer in structure and style.

▶ Fiction is a broad category that includes any work of imaginative prose. This includes novels and short stories of many genres (kinds of literature) such as romance, detective stories, and science fiction. It features narration, description, and dialogue.

▶ A drama is a literary work designed to be performed by actors on a stage.

▶ A speech is a literary work designed to be spoken. A speech shares many of the features found in other literary works.

▶ A rhetorical question is asked for a purpose other than to receive information in return.

▶ Figures of form, also known as *schemes*, are ways of organizing the parts of a sentence—words, phrases, and clauses—to add variety and beauty and to enhance the audience's interest and understanding.

▶ Humor consists of anything that amuses people. It can range from a short "one liner" joke to full-length novels, plays, or films.

▶ A review rates something. The purpose of a literary review is to provide information for an audience so it can decide whether to partake in a literary experience.

Suggestions for Writing

▶ In journal entries, reflect on literary techniques you witness in written works, politics, and advertising.

▶ Write a literary argument directed at a poem, story, play, speech, or comedy.

▶ Write creatively: a modest proposal, a parody, a stand-up monologue, or a humorous rant.

▶ Write a literary argument about Shakespeare's use of insults.

▶ As you draft and revise future essays, look for opportunities to use humor, rhetorical questions, and figurative language.

12

MLA Documentation

Steve Hix/Somos Images/Corbis

{ *Good writers are those who keep the language efficient. That is to say, keep it accurate, keep it clear.*
—Ezra Pound
(1885–1972) }

The Modern Language Association (MLA) system of documentation consists of (1) in-text parenthetical citations and (2) a bibliography (called a Works Cited list) that appears on a separate page at the end of the document. Using this method, each time you quote or paraphrase information from a book, article, or the Internet, you must credit the author and indicate the page on which you found the information. Although it may seem daunting at first, the system is fairly straight forward. If you create your Works Cited list as you write your paper, the process becomes much simpler.

Try following these steps:

1. As soon as you begin to write, move down to the next page and type "Works Cited," centered, at the top of the page.

2. As you write, create your in-text citations. If you leave this step for later, you may lose track of your sources.

3. As soon as you have cited a source, page down to the "Works Cited" list, and create your bibliography in alphabetical order based on the author's last name.

IN-TEXT CITATIONS IN MLA STYLE

In-text citations in MLA style generally consist of an author's name followed by quoted or paraphrased material, with the page number containing that material positioned immediately after the borrowed information. You should be careful to place the citation immediately after the borrowed material so that the reader will not become confused about what information was obtained and from where. You also do not want the reader to be confused about which material you wrote and which ideas you borrowed from someone else.

Avoiding Plagiarism

Whenever you represent someone else's ideas as being your own, you are guilty of plagiarism. In most colleges and universities, the penalties for plagiarism are severe, including expelling a student for a year or longer, or even permanently. Sometimes students will commit plagiarism by accident when they are not careful about citing their sources. In these cases, students will often write a paper first and then intend to go back over the paper and insert their citations and Works Cited entries. During the process of writing a research paper, it is easy to become confused and lose track of your sources. The best way to avoid this problem is to insert your citations and create your Works Cited entries as you write.

Citing Sources

Citing a Work by a Single Author The two most common ways to cite a source in MLA style are (1) to mention the author's name in the text or

(2) to list the author's name in the parenthetical citation. Consider the following sentences:

AUTHOR'S NAME IN TEXT
According to Ruddick, William Golding's *The Inheritors* was unfortunately overshadowed by its predecessor, *The Lord of the Flies* (76).

AUTHOR'S NAME IN PARENTHETICAL CITATION
William Golding's *The Inheritors* was unfortunately overshadowed by its predecessor, *The Lord of the Flies* (Ruddick 76).

If the entire sentence is a paraphrase, then the citation comes at the end. If only part of the sentence is paraphrased, then the parenthetical citation should occur next to the paraphrased material. A comma does not separate the author's name from the page reference, and no indicator for *page* or *pages* (such a *p.* or *pp.*) is used. The period comes after the citation (when the citation occurs at the end of a sentence). Note also that the titles of long works, such as novels, should be italicized, not underlined.

Citing Multiple Sources Although the parenthetical citation often appears at the end of a sentence containing paraphrased material, it is not necessary to always follow this form. Sometimes, the author may follow a citation with commentary, or multiple citations may occur within the same sentence.

Citation with Commentary Sometimes you may wish to comment on paraphrased material within the same sentence. In such cases, the parenthetical citation is best placed so that it is clear where the borrowed information ends and the cited material begins. Though MLA style does not necessarily make this distinction, it is a good practice to avoid confusion between your ideas and the ideas of your source. Consider the following citation/commentary on Ben Bova's book *Immortality: How Science Is Extending Your Life Span—and Changing the World*:

> Although Bova provides a list of his successful predictions to lend authority to his claim that people younger than 50 years of age can look forward to a future of virtual immortality (3–4), there is no current scientific evidence to substantiate his claim.

Most of the first half of this sentence is paraphrased. The material after the parenthetical citation is the author's commentary on Bova's claim.

Multiple Citations by the Same Author Sometimes you may need to cite several different pages within a single article, or you may paraphrase information from several different works by the same writer. Once an author has been introduced, you need include only page numbers in parentheses to indicate material that appears on subsequent pages.

In ancient Rome, the noon meal, *prandium*, was followed by an afternoon nap, the *meridiatio* (Balsdon 25), which itself was followed by a trip to the *thermae*, the public bathhouse (27).

In this example, two pieces of information from two different pages are brought together in the same sentence. Because the first citation mentions the author's name, it is not necessary to repeat his name in the second citation. Note that the Latin words in this paraphrase are italicized. Use italics, not underlining or quotation marks, for words in languages other than English.

Multiple Citations by Different Authors or Works   In some cases, you may cite several authors in one or two sentences, or you may cite information from more than one book or article by the same author. Whenever you move from one work to another, or from one author to another, your parenthetical citation must make the change in sources clear. As you move between works by the same author, you may either mention the title of the work in the text or include a significant portion of the title in a parenthetical citation.

> Everett argues that the Peircian triad can be used as a tool for reader-response critics ("Adopting the Peircian Sign" 129), something he later applied to a reading of *Hamlet*, where he argues that the source story bled through Shakespeare's text ("Two Hamlets" 66).

If works by two different authors are paraphrased, then you can use their last names as you move from one text to another.

> Whereas Chen believes that fast-food ads are to be blamed for the increased rate of obesity among America's youth (26), Nelson argues that sedentary activities such as watching television and spending time on the Internet play a much larger role (113).

Citing Works with More than One Author   When you cite a work written by up to three authors, you may either list all of the authors' names in the text or list just the authors' last names in the parenthetical citation.

> N. Katherine Hayles and Nicholas Gessler have argued that the shifting virtual realities depicted in some contemporary science fiction do not necessarily have to be morally inconsistent because the characters within the shifting realities provide a moral center and a sense of continuity (497).
>
> The shifting virtual realities depicted in some contemporary science fiction do not necessarily have to be morally inconsistent because the characters within the shifting realities provide a moral center and a sense of continuity (Hayles and Gessler 497).

If the work you are citing has more than three authors, then insert *et al.* after the first author's name. Do not mention the other authors.

Citing a Corporate Author Sometimes a source will not credit an individual flesh-and-blood author but rather will list a legal entity such as a government agency or private corporation as the "author." In such a case, you may include the corporate author either in the text or in the parenthetical citation.

Citing a Multivolume Work If you paraphrase or quote material obtained from a multivolume work, then you should make it clear to the reader which volume you are citing. Within the parenthetical citation, give the volume first, followed by a colon and the inclusive page numbers.

> Mesopotamian medicine was more primitive than that practiced by the Egyptians and consisted largely of rituals, though the lack of extant texts limits our knowledge of their pharmacology (*Interpreter's Dictionary* 1: 302).

In this case, the full title of the work in question, *The Interpreter's Dictionary of the Bible,* has been shortened to make the passage more readable. In MLA style it is acceptable to shorten cited titles as long as the citation can be easily located in the bibliography, where titles are not abbreviated.

Handling Quotations While you should use quotations sparingly, these excerpts are sometimes necessary when the language of the original source is memorable, when the passage is subject to interpretation, or when the source uses jargon that would make it especially awkward to paraphrase. Most of the time short quotations are preferred, although longer ones may be necessary from time to time. Remember this rule of thumb: Make any discussion of quoted material at least as long as the quote itself to prevent your quotations from "taking over" your paper.

Short Quotations If a quotation takes up four or fewer lines of text, work it into your prose. Parenthetical citations appear outside of the quotation marks.

> Desmond Morris argues that "The modern human animal is no longer living in conditions natural for his species" (7).

The period does not appear at the end of the quotation, but after the parenthetical citation. Because the entire sentence from the original is used in this example, it is capitalized just as it is in the source text.

Cutting Words Out of Quotations If you cut any words out of the quotation, insert an ellipsis (…) to indicate the omission.

> According to William James, "neither Bunyan nor Tolstoy could become what we have called healthy-minded. They had drunk too deeply of the cup of bitterness ever to forget its taste, and . . . the sadness was preserved as a minor ingredient in the heart of the faith by which it was overcome" (169).

Note that the ellipsis includes spaces between the periods. You can also use an ellipsis at the end of a quotation to indicate that the sentence was cut off in the middle. When the ellipsis occurs at the end, use four periods instead of three. Note that the first period doesn't have a space after the end of the quotation. This is actually a period followed by an ellipsis.

> According to William James, "neither Bunyan nor Tolstoy could become what we have called healthy-minded. They had drunk too deeply of the cup of bitterness ever to forget its taste. . . ." (169).

In this case, the quotation marks and the period go outside the ellipsis. You can use an ellipsis in the same way to eliminate an entire sentence out of the middle of a quotation.

Altering Sources Sometimes it may be necessary to change quotations in some way. For example, if a source contains a grammatical or spelling error, insert the phrase "[*sic*]" next to the error to indicate that the mistake was not yours. To emphasize a particular word or phrase, you can italicize a portion of a quotation and add the phrase "[emphasis added]" to the quotation. Use the phrase "[emphasis in original]" to indicate that italics were not added.

> "For each subject of instruction," Vygotsky writes, "there is a period when its influence is most fruitful because the child is *most receptive* to it" [emphasis added].

> Paulo Freire says that "Revolutionary leaders cannot think *without* the people, nor for the people, but only *with* the people" [emphasis in original].

Sometimes, it is desirable to add bracketed comments to make the meaning of a passage clear.

> According to Dewey, "there are two schools of social reform. One [the theory of innate morality] bases itself upon the notion of a morality which springs from an inner freedom, something mysteriously cooped up within personality" (9).

Long Quotations When you include a quotation of more than four lines, you should block it; that is, you should indent the quotation one inch from the left (usually two tab spaces in most word processing programs). Let us consider James's quotation in full:

> In *The Varieties of Religious Experience,* William James writes that neither Bunyan nor Tolstoy could become what we have called healthy-minded. They had drunk too deeply of the cup of bitterness ever to forget its taste, and their redemption is into a universe two stories deep. Each of them realized a good which broke the effective edge of his sadness; yet the sadness was preserved as a minor ingredient in the heart of the faith by which it was overcome. (169)

In the preceding example, quotation marks are unnecessary because the text is blocked, indicating that it is a quotation. Because the blocked quotation stands on its own, the period comes at the end of the quotation, not after the parenthetical citation. Also, the blocking makes single-spacing redundant, so the quotation is presented double-spaced, just like the rest of the text.

"Quoted in..." You will probably encounter situations where a source you have read quotes someone else you would like to quote. In this case, the best thing to do is to obtain the original source, because the quotation may

---

→ TIPS FOR USING QUOTATIONS

Long Quotations

▶ Block any quotations that are longer than four lines of verse or prose.

▶ Use a colon after a complete sentence to introduce your quotation.

▶ Indent the left margin by one inch and double-space your quotation.

▶ Quote only what is necessary to prove your point.

▶ Use square brackets around changes you make to the text. Don't add quotation marks around the block (but keep quotation marks that appear in the original source).

▶ Place the citation in parentheses after the period at the end of the block.

▶ For electronic citations, mention the author's name or the title of the Web site in the text or in the parenthetical citation. Page numbers are not needed for electronic citations.

▶ Make the discussion following your citation at least as long as the quotation. This helps keep the reader focused on what you have to say, not what your source says.

Short Quotations

▶ Try to keep short quotations to one sentence or less.

▶ Make the quoted material part of the natural flow of your sentence.

▶ Use colons or commas after your material to transition to your cited material.

▶ Place the citation in parentheses after the quoted material. Try to mention the author's name in the sentence, and place the page numbers inside the parentheses.

▶ Place the parenthetical citation before the period.

be inaccurate or the context of the quote may somehow distort its meaning. However, the time constraints of college life do not always allow for such luxuries. If your library does not own the original source, and if you cannot obtain it online or through interlibrary loan, then you may wish to quote the material through another source. Use the abbreviation "qtd. in" to indicate that you borrowed the material from a secondary source, not the source where the material originally appeared. Credit the original source (usually by the author's name) in your prose, but include the title of the source where you found the quote in your parenthetical citation.

> A variety of English teachers have incorrectly applied the word "induction" to the ordering of material within an essay. According to Rorabacher, "In induction we analyze particular instances to establish a general truth" (qtd. in Fulkerson 13). However, the philosophical inaccuracy of this term does not mean it should not be used by writing teachers for other purposes.

Citing Electronic Sources While the Internet has created new opportunities for research, it has also created unforeseen difficulties in citing information. Generally, because Internet sources do not divide material into distinct pages, you can omit page numbers from Internet references, although you should always provide the author's name. A second problem arises when authorship is difficult to determine. In such a situation it is usually best to use the corporate author for the citation. For example, if you cite information from the Web MD Web site that does not include an author's name, you would credit Web MD as the author. Also, because Web sites usually qualify as shorter works, titles are placed within quotation marks. The important thing to remember is to include enough information in your citation so that the reader can easily find the listing in your bibliography (the Works Cited list):

> According to the National Institutes of Health, stem-cell research may one day help prevent birth defects or discover a cure for cancer.
>
> Stem-cell research may one day help prevent birth defects or discover a cure for cancer (National Institutes of Health).

Though the author of the source can either be listed in the text or in a parenthetical citation, it is preferable to list the author in the text.

Note: in many cases you may be able to obtain a PDF form of a printed source. Since the PDF is a copy of the printed source, it should be treated as such and page numbers should be included.

→ CITING BOOKS FROM E-READERS

The recent popularity of electronic book readers like Amazon's Kindle has created a problem for students who need to cite e-books. Though the MLA does not yet have a category for e-readers, it is best treated the same way as source found on the Internet, with no page numbers, as indicated in this chapter. How to list the book (or other work) in the Works Cited is a more significant problem. Because the book is an electronic text downloaded onto computer hardware, we suggest modifying the form for CD-ROM, with the name of the e-reader substituted for the CD-ROM. Use the full publication information of the print version of the source, if known.

The reader would look up "National Institutes of Health" (capitalized in alphabetical order under "N") in the Works Cited list, which would provide information on the Web site, including its date of access and URL.

CREATING A WORKS CITED LIST

Your MLA bibliography is called a "Works Cited" list and is formatted in the following way:

▶ Always title your reference list "Works Cited" (never "Bibliography" or "References").

▶ Double-space all entries.

▶ Use hanging indentation. That is, place the first line of an entry flush to the left margin, and indent subsequent lines by one-half inch (usually one tab space). In Microsoft Word, you'll find tools to change indentation if you click the "Page Layout" tab.

▶ Alphabetize all items. When you have several sources by the same author, arrange the entries in alphabetical order by title. (For example, if Josephine Smith has written articles entitled "Beyond Research: An Introduction to MLA Style" and "Considering Research: MLA Style Revisited," then "Beyond Research" comes first in the list.)

▶ When one author has several subsequent entries in your Works Cited, don't repeat the author's name. List the author's name for the first entry, and use three hyphens to indicate the author's name for the second and later entries.

The examples that follow cover types of citations that are frequently used in college writing assignments. This list is by no means exhaustive, however. Refer to the *MLA Guide for Writers of Research Papers* when you wish to use sources that do not fit the cases outlined here.

Sample Works Cited Entries: Books

In MLA style, a book entry consists of the author's name, the book's title (italicized), and the publication information. Publication information is usually found on the title page of a book. The dates of publication usually appear on the following page.

▶ The list appears at the end of the document.

▶ Entries are arranged alphabetically.

▶ The first author's last name is listed in reverse order. Other authors' names are listed in regular order.

▶ Titles of long works such as books are italicized.

▶ A colon indicates the presence of a subtitle.

▶ If an entry fits entirely on one line, hanging indentation does not apply.

▶ The word "Print" at the end of the entry indicates a print-based rather than electronic resource.

> **Punctuating a Book Citation**
>
> 1. Author: Last name, First name (period)
> 2. *Title and Subtitle* of book italicized (period)
> 3. City of publisher (colon)
> 4. Publisher (comma)
> 5. Publication date (period)
> 6. Medium: Print (period)

Author's name   Title   Subtitle

Degroot, Gerard. *The Sixties Unplugged: A Kaleidoscopic History of a Disorderly Decade.* Boston: Harvard UP, 2010. Print.

Place of publication   Publisher   Year of publication   Print-based source

Book by One, Two, Three, or Four or More Authors Only the first author's name is listed last name first. When citing two or more works by the same person, use three hyphens in the place of the name. When using two or more works by the same author, arrange the sources in alphabetical order by title. If more than three authors are listed for any work, use *et al.* (Latin for "and others") to indicate the second and subsequent authors.

Pinker, Steven. *The Blank Slate: The Modern Denial of Human Nature.* New York: Viking, 2002. Print.

—. *The Language Instinct.* New York: Harper Perennial, 1995. Print.

Roark, James L., et al. *The American Promise: A History of the United States.* 2 vols. New York: Bedford, 2002. Print.

White, Shane, et al. *Playing the Numbers: Gambling in Harlem between the Wars.* Boston: Harvard UP, 2010. Print.

Book with an Editor (No Author Listed)

Burt, Daniel S., ed. *The Chronology of American Literature: America's Literary Achievements from the Colonial Era to Modern Times.* New York: Houghton, 2004. Print.

Book with a Corporate Author
A book is considered to have corporate authorship when it was produced by the membership of a corporation or organization, but the actual writers' names do not appear on the title page. In this case, the organization is considered to be the author. This is different from a book with an unknown author.

American Cancer Society. *American Cancer Society's Guide to Complementary and Alternative Cancer Methods.* Atlanta: American Cancer Society, 2000. Print.

The Conference Board, et. al. *Are They Ready to Work?: Employers' Perspectives on the Basic Knowledge and Applied Skills of New Entrants to the 21st Century U.S. Workforce.* The Conference Board, 2006. Print.

Book with an Unknown Author
Alphabetize works by the first word in the title other than *a, an,* or *the.* When a place of publication is not well known, also include the abbreviation for the state.

Past Worlds: The Times Atlas of Archaeology. Maplewood, NJ: Hammond, 1988. Print.

Book that Is Part of a Multivolume Work
When using more than one volume of a multivolume work, you must give the total number of volumes after the title. If you use only one volume from the set, supply the volume number instead. When citing a multivolume work, indicate the volume number followed by a colon and the subsequent pages. For the example below, the citation would be (Copelston 1: 121–22).

Copelston, Frederick, S. J. *A History of Philosophy* 8 vols. New York: Image, 1962. Print.

or

Copelston, Frederick, S. J. *A History of Philosophy.* Vol. 1. New York: Image, 1962. Print.

A Foreword, Preface, or Afterword of a Book

Goldberg, Natalie. Preface. *The Writer's Handbook 2004.* Ed. Elfrieda Abbe. Waukesha, WI: Writer Books, 2003. 9–14. Print.

A Book with a Title within Its Title

Fish, Stanley. *Surprised by Sin: The Reader in Paradise Lost.* New York: St. Martin's, 1967. Print.

A Work in an Anthology (Short Story, Poem, or Essay)

Mardsen, Madonna. "The American Myth of Success: Visions and Revisions." *Popular Culture: An Introductory Text.* Ed. Jack Nachbar and Kevin Lause. Bowling Green, OH: Bowling Green State U Popular Press, 1992. 134–48. Print.

More than One Piece from the Same Collection

Caputi, Jane, and Susan Nance. "One Size Does *Not* Fit All: Being Beautiful, Thin and Female in America." Nachbar and Lause. 292–311. Print.

Motz, Maralyn Ferris. "Seen Through Rose-Tinted Glasses: The Barbie Doll in American Society." Nachbar and Lause. 211–34. Print.

Nachbar, Jack, and Kevin Lause, eds. *Popular Culture: An Introductory Text.* Bowling Green, OH: Bowling Green State U Popular Press, 1992. Print.

When listing multiple entries from the same anthology, refer to the anthology by its editors' last names and include complete information for the anthology.

Encyclopedia or Dictionary Article With an entry is from a commonly used encyclopedia or dictionary, no page numbers or publication information is required. For more specialized sources, give full publication information. If the article is signed, list the author's name as you would for a book or article. When items are listed alphabetically, you may omit the page numbers. If you cite one of several references from a dictionary, then the abbreviation "Def." and the letter or number that references the definition should follow the word being referenced.

"Elegy." *Princeton Encyclopedia of Poetry and Poetics.* Enlarged ed. Ed. Alex Preminger. Princeton, NJ: Princeton UP, 1974. 215–17. Print.

"Overture." Def. 2b. *Webster's New World College Dictionary.* 4th ed. Print.

"Paella." *Webster's II: New College Dictionary.* 1995 ed. Print.

Translation

Lem, Stanislaw. *Solaris*. Trans. Joanna Kilmartin and Steve Cox. San Diego: Harcourt-Brace, 1987. Print.

A Pamphlet Square brackets are used when information is known but does not appear within the source itself.

What You Should Know about Prostate Cancer. [Los Angeles:] Prostate Cancer Research Institute, 2004. Print.

A Government Publication Government documents present a particular problem because they usually do not list authors and they are often inconsistent in the types of publication information they offer. Generally, you should list the author as being the issuing branch of government (United States, Oklahoma, United Kingdom) followed by the name of the agency, using standard abbreviations as necessary. If a specific author is listed, include that information. If the information was obtained online, the citation should include the date of access and the URL. If you list more than one entry from the same branch of government, use three hyphens instead of the name of the government entity for the second (and following) entries. When citing the U.S. *Congressional Record*, use the abbreviation *Cong. Rec.* and indicate the date of publication and page numbers.

Cong. Rec. 7 Apr. 2004: 3898–914. 20 Sep. 2004. <http://wais. access.gpo>.

—. Federal Register. Equal Employment Opportunity for Individuals with Disabilities, Final Rule. 26 July. 1991: 35725–55. Print.

Sample Works Cited Entries: Articles

▶ To cite periodicals, include the author's name, the title of the article, the title of the publication (italicized), the month (or volume and issue number), year, and inclusive pages on which the article appears.

▶ As with books, the first author's name is listed in reverse order. For works with more than one author, the other authors' names appear in regular order.

▶ Article titles (short works) are put in quotation marks. Publication titles (long works) are italicized.

▶ All months except May, June, and July receive three-letter abbreviations.

▶ When journal volume or issue numbers are used, they are separated by a period.

Punctuating a Print Article Citation

1. Author: Last name, First name (period)
2. "Title of article" in quotation marks (period)
3. *Title of periodical* italicized (one space)
   a. For a journal: volume and issue number with year in parentheses (colon)
   b. For a magazine: date of issue (colon)
4. Range of page numbers (period)
5. Medium: Print (period)

Author's Name   Title

Mitchell, Robert. "Suspended Animation, Slow Time, and the Poetics
    of Trance." *PMLA* 126.1 (2011): 107–122. Print.

Journal title   Volume   Year of   Inclusive Print-based
                        publication pages   publication

Journal Article with One Author (Continuous Pagination)

Everett, Justin Edward. "Adopting the Peircian Sign for a Method of
    Affective Interpretation." *Linguistica Antverpiensia* 25 (1991):
    129–51. Print.

Journal Article with One Author (Separate Pagination for Each Issue) Entries dealing with journals with separate pagination in each issue contain both the volume and the issue separated by a period.

Berlin, James. "Current-Traditional Rhetoric: Paradigm and Practice."
    Freshman English News 8.3 (1980): 1–4, 13–14. Print.

Journal Article with Two or Three Authors As with books, only the name of the first author is inverted. Separate the authors' names with commas, and place a comma before the last author's name, followed by "and."

Flower, Linda, and John R. Hayes. "A Cognitive Process Theory of
    Writing." *College Composition and Communication* 32 (1981):
    365–86. Print.

When an article has more than three authors, list only the first author's name, followed by *et al.* (Latin for "and others").

Article from a Monthly Magazine In the case of monthly magazines, list the month instead of the volume number. In MLA style, three-letter abbreviations are used for the names of months that are more than four letters long; May, June, and July are not abbreviated. Also, popular monthlies will often begin an article on one page, and finish it later in the magazine. In such a case, use a comma in the place of a hyphen to indicate pages that are not continuous. For citing an article from a monthly that was downloaded from the Internet, see "References from Electronic Sources" later in this chapter.

Eilperin, Juliet. "Swimming with Sharks." *Smithsonian* June 2011:
    34–40. Print.

Article from a Weekly Magazine For magazines published more than once a month (weekly or biweekly), provide the publication date (not just the month).

Matthews, Steve. "Escape from the Great American Debt Trap."
    Bloomberg Business Week 11 July 2011: 9–11. Print.

MLA

Article from a Daily Newspaper Entries from newspapers should include the city of publication (in brackets) if it is not a part of the newspaper's title, immediately after the title (example: *Daily Commercial Record* [Dallas, TX]). If more than one edition is available on the date of publication (many papers publish early editions, especially on Sunday), then indicate that fact after the date. Also include the section information. If the section is indicated by a number, use the abbreviation "sec." followed by the number, a colon, and the page number of the article (example: sec. 3: 11). If the section is indicated by a letter, omit "sec." If the paper is not sectioned or the pagination is continuous, then you do not need to include section information.

> Carey, Benedict. "Need Therapy? A Good Man is Hard to Find."
> *New York Times* [New York] 22 May 2011, New York ed., A1.
> Print.

Editorial Editorials are identified with the word "Editorial" placed immediately after the title.

> Satullo, Chris. "Kids' Needs Come First." Editorial. *The Philadelphia Inquirer* 8 Aug. 2004: C6. Print.

References from Electronic Sources

► Citations for electronic sources include the author's name, the title of the article, the print information (if available), the date of access, and the URL (Web site address). The web address is optional, but may be useful to help your reader locate the original source. Keep in mind that web addresses change all the time, and may be "dead" by the time your reader tries to locate your source. When using an article obtained through a search (one that is not in a fixed location on the Internet), include the main Web site's URL. For example, for an article obtained by searching the Web MD site, the URL reported would be: <http://webmd.com>.

Author's Name	Comma	

Title of print source | Horning, Alice. "The Definitive Article ——— Article title
| on Class Size." *WPA: Writing*
Date of access | *Program Administration* | Available
| 31.1-2 (2007): 11-34. | publication
Web-based source | Web. 21 June 2011. | information (page numbers may not be
Web address (optional) | <http://wpacouncil.org/ | available online)
| archives/31n1-2/31n1-2horning.pdf>.

► Some Web site articles have confusing titles (if they have any titles at all) or are not attributed to an author. In such cases, use your best judgment and provide the most complete information you can.

You will not always be able to find full publication information online. However, you should do your best to obtain the most complete information possible to help someone who reads your citation follow up on your source. Remember that the URL may be unreliable or too long to include. It should only be provided if inadequate publication information will make the document difficult to find in a Web search.

A note on page numbers: Online journals, newspapers, magazines, and books often do not include page number references. If the online source where you obtained the text does not provide page numbers, then you may leave the page numbers out of the citation. However, it is preferable to include the original pagination, if possible, by cross-checking the reference in other databases or sources that might include this information in a bibliographic

MLA and URL

MLA style no longer requires a URL (an address) for Web sources listed on the Works Cited page. The rationale is that these addresses change over time, and the same document may be sponsored by more than one site. MLA style further assumes that a researcher can use a search engine to locate a document by using the author and title information.

However, your instructor, employer, or publisher may prefer that you include the URL. If so, place it at the end of the citation after the medium, enclosed in angle brackets, and concluded with a period.

→ UNDERSTANDING A URL

The Web address, also known as a URL (universal resource locator), usually consists of the abbreviation "http://" followed by a series of words or symbols separated by periods and forward slashes. Because Web addresses can be very long and are subject to change, they should be supplied primarily as supplementary information. Most users will locate documents through their own Web search rather than by typing in URLs. Because of this, it is important to include the most complete publication information possible, whether the source is a print-based publication stored online or a Web-exclusive publication.

When including a URL, it is important to know that the forward slashes indicate "levels" in the folder hierarchy of a particular Web address. Anything following a forward slash indicates a permanent place on the Web and should be included in your Works Cited bibliographic reference. The following URL will take you to the online exhibits page for the Museum of the History of Science at Oxford University:

http://www.mhs.ox.ac.uk/exhibits/

Sometimes the symbols in a URL are generated by a search engine when you look for information on the Internet. These symbols (usually a very long string of them) are meaningless as far as the Web address is concerned and should not be included in a Works Cited entry. Here is an example of a URL from a search for "longevity research" conducted on the Web MD site, which located an article entitled "Longevity May Run in Your Blood":

http://my.webmd.com/content/article/75/89691.htm?
lastselectedguid={5FE84E90-BC77-4056-A91C-
9531713CA348}

In this case, the legitimate URL ends with the letters "htm." The material after these letters is computer-generated garbage, so it should not be included in the reference. If you want to test your URL, cut the portion you think is the "legitimate" address and paste it into the address bar of your Internet browser. If it leads you to the article, then you have identified the correct URL. If it doesn't work, then list only the main homepage address (in this case, http://my.webmd.com) in your bibliography.

reference. These days, most archives will provide a PDF of the print-based version of the document (if it exists), which should include the page numbers of the print version. However, Web-exclusive publications—like blogs—will not have page numbers.

Book with Print Publication Information Sometimes you might cite an out-of-print book you found on the Web. In addition to the full print information for the book, you should include the title of the database (in italics) along with the date you accessed it. If the source would normally have included page numbers (such as in a chapter from an anthology), insert "N. pag." to indicate that no page numbers were present. The URL is usually not necessary.

> Darwin, Charles. *The Descent of Man*. 2 vols. New York: D. Appleton and Company, 1871. *Google Book Search*. Web. 12 Feb. 2011.

Article from an Online Database After listing the print information, include the italicized title of the database, the name of the database service, and the date you accessed the article. You will not always have access to all of this information, depending on the service and the place where you access it. Nevertheless, include as much of this information as possible.

> Wilson, Nicholas, Robert Quigley, and Osman Mansoor. "Food Ads on TV: A Health Hazard for Children?" *Australian and New Zealand Journal of Public Health* 23 (2003): 647–50. *ProQuest*. University of the Sciences in Philadelphia Lib. Web. 28 Oct. 2009.

In the preceding example, because "multiple databases" was selected during the search, no database title is included in the citation. Don't forget to include "Web."

Article from an Online Periodical (with Print Source) Follow full publication information with the date you viewed the article online.

> De Lemos, James, et al. "Early Intensive vs a Delayed Conservative Simvastatin Strategy in Patients with Acute Coronary Syndromes." *JAMA* 292 (2004): 1307–16. Web. 20 Sep. 2011.

Article from an Online Periodical If an article is co-published online and in print, include the complete publication information, along with the page numbers, if they exist. If the article exists only online, follow the format for a printed publication and include as much of the information as is available from the online source, followed by the date of access. If the publication is updated daily, treat it as you would a newspaper or weekly/bimonthly magazine, whichever seems more appropriate. If the E-zine ("electronic magazine") is updated monthly, treat it like a monthly magazine. Include "N. pag." if the article doesn't include page numbers.

> Huffington, Arianna. "In Praise of Unruly Women." *Salon.* N. pag. 22 Jul. 2004. Web. 22 Oct. 2010.

> Phillips, Vicky. "Top Ten Bargain Buys: Human Resource Degrees Online." *Virtual University Gazette.* N. pag. Sep. 2004. Web. 17 Sep. 2009.

Article from a Professional Web Site For articles and information published on Web sites, but not associated with an electronic book, magazine, newspaper, or other recognizable print equivalent, provide the author's name, the article's title, the date (the year if a specific date is not published), the sponsoring organization, and the date of access.

> Rubin, Jacob. "Pixilated Breasts and Fountains of Blood: My Strange, Brief Career as a Video-Game Obscenity Watchdog." 2011. Slate. N. pag. Web. 22 May 2011.

> **Punctuating a Short Work from a Web Site**
>
> 1. Author: Last name, First name (period)
> 2. "Title of work" in quotation marks (period)
> 3. Title of Web site italicized (period)
> 4. Publisher of Web site or "N.p." if no publisher (comma)
> 5. Latest update or "n.d." if no date (period)
> 6. Medium: Web (period)
> 7. Access date (period)
> 8. Optional URL in angle brackets (period)

FORMATTING A RESEARCH PAPER: MLA STYLE

Part of becoming a writer involves learning to prepare a professional-looking manuscript; the appearance of the document is your first step toward projecting your authority (*ethos*) as a writer. Fortunately, formatting a research paper in MLA style is a fairly straightforward process. Most of your word processor's default settings conform to basic manuscript specifications, though you will have to make a few adjustments. If you follow these guidelines your paper should be correctly formatted:

Page size and margins: Unless otherwise instructed, set your word processor for 8 1/2 × 11-inch paper. This should be your word processor's default setting. Set margins for 1 inch all the way around (again, this is usually the default setting).

Line spacing and indentation: Set line spacing for double space (this is a setting you will probably have to change, as most word processors are set for single space). Indent all paragraphs by 1/2 inch from the left-hand margin.

MLA

Justify your text to the left margin; text should appear "ragged" on the right margin.

Typeface: Knowing which typefaces are standard in the professional world will help set your work apart from that of amateurs. Times Roman, 12 point, is one of the most common. Avoid smaller typefaces (especially 10 or smaller) because they can be difficult to read. Times Roman is a serif font: it has little "flags" on the ends of the letters that make them easier to recognize. Cambria and Garamond are other serif fonts that are becoming increasingly common as well.

The first page: A title page is not necessary in MLA style. Identifying information, including your name, your instructor's name, class title, and date should be double-spaced in the upper left corner. Two spaces below that center the title, with the text beginning two spaces below that. See the student paper in the next section for an example.

Page numbers: Number every page of your paper, beginning with the first page. Page numbers should appear in the upper right-hand corner, 1/2 inch below the top of the page. (It is easy to set this as part of your page "header" in your word processor.) Put your last name in front of each page number (again, set this in your header) to help identify your pages in case pages get separated.

Tables and illustrations: Tables and illustrations should be placed as close as possible to where they are discussed in the text. Usually, it is best to try to center them in the page, though they may be shifted slightly up or down as needed. Do not let tables "spill over" to the next page, and avoid leaving excessive "white space" on a page whenever possible if an illustration is too large to fit.

Tables are labeled "Table" with a corresponding number (Table 1, Table 2, and so on). Label and title should be justified to the left, with the table appearing below as shown on the next page.

Illustrations may include photographs, maps, flow charts, graphs, drawings, or any other visual representation included in your text. They are labeled "Figure" with a corresponding number (Figure 1, Figure 2, and so on) and may be abbreviated "Fig." (e.g., Fig. 1, Fig. 2). Unlike a table, for a figure the label and caption appear below rather than above. See example of illustration on the next page.

Note: If tables and illustrations are fully documented in the title, then they do not need to be listed on the Works Cited page.

Table 1 The Ten U.S. Metropolitan Areas with the Largest Foreign-Born Population, 1970 and 2006

	1970			2006	
	Total Foreign-Born	Percent of Population Foreign-Born		Total Foreign-Born	Percent of Population Foreign-Born
1 New York-Northern New Jersey-Long Island, NY-NJ-PA	2,285,773	13.7	1 New York-Northern New Jersey-Long Island, NY-NJ-PA	5,304,270	28.2
2 Los Angeles-Long Beach-Santa Ana, CA	876,612	10.6	2 Los Angeles-Long Beach-Santa Ana, CA	4,432,288	34.2
3 Chicago-Naperville-Joliet, IL-IN-WI	604,073	7.8	3 Miami-Fort Lauderdale-Miami Beach, FL	2,023,711	37.0
4 Miami-Fort Lauderdale-Miami Beach, FL	384,539	17.7	4 Chicago-Naperville-Joliet, IL-IN-WI	1,695,417	17.8
5 Boston-Cambridge-Quincy, MA-NH	344,134	9.0	5 San Francisco-Oakland-Fremont, CA	1,235,778	29.6
6 San Francisco-Oakland-Fremont, CA	339,314	11.2	6 Houston-Baytown-Sugar Land, TX	1,193,931	21.5
7 Detroit-Warren-Livonia, MI	308,016	7.1	7 Washington-Arlington-Alexandria, DC-VA-MD-WV	1,078,552	18.0
8 Philadelphia-Camden-Wilmington, PA-NJ-DE	257,824	5.0	8 Dallas-Fort Worth-Arlington, TX	1,063,033	20.1
9 Cleveland-Elyria-Mentor, OH	147,318	6.5	9 Riverside-San Bernardino-Ontario, CA	898,235	22.3
10 Washington-Arlington-Alexandria, DC-VA-MD	132,551	4.3	10 Boston-Cambridge-Quincy, MA-NH	706,586	15.9
			16 Philadelphia-Camden-Wilmington, PA-NJ-DE-MD	504,317	8.7

Source: Audrey Singer, Dominic Vitiello, Michael Katz and David Park, *Immigration to Philadelphia: Regional Change in a Re-Emerging Gateway*, Brookings, 2008; Print; table 2; 6. © 2008 The Brookings Institution. Reprinted by permission.

Figure 1 Brookings Analysis of U.S. Census Decennial and American Community Survey Data

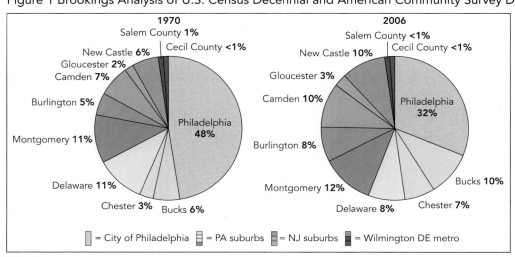

Source: Audrey Singer, Dominic Vitiello, Michael Katz and David Park, *Immigration to Philadelphia: Regional Change in a Re-Emerging Gateway*, Brookings, 2008, figure 4; 13. © 2008 The Brookings Institution. Reprinted by permission.

SAMPLE STUDENT ESSAY: MLA STYLE

Include your last name and the page number in the top right corner of every page.

Your name and other contact information (address or class) go here.

Faith Bruns

Dr. Lamm

EN 102

5 August 2012

Mind Your Manners

Basic manners were once taught in the home and reinforced in the schools. Children learned to say "please" and "thank you" and to address others properly. Good manners were once a sign of good breeding, a good home, and a proper upbringing.

What can you tell about the author from the tone of this paragraph?

Unfortunately, manners have gone out of style. The newest trend is to be different, unique. This can be achieved with manners, but the general public has forsaken polite behavior. Rudeness, according to cofounder of the Johns Hopkins Civility Project P. M. Forni, is an attempt to control others by putting people in an inferior social position (*Civility Solution* 7). In *Choosing Civility*, Forni comments that "[t]he byproduct of doing justice to others is the enrichment of our own lives" (14). Unfortunately, these days many individuals have substituted "politically correct" speech codes for manners, which does consider respect for the individual but lacks civility. In other words, political correctness creates the illusion of civility but actually reinforces the power differential it was meant to address. Moreover, this increase in rudeness has markedly increased within the last generation. In three separate surveys conducted in 1996, 2000, and 2005, 69–80% or respondents indicated that people had become significantly more rude than 20-30 years ago (Walters 64; cf. Forni, *Civility Solution* 5).

Manners cannot be used only on special occasions. They are to be employed at all times and with all people. The way people treat a waiter

Bruns 2

or waitress at a local restaurant should be the same way they treat a client or a supervisor: they should be polite, respectful, and courteous.

Perhaps most important, manners tell others what kind of person you are. According to Emily Post, an expert on etiquette:

> Etiquette must, if it is to be of more than trifling use, include ethics as well as manners. Certainly what one is, is of far greater importance than what one appears to be. A knowledge of etiquette is of course essential to one's decent behavior, just as clothing is essential to one's decent appearance; and precisely as one wears the latter without being self-conscious of having on shoes and perhaps gloves, one who has good manners is equally unself-conscious in the observance of etiquette, the precepts of which must be so thoroughly absorbed as to make their observance a matter of instinct rather than of conscious obedience. (Par. 7)

This means that etiquette makes individuals better members of society by making them aware of how their behavior reflects their moral and social character.

Unfortunately, in the social world today manners are not treasured the way they once were. Mrs. Post and Mrs. Vanderbilt were once consulted daily on the proper way to introduce clients or associates, the correct way to set up and serve a meal, and the best way to send thank you notes or invitations. These gentle graces were not reserved for the women of society, either. Men were quick to note the proper way to conduct business. A major social gaffe, such as a slovenly appearance or rudeness to a lady, was the quickest way to lose a promotion (Allen and Briggs 186).

Manners began going out of style in the sixties, when the youth movement proclaimed that everyone needed to do his or her own thing. Judith Martin, author of the syndicated news column "Mrs. Manners," spoke in an interview about the loss of manners and civility in today's society:

> We have seen, first of all, the result of generations of children being told by very well-meaning parents, "Now you don't worry

The author mentions the name of an authoritative source before going into her quotation.

Block long quotations. Note the distinctive language used here.

When citing from books on the Internet, give paragraph numbers when they are available. Bartleby.com is one valuable source.

Should the author have cited this information about Mrs. Vanderbilt, or can it be considered common knowledge? Is this a case of plagiarism?

Use *and* to connect authors' names in a parenthetical citation. Don't use an ampersand (&).

Bruns 3

about what other people think about you, you go out and search
yourself and get what you want, and never mind what other people
think." So they have done this beautifully and that's the decline...all
the older people joined in; it's not just one generation or two.
(Interview 1)

The problem, as Martin points out, has become infused in society.
Rudeness and self-interest are just the way things are now done. This has led
to a serious problem. When people treat each other without common civility
and respect, how can they be expected, in Rodney King's words, to "just get
along"? According to Allen and Briggs, "The rules [of manners] have changed
as times and conditions have changed, but always the reason for the rules has
been the same—a means of living together with ease, harmony, and
satisfaction" (12). Those who do not learn to treat others with politeness will
find themselves alone in the world playing a difficult game of catch-up.
Students will learn, when they enter the workforce, that civility is necessary to
be socially and professionally successful. Fortunately, help is available. In any
bookstore one may find many different volumes on social behavior and
etiquette. These treasures of wisdom are not outdated modes of behavior;
many of them address such difficulties as job situations, dating, and the idea
of political correctness.

The problem of rudeness in one high school so alarmed the
teachers that they executed a study of student rudeness. In their
article "Situation and Repertoire: Civility, Incivility, Cursing and
Politeness in an Urban High School," Stephen B. Plank and his
colleagues found that while students were more often polite than
rude to teachers, they cursed frequently and were rude to one
another. Still, students were generally polite less than half the time.

Bruns 4

Though most of these students would never use politically incorrect terms to describe people, they are perfectly willing to be rude to each other and curse in public. This is a problem that must be addressed.

For many, the idea of political correctness has eclipsed manners. It is believed by the general public that sanitized labels are equal to good manners. *Political correctness* (or *PC*) is an ideological term, one that has been around for many years and has been associated with a socialist agenda. There are some who attribute PC to the Institute for Social Research in Frankfurt, Germany, which was charged with finding "a solution to the biggest problem facing the implementers of communism in Russia" (Blazquez 1). Bill Lind attributes PC to Karl Marx: "Political Correctness is cultural Marxism . . . translated from economic into cultural terms" (2).

The current trend in our media is to lambaste those who use plain speech instead of PC terminology to get their points across. To not use PC language is erroneously viewed as "bad manners." It may not be politically correct for Bill Cosby to berate other African Americans for what he sees as a decline in civility (cf. Gruenwedel 16), but it is not bad manners. Crosby's remarks were quite the opposite. They were intended to encourage social responsibility and good manners.

Manners are not a set of rules merely meant to force people to behave in a certain way. According to *Miss Manners' Guide to the Turn of the Millennium*, they are inner guidelines that, if taught from an early age, will assist anyone in situations that require interaction with others (Martin 5). Civilization means that the people living in it need to be civil. People need to be aware of their actions and their words. Good manners, not political correctness, are the only way civility will survive.

Note how this quotation is blended into the author's sentence.

An ellipsis is used when something is cut out of the sentence.

Cf. means "compare" (from the Latin conferre, "to bring together, to compare"). It refers to material related to the discussion but not directly drawn from the source.

Italicize the titles of books, magazines, and films.

Don't use a comma before the page number.

MLA

Works Cited

Allen, Betty, and Mitchell Pirie Briggs. *Mind Your Manners*. Chicago: Lippincott, 1957. Print.

Blazquez, Agustin. "Political Correctness: The Scourge of Our Time." 8 April 2002. Web. 29 July. 2012.

Forni, P.M. *Choosing Civility: The Twenty-Five Rules of Considerate Conduct*. New York: St. Martin's, 2002. Print.

—. *The Civility Solution: What to Do When People are Rude*. New York: St. Martin's, 2008. Print.

Gruenwedel, Erik. "Bill Cosby Decries Slumping Urban Civility." *Video Store Magazine*. 25 July. 2004: 16. Print.

Lind, Bill. "The Origins of Political Correctness: An Accuracy in Academic Address." 2000. Web. 29 July. 2012.

Martin, Judith. "Interview with Barbara Lane." 18 November 2002. Commonwealth Club of California. Web. 4 July. 2012.

—. *Miss Manners' Guide to the Turn of the Millennium*. New York: Simon, 1989. Print.

Post, Emily. *Etiquette in Society, in Business, in Politics and at Home*. New York: Funk, 1922. N. pag. Bartleby.com: Great Books Online. Web. 4 July. 2012.

Walters, Julie. "Parlez-vouz Civility?" *Contexts* 9.1 (2010): 64–65. Print.

Looking Back at Chapter 12

► The MLA system of documentation consists of (1) in-text parenthetical citations and (2) a bibliography (called "Works Cited") that appears on a separate page at the end of the document.

► For in-text citations in MLA style, the author's name introduces quoted or paraphrased material, and the page number where the material can be found is placed in parentheses immediately after the borrowed information.

▶ The MLA bibliography (Works Cited) is formatted in the following way:

1. Title the list of references "Works Cited" (not "Bibliography" or "References").
2. Double-space all entries.
3. Use hanging indentation.
4. Alphabetize all items in the bibliography.

▶ Format research essays with 1-inch margins, double-space your text, indent paragraphs, and use Times Roman, 12 point, or similar serif font.

▶ Insert tables and illustrations with appropriate citation. If the citation information appears below the illustration this information does not have to appear in the Works Cited.

13

APA Documentation

Ocean/Corbs

DOCUMENTATION

American Psychological Association (APA) style is popular with social scientists, educators, and certain business-related disciplines. The style is complex, but the essential elements are (1) in-text citations and (2) the references list. Where MLA is an author/page number style, APA is an author/date style. Consider the following examples:

MLA Style

According to one source, today's parents often expect excellence from their children as a way of making up for their own insecurities (Smithers 54).

APA Style
According to one source, today's parents often expect excellence from their children as a way of making up for their own insecurities (Smithers, 2012).

MLA style emphasizes the page on which the information can be located, whereas APA style emphasizes the date of publication. (The preceding example is a paraphrase.) With a direct quotation, the APA citation would be followed by a page reference: (p. 1).

Note on verb tenses: In APA style, sources are generally discussed in the past tense. This is a major difference compared with MLA style, in which sources are usually discussed in the present tense.

IN-TEXT CITATIONS IN APA STYLE

Paraphrasing

Most frequently, writers who use MLA style begin sentences with an author's name followed by the date of publication.

> Smith (2011) has said that the average American eats about 2,750 calories per day.

This approach can be monotonous if it is used repetitively. Another method is to end a paraphrase with the author's last name within the parenthetical citation.

> The average American consumes approximately 2,750 calories per day (Smith, 2011).

Using Direct Quotations

In any type of argumentative writing, quotations should be as brief as possible to prove the point being argued. Long quotations are not encouraged. You should try to paraphrase your evidence when possible. However, when the language of a quotation is particularly important or memorable, you may use the original. Even then, your excerpt should be as brief as possible. Quotations of fewer than forty words are placed within quotation marks and blended in with your prose.

> According to Larson (2010), "*Buck v. Bell* fueled a resurgence of eugenic sterilization lawmaking that led to the enactment of new statutes in sixteen states during the 1920s and 1930s" (p. 182).

If the quotation comes from an Internet source, no page reference is needed.

> Manjoo (2011) has argued that in addition to passwords to protect your online accounts you need "your fingerprint or retina scan, a key fob, or a little widget inside your phone."

When long quotations are necessary, you must block them—that is, indent them from the left margin one-half inch (one tab space on most word processors). Delete the quotation marks, and add a page reference at the end of the block:

Shari Waxman argued that the media cannot be relied on to promote legitimate science:

> Ultimately, the legitimization of pseudoscientific research and paranormal phenomena by trusted news sources cannot occur without the simultaneous devaluation of science and reason. If the trend continues, the American public will be left with two disconcerting options: (1) They can learn to distrust the information provided by the mainstream news sources; or (2) They can learn to readily accept scientifically baseless claims as provided by mainstream news sources. (p. 84)

Citing Sources

Most of the time you will use one of the methods of citation already mentioned. Sometimes, however, you may need to consider a special case (e.g., no author, corporate author, multiple authors).

One Author

> Powledge (2004) reported that a virus may be the cause of obesity in some people.

Two Authors Use the ampersand (&) instead of the word *and* to connect names in APA parenthetical references.

> Guided reading is a process teachers use to help students achieve higher levels of ability by reading with assistance within teacher-led groups (Fountas & Pinnell, 1996).

Three, Four, or Five Authors When a work has between two and five authors, all of the names are mentioned in the text. All are mentioned in the first reference, with *et al.* used in the subsequent references.

FIRST MENTION
(Brundage, Harris, Olson, Paris, & Whited, 2004)

LATER IN THE SAME PARAGRAPH
(Brundage, et al.)

Ampersands

Use the ampersand (&) instead of the word *and* to connect names in APA parenthetical references. The ampersand was used in ancient Rome, where the letters of the word *et* (Latin for "and") were combined into a single figure. It was sometimes listed as the last letter of the alphabet. Its name originates with the phrase "and per se and."

IN SUBSEQUENT PARAGRAPHS
(Brundage, et al., 2010)

Six or More Authors (All References)

(Abrams, et al., 2008)

Authors with the Same Last Name   Use initials to avoid confusion.

T. Hobbs (2009) and J. E. Hobbs (2012) both agree that . . .

Corporate Author   When a corporate name is long and awkward, abbreviate it after the first mention, then use the abbreviation in subsequent references.

FIRST MENTION
(National Council of Teachers of English [NCTE], 2012)

LATER REFERENCES
(NCTE, 2012)

No Author Listed   When an author is not credited in the original source, use the first few words of the title in the parenthetical reference. Place quotations around articles and shorter works, but use italics for books and longer works.

("Cosmic Conspiracy," 1994)

Personal Communication   You may cite letters, e-mails, interviews, blogs, and postings to electronic bulletin boards in the text. Such items do not usually appear on the References page, however.

(R. Lamm, e-mail, June 21, 2012)

Indirect Source   When you cite someone indirectly—for example, if you cite a quotation or paraphrase through a source other than the original—then you must credit the source where you obtained the information.

Victor Barajas of the *Arizona Republic* says rap music is cruel and foulmouthed, but nonetheless entertaining (cited in Hoyt, 2009).

Specific Part of a Source   When referring to information that appears in a specific part of a work, use abbreviations for page (p.), pages (pp.), chapter (chap.), and section (sec.) as appropriate.

Fish (1980) argues that one reads backward and forward at the same time (chap. 1).

Electronic Source When citing information from a Web page or other electronic source, use the paragraph symbol (or the abbreviation "para.") to indicate a paragraph's number.

> Chef Bobo's goal is "to reverse the metabolic disaster of the modern American diet" (Smith, 2008, para. 2).

> If the article is divided into sections across several Web pages (Salon.com and MSN.com are both known for this practice), then cite the section as well.

> (Manjoo, 2012, p. 2, sec. 3)

Multiple Works in the Same Reference When several works are listed in the same reference, they are separated by semicolons. Usually you will include multiple sources in this way when several works address the same topic.

> Several writers have endorsed this approach (Hariston, 1982; Bruffee, 1984; Nystrand, Greene, & Wiemelt, 1993).

> Place works by the same author in chronological order. When you cite more than one source by an author that was published in the same year, give the works the designation *a*, *b*, *c*, and so on. Because works by the same author would be listed alphabetically on the references page, the title of *a* would come before the title of *b*, and so on.

> (Paulson, 2009a, 2009b, 2010, 2011)

Table If you insert a table or other illustration from a source, give the credit in a note at the bottom of the illustration. This source is not listed on the references page.

> *Source:* From J. E. Jordon, *Using Rhetoric* (New York: Harper & Row, 1965), p. 82.

PREPARING THE REFERENCES LIST (BIBLIOGRAPHY)

Books

The bibliography for an APA-formatted paper is titled simply "References." Entries include the author's initials and last name and the date of publication. Book references include a title (in italics), place of publication, and press. Only the first letter of the title and subtitle (following a colon) are capitalized. An exception is made for proper nouns (names of people, cities, countries, and the like).

Author's name	Title	Subtitle
(last name, first initial)	(in italics)	(first letter capitalized)

Allen, D. (2011). *The institutional revolution: Measurement and the economic emergence of the modern world.* Chicago: University of Chicago Press.

Year of publication   Place of publication   Publisher
(in parentheses)

One Author

Mendlesohn, F. (2008). *Rhetorics of Fantasy.* Middletown, CT: Wesleyan University Press.

Two or More Authors

List up to six authors. If a book lists more than six authors, put *et al.* after the sixth name.

Anderson, J., E. Barnes & E. Shackleton. (2011). *The art of medicine: Over 2,000 years of images and imagination.* Chicago: Chicago University Press.

No Author or Editor Listed

2011 factbook. (2011). Philadelphia: University of the Sciences.

Corporate Author

When a corporate entity publishes a book and no author or editor is listed, use the publisher as author and place the word *Author* after the place of publication.

Arkansas State University. (2011). *2011–2012 Undergraduate bulletin.* State University, AR: Author.

Edited Book

Abrams, M. H., Daiches, D., Donaldson, E. T., Smith, H., Adams, R., Monk, S. H., et al. (Eds.). (1974). *The Norton anthology of English literature* (Vol. 2, 3rd ed.). New York: Norton.

When two types of information must be placed in parentheses after the title, separate them by a comma. Do not use two sets of parentheses: (Vol. 2) (3rd ed.).

Work in Several Volumes

Hartshorne, C., & Weiss, P. (Eds.). (1931–1958). *Collected papers of Charles Sanders Peirce* (Vols. 1–8). Cambridge: Harvard University Press.

APA

Foreword, Preface, or Afterword

Meyerowitz, P. (1975). Introduction to the Dover edition. In G. Stein, *How to write* (pp. ix–xxv). New York: Dovers.

Selection from an Anthology
The referenced entry is neither italicized nor put in quotation marks. Even if there are several citations from the same collection, always provide full bibliographic information.

Shakespeare, W. (1974). Venus and Adonis. In G. B. Evans, et al. (Eds.), *The Riverside Shakespeare* (pp. 1703–1719). Boston: Houghton Mifflin.

Article in a Reference Book

Brewer, R. L. (2003). 10 ways to effectively promote your writing through your website. In *2003 writer's market* (pp. 58–60). Cincinnati: Writer's Digest Books.

Unsigned Article
If the article is unsigned, begin with the entry, followed by the publication date.

Rhetoric. (1995). *The new American Webster handy college dictionary* (p. 576). New York: Signet.

Government Publication

United States. (2000). *Guide to the clinical care of women with HIV* (Publication No. 017-024-01656-0). Washington, DC: U.S. Government Printing Office.

Articles

Periodical entries include the authors' names, the year of publication (in parentheses), the title of the work (only first words and proper nouns are capitalized), the title of the magazine (italicized), the volume, and the page numbers.

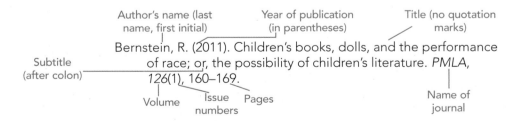

Author's name (last name, first initial)   Year of publication (in parentheses)   Title (no quotation marks)

Bernstein, R. (2011). Children's books, dolls, and the performance of race; or, the possibility of children's literature. *PMLA*, 126(1), 160–169.

Subtitle (after colon)   Volume   Issue numbers   Pages   Name of journal

In this example, a semicolon appears between the title and subtitle, so the semicolon is preserved. In most cases a colon will separate a title and subtitle in an article text. The volume number, but not the issue number, is italicized. If only the volume is listed, then the comma following the volume number is italicized:

> *PMLA, 126,* 160–169.

If the issue number is used, then the comma is not italicized: *126*(1), 160–169.

Article in a Scholarly Journal with Continuous Pagination

> Everett, J. E. (1997). Two Hamlets, one text: A semiotic analysis. *Reader: Essays in reader-oriented theory, criticism, and pedagogy, 37,* 59–77.

Article in a Scholarly Journal with Each Issue Paginated Separately

> Langer, J. (2003). Succeeding against the odds in English. *English Journal, 91*(1), 37–42.

Popular Magazine Article

> Hedegaard, E. (2004, April 29). A magnificent obsession. *Rolling Stone, 947,* 40–50.

For a weekly or bimonthly magazine, the date is given. For monthlies, only the month is listed: (2004, April).

Review Article

> Leland, J. (2004, October 19). I am a woman. Now prepare to die. [Review of the motion picture *Kill Bill*]. *The New York Times,* sec. 9, p. 1.

Newspaper Article

> McWhorter, J. (2003, May 30). Mean street theater. *Wall Street Journal,* p. W15.

Newspaper Article Retrieved Online

> Padawer, R. (2004, March 21). Vendors at same-sex wedding expo in New York City see profits, not politics. *Knight Ridder Tribute Business News.* Retrieved July 1, 2004, from http://proquest.umi.com/pqweb

Letter to the Editor

> Lamanno, R. (2004, June 21). Have ethics become only a legal distinction? [Letter to the editor]. *Wall Street Journal,* p. A17.

Motion Picture

> Gilbert, L. (Producer/Director), & Russell, W. (Writer). (1983). *Educating Rita* [Motion Picture]. United Kingdom: Columbia Pictures.

Television Broadcast

Rose, C. (Executive Producer). (2012, June 23). *Fareed Zakaria GPS*. [Television broadcast]. New York: Cable News Network.

Television Series

Roddenberry, G. (Executive Producer). (1966–1969). *Star trek*. [Television series]. Los Angeles: Paramount Television.

Audio Recording (Entire Album)

Tolkien, J. R. R. (2001). *The fellowship of the ring* [CD]. London: BBC Audiobooks.

Audio Recording (Single Track)   Within the brackets indicate the medium of the recording: record, CD, cassette, and so on. If the date on which the track was recorded is different from the copyright date, then put that date in parentheses following the brackets.

Bach, Johann Sebastian. (1989). Air on a "G" string. On *A little night music* [CD].

Software

Greenfield, S. M., Huntley, C., & Phillips, M. A. (1999). Dramatica Pro (Version 4.0) [Computer Software]. Screenplay Systems.

Internet Sites

Internet sources can present challenging problems for documentation. Material that appears one week may be gone the next. Also, virtually anyone can produce a document for the Web, so you must be careful to make certain that your source is reliable. Many Internet articles do not list authors or do not indicate publication dates. You should do your best to obtain sources with the most complete information possible.

| Author's name (last name, first initial) | Publication date (in parentheses) | Title of article (no quotation marks) | Title of Web page or original print source |

McWhorter, J. (2003, May 30). Mean street theater. *Wall Street Journal*, p. W15. Retrieved October 19, 2011, from ProQuest database.

| Page number for original print source | Date retrieved from the Internet | Name of searchable database or URL |

In your references list, only the first letter of an article or book title, or the first letter of an article or book subtitle following a colon, is capitalized. An exception is made for proper nouns.

Signed Document from a Web Site

Copeland, L. (2011). Get this woman some laughing gas!: Other countries use nitrous oxide in the delivery room. Why don't we? Retrieved June 15, 2011, from http://www.slate.com/id/2294978

Document from a Web site with No Author or Date

Branding yourself: Making the choice. (n. d.). Retrieved June 23, 2009, from http://www.bmezine.com/scar/A40510/scrbrand. html

Document from a Corporate Web Site

National Institutes of Health. (n. d.). Research ethics and stem cells. Retrieved July 30, 2010, from http://stemcells.nih.gov/info/ethics.asp

Internet Version of a Print Article You should add the words *Electronic Version* in brackets after the article's title. If the electronic version differs in any way from the print version, you should indicate the date it was retrieved and the URL.

Byrne, R. (2006, February 10). Rebuilding Balkan bridges. [Electronic Version]. *The Chronicle of Higher Education, 52*(23), A12. Retrieved February 14, 2010, from http://chronicle.com

With articles retrieved from the Internet, unless you are absolutely certain the Internet version is identical to the print version, (including pagination and illustrations), it is always a good idea to include the Internet information.

Article from an Electronic Journal (E-zine)

Zebrowski, G. (2004, June 21). Ray Bradbury, looking back on a lifetime of science fiction, says that for better or worse, the future is now. *Science Fiction Weekly, 10*(25). Retrieved June 22, 2011, from http://www.scifi.com/sfw/current/interview.html

Document from a University Web Site

Swadley, S. (n.d.). Classical rhetoric: A brief overview of the five canons. Retrieved May 28, 2010, from University of Oklahoma website: http://www.ou.edu/S/Charles.R.Swadley-1/classicalrhetoric.htm

Printed Article from a Database

Clarke, P. (2001). Medical marijuana and the compassion clubs. *Medical Post, 37*(25), 22 [Electronic Version]. Retrieved October 24, 2009, from ProQuest database.

APA

FORMATTING A RESEARCH PAPER: APA STYLE

Part of becoming a writer involves learning to prepare a professional-looking manuscript; the appearance of the document is your first step toward projecting your authority (*ethos*) as a writer. A research paper that follows APA style is divided into four main sections: The title page, the abstract, the body, and the references.

Page Format

All pages of an APA-style paper adhere to the following guidelines:

Page size and margins: Unless otherwise instructed, set your word processor for 8 1/2 × 11-inch paper. This should be your word processor's default setting. Set margins for 1 inch all the way around (again, this is usually the default setting).

Line spacing and indentation: Set line spacing for double space (this is a setting you will probably have to change, as most word processors are set for single space). Indent all paragraphs by 1/2 inch from the left-hand margin. Justify your text to the left margin; text should appear "ragged" on the right margin.

Typeface: Knowing which typefaces are standard in the professional world will help set your work apart from that of amateurs. Times Roman, 12 point, is one of the most common. Avoid smaller typefaces (especially 10 or smaller) because they can be difficult to read. Times Roman is a serif font: it has little "flags" on the ends of the letters that make them easier to recognize. Cambria and Garamond are other serif fonts that are becoming increasingly common as well.

Running head and page numbers: Number every page of your paper, beginning with the title page. Page numbers should appear flush right in the upper right-hand corner, and the title of your paper, in ALL CAPS, should appear flush left in the upper left-hand corner. This header, with your paper title on the left and the page number on the right, is called a running head. See the section that follows on the *title page* for formatting the running head on that page. (Use your word processor's header function to set the running head; remember to format it correctly for the title page separately from the other pages.)

Title Page

Research papers formatted in APA style must begin with a title page containing the following information:

Running head: The running head is formatted exactly as it is on other pages EXCEPT that the words "Running head," followed by a colon, appear in front of the title.

Running head: IMMIGRATION REFORM IN ARIZONA   1

Note: The running head is only formatted this way on the title page.

Paper title: Center the title, capitalizing significant words, with the longest line on top if the title is more than one line (make it look like a wedge shape). The title should begin approximately one-third of the way down the page.

Author's name: Your name, as author, appears below the title.

Affiliation: In an APA paper, your institutional affiliation (where you go to school) should appear below your name. Your instructor may also wish for you to include other information here, such as the class title and date.

   See the student paper in the next section for an example of a title page in APA format.

Abstract

All research papers in APA style include an abstract, or formal summary, of the content of the essay. Center the word "Abstract" at the top of the page (on the first line of text, directly under the header). On the next line begin your abstract. The text should be flush left, double-spaced, and the first line should not be indented 1/2 inch as a paragraph in the body of your researched argument would be indented. The abstract should be approximately 150–200 words in length and should summarize the paper's main ideas. (For more on writing effective summaries, see Chapter 8, Using Sources, Avoiding Plagiarism.)

APA

References

The word "References" should be centered immediately below the running head. Double-space all entries as described earlier in this chapter. Do not single-space entries or insert additional spaces between the entries. Do not title your references list "Bibliography" or "Works Cited." This is a common mistake made by students learning APA style.

Tables and Figures

As a documentation style associated with the social sciences, APA is frequently used in empirical research where complex data must be easily understood at a glance. Tables and figures should be used if the information they contain is necessary to understanding the argument. All information in the tables and figures should be documented, and should be able to stand alone so that the data can be understood without having to read the accompanying text. All the same, tables and figures should be placed as close as possible to where they are discussed in the text. Usually, it is best to try to center them in the page, though they may be shifted slightly up or down as needed. Do not let tables "spill over" to the next page, and avoid leaving excessive "white space" on a page whenever possible if an illustration is too large to fit. Size illustrations to fit the page. Make sure that the text in illustration can be easily read without causing eyestrain.

Tables Tables are representations of data set out in rows and columns. The table should be necessary in order to understand the paper's argument but should also be clearly labeled so that the data can be independently understood. To format a table properly in APA style, follow these guidelines:

Label: Each table should be labeled by number (Table 1, Table 2, etc.) on the first line with a descriptive title below the label.

Headings: Columns and rows should have headings that make the data easy to understand.

Format: Tables should be formatted consistently within the document so they all appear the same.

Notes: If explanatory notes are necessary to understand the data in the table (such as the use of special abbreviations), this information should appear below the table.

Table 1 The Ten U.S. Metropolitan Areas with the Largest Foreign-Born Population, 1970 and 2006

	1970			2006	
	Total Foreign-Born	Percent of Population Foreign-Born		Total Foreign-Born	Percent of Population Foreign-Born
1 New York-Northern New Jersey-Long Island, NY-NJ-PA	2,285,773	13.7	1 New York-Northern New Jersey-Long Island, NY-NJ-PA	5,304,270	28.2
2 Los Angeles-Long Beach-Santa Ana, CA	876,612	10.6	2 Los Angeles-Long Beach-Santa Ana, CA	4,432,288	34.2
3 Chicago-Naperville-Joliet, IL-IN-WI	604,073	7.8	3 Miami-Fort Lauderdale-Miami Beach, FL	2,023,711	37.0
4 Miami-Fort Lauderdale-Miami Beach, FL	384,539	17.7	4 Chicago-Naperville-Joliet, IL-IN-WI	1,695,417	17.8
5 Boston-Cambridge-Quincy, MA-NH	344,134	9.0	5 San Francisco-Oakland-Fremont, CA	1,235,778	29.6
6 San Francisco-Oakland-Fremont, CA	339,314	11.2	6 Houston-Baytown-Sugar Land, TX	1,193,931	21.5
7 Detroit-Warren-Livonia, MI	308,016	7.1	7 Washington-Arlington-Alexandria, DC-VA-MD-WV	1,078,552	18.0
8 Philadelphia-Camden-Wilmington, PA-NJ-DE	257,824	5.0	8 Dallas-Fort Worth-Arlington, TX	1,063,033	20.1
			9 Riverside-San Bernardino-Ontario, CA	898,235	22.3
9 Cleveland-Elyria-Mentor, OH	147,318	6.5	10 Boston-Cambridge-Quincy, MA-NH	706,586	15.9
10 Washington-Arlington-Alexandria, DC-VA-MD	132,551	4.3	16 Philadelphia-Camden-Wilmington, PA-NJ-DE-MD	504,317	8.7

Source: Singer, A., Vitiello, D., Katz, M., & Park, D. (2008). *Immigration to Philadelphia: Regional change in a re-emerging gateway*, Brookings. Print; table 2; 6. © 2008 The Brookings Institution. Reprinted by permission.

Documentation: If the table comes from another source, provide source information at the bottom of the table below the notes. If the table is from another source, it should not be reformatted, but should appear exactly as it does in the original source. Provide documentation information in APA style.

Figures In APA style, figures are usually visual representations of data that may include graphs and charts but may also include photographs, maps, flow charts, drawings, or any other visual representation included in your text. In a fashion similar to tables, they should be necessary to the argument but should also be self-explanatory and easily understood alone.
They should be clearly labeled and easy to read. To format a figure properly in APA style, follow these guidelines:

Size: Figures should be between 4.25 and 6.875 inches wide.

Labels: Labels should be in a sans serif font (such as Arial) between 8 and 14 points in size.

Format: Figures used in your paper should be stylistically compatible with each other. If one figure is in color, then the other figures should be in color as well.

Position: Center the figure on the page, and do not wrap text around the figure. Try to position the figure in the center of the page whenever possible.

Caption: Include a figure number and caption or title below the figure. Label figures by number (Figure 1, Figure 2, and so on). Italicize this label, but do not italicize the title as follows, flush left:

Figure 1. 2010 census data on immigration to Philadelphia.

Documentation: If the figure comes from another source, document the source properly in APA style.

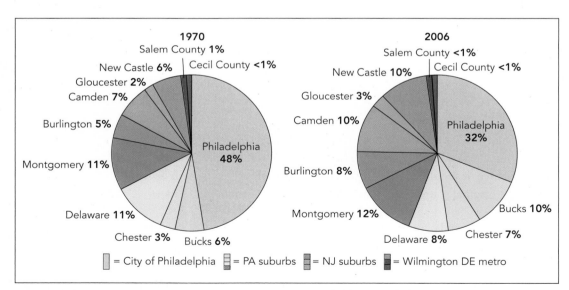

Figure 13.1   Share of Foreign Born by Jurisdiction, Philadelphia Metropolitan Area, 1970 and 2006
Source: Singer, A., Vitiello, D., Katz, M., & Park, D. (2008). Immigration to Philadelphia: Regional change in a re-emerging gateway, Brookings. Print; figure 4; 13. © 2008 The Brookings Institution. Reprinted by permission.

STUDENT ESSAY: APA STYLE

running head: BLAME GAME   1

The Blame Game of Blaming Games

Charles Mueller

English Composition

Professor Everett

October 10, 2012

Include a short version of the title and the page number in the top right corner of every page.

Center the title in the upper half of the page, followed by the author's name and course information.

BLAME GAME   2

Abstract

Blaming violent video games for game-players' violent real-life crimes could lead to future tragedies if (a) the video games are not the actual cause of real-life violence and (b) it misdirects us from seeking the true causes and solutions. Unfortunately, the case against violent video games is shaky and pushes the issue of parental influence into the background. Parental involvement takes not only time but *quality time*, which would necessitate parents sharing activities with their children. As a role model, a parent can demonstrate to a child the intended use of video games as a mode of entertainment and instill that they are not to be used as a standard of real-life conduct.

Center the title at the top of the page.

Do not hyphenate words at the end of lines.

Multiple citations are separated by semicolons.

In APA, page numbers are given only for direct quotations.

Titles are italicized, not underlined.

After paraphrases, cite the author's last name and the date of publication in parentheses.

The Blame Game of Blaming Games

In Arkansas, two Westside Middle School boys with powerful hunting rifles wore camouflage and concealed themselves behind bushes like hunters, but their prey was their own classmates and teachers on the playground. In Colorado, another pair of boys dressed in trench coats and stalked through Columbine High School while shooting their own classmates and teachers. When the public's initial shock from these school shootings wore off and people began to ask questions about the causes of the rampages, many fingers were pointed at the violent video games that were played occasionally by these boys prior to their murder sprees.

Certainly when consequences are serious, fixing blame is vitally important. Certainly the tragic slayings in our schools demand that we understand the causes and take action. However, blaming games could lead to future tragedies if (a) the video games are not the actual cause of real-life violence and (b) it misdirects us from seeking the true causes and solutions. Unfortunately, the case against violent video games is shaky (Reichhardt, 2003; Rimensnyder, 2002; Wagner, 2004; Ferguson, 2011), and it pushes the issue of parental influence into the background.

Authorities have several concerns about video games. First, they are shocked by the content of particular games such as *Grand Theft Auto: San Andreas*, which includes nudity, gambling, and an array of violent scenarios (Reichhardt, 2003). *Grand Theft Auto* players earn money by committing crimes such as stealing cars, running over pedestrians, physically beating other drivers, and killing police officers. In the game *GoldenEye 007*, a player assumes the role of James Bond or one of his counterparts. The object of this game is to uncover as much ammunition as possible and kill your opponent in a set time frame.

BLAME GAME 4

Finally, in the game Twenty-five to Life the players shoot policemen and use civilians as human shields. According to Shirley Gibson, the national president of Concerns of Police Survivors, "It is unconscionable and unacceptable for [the game producer] Eidos to promote violence against the men and women behind the badge who devote their lives to serving and protecting our communities" (Concerns of Police Survivors, Inc., 2005).

More specifically, authorities are concerned about the short-and long-term psychological effects these games have on players. According to the American Psychological Association (APA), "Violence in video games is bad for children's health," largely because "violent acts [are shown] without consequences" (qtd. in Less Videogame, 2005). The APA further claims that "violence in video games increases aggressive thoughts, aggressive behavior, and angry feelings in children" (Video Wars, 2005). Lieutenant Colonel David Grossman (1995) describes these games as "violence enabling," a form of psychological conditioning similar to the way real-life soldiers are trained to kill:

> The kind of games that are very definitely enabling violence are the ones in which you actually hold a weapon in your hand and fire at human-shaped targets on the screen. These kinds of games can be played on home video, but you usually see them in video arcades. There is a direct relationship between realism and the degree of violence enabling. (p. 315)

Although the authorities' concerns make sense on an intuitive level, their conclusions have been challenged by researchers who see no clear cause-effect connection between game playing and real-life violence. "Chasing the Dream," a report in The Economist (2005), suggests that

Square brackets are used around changes made within a quotation.

Quotations from an online source do not include page numbers.

If the name of the source is given in the text, cite only the publication year in parentheses.

Quotations of fewer than 40 words are not blocked.

Quotations of more than 40 words are blocked.

The page number is given after the period at the end of a blocked quotation.

research that shows a correlation between video games and violence may be due to a focus on short term rather than long-term studies. Further, the report states, researchers who have found a positive correlation between video games and violence have also failed to differentiate between different kinds of games, and researcher Marko Skorrik of the University of Michigan has failed to find signs of increased aggression on the part of players of violent video games. C. J. Ferguson (2011), in a study of Hispanic youth, found that while depression was a positive predictor of youth violence, neither television nor video games had the same predictive power.

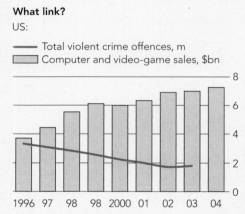

What link?

US:

— Total violent crime offences, m

▭ Computer and video-game sales, $bn

Figure 1   Linkage Between Violent Crime and Video Game Sales
Source: Anonymous. (2005, August 6). Chasing the dream: As video gaming spreads, the debate about its impact is intensifying. *The Economist.* **376, 66. Retrieved from http://www.economist.com/node/4246109 . © The Economist Newspaper Limited, London 2005.**

As the negative correlation between social violence and video games seems to suggest (Figure 1) while some video games may be blamed for isolated incidents of violence, in general there is little data to suggest that video games incite violence in society at large. Indeed, as expert witnesses in a court case challenging a California law banning selling video games to minors attested, similar tendencies toward aggression were observed for reading violent passages from the Bible (Sullum, 2011).

An increasing number of researchers believe that violent fantasies actually may be beneficial, providing a vent for aggressive-yet-normal feelings. According to psychologist Kevin Durkin, "Despite much debate about the consequences of playing games with aggressive content, the evidence available to date to support claims of harmful effects upon children is modest" (qtd. in Reichhardt, 2003, p. 368). Gerard Jones, author of fantasy and science fiction stories, asserts that violent entertainment may even have healthy benefits:

> We're trying to control and eliminate real violence in society, and that's a good thing. But in our zeal to do that, we go after everything that resembles violence or seems to glorify it. We forget that one of the main functions of fantasy is that it enables you to take your antisocial desires and dispel them outside of the real world. (qtd. in Rimensnyder, 2002, p. 15)[*]

Steven Johnson goes further in his book *Everything Bad is Good for You* (2005) in which he argues that the complexity of plot lines on television and the sophisticated interactivity of video games like Zelda actually build high order critical thinking skills. As an example, he compares the relative simplicity of following a *Starsky and Hutch* episode to the convoluted and difficult plots of *The Sopranos*.

Video games may be scapegoats for a deeper societal problem, one that will not be solved as easily as unplugging the X-Box. If games are not the root cause of violence in real-life situations, what is? What if the cause

For quotations from an uncited source, "qtd. in" indicates where the quotation was seen.

Block quotations are indented half an inch (usually one tab space).

---

[*] Quoted in "Bang, you're dead - Soundbite—media violence—Interview," by Sara Rimensnyder. *Reason*, November 2002. Reprinted by permission of Reason.com.

is not so much violent entertainment but the lack of parenting that helps young people distinguish fantasy from reality and immorality from morality?

Parental involvement takes not only time but *quality time,* which would necessitate parents sharing activities with their children. Unfortunately, young people spend more quality time with their games than they do with adults: "Teenage boys play video games *for around 13 hours a week*" [italics added] (Breeding evil, 2005). Restricting the kinds of entertainment pursued by young people makes sense only if the parents replace that time with something constructive and meaningful—something that includes their presence and interaction. Of course, some parents feel that being actively involved inhibits their children's development. In actuality, responsive, involved parents can provide an example of what it means to be a model citizen—a real example to contrast the fictional characters of video games.

Parental involvement in youths' lives can lay a solid foundation that would influence them toward becoming positive members of society. As a role model, a parent can demonstrate to a child the intended use of video games as a mode of entertainment and instill that they are not to be used as a standard of real-life conduct. "Playing the blame game" about playing video games is quick and easy but probably ineffective. Quality parenting—far from quick and easy—is the best solution.

Words may be italicized to add emphasis.

Square brackets and the words "italics added" show that you italicized words in a quotation for emphasis.

BLAME GAME 8

References

Breeding evil? Defending video games. (2005, August 4). *The Economist, 376*, 9. Retrieved September 30, 2011, from the ProQuest Database.

Chasing the dream: As video gaming spreads, the debate about its impact is intensifying. (2005, August 6). *The Economist. 376*, 66. Retrieved September 31, 2011, from http://www.economist.com/node/4246109

Concerns of Police Survivors, Inc. (2005, July 19). COPS opposes violent new video game [Press release]. Retrieved October 2, 2005, from http://www.nationalcops.org/pr04.htm

Ferguson, C. J. (2011). Video Games and youth violence: A prospective analysis in adolescents. *Journal of Youth and Adolescence 40*(4), 377–392.

Grossman, D. A. (1995). *On killing: The psychological cost of learning to kill in war and society.* Boston: Little, Brown & Co.

Johnson, S. (2005). *Everything bad is good for you: How today's popular culture is actually making us smarter.* New York: Riverhead books.

Less videogame violence is urged. (2005, August 18). *Wall Street Journal*, p. E1. Retrieved September 30, 2011, from the ProQuest database.

Reichhardt, T. (2003, July 24). Playing with fire? *Nature, 424*(6947), 367–368.

Rimensnyder, S. (2002, November). Bang, you're dead [Interview]. *Reason, 34*(2), 15.

Sullum, J. (2011). The Terminator vs. the Constitution. *Reason, 42*(9), 60.

Video wars [Editorial]. (2005, August 25). *Knight Ridder Tribune Business News.* Retrieved September 30, 2011, from the ProQuest database.

Wagner, C. G. (2004, July–August). Aggression and violent media. *The Futurist, 38*, 16.

APA format is designed to document the results of formal studies in the social sciences. Papers are often divided into several independent sections, each with its own heading, including an introduction (not titled), method, results, and discussion. Each section can be further subdivided as necessary. Of course, APA style may be used without this approach to organization, as the student essay demonstrates.

Looking Back at Chapter 13

► For in-text citations, APA style uses an author/date system.

► The bibliography for an APA-formatted paper is titled "References."

► Bibliographic entries include the author's last name and initials and the date of publication.

► Book references include a title (in italics), place of publication, and publisher.

GLOSSARY

A

analysis The study of the parts of an object of learning (like an argumentative essay) to understand how the different parts work together to contribute to an understanding of the whole. One of the elements of **Bloom's taxonomy**.

anecdote A brief narrative that can be used in an informal way to begin an essay or illustrate a point.

annotate To write notes in the margin of a text as it is being read.

appeal to authority A logical fallacy that relies on expert opinion when the authority is not actually an expert on the subject. Also called *argumentum ad verecundiam*.

appeal to faith A logical fallacy that relies on a previously held belief rather than evidence to support a claim. Also called *fiatism* or *blind faith*.

appeal to fear A logical fallacy that relies on fear rather than evidence to persuade an audience to accept a claim.

appeal to pity A logical fallacy that relies on the likelihood that an audience will sympathize with someone or something as the basis of convincing that audience to accept a claim. Also called *argumentum ad misericordiam*.

appeal to popularity A logical fallacy that relies on the wide appeal of a particular position to persuade an audience to accept the validity of a claim. Also known as *argumentum ad populum* and *bandwagon fallacy*.

application A way that knowledge can be applied in a practical way. One of the elements of Bloom's taxonomy.

argument The process of providing claims, giving reasons, and supplying evidence to change the way someone thinks or acts.

argumentative thesis An assertion that needs support—specific reasons—to be accepted as true. Also called a *claim*.

attacking the person A logical fallacy that relies on a criticism of a person's character, rather than on the validity of his or her argument, to persuade an audience. Also called *argumentum ad hominem*.

audience The people who are intended to read a piece of writing.

authority The degree of faith or the level of trust that an audience has in a writer. Also called *ethos*.

B

backing In Toulmin's system of argumentation, an additional argument that is needed to convince a skeptical audience that a particular **inference**, or *warrant*, is valid.

begging the question A logical fallacy in which the conclusion and premise of a logical statement are the same or similar. Also called *petitio principii*.

block method An approach to organizing an argument by comparing divergent views (opposing arguments) by analyzing them in large "chunks" rather than breaking them down side-by-side. With this approach, each view is taken as a whole and analyzed before moving on to the opposing view.

Bloom's taxonomy A system developed by Benjamin Bloom that describes how people acquire and use knowledge. The elements of Bloom's taxonomy are **knowledge, comprehension, application, analysis, synthesis,** and **evaluation**.

C

card stacking A logical fallacy that relies on giving the impression that all sides of an issue are being fairly represented while actually selecting evidence that favors a particular viewpoint. Also called *cherry picking*.

cause claim A claim that focuses on the source of a particular effect. With a cause claim, the effect is generally known, but the cause is open to debate.

cause-and-effect claim A claim that connects an action with a result. Such claims can focus on a cause, an effect, or both.

chart A visual representation of numerical data as it changes over time, such as a chart displaying the history of stock prices. Sometimes used interchangeably with **graph**.

claim An arguable idea that you want your audience to accept as true.

classification claim A claim that organizes collections of people, concepts, or objects into identifiable groups.

comparison and contrast claim A claim that identifies one thing in relation to something else.

comprehension The understanding of the meaning of an object of knowledge and ability to rephrase that information in your own words. An element of **Bloom's taxonomy**. Also called *interpretation*.

counterargument An argument that differs from your own argument, usually by arguing a contrary position. See also **refutation.**

critical reading Reading in an active mode with the idea of understanding, analyzing, and evaluating a text.

D

definition claim A claim that identifies something by outlining its distinguishing features.

drafting The second major stage of the writing process, following **planning** and coming before revising.

E

editing A terminal stage of the writing process that is engaged in only after a draft has been thoroughly revised and polished.

effect claim A claim that focuses on the result of a particular cause.

emotion A persuasive appeal that helps an audience sympathize with the author's point of view. Also called *pathos*.

enclosure In document design, enclosing page elements in a box (or between lines or other separators) to isolate it as separate, but supplementary to, the main text.

enthymeme An incomplete logical statement consisting of a **claim** but omitting the **reason**, the **warrant**, or both.

evaluation A determination of the value of an object of knowledge. An element of **Bloom's taxonomy**.

evidence Any information that can be used to support a claim. Common types of evidence include anecdotes, examples, expert opinions, facts, history, scenarios, and statistics.

F

fact A piece of information that is looked on as being true and generally is not open to debate or interpretation.

fact claim A claim that tries to determine whether something is real or true.

fallacy An abuse of logic that undercuts or replaces an argument based on claims supported by evidence.

false cause An assumption that a first event causes a second event just because the first event happens before the second event. Also called **post hoc fallacy**.

false dilemma An artificially limited choice. Also called **false choice**.

figurative language Words and phrases that mean something other than their literal meanings.

figure of form A series of words that are rearranged in a way that alters their meaning or creates an aesthetic effect. Also called **scheme**.

figure of speech A word, such as a metaphor or simile, used in a nonliteral way that expands its meaning or effect. Also called **trope**.

G

graph A visual representation of data that demonstrates differences in proportions or values, such as a circle (or "pie") graph that illustrates the percentage expenditures for an organization's budget. Sometimes used interchangeably with **chart**.

grounds In Toulmin's system of argumentation, the **evidence** that is provided to back up a **claim** and its associated **reason**.

guilt by association A logical fallacy that diverts attention away from arguable issues by discussing the negative reputations of others who supported the claim.

H

hasty generalization A logical fallacy that assumes the truth of a claim based on insufficient examples.

I

identity claim A claim used to identify what something is by understanding its dominant features.

irony A dramatic, situational, or verbal contrast between the expected and the actual.

issue A subject that can be debated and argued.

K

knowledge An accurately recalled or reported piece of information. One of the elements of **Bloom's taxonomy**.

L

lead A sentence (or group of sentences) placed at the beginning of an essay designed to engage the reader's interest and provide an idea of the argument's key issues.

logic The science of establishing relationships between ideas. Also called *logos*.

M

main idea One or more sentences in a paragraph that states the paragraph's rhetorical purpose. In arguments, main ideas frequently take the form of minor claims that serve to support the argumentative thesis, the major claim. Though frequently placed at the beginning of a paragraph, main ideas can be stated at the end, delayed until the middle, or even implied. See also topic sentence.

major claim The thesis statement of an argument; a statement of the idea that you want your reader to accept when he or she is finished reading your essay. Also called an **argumentative thesis**.

moral and ethical claim A claim that proposes to judge human behavior on the basis of a religious or philosophical system.

N

non sequitur An argument that presents a conclusion that is not supported by the evidence. Literally, "does not follow."

O

objection A potential argument that may be raised in objection to your argument and that must be answered with an argument of your own in the form of a rebuttal.

overall design In visual argument, the structural relationship between text, image, and color that binds the elements into a single, coherent composition. **Viewing order** is a primary element of page design.

P

paraphrasing The process of taking information from a source and putting it in your own style. Paraphrases should be approximately the same length as the original material and should not distort the original source's meaning.

plagiarism The insertion of information from another source into your own work and the representation (either intentional or unintentional) of it as your writing or ideas.

planning The first stage of the writing process, which is followed by **drafting** and **revising**. Also called *prewriting*.

point-by-point method A method of organizing an argument by comparing divergent views (opposing arguments) by analyzing the breakdown of the argument one piece at a time, comparing the similarities and differences between the views.

poisoning the well The process of discrediting an opponent before the audience has had a chance to consider the opponent's arguments. A form of **attacking the person** (*argumentum ad hominem*).

policy claim A claim that proposes rules, guidelines, or laws to govern a particular situation.

procedure claim A claim that argues how a particular policy should be carried out.

proximity In visual argument and document design, placing page elements next to each other so they will be naturally related by the reader, such as placing a photo next to text where the subject of the photo is discussed.

publishing The act of presenting writing to an audience through various media, including web pages, blogs, letters to the editor, or other means.

purpose The belief that you want your audience to have when they finish reading your writing (or listening to your speech).

Q

qualifier A term inserted in a logical statement that limits its application.

quoting The practice of reproducing words from a source and using them to support your arguments.

R

reason A statement attached to an argumentative claim that is used to support the validity of a **claim**.

reflecting An essential part of the writing process involving writing meaningfully about the writing experience.

rebuttal In Toulmin's system of argumentation, an argument made to respond to a particular **objection**.

red herring A secondary issue that distracts from the claim at hand.

refutation The part of an argument involving arguing against an opposing position. See also **rebuttal** and **counterargument**.

re-paragraph Use a different paragraph organization.

research question An issue for argument phrased as a question rather than a statement in order to facilitate research to locate sources of evidence to support an argument.

resemblance claim A claim that helps the audience understand something unfamiliar by comparing it to something familiar.

re-sentence Use different sentence patterns.

revising The third stage of the writing process, which follows **planning** and **drafting**. Revising involves thinking about what you have written (how well it accomplishes your **purpose** and communicates with your **audience**) and making changes, both large and small, to fine-tune your text. Also called *revision*.

re-word Use synonyms for words or phrases.

S

scenario A hypothetical situation that has not happened but could occur.

slippery slope A logical fallacy that assumes that if one step is taken, or one concession is made, it will lead to a series of new events or concessions, akin to a stack of dominoes falling down.

statistics A form of evidence that uses numerical data to support a claim.

straw man A logical fallacy in which an arguer misrepresents an opposing position in an inaccurate or simplistic way that will make the counterargument easy to discredit.

structure The organization of an argument—how the parts are arranged into an effective and persuasive whole.

style The effective arrangement of words so that they are engaging, eloquent, clear, persuasive, and appropriate for the target audience.

summary A condensed version of a source with the idea of capturing the essence, main ideas, and emphasis of the original.

supporting claim A secondary claim that appears in an argumentative essay's body paragraphs and usually takes the form of a topic sentence. Also called a *minor claim.*

syllogism A complete logical statement consisting of a major premise, a minor premise, and a conclusion. See also **enthymeme**.

synthesis The comparison and contrasting of an object of knowledge with other, similar objects. An element of **Bloom's taxonomy**.

T

tag Attaching one's own words to a quotation. It tells something important about the source, and helps the reader see how the quotation connects to the rest of the text.

topic A general, nonarguable subject.

topic sentence A sentence in a paragraph that states the paragraph's rhetorical purpose. In arguments, topic sentences frequently take the form of **minor claims** that serve to support the **argumentative thesis**, the **major claim**. See also **main idea**.

V

value claim A claim that tries to determine the worth of something by measuring it against a standard or scale.

viewing order The "reading order" of a visual text. May be top to bottom, straight to center, diagonal, or in a "Z" the directs the eye across the page. Careful placement of elements determines implied viewing order.

visual argument An image (such as a photograph, editorial cartoon, or public service advertisement) that states or implies an argument using means in addition to, or in the place of, written text.

voice The unique tone created by a particular writer's **style**.

W

warrant An underlying assumption that allows a reason to support a claim.

Z

zone of reasonable skepticism The position an audience must take in order to be persuaded. "Reasonable skeptics" are not already convinced, but are willing to fairly weigh the evidence and are open to persuasion.